~1-C—T-A—BILITY

ng whore ~)
~~xxxx~~ ~~xxxxxxxxxx~~)

L—E—C—7R—1-C77
nd) — your out the door

r up A—S—P—1—R=1-1
yourself.

:—E—A—L—1T—Y.
shelf.

=O
=C—K—E7—(oh)

hoyn! oh?

DEFYING GRAVITY

JORDAN'S STORY

DEFYING GRAVITY
JORDAN'S STORY

JORDAN MOONEY
WITH
CATHI UNSWORTH

OMNIBUS PRESS
London / New York / Paris / Sydney / Copenhagen / Berlin / Madrid / Tokyo

With thanks to my mum and dad,
Rosalind (Linda) Rooke and Stanley James Rooke.

With such gratitude to my mum,
for letting me learn to dance,
and to my dad,
for quietly supporting me when
times got difficult with my mum.

What a pair. xx

CONTENTS

CREDITS AND CAPTIONS

Photographs

Page xviii: Mum's haircut, circa 1961.

Page 14: First time as a bridesmaid. Showing my pants from an early age.

Page 22: Teenaged me. Beehive in the making.

Page 26: Played right forward, famous for smacking ankles (sorry ref!). Second from left on the front row.

Page 38: As Derek Jarman would say, "studied at Miss Angela's school of dance".

Page 53: City Lights trousers, Biba jacket, alligator handbag. Wishtower in Eastbourne, circa 1973.

Page 56: [Jane England]

Page 70: Boots dangerously long for me. [Mirrorpix]

Page 72: Touching up the Mohairs. [Mirrorpix]

Page 80: Let it rock. [Sheila Rock]

Page 88: Not a hair out of place. [Harri Peccinotti]

Page 104: Clearly I've heard the joke before. With Malcolm McLaren. [Joe Stevens]

Page 106: Lucky the basque was boned. [Joe Stevens]

Page 115: Tits and arse, to quote Lenny Bruce. With Chrissie Hynde and Vivienne Westwood. [David Dagley/REX/Shutterstock]

Page 326: Yves Saint Laurent earrings at Adam and the Ants. [Peter Anderson]

Page 330: With my dear friend Anna Melluso.

Page 344: O level needlework came in handy.

Page 349: With Kevin Mooney, Anna Melluso and Michael Collins in Hyde Park Square.

Page 360: Pirate love. [Derek Ridgers]

Page 375: *Farque* in Zandra Rhodes.

Page 378: Spaghetti Bolognese for Luca Melluso.

Page 381: Naughty me, bought some Tiger stripe. For the Billy Hyena video.

Page 394: *Last of England* by Derek Jarman. [Mike Laye/imageaccess.net]

Page 397: My one in a million cat, Berry.

Page 416: Taking up space at the Chelsea Space. [Sheila Rock]

Page 425: Tits and aerosol. [Etienne Gilfillan]

Page 431: It's in the can. [Jef Aérosol]

Lyrics

'Lou'
Words & Music by Adam Ant
© Copyright 1984 Tamadan Ltd.
Universal Music Publishing MGB Limited.
All Rights Reserved. International Copyright Secured.
Used by Permission of Hal Leonard Europe Limited.

INTRODUCTION

JON SAVAGE

We could be talking about Riah.

In the summer of 1973, Pamela Rooke left school with six O levels and two A levels. It was a pivotal time: in late May she'd seen David Bowie on his final Ziggy tour. Already obsessed with appearance as a statement beyond mere fashion, she went in 'a three-quarter-length Biba jacket, no lapels, brown with big beige musical notes all over it, and beautiful padded shoulders; not too much, not too little, just perfect. A pair of beige Oxford bags, a massive pair of gold platforms and of course, my red-and-pink razor-cut hair.'

Completing the look was a homemade earring constructed 'out of starling's feathers, helpfully left for me by my cat, with pearls sewn into them from a necklace I'd taken to bits'. Noting that, in his current publicity photos, Bowie was wearing a Yamamoto suit with cherry blossom details, Pamela and her friend Sally Reid gathered all the cherry blossom they could find and, at a key moment, threw them all over the singer: 'through a shower of falling petals, he took my hand and asked me if he could have my earring. I shook my head slowly and said: "No".'

Encouraged by Bowie's hyper speed transmogrifications, Pamela was experimenting with a new identity. At the time of the Bowie concert she was known as Jipper: 'a deliberately androgynous name.' As Sally Reid remembers, 'we went through a myriad of names. Riah was one of them – the Polari slang word for 'hair', which would have been good.'

However, Jordan's new identity would come from another source – a classic of American literature that, she recalls: 'was inspired – and I took that inspiration and ran with it.' This source is revealed here for the first time.

The name would take a few permutations, but the script was already there: the androgyny of Bowie and his followers, given depth and toughness through a thorough immersion in the gay culture of the time – hence Riah. One of the many pleasures in this memoir is the period cartography of gay bars: the Palace, the Curtain Club and Tricky Dicky's disco in Brighton; the Masquerade, Maunkberry's, the Catacombs, the Regency, Gateways and Louise's in London. A favourite haunt was El Sombrero in Kensington High Street, haunted by Nureyev, Jagger and Mercury.

From the still underground gay world of the time Jordan took the sense of outsider community, and the toughness to deal with any adverse reaction: from gestures to verbals to actual violence. In the mid-seventies, she was fearless, Amazonian, 'like a Marvel superhero' as journalist and witness Jonh Ingham observes. Already a firm King's Road habitué, she came into the orbit of Malcolm McLaren and Vivienne Westwood during 1973, and quickly became the figurehead for the shop at 430 King's Road: the first Sex Pistol.

Her sheer being set the style for this most confrontational of shops: 'people were terrified of coming in,' she told me. 'I'd heard reports from people who later became friends, that people wouldn't go in because of me, that I wouldn't say anything to them, I'd be horrible. It was just my attitude. I thought I looked better than anyone else. I was very introverted, I know people thought I was an exhibitionist, but I was pretty stand-offish. I felt powerful, and I think I looked powerful, I know I looked very intimidating.'

By 1974/5, London seemed like a wasteland, drained of colour. There was nothing going on. As Jordan observes, 'in a way, we were isolated. There is a picture of me walking up the King's Road, looking very much like I did when Derek Jarman first saw me, with that see-through net skirt on, and what is interesting to look at now is what's going on in the background – it's really grey, with corrugated iron, almost like a bomb site – and that was me walking on my own like that. We were very much on our own to start with.'

With her luxuriant, swept up blonde hair and tight, form-fitting clothes – which mutated from sports/fifties styles into the rubberwear sold in McLaren and Westwood's third incarnation of 430 King's Road, Sex – Jordan looked like no one else. Seen in scattered press shots and in the flesh, her presence was at once sexual – very much a dominatrix, although she shied away from any practice – and science fiction: she seemed beamed in from a future that was at once retro and highly unsettling.

As The Sex Pistols were beginning, Jordan was the face you saw: the visual hook. She was the standout presence at the Valentine's Day 1976 group appearance at Andrew Logan's loft: interacting with Johnny Rotten on stage in a staged moment of outrage, bursting out of the *Sunday Times Colour Magazine* in a candid shot with David 'Piggy' Worth. She mirrored the appearance of Mrs Thatcher, then rising to national prominence – a visual coincidence caught in a contemporary painting by Adam Ant, with Mrs T pictured as a dominatrix.

From her stage invasion in The Sex Pistols' first TV appearance for Granada, her modeling of Malcolm McLaren and Vivienne Westwood's startling bondage collection for Seditionaries, and her constant presence, along with Michael Collins, as front person in Sex and Seditionaries, Jordan was a major face in 1976. As Adam Ant remembers, 'Jordan created punk rock, she was literally selling it on the front line, she was living it on public transport when other people were just dressing up.'

As The Sex Pistols and Punk went nationwide during 1977, she began to withdraw from the group. The Sex Pistols' boat trip on the Silver Jubilee weekend was the final straw: as she told me, 'I just thought there was doom coming, after the boat trip. John was being really obnoxious to everybody. It was the star trip, and him thinking that everything had got too commercial. I don't think he could quite handle it. I think he'd lost it by then, he'd lost the need to do it.'

Although continuing to work in 430 King's Road, Jordan refused any involvement in *The Great Rock'n'Roll Swindle* – 'it was obviously going to be really shit' – and focused on Adam and the Ants and her starring role in Derek Jarman's *Jubilee*: a fascinating film of which the highlight is her dance in a disused Deptford dock. 'Derek Jarman was a beautiful man,' she says: 'The way he would throw his head back and laugh, he was wonderful – "wonderful" being one of his favourite words. I will always miss him.'

Jordan remained at 430 King's Road until her marriage to Kevin Mooney in summer 1981, when Vivienne Westwood promptly sacked her. By then she had witnessed and participated in Adam Ant's rise to superstardom. Striking out with Kevin Mooney and the new group Wide Boy Awake, she slowly became mired in heroin addiction – which, with typical fortitude, she kicked cold turkey, before totally changing her life and becoming a veterinary nurse and a breeder of Burmese cats. Jordan was always good at saying 'no'.

As if this story wasn't enough, there are many other pleasures here: details of how Vivienne Westwood and Malcolm McLaren made the extraordinary clothes that they sold in 430 King's Road from 1973 to 1981; a full account of life at Linda Ashby's flat in St James's, where Jordan lived with Johnny Rotten, Derek Dunbar, Simon Barker and Sid Vicious – a punk nest in the heart of the English establishment; stories about nearly forgotten but fascinating characters like Tracie O'Keefe, Debbi Juvenile, and Vikki De Lambray.

Transformation was the name of the game in this classic era of pop culture as urban, suburban and exurban adolescents responded to the only thing in the culture that spoke to them: refashioning themselves into heroic, superhuman, fantastic creations. This book is the story of how the nature-loving balletomane Pamela Rooke from Seaford on the South Coast became the striking figurehead of her generation.

1

SEAFORD BOULEVARD

Childhood on the wild Sussex coast (1955–66)

A dance to the music of time

Simon Barker said he could remember the night before we shot the *Jordan's Dance* sequence for *Jubilee* at the flat at St James. Everyone was there – the Pistols, Sid, Adam – and there's me sewing all these ostrich feathers on a tutu at three or four in the morning! It was my original tutu, which I'd worn when I used to perform in competitive ballet, along with the tiara, which was made of crystal and bought at great expense for me by my mum. It's the one part of the outfit that I still have today. I did all that myself, the night before we shot the scene. I should have been thinking about the next day's shooting! But I still remember the smell of new ballet shoes, new satin. It's a most wonderful smell. And it takes me back in time…

I was probably about 6 the first time I encountered it. There was a little shop called Dancia, just off the Western Road in Brighton, not far from my hometown of Seaford on the East Sussex coast, which was probably the most exciting thing you can imagine for a little girl who loved ballet. I got a tutu made to order there with a satin top and Fabiola ballet tights in very, very pale pink. Some of the shoes were kid leather, the little flatties, whereas the pointe shoes were pink satin. It smelled beautiful when you walked in.

Before I was taken to this emporium to buy proper dancewear, I would make my own outfits. Chiffon scarves were very fashionable and Mum had several; they kept your wash-and-set in place because they were light, and they came in so many colours. So I would put all of hers together, tie them to a little belt around my waist and do the 'Dance of the Seven Veils' on the landing! The soundtrack was my first ever record, Tchaikovsky's *Nutcracker Suite*, floating out from my sister's little record player. I would dance away up there, back and forth… It wasn't the carpet and the banister I was seeing – in my mind I was dancing in the middle of an amazing stage set. Those are my earliest memories of really being in love with a piece of music, and it's probably not what people would expect. But, in many ways, my childhood was like one long fantastic dream.

My heart Cinque

Seaford, in East Sussex, where I was born, is a place with a history of rebellious behaviour. In a part of the country that was most open to invasion by sea, it became one of the region's Cinque Ports[1] that have banded together to defend the coast since Saxon times. That spirit still lingers in the salty air. The seafront has barely changed at all since I was born, on 23 June 1955, though there have been some awful storms out at sea. In 1987, they built the beach up level with the promenade. It cost millions of pounds, and about a week later, the hurricane hit and all of it disappeared overnight. I think it ended up somewhere like Dungeness – in Derek Jarman's garden, probably.

But, when I was little, it was a lovely big drop down to the beach with lots of groynes going out to sea. I had many very happy days down at the beach – as well as one memorable day of terror, when I was 8 years old and the lilo I was floating on got caught in a riptide. My brother Roger had to swim out to sea, catch it and haul me back to shore – risking his own life in the process. But in those days,

---

[1] The Cinque Ports were a confederation of maritime towns and villages in Sussex and Kent that joined forces over a thousand years ago to provide a fleet for the King in case of need.

parents would let their children go off on their own like that, and I used to spend hours down there. It's a feeling of freedom. It probably sounds strange, because I know the sea is a sort of full stop in a way, a full stop to the land. But to me it feels different; it feels like freedom and I don't feel hemmed in.

From out of the past

The night I made my entrance into the world, there was a dense sea fog hanging over the town. We didn't have a car, so Dad had to ring for a taxi, an extravagance for us – but the hour was late and my arrival was imminent. Mr Squires, the taxi driver, got to East Dean, about halfway from Seaford to the hospital in Eastbourne, and announced that he couldn't go any further, the visibility was too bad.

My dad went mad.

"What do you think we're going to do?" he asked him. "We can't turn back, she's having a baby!" Obviously, the driver was persuaded to soldier on. My brother Roger, who was 8 at the time, remembers the next morning, when Dad got home:

ROGER ROOKE: He seemed quite pleased with himself. But the only thing he would say was that you looked like a skinned rabbit! He didn't say what a bonny baby or beautiful little girl you were. I remember the day that you were brought home from the hospital, because it was a lovely day, very hot and sunny. We'd been out, all us children who lived round about, to a Donkey Derby in the fields past the hedgerow. And when I got home, you were there. I remember being a bit mystified by it all, because times were different then. I was kept right out of the fact that Mum was even pregnant. I knew nothing about it until about four days before you were born.

Perhaps this is not so surprising – there is a lot of mystery in our family, some of which we still have yet to get to the bottom of. As the newly arrived Pamela Anne Rooke, I was the youngest in a tightly knit, self-sufficient family. My dad, Stanley James Rooke, was a proper Cockney, originally from Tottenham, who had been billeted in Seaford during the Second World War and preferred to settle down there than return to London. My mum, Rosalind Jean Needham – although everyone called her Linda and she was actually christened Rose – was originally from Islington, the area around King's Cross and the Caledonian Road. A professional seamstress, she was the driving force in the house. Later, when I was a teenager, she often got very, very upset about how I looked. But Dad always, in his own way, tried to smooth things over and stand up for me. Not that I needed it, really.

I was born very late in my mum and dad's life – Mum was 41 when she had me, which in those days was really risky. I was the fourth of four children, one of whom didn't survive. I had my brother Roger and my sister – also called Rosalind, but we've always called her Jeannie – and between them was a little boy, Michael, who died at 18 months of scarlet fever. My mother took him to the doctor and he told her there wasn't anything to worry about. Then, twenty-four hours later, Michael died in her arms. It made her dislike doctors for the rest of her life, she was never able to trust them. Jeannie remembers that she wouldn't have any painkillers when she gave birth to me, which shows you how deep that distrust ran and how long it lingered.

JEANNIE CRAVEN: That was a dreadful burden for Mother, dreadful. That's my first memory of us moving to Seaford... her crying, not wanting to get out of bed, because she had lost Michael that way.

So I was brought up as a bit of an only child really, but with an older brother, and a sister who was quite boyish – Jeannie liked to play cricket with the boys. That was an era when kids could play cricket and football in the streets without anyone worrying about them.

When I say we were close, I really mean all I've got is my parents. I never knew my grandparents; I never had any family stories from them, which are really quite valuable when you're growing up, though Roger's research into the family tree, as well as his own longer memory, have shed some light on matters.

A family affair

Nobody seems to know how Mum and Dad met, although we think it would have been when they were still in London. Roger says that Mum always went a bit coy when he asked her. It was an unusual

4

sort of relationship in the fact that, while Dad was only 5′2″, Mum was over 5′6″, which was considered strange then and probably still is today, with the ridiculous parameters people put on relationships. But she loved him because he was a good man. I also get the feeling that he made her feel safe, and that going to Seaford was a way of getting away from her family, who she fell out with irrevocably after the death of her father.

ROGER ROOKE: Our grandfather, Edwin Needham, committed suicide on 25 August 1929, when Mum was only 13. He put his head in the gas oven and Mum was the one who found him. His wife Jane had died two years previously, leaving him to bring up seven children, and it was two days after what would have been their wedding anniversary, so I think that was the possible reason. It states on his death certificate that he died of carbon monoxide poisoning from coal gas, administered by his own hand while of unsound mind. Jean Goddard, the daughter of Mum's sister Daisy, told me that he died of a broken heart. There was a big stigma about suicide in those days: it was a crime, and if he hadn't succeeded in taking his own life he could have been locked up for it.

Mum never directly told me anything about it, but she mentioned it to a friend while I was there, one of our neighbours, Gladys Rose, a 'cup-of-tea-confidante' who used to drop in every now and again – a big old lady with grey hair and a pinny with only one of her front teeth left. I think Mum was feeling a bit down and she said she felt like doing away with herself. Gladys said: "Oh, don't be so silly." And I remember Mum saying: "Well, my Dad did. And I was the one who found him."

My maternal grandmother Jane died of erysipelas, also known as St Anthony's fire, which today would be cured easily by penicillin. It's basically cold sores that burst and get into your bloodstream – something as simple as that could kill you back then. She was 51. And, with seven children, he had quite a job on his hands, did my grandfather Edwin, who worked making wheels in a cycle factory. Roger's research pointed to the fact that Edwin, who was born in the workhouse that served as a hospital in those days, probably had an Italian father, but he was illegitimate, so this has made tracking down his birth certificate impossible so far.

Mum had three sisters, Lilian, Bertha and Daisy, and three brothers, Sidney, Frederick and George. Roger thinks Sidney was her favourite and I can remember seeing a photo of him, dressed in a naval uniform, that she kept in her purse. She would take it out from time to time and look at it with a wistful expression. But, whatever happened between Mum and her siblings, she never had anything more to do with them.

I did hear that one of the sisters came down to Seaford and Mum wouldn't go to the bus stop and meet her. And I have one very strange, abstract memory of being taken up to London to see one of them, who lived in the sort of tenement block you'd see in 1960s 'kitchen sink' dramas, with no decorations indoors, just stone walls. It was pouring with rain.

Mum was tight-lipped about her family, but Roger has since discovered we have a second cousin on her side, Derrick Howlett, who was the son of her sister Daisy, born when she was 16 and given up for adoption. They met when Derrick's daughter started to do some research into his birth mother while, at the same time, Roger was researching our family tree. Sadly, they didn't get to meet Daisy, but according to Roger she had lived quite a life. She had three partners and seven children, of which Derrick is the oldest. Because she kept changing her name, by the time they tracked her down, Daisy, now calling herself Elizabeth Karim, had already died in a care home, so Derrick never did get to meet her.

We do know a bit more about Dad's family. His father, Arthur, was a leather gilder, who engraved book titles in gold onto the leather bindings. By strange coincidence, the place where he worked on Poland Street would later become Louise's, the key club of the Sex Pistols era. Arthur was married to Sarah Jane, who came from a small Hampshire village called Denmead, where her family worked as farm labourers. Jeannie said that Dad thought the world of his mum, and that she worked herself to death – she died in her sixties of cancer. All that remains is some photos of her as a tiny, pretty young girl and a worn-out old lady looking much older than her years. Arthur became a bit of a drinker, and legend has it that he died on the way back from the pub. Dad told me once that he was reading a report in the back of the *Evening Standard*, on a section of the paper they printed last for breaking news, about a man collapsing and dying in a certain area of London, and he just knew it was his dad.

Dad had two brothers and both of them were rather strange. Uncle Ted was a philatelist who actually made a living out of collecting stamps. Ted lived his whole life with his older brother, Uncle Frank, who was a racetrack bookie and was married to Auntie Maud. She was quite unusual, as she only ate bananas. Even at weddings! At the reception on Roger's big day, she gave me her coq au vin, and got her bananas out of her handbag to eat instead! I don't know where he found her. In a fruit shop?

> **ROGER ROOKE:** Auntie Maud was a bit of a one-off, and I often wonder whether Ted was actually gay. I had a surprising insight into their lives when I went to stay with them in London for a week on my own when I was about 16... Maud came out with some extraordinary things. Right out of the blue, she said: "Some people think that Ted's a dirty old man, but he's not you know, he's just going to see his friend." I didn't quite know what that meant. And then another time, over breakfast she said: "My marriage has never been consummated, you know." I was trying to reach for the dictionary to check she meant what I thought she meant. I was absolutely gobsmacked. She followed that up with: "You know, they sit and watch television and if there's anything about sex on they both look away, as if it's disgusting." I only went up there for a week to get over splitting up with my girlfriend. I thought it was going to be a refuge!
>
> But actually, I got talking to Ted a couple of times during that week and was quite amazed at his depth of knowledge in politics and literature, when he was in the mood. They'd both worked as tic-tac men, mostly at the dog tracks, working for bookmakers.

Dad also had a sister, Auntie Grace, who was a lovely woman. She and her husband Leslie adopted a little boy, Barry, but it was a hard life for Grace, too, as Leslie died quite young and she never remarried, bringing Barry up alone.

My old man

It's fair to say that my dad, Stan Rooke, was the adventurer in his family. Before the war, he'd worked as a Prudential insurance agent and, from when I was born until his retirement, he worked for the NHS Dental Board. But, in those wartime years between, he'd certainly seen enough excitement. Dad joined the regular army in 1940 and volunteered for the newly formed No. 4 Commando, a highly skilled combat force raised to carry out raids on German garrisons in occupied France. He rose in rank to Quartermaster Sergeant, in charge of appropriating troop rations and provisions. He'd originally wanted to be in the air force but, because he was short, he wasn't eligible, which in retrospect probably saved his life. When you think how many of those airmen actually came back, I probably would never have been born.

He was one of the very few who stuck the whole war out in No. 4 Commando. If you couldn't hack it there, which many people couldn't, you could be Returned To Unit (RTU) without anything bad going on your service record, because you had volunteered. Dad was perfect for it – any self-defence moves were useless on him because he was so short you couldn't get purchase on him. There was no leverage; he was like a rock. Adam Ant would always jokingly say to him: "Stan, admit it, you're in the 4s."

He told me a lot of funny stories about his unit. Once, they were on a ship going to do a raid on a German fuel depot in the Lofoten islands, in the Norwegian fjords. The cook had roasted all these legs of lamb, but the weather was so bad that most of the soldiers onboard were dreadfully seasick. So Dad sat in the mess and ate *everybody's* lamb! Then he was almost sick too, from eating so much.

He nearly died on a training exercise, where he had to jump off a landing craft with a Bren gun and run up the beach – and he just plummeted to the bottom of the sea with this big weapon on his shoulders and had to pull it off to stop himself drowning. Then he was up on charges because he'd lost a bit of important equipment! He was let off, but that's how serious it was, as he had to go through the whole process of proving he had to take this gun off to save his life.

He was suited to the life of a quartermaster, as he was a bit of a wheeler-dealer. If they had too much butter to carry around with them, for example, he'd go into the local community and do some deals – he said he could remember buckets of oysters in Amsterdam. Once, he managed to appropriate an entire ration of butter that had been designated for pregnant women – that was one I think he had to hand back. Another time, he had a lot of cigarettes that he swapped for a beautiful ring, solid gold with a big diamond inset. Funnily enough, back at home in peacetime, he lost the diamond ring gardening and spent years looking for it. I still think about that ring. A mole could come up one day like Paul Simon, with a diamond on the end of his nose!

While Dad was out in the field, Mum was left to have their first child on her own. They moved around a lot in the war, making life even more difficult and uncertain. From London, Dad's first posting was Weymouth in Dorset. Mum told stories of being chased down the street there by a Messerschmitt when she was pregnant with Jeannie. Dad sent her his army pay so she could save up and buy what she needed for herself and the baby. When he came home on leave, she went to meet him wearing this silver fox fur – the full works, with the head and paws all dangling down. He looked at her awestruck. That was where all his money had gone.

My dad was short, strong and very, very tough – though not in his heart. I remember him usually being the peacemaker at home. Roger's memories of the times before I was born and when I was only a toddler reveal darker currents to my parents' marriage than I had realised before I started work on this book.

ROGER ROOKE: I must admit we were a family who got a little bit dysfunctional. There was a bit of conflict between our parents. I think Dad would have preferred it if Mum would have been a stay-at-home mum. I remember them having, let's say, lively discussions about her going back to work. I mean, she was a great mum, she was an excellent cook and really did feed us well, proper, home-cooked food, and she was always darning socks and sewing buttons on, nothing got thrown away quickly. But I think she really liked the buzz of working in the pub, the banter and just the liveliness of it all. She was not comfortable with just being at home. She was more aspirational than Dad was, ever. I can always remember them talking about decorating the house, and her saying to him: "I suppose you'd be quite happy with orange boxes for tables and jam jars for glasses, wouldn't you?"

Dad would take me to the library every Saturday and, on the way back, we'd stop at the garage and he'd spend about quarter of an hour looking at the cars, all black and shiny and new. We never had a car, but obviously it did cross his mind… But it was all too much money out of his budget.

We didn't even have a fridge for ages, and when you think there wasn't a shop on the estate… the shopping had to be done every one or two days and then carried home on the bus, I don't know how Mum kept on top of it.

There were periods, quite frightening to me, when she went through a time of not getting out of bed and the whole of the bedroom floor was littered with cigarette packets. There was a very difficult period where there were a couple of fairly vicious rows. Not physical, verbal, but enough to make me feel really uncomfortable, awkward and not know where to put myself. That coincided with Mum disappearing.

I was probably the last person to see her before she went. I have a recollection of being at home as she came back from work in the pub in the afternoon. I can't remember what she said to me, but she went upstairs and then fifteen minutes later she'd gone again and that was it. She didn't come back.

She'd had an affair with a person she worked with, the landlord of the pub, the Hole in the Wall, and he left his family too. They went to Hastings and she was gone for a couple of months. Of course, Dad was devastated. He went down with shingles.

But I think what must have happened was, at the pub they put two and two together, that they must be somewhere together, and somehow they found out where that was. Now I guess Dad persuaded her to come back, which everybody must have known – Seaford's only a small town. It's quite a big thing to do, isn't it? To forgive somebody and say: "The family needs you here." But he wanted to keep the family together at any cost, so he eventually persuaded her to come back. I can remember a great feeling of relief because there were no more rows, and I think the teachers all knew at school what had happened, so I was given a bit of leeway, a bit of sympathy, I guess.

I have absolutely no memories of any of this happening, but it explains a lot. I remember, in later life, Dad telling me that he had called the Salvation Army to help him find her – he had been absolutely distraught, he loved her desperately. He was a bit at sea, a bit lost without her, and once she died, he started to drink even more than he did before. He didn't know what to do with his life except drink. And as a poignant coda to Roger's story about the cars, in the last few days of Dad's life, when he was in a hospice, he had some intensely vivid dreams, one of which was about buying a motor from a car sale on Seaford seafront and driving off in it. Maybe that was his vision of what heaven was really like.

But I had no idea Mum had been so depressed that she'd considered taking her own life. I can only guess that, when I came along, Mum thought it would mark a new beginning. That it would be really nice if I was a sweet little girl, not like my tomboy sister Jeannie, who was not your average schoolgirl of 1960, but the little girl she'd always dreamed of. A girlie-girl.

Only it didn't quite work out that way…

Dance, ballerina, dance

My first memory of clothing, which would have been when I was little more than a toddler, was a little pink cape I saw in a shop. It was fuchsia, or even cerise, bright wool, with a mandarin collar in black velvet and a little cap that went with it. It had lovely lining too. Another thing I can still smell to this day.

My first soundtrack to dressing up came courtesy of my Triang, a child's record player that played nursery rhymes on brightly coloured red and yellow plastic discs. 'Dashing Away with the Smoothing Iron' is one that I really remember, that I used to play over and over again. Jeannie had a record player – it wasn't a real Dansette, because I don't know if Mum and Dad would have been able to afford one – but Jeannie made it look like one, by covering the maroon lid with white Fablon, putting it all round the edges. It looked so good by the time she finished that it became a source of real argument when she split up with her boyfriend Morris and he claimed it was his in the first place. Jeannie remembers it costing £27, a fortune in those days! It was on this customised contraption that I would play my first proper record, *The Nutcracker Suite*, which came from a whole album of excerpts of ballet music, and which meant so much to me.

I was probably about seven or eight when I started doing ballet classes with Angela Bolsch, at Miss Angela's School of Dancing in Eastbourne. When they knew I was really taking it seriously, Mum

11

and Dad let me have *Dancing Times*, an expensive, glossy monthly that had the results of all the competitions in it. It also had lots of articles about dancers, and it was there that I first read about Margot Fonteyn.

There are, in my mind, very few dancers who had everything. Margot Fonteyn is one, and so is Natalia Makarova. These dancers were perfect in their technique but also showed great verve and character. Then I saw the film *Romeo and Juliet* with Rudolf Nureyev and Fonteyn, and I was just enchanted.[2]

One of the most exciting moments of my life was one day when I'd been to school, done my athletics practice, got on the bus, been to my ballet practice, and Mum suddenly turned up at the ballet school. She had never done this before: I would normally get the bus back home. But she said: "We're going somewhere." She was taking me, for the first time ever, to see a ballet. It was the Royal Ballet in *Coppélia* at the Congress Theatre in Eastbourne. She just turned up and said: "We're off!" I finally got to see real ballet dancers on-stage and I was in total ecstasy.

Mum and Dad always went the extra mile to get me the ballet lessons and the beautiful clothes and shoes that went with it. I could never thank them enough for that, and I encourage anyone who's got a child with such an inclination to scrape the money together somehow, because you've opened up a whole different world for your child. Ballet was everything to me, really.

When I was a little girl, the country was still recovering from the Second World War, when people had been dying in their thousands and cities had been bombed night after night. What my parents' generation went through was incredible; they felt lucky just to have survived. So I was a product of that post-war environment.

'Make do and mend' is one wartime slogan that has stayed with me. I always used to darn all my own ballet shoes, because they're very expensive, new pointe shoes. You can't just let them wear out quickly – a few dances and all that satin would go. With a special

---

[2] Years later, Derek Jarman took me to the Royal Ballet in London, where I met the choreographer and director Sir Frederick Ashton, who had so often worked with Margot Fonteyn. It was quite a moment for me.

Prima ballerina: Dame Margot Fonteyn

Dame Margot Fonteyn was the daughter of an Irish mother and Brazilian father. She took her first dance classes at the age of 4. She showed such talent that, at only 14, she was enrolled at the Sadler's Wells Ballet School. Margot began performing with Ninette de Valois's Royal Ballet and devoted her entire career to the company.

Her debut was as a snowflake in *The Nutcracker* in 1934, followed by parts in *Sleeping Beauty, Giselle* and *Swan Lake.* Her first major role was in Sir Frederick Ashton's *Le Baiser de la Fée* in 1935, and she became Ashton's muse. He created leading roles for her in *Apparitions, Nocturne, Les Patineurs, A Wedding Banquet* and *The Quest,* among others. During the Second World War, she continued to perform a full schedule, including entertaining the troops.

In 1961, when Margot was in her forties, she had just started to think about retirement when she met the Russian Rudolf Nureyev, who had defected at the age of 23. They became the most dynamic and popular couple in the ballet world, performing *Swan Lake, Giselle* and *Romeo and Juliet.* For the next fifteen years, they performed together all over the world, until, at the age of 60, Margot gave her farewell performance at the Royal Opera House.

The reason Margot danced on for so much longer than any other ballerina was for love. In 1955, at the age of 36, she married a man she had met in her youth, Roberto Arias, the son of the former president of Panama. He led her into a life of trouble and danger. She was arrested in Panama in 1959 while helping him attempt a failed coup against the government and then, in 1964, a rival politician shot Arias, leaving him a quadriplegic for the rest of his life. Margot retired to Panama to be close to him. With no pension, she spent her savings looking after him for the rest of their lives.

Margot received the title of *prima ballerina assoluta* from the Royal Ballet in 1979, one of only three women to receive that distinction in the twentieth century. This brave, brilliant, remarkable woman took her final bow on 21 February 1991.

thread, you'd make a chain stitch going round in a circle, right round in the middle, and that reinforced the whole tip of the pointe shoe. I spent hours doing it on every new pair. I can darn a pointe shoe

with my eyes closed now. Then you had to put your own ribbon on, just angled right for your ankle with no puckering, double-sewn over the top, because it takes a lot of stress as well. That's how I could spend all night stitching before the major scene in *Jubilee* – it was like second nature to me by then.

Playground twist

I started school at Chyngton Primary, conveniently located at the end of my road. I can still remember some of the first clothes I really liked to wear. Along with the pink cape, I used to wear these little sticky-out dresses and, because of that, I was regarded as being unusual and even started to get into a bit of trouble.

Luckily, I had a good friend in Glynis Rundell, an older girl who was a bit of a minder, so if anyone did anything to me, she would have them – she once had someone up against the wall by their throat because they were picking on me. And that had a knock-on effect because, by the time I got to secondary school, if anybody picked on one of my friends, I'd be the person to protect them. It taught me about standing up for people who can't do it for themselves.

I was average, I should think, at primary school. I would say, truthfully, I was rather more into literature than maths. Though I did get picked for one special occasion. There was a big school celebration, I guess it might have been an anniversary, and the headmaster wanted somebody to present a bouquet to his wife. So there was a curtsying competition to see who was graceful enough for the task and I won. I'd done a lot of ballet practice by then.

My main focus was on sports. I was training daily. I won a race down my street and first prize was a pencil case, second prize was a pencil case, third prize was a pencil case. It was hard to see the incentive in that. I should have at least had some pencils in my pencil case! That may have been the beginning of the trend in which no one can be a loser, which then results in no one being a winner. You should really, really encourage talent. You can't do that if you're trying to equalise everyone.

The time of the season

The summers of my early childhood were spent at the pubs where Mum worked. I spent hours and hours of my life at the Cinque Ports, in Seaford – which is still open, quite something in these days of pubs closing hand over fist. I would be upstairs with the lady who owned it, Ma Turner, while Mum ran the bar. There used to be a great big wooden gate, where the brewery people came in to deliver, and my Dad got worse for wear there once and tried to jump over it! He'd had a works do with the Dental Board and was so drunk that a work colleague tied him to the back of a motorbike and drove him home from Eastbourne.

Then there was the Old Tree, which is now a mobility scooter outlet – a burgeoning enterprise on the south coast, unlike the pub trade. Mr and Mrs Reed owned that and, although it was pebble-dashed on the outside, inside it had all the old beams and low ceilings. It was really lovely.

For many summers, Mum and Dad used to take over a pub called the Brewers Arms in Mayfield, a little village up in the High Weald of Sussex with an intriguing history. In the eighteenth century, it was at the heart of silk and brandy smuggling, a practice they used to call 'owling'. Very much a hotbed of dissenters, the village was also involved in the Swing Riots in 1830, when agricultural workers revolted against landowners across the south and east of England, striking terror into the ruling class, who feared a replay of the French Revolution on English soil. It still has the feel of a Hammer horror film about it, especially on Bonfire Night, when the town takes part in the Sussex tradition of torchlight procession and fireworks display.[3] We used to stay there for our summer holidays while the landlord went on his, living in the pub for three weeks or a month. I remember the mynah bird they used to have that would copy the things you said to it; and long hot days spent playing in haystacks and scrumping apples, and my dollies Linda, Diane and Miré, who Dad bought me one time when we were staying there. It was only me who would go with Mum and Dad to the Brewers Arms, and this was really the closest thing I had to a family holiday. Jeannie had already married her first husband James and gone to live in Scotland, where he worked for British Aerospace; and Roger, now an amorous adolescent, had his own plans for staying home alone.

ROGER ROOKE: I was particularly pleased one year, because I had a girlfriend, and I thought: Yes, at last! We don't have to go in the bus shelter! Of course, I didn't waste any time: the very first day you were away, I told this girlfriend she could come up to the house. So I went to

---

[3] Lewes holds the biggest parade of them all and has several different factions competing to blow up effigies of the Pope and any current authority figure considered worthy of being stuffed with gunpowder and set alight.

where she lived and walked back with her, and as I walked around the corner there was Jeannie's car parked outside. She hadn't told me, but Jeannie had this plan that while they were away she would redecorate the bathroom. So that was that. I had to turn straight back round and walk this girlfriend home.

JEANNIE CRAVEN: Well, it was a week's work, and it was hard work. When it was done, I gave Mum and Dad the bill – £19, it was. I had to pay for the paint. I had no idea that Roger was going to bring his little friend round.

After the pubs, Mum worked for years in a haberdasher's shop, selling curtains, towels, linens, all sorts of things. She made me a dress with Velcro cuffs, which amazed my schoolfriends when I pulled them open to show them how it worked. Over the road from that shop was the salon where she used to get her hair done. Mum was always very careful about her appearance, and her hair was central to that. The proprietor was a guy called Michael Anthony, who used to do her hair in rollers, with the hood dryers, the whole thing – and, of course, the Marcel wave, made with special iron tongs. She had a lovely head of hair, my mum, really thick, and she stayed dark, she never went grey. I've inherited that.

Wondrous place

Dad prided himself on always being able to provide for us. The generation who came back from the war made sure their gardens were full. Out front was always planted with regiments of beautiful flowers, like dahlias and roses, but the back was the veg, the business end of the family plot. I used to get sent out on Christmas morning to get the Brussels sprouts. And he'd always say: "Pick the big ones!" I'd have to look at every stalk, so they'd fit on the plate with the twelve other vegetables.

JEANNIE CRAVEN: James once whispered to me at Christmas dinner: "There are thirty-one Brussels sprouts on my plate!" In his house it was the opposite: his mother never gave him enough to eat. Twelve vegetables including thirty-one Brussels sprouts. Food was the best part of the family, wasn't it?

Although Dad had green fingers, he was useless at any kind of DIY. I once came home to find him wandering around looking puzzled. One of the Bakelite tiles had come off the skirting board and he'd tried to fix it with the type of glue you have to put onto both surfaces and then leave for ten minutes before pressing them together. Dad had wandered off to have a cup of tea and come back to find the tile had vanished. He looked everywhere for it – even in the airing cupboard – until I saw that it was stuck to the back of his waistcoat.

He didn't like to spend any money on tools, either. He had one handy screwdriver, which Roger watched him lose while trying to put a tile back on the roof. It went straight down a drainpipe, at the bottom of which it probably remains to this day. I've had similar excruciating experiences watching him try to change a plug.

But one thing he was brilliant at was catching shellfish. He used to pick winkles, take them to Eastbourne to a fishmonger's there and sell them, to pay for Jeannie's cricket coaching. He also used to go prawning, so we had fresh prawns for ourselves. This was quite an alarming feat, because you had to work with the tides and sometimes it can be pretty dangerous. If the tide was right, he would go out at one in the morning, in the dark, and it's really treacherous down there, all jagged rocks covered in seaweed. He used gin nets, which are the ones you dip into the water and wait for the prawns to take the bait, so it wasn't just a matter of scooping a big net along the sea bottom. This took patience, skill and daring.

There's a kind of link to London in it, too – it was always a very big London thing, getting cockles and winkles and jellied eels to be served in the pubs. So there was probably something there that fed Dad's own memories of childhood.

As soon as he considered I was old enough, which would have been when I was about 10, I would join him. Some of the happiest days of my life have been spent under the gullies of the Seven

Sisters, perhaps the most wondrous – and dangerous – spot on the Sussex coast.

Grab the crabs! Kill! Kill! Kill!

We used to ride down to Seaford Head on our bikes, with the nets on the handlebars. A steep enough journey through the heathland going up the cliffs, but that was nothing compared to coming down. They've got proper steps here now – health and safety, of course – but then it just used to be rugged, irregular pieces of stone that you had to pick your way around. The prawns were all down there in the gullies to the north. The whelks were over to the south somewhere. They were separatists.

Once we were in the prawning grounds, we'd get straight down to business. Dad had a round net, and he would make a little rod that went through it, with a notch cut into it, so that you could rest it in the net. You'd catch crabs first, bait them with some old fish or whatever he had to hand. They would go straight for it, then you'd grab the crabs, crack them open, break all their legs off, halve them and spear them on this stick, put the stick in the net and that's what the prawns go for. It was a killfest!

You'd have a little float on the end of your net, so you could see where it was, though at night-time it was quite difficult, and there have been many times where I've had to wade out, quite dangerously, in order to get the prawns – you could just see the cork bobbing where they were biting. Otherwise you've lost your net.

I didn't have any special waterproofs for these manoeuvres, just a pair of trousers and some wellies, which weren't really all that good for it. The best thing would have been hobnail boots, because you can so easily jam your ankle between the rocks. And it's a real ankle-breaking sort of place. I used to get so wet, and so cold!

If I bunked off school, I would always go somewhere around the Seven Sisters. My best friend Sally Reid and I used to walk all the way along the cliffs, with my big bag of Tom Thumb drops and Tizer, like the Famous Five or the Secret Seven. When I moved back to Seaford in the eighties, it was a kind of therapy to see it all again; to be out in this wild place, with the skylarks and the

19

swallows all ducking and diving around. Dad's still with me when I come back here now. It's where we scattered his ashes, down where he used to go prawning.

After a long night's vigilance, once we had gathered our nets, Dad used to put all our bounty in an old Second World War gas-mask bag. I've still got it, and his Commando knife in its leather sheaf. I feel perfectly safe with that in the kitchen drawer…

Then we'd bring back the prawns to the sink at home, still alive.

Put 'em in a box, tie 'em with a ribbon

One special occasion I'll never forget was buying my first ever bras, in Colliholes on the High Street. I was well endowed for a young child of 9, quite far ahead of some of the girls in my primary school.

Funnily enough, the experience was very much like going into the SEX shop would later be. It had those lovely big old wooden cabinets, sometimes with a glass front on the door, and stocked very large ladies' knickers and Cross Your Heart bras, and a lot of support garments – this was the era when women had to wear their girdles. Again, this was a thing that you'd later see in SEX, models wearing corsets and suspender belts. Malcolm McLaren appropriated a lot of things from those days.

My first bras were Berlei, size 30AA, in a sort of nylon fabric – it was that time when everything changed from old cotton into drip-dry fabrics. One was turquoise and white; the other one was lilac checked gingham. They were little tiny Doris Day bras, and very good-quality garments. My parents' approach to clothes was always to save for something that would be better made than the cheaper alternative, and it's something that I've stuck to all my life.

Dad's biggest outlay was the suit that he had to wear to work, and you couldn't just get suits off the peg. Montague Burton started the idea of being able to buy your suit piece by piece, until you'd got the full monty from his chain of Burton's shops, but Dad used to go to a little place called Hepworth's, which made suits to measure. It would have cost him a month's wages, a serious consideration, but it would be made to last for years and years. This is why I am in total agreement with what Vivienne Westwood has always said

20

about clothes – that you should buy things in a considered way. They might be expensive, but they're something that you will really love and value.

Already, the instincts and aesthetics that would guide me in later years were quite clearly formed in my mind.

2

HIGH SCHOOL CONFIDENTIAL

I was a teenage alien (1966–70)

Girl trouble

By the time I left junior school, I already knew I was going to do something different with my life.

I didn't pass my eleven-plus and went to Seaford Head Secondary, where I first met my friend Sally, and Gillian Payne, another girl I'd been friends with at juniors, who often lived up to her surname. I did really quite well to begin with – I was in the A stream – but it was a real eye-opener going from quite a small school at the end of my road to a big comprehensive full of loud, clamouring voices. At times, my secondary school days closely resembled the Bash Street Kids strip in the *Beano*. I didn't have many friends, but one of the best was Lesley Foster, who would be there for me in some crucial moments of my young life, and still remains very close to this day.

LESLEY FOSTER: My first memory is sitting in the school playground with Gillian Payne, her of the limp. I had started a term after you, so I was new there and she always tagged on to new people. I can remember sitting in the playground with her while the rest of you all 'limped' from one corner to another. [You and I] just hit it off and I don't think in fifty years we've ever had a cross word.

Lesley, Sally, Gillian and I shared a binding passion – *Star Trek*. We'd watch episodes together round mine and I'd record them all on a Binatone – a horrible little tape recorder with a button you pushed up to play and then you brought down to the left or right. Then we'd transcribe the scripts, word for word, and make up our own stories that spun off from the episodes on TV. I was always Spock, my favourite character and the reason I remain an avid Trekkie to this day; Lesley was always Scotty, and Gillian – well, she had a new character of her own to play.

LESLEY FOSTER: Jim Kirk had a wife called Julia – that was always Gillian. But we never had a Kirk, and I don't think we had a Bones either. I had a Saturday job and managed to wangle it so that I started early and finished in time to get to yours to watch *Star Trek*. Staying at your house for weekends, I remember, 'cos your mum used to make the best bacon sandwiches on a Sunday morning. I've never had bacon sandwiches like it since. The smell, as she brought them up with a cup of tea for us...

My bedroom was by then decorated with blue, turquoise and green wallpaper, and a rotating, *Barbarella*-type chair, made of polystyrene and covered in blue canvas, with a white plastic moulded base. Sitting in there, listening to *Leonard Nimoy Sings Songs from Outer Space*, imagination might allow you to think that you were on the bridge of the Starship *Enterprise*.

We also used to spend long hours at the cinema, either at the Curzon in Eastbourne or our local fleapit in Seaford, the Ritz. Then we used to get fish and chips and walk to the swings, where we'd sit making up more *Star Trek* stories.

LESLEY FOSTER: How many times did we see *Paint Your Wagon*? At least nine. We went to see *Midnight Cowboy* and we were extremely under age. It was on with *Women in Love* at the Curzon. When we got there, they asked us how old we were and, 'cos your brain works quicker than mine, you reeled off your date of birth with a couple of years added. Then they

The search for Spock

Leonard Simon Nimoy (1931–2015) was best known for his role as Spock in *Star Trek*. This began with the original TV show pilot *The Cage*, directed by Gene Roddenberry, shot in 1964, and ended with his final performance in the film *Star Trek into Darkness*, directed by J. J. Abrams in 2013. Spock, the Science Officer on the USS *Enterprise*, who would rise in rank from Lieutenant Commander to Captain over his time in the Starfleet, is of mixed race, his father a Vulcan and his mother a human. The troubles he endures because of this inform several plotlines, drawing parallels with the America of the 1960s.

Spock has many endearing talents, including the 'Vulcan nerve pinch' to disable his foes, the 'Vulcan mind meld' to access information from the brains of others and a logical mind to counterpoint the more red-blooded instincts of his Captain, James T. Kirk (William Shatner).

In real life, Nimoy was born in Boston to Jewish Ukrainian parents who had fled the pogroms of Tsarist Russia. He took drama classes at Boston University and voiced radio shows for children on local stations, often reading stories based on the Bible. His co-star William Shatner later noted in his book *Leonard: My Fifty-Year Friendship with a Remarkable Man* (St Martin's Press, 2016): "Obviously there was something symbolic about that. Many years later, as Captain Kirk, I would be busy rescuing civilizations in distress on distant planets while Leonard's Mr Spock would be examining the morality of man- and alienkind."

Nimoy wrote two autobiographies in which his Vulcan alter ego took centre stage, *I Am Not Spock* (1975) and *I Am Spock* (1995). In 1995, I stood in a queue around the block at the Forbidden Planet comic emporium in London to get my copy of this second tome signed by the great man himself. I had been on TV in Paul Tickell's *Punk and the Pistols Arena* documentary a couple of weeks before, and I was standing out from the crowd with a red wool blazer and long white ringlets. Right at the moment I got to Leonard Nimoy, a bloke came out of nowhere and said: "Jordan! Can I have your autograph?" That was too much for me. I said: "Can you just FUCK OFF! Go away and wait until I've spoken to Spock!"

I did get a kiss off Nimoy, so it was worth it in the end. And I signed the autograph for the fan, too. He was lucky.

looked at me and said: "What about you?" and I said: "Same as her! We're twins!" The bloke looked at us. I said: "We're not identical!" We got in – just in time to miss the nude wrestling scene in *Women in Love*.

This sporting life

I continued to be very sports-orientated and Seaford Head was well equipped for such endeavours. It had a really good running track, with a long-jump landing pit on the side of it. Across the road was the hockey pitch, netball and tennis courts – I was the captain of the hockey team, too. We had a gym equipped with climbing bars and rings and a swimming pool, which was really something in those days, although it was an outdoor one.

I was very, very busy with athletics at school. I would do hurdles – the 100-metre hurdles is a very quick race and, because they could see that I had some talent, the sports teacher would stay behind and tutor me after school, at hurdling in particular. I used to train with pegs on my nose to make me breathe properly!

I was probably one of the first people to have a pair of spikes in school. My parents had to really save up for those. They came

home one day with this beautiful pair of spikes, they were Slazenger, leather, black and white. And I was so thrilled with them, I took them to school – and my teacher said: "I'm sorry, these are cross-country ones, they're not for sprinting on track, the spikes are too long."

Dad had saved up and saved up for these – but he took them back and came back with a pair of spikes that were meant for track. They were Gola, maroon and white. I can remember more about my sportswear than anything else about school!

After athletics practice, I'd get on the bus and go to ballet, doing my homework on the bus. I did a lot of duets with Caroline Tarbuck, my partner in dance, including *War and Peace* and *Exodus*. All told, it sounds like a tough workload, but if you really, really enjoy something, then it's not work. I'm eternally grateful that my parents allowed me to do it, especially when we had so little money.

Back in the jug agane

Alongside all these advantages, there was one major drawback to my high school life. Mr Alexander, my Maths teacher, lived next door to me. He was a force to be reckoned with, was Alex. Old school. Ex-army. "I fought seven years in the war for you lot," he constantly used to remind us. "What am I standing here for with you load of twits? I could be up there playing golf." This was delivered in a really venomous way. Alex terrorised Sally, and the reason she was always going up and down between streams was largely down to him. I remember once when Jeannie and her husband James came home for a weekend, James, who was a total maths genius, helped me with my homework. Alex marked it: "A+. Well done, James."

We were disruptive at school, but it was the teachers as well as the pupils who gave Seaford Head its comic-strip atmosphere. We used to chop up little bits of rubbers and surreptitiously put them on the top of the boiler rack. Obviously, they began to smell. After a while, Alex would get up and sniff his jacket, and then his armpit. When he finally sussed out what was going on, a blackboard rubber would whizz past the side of my face, missing me by millimetres.

Richard Gillett and I were on the school's public speaking team. Now Richard teaches circus clowning – and I reckon he got his start in the classroom. Alex once pulled him out of his desk, dragged him to the front of the class and smacked him so hard his bum landed in the waste-paper basket and he got jammed in there. When he stood up, the bin was still attached. Not to be upstaged by this unintentional comedy moment, Alex smacked him all the way out of the class and all the way downstairs. Anger management wasn't on the curriculum in those days.

Our Geography teacher, who also lived on the same estate as us, used to invite girls into his stationery cupboard – but not me and Sally. We used to feel left out because of this, but now realise we probably had a lucky escape. Not that we ever saw what went on – we only heard the rustling of papers and the sharpening of pencils – but I reckon he probably asked the girls who were chosen for this honour to look on the tops of shelves for things, while he accidentally dropped something on the floor…

Then there was Mr Griffiths, our History teacher, who used to hide in his cupboard, having a smoke. Those were the days when you had a teacher who would say: "Good morning, you lot – now get in your holes, you rats." And then, when the lesson was over, say: "All right, you rats, off you go."

But I did actually work hard in lessons I liked. English was one of my strong subjects; another one was art. Sally and I had a way of remembering art history, by making up word associations that we'd score points for. The best was the mnemonic "1240, Charles Hawtrey", which was the date of birth of Cimabue, the Florentine painter and mosaic artist, whose life and work were an inspiration to me. Cimabue was a real rebel, one of the first people I would consider to be punk. There have always been people who've balked against the Establishment and it doesn't matter when they existed, only that they *did* exist. We remembered his date of birth by rhyming it with Charles Hawtrey – and it worked. Look it up now and you'll see I'm right.

I had a very fine art teacher, Mrs Scott, a sweet lady who got hell from a lot of the students who weren't interested in the subject. I learned a lot from her – pottery, screen-printing, all sorts of painting techniques from watercolours to gouache. She came to the Crypt in Seaford when I gave my first real talk about my past, all those years later in 2015. She was there in the front row.

So it really upset me that, when I did my three A levels, the one that was a sure thing as far as all the teachers were concerned was Art – and it was the only one I didn't pass! It just goes to prove how subjective it is, and how difficult it is to judge, because obviously what I did wasn't what they wanted to see. I was doing quite a lot of abstract and acid etchings. I'd had art prizes every year, really big prizes, up until then.

The A levels I did pass were in English and Law. Sally and I had to go to night school in Lewes to study Law, as it wasn't something that was on the school curriculum, but our Religious Instruction teacher, Mr Forsyth, had studied it himself and thought we would be good at it. My sister Jeannie studied Law – she became one of the first female Assistant Justices of the Peace in Britain – so it runs in the family.

Law is very interesting if you've got an analytical mind. It's basically a history of precedents rather than making a moral judgement on what's wrong or right, which is something that a lot of other students found difficult. Sally and I loved it. We got obsessed with Lewes Crown Court and spent all our spare time there. When you do the 'General Principles of English Law', you have to do all sorts: contract law, property. There's not a great deal of criminal law, so we thought we'd do a day's worth of criminal law in our lunch breaks. There was an attempted murder case, the Bounder Binder, who tried to kill his sister and bury her at Devil's Dyke. He dug a hole, hit her head really hard, but she didn't die. So then he decided he'd drive her to Devil's Dyke and push her and the car off the cliff. It all failed, though. He didn't manage to kill her, despite making about four attempts in one day.

SALLY REID: There was a Green Shield Stamp fraud, as well. Not quite so interesting.

But, although I was excelling at all these things, there was trouble ahead. I was a prefect when I was asked to leave on account of my hair. But the seeds of rebellion had begun sprouting in my mind long before then. A certain film, by one of history's most notorious directors, had given me an idea…

Mama Mia

The first time I had what you could call a radical hairstyle was the summer of 1968, when I was 13, and Roman Polanski's *Rosemary's Baby* had just come out. The adaptation of Ira Levin's novel, about a young wife who believes she has fallen under the spell of a Satanic coven who share her apartment block in New York's Dakota building, was a controversial hit and the film that made Mia Farrow a star.

For her role as Rosemary, she had her hair done in a really boyish crop, an ultra-short-back-and-sides that really suited the angles of her face. Roman Polanski flew in Vidal Sassoon to do the cut as a PR stunt on the Paramount lot, in a boxing ring set up as a stage. They called it the 'Pixie crop' and, though legend has it that Mia's then husband Frank Sinatra filed for divorce over it,[1] I thought it was the hairstyle for me.

Obviously, I couldn't possibly have seen the film at the cinema back then, but Jeannie was very into Frank Sinatra and I think the first time I saw a photo of Mia with the crop would have been in one of her magazines. I saw Mia very, very clearly, as someone who knew her own mind.

I was on holiday with my mum. It was the first holiday I'd ever had, and it was just me and her. I've never been absolutely sure whether this was the result of a row between her and Dad, or perhaps, as Roger thinks, that it was just because I was old enough for the two off us to go off together and she wanted to spend the time with me. We shared a room, which was the first time I'd ever shared a room with her, and actually it's the first time I can remember seeing my mum's bosoms. I was quite shocked – she was a big-breasted lady and obviously I wouldn't have shared a room with her at home; nobody flounced around with no clothes on there. I was quite amazed!

We went on a little coach tour of the West Country, Seaton, Dartmouth and Paignton. We'd been on a coach trip to the Donkey Sanctuary and, after that, we were walking through the town and

---

[1] Bizarrely, despite many photographs and documentary evidence shown in the 2011 film *Vidal Sassoon: The Movie*, when Sassoon died in 2012 Mia Farrow claimed that she did the haircut herself, in a tweet that stated: "Ppl ask: Vidal Sassoon trimmed my inch long hair as publicity prank 4 RosemrysBaby Actually I cut my own hair 2yrs earlier. He was nice. RIP".

30

saw a hairdresser's. I turned and said to my Mum: "I want my hair cut like Mia Farrow."

I think back now, and wonder – how did she put up with that? But Mum was all right with it – she must have been, or it wouldn't have happened. I went into this little hairdresser's with fairly short hair and came out with the Mia Farrow crop. Mum liked it because it suited me.

But when I went back to school, people were just so shocked... No other girl would have looked like that in those days, the short hair and the big shoes that I wore. They all thought I was bonkers. I would be running, wanting to do really well at sprinting and that, and all the other girls would be giggling at the side of the running track, wearing the shortest shorts they could find, with ponytails, looking as feminine as they could. I was exactly the opposite and that hair was just the finishing touch. I felt great, and I absolutely loved it. It empowered me, instantly.[2]

Sisters by choice

Between school and home, another big change occurred when I asked Mum and Dad if Sally could come and live with us. At the time, she was in a children's home in Seaford. Sally's dad had died when she was very young and her mum became unable to take care of her through ill health, so she had been put in this 'home', for want of a better word. There comes a time, when you reach a certain age, that you need your own space, and the lack of that was making her unhappy.

Mum promised she would look into it, and she bloody well did, straight away. Even in those days you had to jump through hoops to adopt a child, there were really strict criteria with lots of rules, but we did it and Sally came to live with us for many years. So she's a sister by choice, and I call her my sister. People do get confused, because there's only three months between our ages, so we couldn't actually be sisters. But you can't fault my mum and dad – they'd already had

---

[2] When I did finally get to see *Rosemary's Baby*, I thought it was a great film and the detail was amazing. The Dakota Building, the brilliant cast — and it really freaked people out. Films like that portray a loss of control of the mind; they are to do with possession, the fear of the unknown, which terrifies people more than getting jumped on by a monster.

three children of their own, but they were happy to welcome Sally, who has always been a very important part of my life. I loved her being at home. We did so many things together that I wouldn't have done on my own: going to gigs, shopping in London, the ballet, all sorts of lovely things. Sally also made the most wonderful daughter to my mum and dad.

In the drink

Most people can probably remember the first time they got roaring drunk. But how many can say it was their mother who got them into that state – and in a job interview situation, to boot? When I was 15, Mum was working at The Buckle pub in Seaford when she decided I needed a summer job, and took me for an interview to work in the kitchen. It was a boiling-hot day and I can still remember what I wore to try and make a good impression on the landlord, Mr White: a seersucker skirt that went all the way to the floor, cut on the bias, with yellow and green stripes that went round, and a pair of yellow patent Ravel cork-heeled wedges.

But, rather than just introducing me to my prospective employer, Mum sat me down at the bar and proceeded to order drink after drink until I didn't know where I was. I don't think she realised I just couldn't drink that much. But it was unbelievable. It still shocks me to think about it. And I got the job! When I got home I had to go back and play stoolball[3] with Sally, riding my bike to get there. I was *so* ill. I was *so* drunk.

Crash

There are some things in your life that you have no control over, and that can change everything in an instant. One happened to me on 4 July 1970.

---

[3] Stoolball is a game native to Sussex, dating back to the fifteenth century. It is said that milkmaids used to play it using their stools as the wicket. It's similar to cricket, but you have raised stumps in a square. It can be quite dangerous. While fielding in the equivalent to the wicket-keeper position, I once got hit straight in the forehead by the bat. Sally stayed up all night with me to make sure I didn't have concussion. See www.stoolball.org.uk for more information.

It was really near my home, on the main A259 road, and I was running to get my dinner before I went on a school outing to see *Peer Gynt* at Chichester Theatre. It was a hot summer's day and there was a long stream of traffic as I approached the bus stop almost opposite where I live. I didn't look left or right – whether my brain had told me there was a gap in the traffic, I have no idea – but I was thinking about something else and I just ran across the road without looking.

I still remember each second of what happened next. A car hit me, a white Vauxhall Viva. It was probably coming at 30–35 mph and I collided directly with its headlights. Things went flying everywhere – they found clothing fifty, sixty, seventy metres down the road, and my shoes and glasses.

Lesley had been standing right next to me.

LESLEY FOSTER: I'll never forget it. I was here, my bike was next to me and you were next to my bike. The day before, you'd stopped me getting knocked down by a bus in exactly the same spot. You ran out and there was this incredible bang and you went flying… I thought it was further than it was. When I've seen the bus lane since, it wasn't as far as I thought. But my bike went flying behind you. I went over to you and you said: "I think I've broken my leg." I took my coat off to cover you up, so you were modest. Someone from somewhere came out with a cushion to put under your head and I think I just sat there and held your hand and yelled at Gillian, who was at the other end of the bus stop, to go and get your mum.

I tried to get up and immediately fell down again. It was the most unusual feeling, not having any power in my legs at all. I tried to get up to run away from the scene without realising that I had three fractures to my pelvis and my pubic bone had crossed right over – which meant I couldn't lie down on my back either, I had to stay where I was, with one leg underneath me and one leg sort of propping me up. Any other movement was agony. The thing that saved me from an even worse injury was that I had my Adidas sports bag resting on my hip at the point of impact, with all my homework in there. That really thick plastic bag with a heavy book inside it probably saved me from losing a leg, or worse – though afterwards I was pissed off that the bag was broken. There was a massive V-shape cut into it from the impact. But, then again, my doctor said if it had been a sports car, it would have gone straight into my femur and smashed it to pieces. I would have either lost my leg or it would have been a whole lot shorter. And, if it had been a lorry, I would have been dead.

I can remember Lesley turning as white as a sheet. I was spitting blood out onto the road – they thought it was internal bleeding, but I'd bitten my tongue really badly and damaged my elbow.[4] I have a surreal memory of my teacher, Mrs Watkins, leaning over me and saying: "I suppose you won't be needing your ticket for tonight after all, then?"

Mum came running out and then had to send Gillian back again to the house. Because I had to eat quickly and then go back to school to get to Chichester, she thought she'd left my dinner under the grill and it was going to burn the house down. I had to stay under my coat covering until the ambulance arrived.

They couldn't give me any pain relief in the ambulance at all; my only consolation was that Mum was there with me. Although I had to actually ask her if she would hold my hand – Lesley gave me more affection that day than she did. It was because she was in shock – she'd run all the way from home, I had blood coming out of my mouth. All sorts of horrible things.

The ambulance driver said: "I'm going to go very slowly, because there are fractures here, we just don't want to make it any worse." So they put the sirens on, but they went really slowly. I remember every pothole, every jolt, all the way to the hospital.

Meanwhile, Lesley and Gillian were left standing on the pavement in a state of shock. Then an unlikely hero stepped into the breach.

LESLEY FOSTER: When the ambulance came, your mum went in there. But they wouldn't let me or Gill come with you, so we were both a bit shocked. You went off, I left my bike at your house and Alex took us in next door. He was absolutely amazing. He and his wife made us sit down and gave us a cup of tea. He smoked; I always remember I had cigarette

---

[4] My elbow is still numb to this day at the point where it hit the road. I still can't sleep on my back, either, because of the amount of time I spent in traction. I've got a souvenir bruise on my right thigh at the point of impact with the car, deep tissue damage that will never heal; and my right leg turns out more from the hip.

ash floating in my tea. Then he took us home in his car and he told my mum what had happened. He was extremely kind. He was saying how well I'd done, and all I'd done was covered you up and held your hand. Made sure you didn't fall over. Then he took Gill home. I was a mess, really. My worst thing was seeing the ambulance go off with you in it, but this cemented our friendship and the feelings that I have for you and I've had for you since. In adversity...

As soon as we got to A&E, they gave me big injections into my thigh. They had to cut all my clothes off and turn me onto my side, which Mum and I would never forget – Mum heard my screams coming all the way down the corridor. I don't think that would happen these days; you'd immediately have a scan and an MRI for internal bleeding, but there was none of that in 1970. I just had to have X-rays, where they found the three fractures. I was put on traction, where they pull the socket of your thigh out so that your pelvis can move back to the correct position.

The police took a statement from me, in which I said that it was my fault. I was really clear that no one was going to get the blame for it. The person travelling in the back of the car was fairly elderly and apparently had a heart attack afterwards; it was such an enormous shock to see someone fly over the bonnet like that.

LESLEY FOSTER: I think Mum phoned your mum later in the evening to see how you were. There was talk that you might have to have an operation because it was your pelvis.

After the initial pain of the pelvic break, it was the pain of lying on my back that was unbearable. I lost two or three vertebrae on the base of my spine and my coccyx, because of the pressure.

LESLEY FOSTER: I wasn't allowed to go and see you on the Friday; I came in on the Saturday and you were all laid up in your traction. They said that you probably wouldn't dance again.

I had bedsores, I had to have four nurses to lift me onto a bedpan and they had to be coordinated to tilt me the right way. Dreadful constipation and things like having periods were really awful. Worst of all, I had an American girl opposite me who was a really big cry-baby. I was trying to be as brave as I could and, eventually, the nurses knew that I was crying quietly while she would be yelling out. Apart from her, I was on a geriatric ward, with people dying around me. Instead of being able to see out of the window, they'd put me facing another building, so all I could see was bricks.

Any optimism I had that I might be getting better and going home again soon vanished when the consultant came round to do a review of my case. He didn't look at me while he was talking. Instead, he said into his Dictaphone: "I'm going on holiday for six weeks – I'll review this patient when I come back." I was dreadfully crestfallen, just devastated. Mouth wide open. I was going to be stuck there for the whole of that long, hot summer…

3

I HEAR A NEW WORLD

Teenage adventures in clubland (1970–73)

Notes from underground

In a few years' time my own face would be staring back at me from its inky pages. But, in 1970, the weekly music press was an information beacon, flashing out to teenage minds across the darkest recesses of the land. And in the summer of that year, my fifteenth, I was in a pretty dark place: lying in traction on a hospital bed, in the geriatric ward of Eastbourne General Hospital.

I ended up spending ten weeks lying on my back with my leg in the air, while my pelvis gradually knitted itself back into position. As if to remind me of how lucky I had been, I had to witness several of the elderly people on the ward breathe their last through those long days and nights. There was a grim ritual to it: the closer they came to death, the nearer they got to the door, so that the nurses wouldn't wake us up when they had to wheel them away. Not that I knew such a thing as peace. There were families coming in to grieve, knowing that they would not be taking their loved ones back home; people with dementia who were in pain, waking up screaming in the middle of the night. In the daytime, it was hot – and I would get wheeled through the men's ward in my traction out onto the patio. I got a lovely tan on one leg, while the other wasted away.

But my friends who had been with me when the accident happened and looked after me then all came to visit. There were so many of them that they had to come in groups. They would bring with them the music papers that were a lifeline to the world outside. Through the pages of Sounds and NME, I was able to see into all the clubs, dance halls and festivals I was missing out on. It was a bloody – and muddy – world out there, too.

The bright sixties pop sounds that had soundtracked my childhood took a darker swing as the seventies arrived, heralded by events at Altamont, where murder was just a kiss away, and washed-out Woodstock. In an English echo, the third Isle of Wight festival had brought together Jimi Hendrix, Miles Davis, Leonard Cohen and The Doors with Pentangle, Procol Harum and Tiny Tim – and then had its idealism, along with its security, ripped to shreds by an invading force of anarchists, Hells Angels and White Panthers. Jimi Hendrix would be dead within a month of his appearance there, his meteoric career framed by iconic festival appearances.

Across the Atlantic Ocean, a new scene was taking shape. A band called The New York Dolls – singer David Johansen, lead guitarist Johnny Thunders, rhythm guitarist Sylvain Sylvain, bassist Arthur Kane and drummer Billy Murcia – were playing their first gigs in the Oscar Wilde Room of the Mercer Arts Center in NYC. Their outrageous, dragged-up, stack-heeled look, combined with the raw power of their primal rock'n'roll sounds, was attracting an equally outré audience that included Andy Warhol's Factory crowd, Lou Reed, David Bowie and the photographer and manager Leee Black Childers, who gave the Dolls the soubriquet 'glitter rock'.

In England, myriad new sounds and scenes were emerging from the smouldering ruins of the hippy dream. There was one man, forged in the cusp between blues and soul and the emergent dandyism that was about to become glam rock, who really took my eye. Rod Stewart had made a name for himself with Long John Baldry, Brian Auger and Julie Driscoll's Steampacket, gone on to sing for Jeff Beck's group and was just, I read with interest, replacing Steve Marriott as the new Face in town. It was his style I particularly liked – short, spiky hair and Great Gatsby jacket. I could do that, I thought. It was one of the ideas I had in hospital that really kept me going.

Beam me up, Scotty!

When visiting time was over, another way I tried to keep my mind off the agony of daily existence was knitting by mirror. When your head's lower than your legs because of the traction, you can't hold your arms up, so I had to use a mirror to do everything, including eating. It was beside my bed so I could see into it sideways, but I dropped a lot of stitches – and a lot of spaghetti Bolognese. I had to drink out of a baby's beaker because otherwise it would go all over me – lumpy soup that used to get stuck around the nozzle. Sometimes I used to think I might as well tip the food on my clothes, my nightie, and just eat it off that.

Apart from the music press, my most valuable reading matter was Professor Christiaan Barnard's biography *One Life*, about all the groundbreaking heart transplants he did. The nurses put it on a music stand at the side of my bed for me to read from. It really gave me hope.

The other thing I used to do was write a lot of stories. I was missing *Star Trek* terribly, so when Lesley visited we practically wrote an entire series together.

LESLEY FOSTER: I've still got some of the letters you wrote me while you were in hospital. One of them was a letter from Sarek to Amanda and you put a little note in explaining what the letter was about, and you wrote: "Answer this seriously." So I did and you sent me a reply. But I had to try and be logical, which for me is not at all easy. I've still got those; they were written on pink notepaper.

One person who couldn't hide her distress when she saw me was my dancing teacher, Miss Angela. She brought me a pot plant to put by my bed, but the look on her face was deep sadness. She was absolutely devastated, because I was, in a way, her protégée. I did eventually learn to dance again, but first I had to remember how to walk – that was another ten weeks on crutches and I wasn't allowed to put any weight on my leg, because my pelvis was healing. It would be a long, hard road back out of there.

Back in black

When I finally did leave hospital, it was music that welcomed me home – Mum and Dad had saved up and bought me a radiogram. Standing proudly in the kitchen to greet me, it was a long wooden construction, with a heavy lid, under which lay album racks, a turntable and the radio, with big dials and knobs on. Dear old Alex and other neighbours had chipped in to help me bolster my existing record collection. They'd bought me *No One's Gonna Change Our World*, a World Wildlife Fund charity album put together by Spike Milligan which featured a combination of actual Goons and tunes by Cilla, Lulu, The Beatles and Cliff – which just about sums up the strange hierarchy of showbiz royalty as it stood at the end of the sixties.

I had to have my bed downstairs because, obviously, with my crutches, I couldn't get upstairs. I didn't dare do anything that might have made me fall over or lose my balance. If I put a foot on the ground, it might have fractured my pelvis again, so I really had to keep my wits about me. Many a time I'd go to get up, half stand up and think: Why did I do that? It was just instinct.

Towards the end of that long, hot summer, we went on a family trip to Longleat for the day, in Jeannie's Mini. There was my sister, me, Dad and Mum in this small car, going through the monkey enclosure, where they all tried to rip things to pieces. Then we went through the lion enclosure and one lioness jumped on the bonnet, while another one tried to pull the rubber off the seal on the back window. We were like sardines in there, getting hotter and hotter and more and more shit-scared. My dad was going: "What are they doing? Jeannie, what are they doing? What are they DOING?" Getting more and more hysterical, pumping out sweat.

I didn't realise, until we drove away with bits missing off the car, that it was one of those old Minis where you had a drop-down handle on the outside that opened a string on the inside – and my door wasn't locked. We thought we were all going to die and I nearly could have, if one of those lionesses had put her paw on that handle. I could have survived my accident and Dad could have lived through all the perils of the war – only to get eaten by a lioness. But this wouldn't be the last time I would face mortal peril with an animal at Longleat…

One of the very first things I did when school started again in September was to go to the local cinema, the Ritz, to see Olivia Hussey in Franco Zeffirelli's *Romeo and Juliet*, on another trip organised by the school. I dressed from head to foot in the spoils of the shops I'd found in Eastbourne – and perhaps the constant presence of the Grim Reaper hanging over my shoulder all summer might have influenced my look. I had a pleated black ciré skirt, a very shiny type of plasticised synthetic that resembles crinkled patent leather. I'd found a coat in crinkled black PVC that went very well with it, and matching gloves and patent leather shoes from Ravel – along with my crutches.

My friends were delighted to welcome me home. Only many years later did one of them make the observation that, in her opinion, I had become a different person when I returned.

Maybe I'd got tougher.

First step

It was four months before I could walk properly again, but I didn't lose track of the objectives I'd made in hospital. I had to learn ballet all over again, right from baby classes. Because all my ligaments were strained on my right-hand side and my leg was out for so long, I had go back to the basics. My leg had lost all its muscle; it was just a stick. Once I'd got my balance back, I started to work on my competitive ballet again. I was doing a routine for an exam where I had to do a high kick on the right leg that completely took the left leg away from under me, right in the middle of the exam. But I passed – with honours – my Modern Ballet, and it was only afterwards that Miss Angela told the examiner that I had broken my pelvis. I don't think she thought I would ever dance again. However, not only did I dance, but I won a major prize at the Eastbourne Festival, pitted against a girl who was perfectly formed and obviously made to be a ballet dancer. She told me backstage, in a rather superior way, that she had been accepted for the Royal Ballet School, thinking this might put the heebie-jeebies up me. But it didn't; it just made me even more determined to beat her. I think I got the highest marks of anybody at the whole festival – 98 out of 100. I couldn't believe it.[1]

> **SALLY REID:** The competition was over two days and on the first day you came second against that girl. The next day it was a different piece and the judge said she'd noticed something in you that she hadn't seen the day before and had no hesitation in awarding you the prize. Your mum was so thrilled. All those bus rides in the snow, all that training, it had all paid off.

On Saturdays, I bolstered my record collection by following Roger and Jeannie's tracks up the narrow little staircase that led from the downstairs bookshop to the listening booths in Dunn's record shop on Seaford High Street. Through this magic staircase, and the clubs that lay beyond my hometown, down the coast in Brighton and up to London, I would soon make up for lost time.

I didn't have any boyfriends at school. Not one – which was out of choice. There once was a boy brave enough to ask me on a date: Kevin Cann. At the time, I'd gone to great lengths to make myself a dress in sewing class, out of a sort of synthetic python-skin material. I'd spent my entire pocket money on it. It was A-line, fully lined, French-seamed with brown sleeves – I absolutely loved it. And what did Kevin do? Dumped me for Gillian Payne. Why? Because of that dress: I was too way out there. He'd rather go for someone conventional. But that sort of thing makes you think you're on the right track, because he wasn't anything. Though it maybe should have served as a warning to me about boys called Kevin… I turned my attention swiftly back to Rod Stewart.

---

[1] I did actually audition for Sadler's Wells. But the physical parameters are exacting: they do an anatomical examination of you right down to the gaps in your vertebrae, and they also want to know your prospects for growth. Although I was the perfect height, you also have to have the perfect conformation, which I didn't after the accident. So I knew it was a bit of a long shot. But it was nice doing it. I also auditioned for Central School of Speech and Drama, but that didn't go too well. I came in looking like Marilyn Monroe in a polka-dot dress and bolero – everyone else was wearing dungarees. I guess I wasn't the blank slate they were looking for.

One of the very first concerts I went to was The Faces in action at the Sundown in Edmonton. In the flesh, Rod and his rockers were louche wastrels, dressed in satin and ostrich feathers. They looked pissed while they were singing and passed round bottles of Blue Nun to the appreciative audience, who threw back packets of fags in return.

It wasn't just Rod's gasoline-soaked voice and tales of rambling roguery that I found inspiring. His look was kind of viable. You could buy those sorts of jackets with the padded shoulders in Biba; there was also a brand called Stirling Cooper that did some really nice fitted jackets, with padded shoulders and wide lapels, designed by Roxy Music's future tailor Antony Price. You add all that lot together with some big platform shoes…

I found my way to Carnaby Street and a salon that could razor me a spiky Rod crop. Again, a lot of girls at school thought I had gone mad, because they were so opposite, so feminine. But I knew it suited me. The Stewart barnet was only the beginning.

Fish, chips and sweat

I rocked out with Rod up in London, but Brighton was where I cut my clubbing teeth. Here I met David McDonald, a young gay man who worked as a nurse at the Valley Hospital in Newhaven. David introduced my 16-year-old self to the many different artificial paradises that beckoned beyond the neon wink, fairy-light dazzle and 'kiss me quick' amusements of the seafront.

This was a world of velvet suits and long lurex dresses, go-go dancers in platform boots and DJs in white jumpsuits, where venues alternated between live music on weekdays and discotheques at the weekends, and the bouncers did a good trade in renting out ties to those not adequately kippered. Most of the legitimate places provided you with chicken in a basket or burger and chips, which you were supposed to eat in order to keep the place legal. Not many of them bothered to check your age when they let you in.

The early seventies was a raw time, with as much violence as thrills. Razor-wielding lads from London would take a train ride down for a seaside rumble; the tradition of the Mods and Rockers bank holiday fights kept strong. Bikers hung out by the clock tower at the bottom of London Road, heavy metal music booming out of the Hideaway, a converted warehouse nearby. Skinheads stalked the Beer Keller at the Queen Anne pub, while, next door at Sherry's, resident DJ Kenny Lynn rocked the white jumpsuit look. Brawlers were known to go flying over the balcony, land on the tables below and still come back up for more. Apart from all that, there were those other seventies staples: IRA bomb threats, football hooligans and the riot squad.

I met David in the Revolution, a straight club situated by the seafront. It had a low ceiling and a round dancefloor and played a lot of Tamla Motown, plus incongruous rock songs by Johnny Winter or Status Quo, dropped in, it seemed, for those who wanted to practise their air guitar. They were also over fond of playing James Brown and Billy Paul's 'Me and Mrs Jones', the sounds of which would drive us out to Tricky Dicky's gay disco every Friday night at the Stanford Arms. Like most of Brighton's gay clubs, it was slightly more cutting edge – though the chicken in a basket was mandatory and you were taking your life into your hands doing the conga – and all for 15p entrance. You had to buy a raffle ticket on the way in and Tricky Dicky used to shout out at the end of each evening: "Now who's got number 69?"

Soon there was a little gang of us – myself, Sally, David and his boyfriend Peter, Deaf Alan and the two Toms, one of whom Sally was in love with, even though she knew it was futile. But she was always falling in love with gay men.

We would often go en masse to the Curtain Club, underneath the Queen's Hotel, through 'the twittens', as the locals call them, of Ship Street Gardens and Black Lion Lane. Its entrance was in an arcade that led down to a little basement labyrinth of bars and dancefloors. It had been established when being gay was still illegal and no touching was allowed on the dancefloor. Next door was the Palace, run by a man who rejoiced in the name the Honourable Darrell Sebastian Jerome de Quincy de St Martin, which catered for a younger gay and glam crowd. It was here that I first met Anton Binder (no relation to the Bounder Binder from Lewes). Now a playwright, actor and stage magician, Anton was in those days a David Bowie lookalike who, through his gay friends, also found refuge in those clubs. He has strong memories of our first meeting, and of the scene that was rapidly inventing itself in these locations back then.

ANTON BINDER: It was the Palace Club, and I was at the bar, getting a drink. I looked around and saw you holding a clutch bag that was like a rolled-up magazine, it looked like *Vogue*. I couldn't believe my eyes when you opened it up and paid for your drinks out of it, how it was revealed to be a clutch bag.

If you looked like us in those days – and I was a complete Bowie casualty – then you were only safe in a gay club. There were no punk clubs to go to then, it was an edge-world, for gays and people who just didn't fit in. It was all about taking lots of speed and dancing ourselves stupid, looking as daft as we could. I used to love watching Deaf Alan and Tom sign to each other – they were the only people who could talk to each other above the sound of the music. They'd be screaming at each other in sign language!

The Curtain Club was very much old queens of the Quentin Crisp variety, sipping G&Ts, looking at young twinks on the dancefloor – and there was actually a curtain. The door policy wasn't quite Steve Strange at the Blitz yet, but if you didn't look right, then you weren't going to get in. The Palace was a bit of a reaction to that; it was for younger people, a more glammy gay crowd. There were different dances every night there; the queens somehow knew how to learn them. Strangely, there were no gay women in those days, they didn't seem to exist. But girls down the gay clubs – the polite term for them was 'fruit flies' – they had a definite look. They liked dancing and they liked dressing up and looking at the pretty boys. I did quite well out of that.

Anton might not have had all the same experiences as me and Sally; as we can remember there were definitely gay women at Tricky Dicky's. There were a couple of butch women who were always over friendly in the toilets, and a woman in white jeans who always jumped in right behind us when we did the conga, for some reason.

We'd also go to the Spotted Dog pub, run by a little old lady, which probably had the best jukebox in Brighton at the time. That's gone now, but the Heart and Hand pub still does have its jukebox, with Roy Orbison and Gene Vincent 45s in situ. For live music, the Inn

Place on the seafront had an upstairs room for bands that would later become part of the punk circuit. Anton can recall being bothered by Bernie Rhodes and a young Billy Idol in there some years later, and being one of only three people drinking downstairs who took the opportunity to go up and see Generation X.

The Forty-Two Club was the oldest gay club of all, but had a more militant edge: the Gay Liberation Front's British wing was founded here in 1971 by students at Sussex University, who would go on to stage the first Gay Pride march in the summer of 1973. I discovered that, like the hall of mirrors on the seafront funfair, there were always parallel universes within parallel universes.

I'd walk into straight clubs in Brighton and the DJ would clap because I had arrived, whereas in the gay clubs I felt more relaxed and there was better music to dance to. There was no threat for a gay man in the early seventies to have me standing next to him. In fact, the way I looked – dressed in 1940s and 1950s skirts, jackets and suits, found in abundance in the second hand shops of the Lanes – they thought it was great.

ANTON BINDER: The thing was, you could not be seen twice wearing the same thing in those days. You would be a pariah, because these queens were vicious: "Oh, I never tire of seeing you in that, darling!"

There was a shop in Ship Street called Uncle Sam's that had their own T-shirt printing and iron-on transfers, but they had these old 1950s bowling shirts as well. I think the owner was actually American, unless he was putting that accent on. But one of the designs he had was the cover of Guy Peellaert's *Rock Dreams* and I remember saying to the guy, "Could you put that on the back of a bowling shirt for me?" And he did, and that was my pride and joy.[2]

There used to be a big thing back then about those bowling shirts. David McDonald used to wear one with peg trousers and two-tone

---

[2] Guy Peellaert (1934–2008) was a Belgian pop artist famous for his album covers, film posters and paintings, including David Bowie's *Diamond Dogs* cover. In 1973, he collaborated with Nik Cohn on the book *Rock Dreams*, a visualisation of the rebel heritage of rock'n'roll, R&B and pop that sold a million copies. The book was reissued by Taschen in the UK on its thirtieth anniversary, but it's currently out of print.

bowling shoes. Until recently, I still had one with 'Yonkers Bowling Club' on it; it was white with an olive green trim. There was also a brief fashion of people turning up with toothbrushes in their top pockets, showing that they were ready to stay out overnight. That was their little signal. I once bought this amazing ballgown in black-and-white heavy satin, almost like something out of *Cinderella*. It was really full and gathered at the waist, with a bodice. I didn't wear too many ballgowns, but this was something else.

I've still got an original pair of 1940s suede wedges I wore back then, with cut-outs and little bows. They were beautifully made and really comfortable. My favourite outfit was a wonderful black 1940s suit with a pencil skirt, and a jacket that had slightly rounded lapels – much like Vivienne Westwood's heart-shaped lapels – a really cinched-in waist and black-faceted buttons; delightful in its simplicity. And it suited my shape.

Not everyone appreciated this. Roger can remember a serious run-in between Mum and me over a little black number I found in the Lanes, a late 1960s Courrèges dress. The whole midriff was see-through black chiffon and the next bit was cotton. But the top panel just came under my bosom, so you could almost see a bit.

ROGER ROOKE: That was quite a serious row – but you stood up for yourself, if I remember rightly. Both Mum and Dad had trouble adjusting to those times, but I guess all parents were like that; it was such a time of change. I remember Dad saying to Mr Alexander next door: "These times have really taken us by surprise. We don't seem to have the control any more."

It was as if the floodgates had opened on fashion and music. Much as I loved the 1950s look, the guys with the drapes and the girls with the leopardskin swing coats, there was still a definite sexual inequality in those clear lines of masculinity and femininity, something punk would go on to subvert, that owed something to my days slipping between the shifting worlds of Brighton's pleasure palaces.

The clubs all closed around midnight to one o'clock on weekends, two o'clock at the latest. There were a lot of parties at people's houses after that. I once went to a party on acid. It was a white party – everything was painted white and everyone was asked to wear white. Well, it wasn't very good. I had to get outside quickly, where I spent the next half-hour having a very good conversation with a postbox before I realised, eventually, that it wasn't answering, and it wasn't a human being.

If there was no party to go to, you'd buy chips if you were hungry and hitch back to Seaford. I'd often do that on my own, which in those days wasn't a prospect to be worried about. When I was getting ready for a night out, there was never any thought about how I'd get home again afterwards. That would be the last thing on my mind.

Which is not to say there weren't a few adventures along the coast road. I got arrested once while hitching home, for loading bollards onto the back of a fish truck. They put me in the cells for two hours before letting me go. Then there was the time some bloke took me onto his pontoon in Eastbourne harbour – I just followed him there, across the water, until we got to his boat and it suddenly hit me that it might not be a good idea, since I had only just met him, and turned back and ran away.

Sometimes walking home was preferable to the lifts I got offered – for instance, the night an RSPCA officer loaded me in the back of his van and locked the door. Or the time I was on the main A259 and this car screeched to a halt next to me. The driver wound down the window and went: "Bend over and I'll drive you there!" I thought that was one of the best one-liners ever.

Further perils waited at home. One night, Sally and I took David and Tom back home to Seaford. We crept in, went up to bed – and of course nothing was going to go on because they were both gay – but we were sleeping top-to-toe in the bed when my dad burst in. We had all been trying to be quiet, but I suppose we were giggling a bit. Dad went absolutely and utterly bonkers. Told them to get out – this was in the middle of the night and they lived in Brighton. I was standing there in my pyjamas telling him there's nothing going on, but he just didn't like the idea of it. I mean, it could have been an alien in there and it would have been just as bad.

50

Remake/Re-model

The reason that DJ in Brighton used to cheer me onto his dancefloor was the same reason why I got suspended from school – and you can thank the music press for that, too. In the spring of 1973, I'd just been up to London and had my hair done: bleached and dyed pink with a red stripe across the top, razor cut at the sides. Andy Mackay, the saxophonist from Roxy Music, had that haircut and I found out who was responsible for it: Keith Wainwright from Smile, the most influential stylist of the era. I made my way to Knightsbridge and his beautiful salon near Harrods.

The first day I turned up for school with my new look, I was asked to go home again. I guess the headmaster, Mr Carlisle, had a job to do and he had to be seen to be doing it. He came round to my house to try and get me to change, but I wasn't going to budge on it. The solution he came up with was for me to wear a headscarf, in class and between classes, so that nobody else could see the cerise-and-scarlet woman beneath. I thought the way to get around that was to

Give us a Smile

Keith Wainwright MBE left school at the age of 15 with no qualifications and was apprenticed as a hairdresser in Leonard's ladies salon in the West End, where he first introduced the idea of cutting men's and women's hair in the same salon. With his two partners, Leslie Russell and Paul Owen, he opened Smile in Knightsbridge in 1969 at the age of 25 and attracted everyone from Bryan Ferry to Anita Pallenberg. The haircuts were cheap (£3.50!) and there was a relaxed, clubby atmosphere, with great records playing. In 1972, he was the first hairdresser to be credited on an album sleeve on *Roxy Music*. He did the hairstyling for Derek Jarman's *Sebastiane* (1976) and *Jubilee* (1978) as well as consulting on *The Great Rock 'n' Roll Swindle* (1980).

Keith specialised in outrageous colours, going where no other hairdresser had dared to venture, for which he deserves massive credit. He had no idea that the colours he did for me back in the day had got me into so much trouble at school.

get out quicker than anyone else, lose the headscarf and stand just outside the gates, where everyone could see me.

But what I did get, surprisingly, was a good report. I think Mr Carlisle appreciated the fact that I could argue my point – I did win an award for public speaking, after all. But what was difficult was that he had to come to my home, because it wasn't something Mum or Dad had been expecting, either; they were just as shocked by it. At the time, it felt like everyone was against me.

LESLEY FOSTER: Let's face it, I was about the only person who would walk down the road with you at that point.

There was a major issue with Mum being seen out with me in public. She would tell me to keep several yards behind her. We used to go to the races quite a lot – Epsom, Brighton, Fontwell – and she wouldn't leave me at home, but she wouldn't be seen with me, so I had to be kept away from her immediate vicinity. She was very conscious of keeping up appearances.

SALLY REID: She was horrified. Mortified. She would have liked to have belonged to a more upper-class set and I think she was very sensitive as to what her friends and neighbours would think. You seemed oblivious to it.

Yet, on the other hand, she was so good at allowing me freedom. She would be cross with me hitching back from Brighton, but she wouldn't scream and shout at me the way she did over my clothes and hair. That's why I was so annoyed with my headmaster. He said: "You can't look like this at school; if I let you, then everyone's going to want to copy you."

I just burst out laughing. "You must be joking. They're not doing that, they're laughing. Can't you see no one's going to copy me?"

It was quite a big decision to make and I made it without being influenced by anyone. I was very set apart in my life, at school, in my early days. The decisions I made then were very clear and I can remember why I made them. I remember thinking: I'm not going to be just a girl who is picked up by some bloke at school. I saw these girls who were desperate to get married and have babies and I really didn't want any of that. I wanted to excel at something. I wanted to dance, I wanted to be athletic and I wanted to be my own person. So I made the decision to be nothing but my own person. If you're happy with what you're doing, then who cares if nobody wants to walk down the street with you? It's never been of consequence to me. I've never courted hangers-on.

The prettiest star(ling)

David Bowie played two shows at the Dome in Brighton on 23 May 1973. The month before, when the tickets went on sale, Sally and I had to queue up all night for our tickets, and when the day finally dawned, Brighton's streets were awash with girls with bright red hair and boys who'd raided their sisters' wardrobes, trying to emulate Aladdin Sane. I had taken special care with my appearance. I don't like to boast, but I looked so fucking good that night, it's untrue.

I'd made an earring out of starling's feathers, helpfully left for me by my cat, with pearls sewn into them from a necklace I'd taken to bits. I had a three-quarter-length Biba jacket, no lapels, brown with big beige musical notes all over it, and beautiful padded shoulders; not too much, not too little, just perfect. A pair of beige Oxford bags, a massive pair of gold platforms and, of course, my red-and-pink razor-cut hair.

Bowie had just gone from Ziggy Stardust into Kansai Yamamoto, and had publicity photos done wearing a satin suit with cherry blossom all over it – a natural bounty that was in season at the time. Sally and I climbed up a tree at the end of my road to get all the cherry blossom we could carry. It wasn't easy getting into the Dome that night, even with a ticket: the crush outside was intense and, once inside, the bouncers were displaying their usual thuggish disregard for dancing – along with the sign on the side of the stage that warned any such activity would result in the gig being stopped.

Doing my best to ignore all of that, I walked through to the front of the stage, where Bowie was wearing his cherry-blossom outfit, and threw my offering all over him. Through a shower of falling petals, he took my hand and asked me if he could have my earring. I shook my head slowly and said: "No."[3]

Biba, the source of this outfit, was in its full pomp on Kensington High Street then. Barbara Hulanicki had created an Art Deco emporium inside the old Derry & Toms department store, which had itself been redesigned in the early thirties by architect Bernard

---

[3] Years later, I met David Bowie at the 1978 Cannes Film Festival, and then again at Live Aid in 1985. If only he'd known I was that girl with the starling-feather earring.

George to the height of chic utilitarianism. Close by was Mr Freedom, on Kensington Church Street, owned by Tommy Roberts, who first opened the Kleptomania boutique on Kingly Street in 1966, stating his ambition to run it "like a circus".[4] There's a great photograph of me at dancing school, wearing a Mr Freedom top and an orange-and-white satin dress with white-framed sunglasses and white platform boots – I look like a Volkswagen Beetle. Mr Freedom went out of business in 1972 and re-emerged the same year as City Lights in a former banana store in the unreconstructed fruit and veg market of Covent Garden. Bowie was a big customer of his; he did lots of lovely coloured satin, really thick, with good shoulders. Tommy was attracted to maverick musical talents, and in the years to come he would manage Kilburn and the High Roads.

These were some of my favourite shops, though trips to London weren't complete without a visit to Granny Takes a Trip and Alkasura, on a stylish thoroughfare where Roberts had operated an earlier incarnation of Mr Freedom. These boutiques, and the people I met shopping and working there, were signposts to where life would take me after I left school. They all pointed in the fabled direction of King's Road, SW3.

---

[4] See Tommy Roberts obituary, *Guardian*, 18 December 2012.

4

A WALK ON THE WILD SIDE

Arriving in London (1973)

Becoming Jordan

I left school at 18, in the summer of 1973. I was now qualified with six O levels and my two A levels in Law and English, and spent the summer holidays doing admin work at a dental practice in Seaford and working behind the bar at the Mercury Motor Inn in Newhaven. Lesley was doing her training as a nurse and she used to sneak me into the nurses' home when we went out of an evening. Not an easy job, though she was obliged to wear a cape, which has its advantages in these situations, as any stage magician can tell you. Most of my wages went on expanding my wardrobe, with an eye to getting a job in London.

While I had been experimenting with hair, make up and clothes to transform my appearance, I had also been considering a new identity. I went through a few alternatives – I was calling myself Jipper at the time of the David Bowie gig, a deliberately androgynous name. Pamela Rooke finally became Jordan in the summer of 1973 and the inspiration came from the same place as Rod Stewart's tailoring – F. Scott Fitzgerald's *The Great Gatsby*. It was Sally who hit upon the

---

A sporty little number

Jordan Baker is a character in F. Scott Fitzgerald's 1925 novel *The Great Gatsby*. She's a professional golf hustler, with a cool, cynical edge that draws in the book's narrator, Nick Carraway, when he first meets her at a party on Long Island. Jordan, who seems to know the secrets of the mysterious elite who live in the mansions of the fictional town of East Egg, where the book is set, leads Nick into a world of intrigue that centres around reclusive millionaire Jay Gatsby.

Fitzgerald based Jordan on the real-life golfer and socialite Edith Cummings (1899–1984), the first female athlete to grace the cover of *Time* magazine in 1924. Her name was a combination of sports car manufacturers Jordan and Baker, an allusion to the new freedoms women were finding in the America of the Roaring Twenties.

---

name, inspired by the enigmatic Jordan Baker, a shrewd golf hustler who knows what really goes down in the clandestine world of the title character's glamorous milieu. Jordan was the name of a sports car that was very popular in 1920s America, when the book is set, so it wasn't a sexual definition, it was a brand name. It was inspired – and I took that inspiration and ran with it.

SALLY REID: We often talked about what we could call you, and we went through a myriad of names. Riah was one of them – the Polari slang word for 'hair',[1] which would have been good, but then I came up with Jordan after reading *The Great Gatsby*. She was a powerful character and we both thought her name was really striking. It wasn't a name you really heard in those days.

---

[1] Polari is slang used in Britain predominantly by show folk, market traders, criminals and the gay subculture, all of whom wanted to communicate without being understood by mainstream society. It is a mash-up of Italian, Lingua Franca, Yiddish, Cockney back-slang and rhyming slang, and Navy terms. It is strongly associated with Punch and Judy shows and the popular 1960s BBC radio comedy *Round the Horne*.

Way-out Way In

Now married to Linda, Roger had moved up to Canning Town, near West Ham, and I was keen to join him in London. When I saw a vacancy advertised, I applied for a job at Way In at Harrods. This was a boutique floor that was launched in 1967 as a place where the in-crowd could mingle, listen to records spun by a DJ, sip fruit cocktails, try on make-up and sample the first ready-to-wear designs for both men and women that this upmarket store had ever sold. It was a sign that even the giants of respectable retail were serious about the young designers nipping at their heels.

By 1973, they were selling a very eclectic collection of clothes, as well as the ones for ladies who dressed nicely in velvet paisley suits. What I liked most was that, as you came in, there was a great big glass dome with little models of all The Faces underneath it.

As I left for my interview, my mum waved me off with the encouraging words: "There is no way you're ever going to get it, looking the way you do. Why are you wasting your train fare?" I had transformed my look from the red-and-pink Andy Mackay cut done by Keith from Smile to pale green make-up and a blonde bouffant hairstyle by Ricci Burns, a former apprentice of Vidal Sassoon who had become one of Swinging London's most sought-after stylists. The idea was that I wanted it to look like a really big wave.

Ricci had a young stylist working for him then called Robert Lobetta, who was truly amazing. He went on to create some fantastic styles with me when he opened his own salon in Berkeley Square. Some of my most-copied looks originate with him, and he would always go the extra mile for me. I would arrive at his salon about six or seven o'clock at night and he would stay open just for me, to do whatever I wanted. He would take hours over a cut, literally hours – a true artist. And he wouldn't charge me. Never took a penny.

The idea for the make-up I took from an issue of *Vogue*. There was a guy called Serge Lutens who worked for Yves Saint Laurent; he had done a sort of Cleopatra look and I thought: It's good, but it's a bit weedy – I can do it miles better. But it gave me the idea.

Unlike Mum, Harrods approved of this look. They gave me a job as sales assistant there and then. At first, I moved in with Roger and Linda in Canning Town.

> **ROGER ROOKE:** We didn't see much of you, because you were out all day. We were terrible, really – we didn't even have a proper bed for you. We made it up out of those Habitat cubes with foam on the top. We had some very good friends who lived in the flat above us, Diane and Maureen, both teachers like ourselves. And we got the mischief in us one night and Linda dressed me up in some of your gear, a big, furry bolero sort of thing, and put quite a bit of make-up on me. Then we invited them down for a coffee and I was sitting on the sofa. Diane and Maureen came in and Linda introduced me as one of your friends! They were so polite. They either really did think that it was someone else, or they thought: Oh my goodness, he's gone trans and this is their way of telling us!

Back home, Mum, Dad, and especially Sally, took my leaving home hard.

> **SALLY REID:** I was absolutely devastated. But at least you went to Roger's; it wasn't as if you were suddenly in the middle of London with no one to look after you. So Mum and Dad were OK about that, but they were very sad. Then, the relief of not being embarrassed about how you looked took over for Mum. They loved you coming home and being in the house, but Mum especially couldn't do with going out with you.

I didn't stay at Roger's for long. The trek to the Tube and back in high heels started to grate after a while. I remember coming home from Plaistow station in a pair of Terry de Havilland shoes, all the way to Canning Town, smashing them to pieces halfway through and walking the rest barefoot. My feet were so sore. So I got myself a room in a serviced flat at 35 Draycott Place, Chelsea, with the girl I was working with, Liz Challis, who called herself Swedish Elizabeth, even though she wasn't – 'Mad Elizabeth' might have been more accurate. I got into real trouble with her once, when we took home a tester lipstick and the security guards clocked us. I didn't realise how long the arm of the law was in those days, until Jeannie told me how she came to hear about this incident during the writing of this book.

JEANNIE CRAVEN: The bit that you don't know is that two policemen came to my door, all the way up in Scotland, and I had to pay the fine. Forty pounds, it cost. Things were very different in those days.

My world was crammed into a tiny bedsitter with a Primus stove serving as the kitchen. But it was in a great location, just about equidistant from Harrods on Brompton Road and the King's Road, where a new rebel fashion aesthetic was brewing, thanks to a couple named Malcolm McLaren and Vivienne Westwood, who had taken up residence at the World's End corner, 430 King's Road.

Rocking and reeling

Malcolm and Vivienne were an unlikely couple – he was an ex-art and drama student from London with a head full of ideas about Situationism and film making; she was a former schoolteacher from a small village in Derbyshire. Vivienne was running away from her first husband, Derek Westwood, and took her young son Ben to stay with her brother in London, where she met Malcolm. One of the central enigmas, to me and to everyone else I spoke to during the writing of this book who knew them as well as I did, was how those two strange opposites attracted each other in the first place. Suffice to say, Malcolm took the first steps towards their eternal infamy by persuading Vivienne to take pattern-cutting lessons, in order to make him an Elvis Presley-style blue lamé suit. Vivienne had studied silversmithing at Harrow School of Art as a teenager in 1958, but abandoned the course, convinced that she could never make a living in the art world. Malcolm was about to prove that notion wrong.

The shop at no. 430 had previously been Tommy Roberts' Mr Freedom, where I'd bought some of my favourite dancing clothes. When Tommy moved on to 20 Kensington Church Street in 1971, his former business partner Trevor Miles took over the premises at the far end of the King's Road, a mile's walk up from Sloane Square. He called it Paradise Garage.[2] His shop was decked out like a beach shack, with a green corrugated-iron frontage and its name spelled out in letters made from bamboo. An American petrol pump stood outside, along with Trevor's customised, tiger-striped Mustang. He sold vintage American denim, boiler suits and screen-printed T-shirts to a soundtrack of surf music – there was even a tiny dancefloor in there. This fifties Americana vibe attracted the now drape-suited Malcolm and Vivienne, who leased a small space at the back of the shop to start selling rock'n'roll records, usually picked up from Chiswick and Ace Records founder Ted Carroll's Rock On stall in Golborne Road indoor market, along with other stylish period objects and ephemera. At the end of 1971, Trevor Miles left London and Malcolm and Vivienne took over.

VIVIENNE WESTWOOD: The King's Road was wonderful when I first went there; it really was something else, really different and special. Like it is now, it was full of little shops, the side streets as well. Ossie Clark and Alice Pollock had Quorum, and of course Mary Quant's first shop was there. One of the first ones was Granny Takes a Trip, run by my friend Gene Krell.[3] Gene opened this shop with twelve pairs of velvet trousers and they sold them in minutes, it was all word-of-mouth. He had more influence on the fashion of the 1960s than anybody. Whatever The Rolling Stones looked like, it was what Gene was wearing. He really dressed incredible. You know that white dress that Mick Jagger wore in Hyde

---

[2] In two acts of serendipity, the name 'Paradise Garage' was adopted in the mid-1970s by a New York gay club at 84 King Street, Greenwich Village, where disco giant Larry Levin was a regular DJ. It was then snaffled by ex-Amen Corner saxophonist Allan Jones for his punk shop in Cardiff, which attracted the likes of the young Steve Strange.

[3] Granny Takes a Trip was first opened on 488 King's Road by artist and designer Nigel Waymouth, his girlfriend Sheila Cohen, who had amassed a collection of vintage clothes, and Savile-Row-trained tailor John Pearse. In late 1969, they sold the business to American entrepreneur Freddie Hornick, who brought over Gene Krell to run the shop. Their velvet dandy outfits were immediate hits with The Rolling Stones, The Faces, Marc Bolan and Elton John. Gene then worked for Vivienne at World's End and Nostalgia of Mud until 1982, and wrote the book *Vivienne Westwood* (Universe of Fashion, 1997).

Park? That was Gene's thing... Granny Takes a Trip was famous for its boots, especially the ones made out of flowered velvet.

The first week when we were in the shop, Gene came... and introduced himself. He became my best friend. One day, Mick Jagger was in his shop and he said: "Go down there and have a look in that shop." Mick Jagger stood in the doorway and went back to Granny's, just a block away from us. Gene said: "How was it?" And he said: "Oh, it's great." But he didn't actually dare come in. It's true, that.

All these people were friends with drag queens, especially the fashion people. People like [shoe designer] Manolo Blahnik and [blue-haired *Vogue* writer] Anna Piaggi; they were all very friendly...

Then there was Anna Piaggi's friend Vern Lambert, who had a stall in Antiquarius Market. You went up these little tiny dark stairs like you were going up to an attic, and you'd see a flamenco dancer's dress there, things like that. He bought a whole batch of old sailor's bell-bottoms and got them all dyed different colours...

Just round the corner from World's End was Emperor of Wyoming and it had all this cowboy stuff in it, the boots, shirts with poppers on and lasso neckties, it was *so* brilliant. Then there was another one called Alkasura, which was kind of magical. They had the most really good designs by this guy called John Lloyd, who tragically died. I think he committed suicide.[4]

But the best of all was Mr Freedom. That's where I found everything that I wanted... I looked like a space-age princess. By then I had done my hair spiky and I had a pair of velvet leopard trousers...

Then there was the cruising, the cars going down the King's Road. Trevor Miles, his car was painted with tiger stripes all yellow and it was a coupé, so people were all sitting on the back posing as they went down the King's Road. It was amazing. Trevor was a really clever person, he was... the first in London to make used jeans into miniskirts and bags. People had such good ideas. The whole King's Road was like this.

---

[4] John Lloyd did commit suicide, and in a most alarming way. Obsessed by religious cults and portents, he took to tramping the King's Road wearing a monk's habit and, convinced he was possessed by the Devil, set himself on fire on a building site just around the corner from Alkasura (304 King's Road) in November 1975. Satan had taken a trip to these environs previously, as Christopher Lee in *Dracula AD 1972*, when followers of a teenage cult led by the backwards-masked Johnny Alucard met for coffee at the Cavern (372 King's Road).

Michael Costiff, whose arrival in London from his and Vivienne's native Derbyshire at the height of the Swinging Sixties eerily mirrors the plot to the George-Melly-scripted film *Smashing Time*,[5] was by then working with his German wife Gerlinde on their stall in the Antiquarius Market, near the World's End corner of the King's Road. He soon noticed the new couple.

> **MICHAEL COSTIFF:** We moved here in 1972, so we passed World's End every single day; that's how I knew what was happening. When I first came to London, 430 had all carpets on the floor and cushions, it was like a real hippy coffee shop. Everybody tells me that was next door, but in my head it was exactly that spot in 1969. When Malcolm and Vivienne arrived, they were doing 1950s stuff, brothel creepers, Teddy boy clothes, and Vivienne was in a big skirt, sat at the machine sewing in the back. Loads of couples did things like that at the time, young people having a go at shops – it was cheap to do it and we soon made friends with them.

From the beginning, everything they did was a reaction against the flower-power end of the 1960s. This was inspired both by Vivienne's love of the music of her youth and the nascent rock'n'roll revival of the early seventies that was being fuelled word-of-mouth by aficionados of Ted Carroll's imported US records. All of which further chimed with Malcolm's obsession with early British Beat Svengali Larry Parnes and the stable of rockers, such as Billy Fury and Marty Wilde, with which he had dominated the charts over a decade before.

The couple took down the bamboo, painted the frontage black and spelled out the name of their new enterprise in shocking pink letters. Inside the shop was remodelled to resemble a Modernist 1950s front room, complete with Trevor Miles's jukebox, guitar-shaped mirrors,

---

[5] In Desmond Davis's 1967 movie, northern lasses Rita Tushingham and Lynn Redgrave come down to London looking for a flat on Carnaby Street and careers as models and pop stars. Tushingham is reunited with her old *Taste of Honey* beau Paul Danquah and flatmate Murray Melvin at a boutique on the King's Road called Too Much.

rock'n'roll posters and photographs. Malcolm would often spend all of Friday night and well into Saturday morning preparing eye-catching displays of clothes for the biggest shopping day of the week – a tradition that I would soon become part of.

The curator and collector Roger K. Burton, who would refit the shop when it turned into World's End in 1980, was then dealing in vintage clothes from his hometown of Leicester. Inevitably, his path crossed with Malcolm's.

ROGER K. BURTON: At that time, 1972–3, I was heavily on the road, buying dead stock from all over the country. I remember turning up in this warehouse I'd heard about, a jeans manufacturer in Portsmouth, who had all this stock of 1960s shirts, still brand new, from the period, box-fresh... The first time I went there, the guy said: "Oh we just had some other guy down here from London, skinny guy, fast-talking, ginger hair." And of course that was Malcolm. So he'd been buying these shirts and selling them to Teddy boys, but, like everything else, he overbought and couldn't sell them all... I'd been selling them as the genuine article for the Japanese market and they were very happy with them. Malcolm would end up changing his surplus into the Anarchy shirt. I've still got one of the originals, white with a fine red stripe going through it, and a picture of Malcolm wearing one before it was customised.

Vivienne can remember how assiduously Malcolm courted a Teddy boy clientele – or, rather, got her to court them for him.

VIVIENNE WESTWOOD: When we first opened up Let It Rock, we opened it with the idea of selling old records. At that time, you did not have 1950s music anywhere at all, not on the radio, nowhere. Malcolm had the idea that we would collect these old records. This was the second wave of Teddy boys – not the originals, who were like a caricature of the first, much bigger hair, much more hairspray.

Malcolm was scared of going to their pub, the Black Raven, so he got me to go in there and invite them to come to the shop. He thought they'd be really rough and they wouldn't really like us. But they were just so happy and they came down straight away. This shop selling old records and some drapes in there and old-stock jeans. Soon after that, they came in coachloads from up north – all the Teddy boys used to come down from up there and stand in the shop all day listening to all these old records. So that's what it was all about.

A couple of streetwise scamps from Shepherd's Bush had also made their way to the far end of the King's Road, in search of something stylish to wear. They were quickly drawn into the shop at World's End and the environment Malcolm was creating there.

PAUL COOK: Me and Steve [Jones] were totally into the clothes when we was kids. We always had to have the best clothes, the latest gear. We were skinheads first, when I was at school – it was all ska music and all the old soul stuff, that's what I grew up with. Music and fashion was our passion! We were very aware that Malcolm's shop was happening, and the place to be. It was Let It Rock when we first used to go there, when they was selling Teddy boy stuff. We just connected. We used to go there every Saturday, down the King's Road posing about, and we'd always end up in Malcolm's shop. You could hang out and Malcolm didn't just want your money. He was interested in where you were from and what you were doing. He had a great jukebox in there, you know. So we was well aware of the importance of Malcolm and Let It Rock. We thought it was a cool place to hang out. This is before we even had the idea of getting the band together.

The first I ever heard of the place was when I was in Brighton, wearing an original 1950s skirt with gold filigree musical notes on it, and someone asked me if I'd bought it from Let It Rock. I hadn't – it came from the Lanes in Brighton – but I was after a good net petticoat to go underneath it, so I travelled to the far end of the King's Road to investigate. That was the one thing I really wanted from the shop but never got – there were lots of them hanging up from the picture rails. But I didn't have enough money on me to buy one.

VIVIENNE WESTWOOD: Oh yeah, I used to make them meself. The amount of time they took me to do and I sold them for £6. That was something in those days; it was a lot of money. You could live on £6.

The next time I went along, the store was closed and the sign above the door was being painted over. This was because, despite Malcolm's initial stylistic sympathies, he and Vivienne had begun to find their core customers tiresomely purist in their outlook. They had had a massive batch of Let It Rock T-shirts made up for the huge Rock'n'roll Revival show headlined by Little Richard, Jerry Lee Lewis and Chuck Berry that took place at Wembley Stadium on 5 August 1972.[6] The stall was a success in that they attracted plenty of customers who found their way to no. 430 and made the shop their meeting ground of a Saturday afternoon. This was when Malcolm and Vivienne first came to the attention of journalist Peter York, who would go on to pen some of the most perceptive cultural analysis of the tribes found down the King's Road.[7]

PETER YORK: I used to live around the corner, at the point where World's End curls around the King's Road. I can remember buying something in order to go appropriately dressed to the big rock revival gig at Wembley. That's when I first got to know them, and I would go in and talk to Malcolm and Vivienne. My little friend at the time had a wonderful expression she used about them. She used to say they were plunging themselves headfirst into legend.

Shortly afterwards, film costume designer Marit Allen also called in. She was looking for clothes for a film she was working on with her husband Sandy Lieberson and director David Puttnam about 1950s juvenile delinquents. *That'll Be the Day*, starring David Essex, Ringo Starr, Keith Moon and Billy Fury, ended up boasting a number of Let It Rock originals in its wardrobe.

---

[6] You can see footage of Malcolm's Let It Rock stall in Peter Clifton's 1973 movie *The London Rock & Roll Show*.

[7] Peter York's essays from the mid- to late 1970s were collected together in his 1980 book *Style Wars* (Sidgwick & Jackson), which featured me and my opposite number from Sloan Rangerland, Arabella Scott, on the front cover. It's still essential reading.

Despite this living link to British Beat's Larry Parnes, Malcolm had changed his mind about the validity of Let It Rock. In 1973, he and Vivienne changed the name of the shop to Too Fast To Live, Too Young To Die and brought in a range of tougher, more fetishistic-style bikers' leathers, American zoot suits, flecked jackets and peg trousers. The corrugated iron above the door was repainted again, this time with the new name and a skull-and-crossbones motif in the middle, so that it resembled the back of a biker's leather jacket, the inspiration for the name and the shop's new direction.

Reading about *That'll Be the Day* in *Club International* and clocking the pictures of Essex and Ringo suited and booted drew another young man who would soon be on his own musical mission out from the suburbs to make the SW3 pilgrimage.

MARCO PIRRONI: It was a Tuesday afternoon and I actually went down in my school uniform. I think I'd just turned 14. I'd never been to the King's Road and I had to go from Harrow, get off at Sloane Square and walk all the way down, thinking: Where the fuck is this place? You have to go round the corner, thinking you've missed it and [I was] about to turn back, when I saw the skull and crossbones. I just wanted some brothel creepers, but they didn't have the ones that I wanted. I bought some luminous socks instead, which I think were about 5p. But I had to go back the next week. It was like a drug. You had to get up there every Saturday, and then it became twice a week, then it was three times a week, then it was every day… You just had to be there. It was the place you wanted to be; it was the place that most excited you when nothing else did.

Between closing the first incarnation of the shop and opening the second, Malcolm and Vivienne encountered a renegade teenager in a West End nightclub who would have a pivotal effect both on them and my own future. Michael Collins wouldn't mind me saying that he had what could be described as a feral upbringing. More or less abandoned by his real parents, the circumstances of his youth were not far from the gangs of Dickensian street urchins that so fired up

Malcolm's imagination. Michael remembers that he was running a night at the Subway club in Greek Street, Soho, when they all met for the first time.

MICHAEL COLLINS: I knew a guy called Timmy, mixed-race Timmy, part of a whole gang of us West End boys who were hanging out, doing the club scene. Timmy went to work with Malcolm and Vivienne in Let It Rock with Elaine, a rocker girl from Hammersmith. He did it for about a year and then he didn't bother turning up – didn't like any of the clothes and never wore any of them, which was quite weird. But when they changed the shop to Too Fast To Live Too Young To Die he got me in.

By this time I was going to Alkasura and I had these satin snakeskin skintight trousers – Marc Bolan and me fought over them and I nicked them off him while he was in the changing room and ran out of the shop. I was wearing these and I had really short hair, which I'd bleached and permed into these tiny little bubbles. I had lots of piercings and stuff before piercings were really fashionable, and I had [Vivienne's] cards/zips T-shirt which Timmy had got for me, and the Japanese clogs they sold. So it was a strange mixture and there wasn't really anyone wearing anything like it. I was on acid most of the time; completely tripped out. Vivienne fell in love with my hair. She said I looked like a Greek god.

So that was how I started out there, and I got offered a job straight away because of the way I looked.

Too Fast To Live Too Young To Die marked the point where Malcolm and Vivienne became more involved in the process of designing and manufacturing original clothing, a process that grew out of revamping vintage items beyond recognition. They began customising their own leather-studded mini skirts and jackets, adding ball-and-chain zips to T-shirts and making slogans that drew on the brand names of popular British motorbikes with sexual connotations, such as the Norton 'Dominator'. Mohair jumpers, assembled by an army of housewife knitters recruited by Vivienne, and perfect American stiletto shoes in red, green, gold and black patent leather proved big sellers.

This would lead them in turn to the outer reaches of fetish fashion. The hidden world of leather and rubber wearers that lurked behind the twitching curtains of England's suburbs would prove the inspiration for the shop's next, and most radical, rethink yet.

Which is where I come in.

5

LET'S TALK ABOUT SEX

Behind the counter at 430 King's Road (1974)

When 430 King's Road reopened in 1974 as SEX – another radical shopfront overhaul, announced by three plump pink vinyl letters over the front door – I knew I had to work there. A lot of people have said how intimidating they found the new look of this place, like a sex shop mixed with a dentist. But I just walked in and introduced myself to Michael, who was sitting on the metal medical bed that had become part of the new interior decor. We hit it off instantly and ended up talking for hours – perhaps because he was as unfazed by the shop's atmosphere as I was.

MICHAEL COLLINS: It was down to me to employ people. I was left in the shop on my own, so I was running the whole thing. I didn't have any training, I'd never worked in a shop before, I was just making it up as I was going along. Mixing with Bianca Jagger and all those famous people of the early 1970s, and I didn't give a fuck about any of them. They were just ordinary people to me. If I'd seen them in a club I would have ignored them. I escorted so many people out of the shop, Bianca Jagger being one, because she had so many airs and graces and it didn't rub up well with me... I much preferred the kids who came in who had saved up all their benefits money to buy something. Or even tried to nick something – at least there was some passion there.

I used to get quite lonely in there, because sometimes people were too scared to come in… But when you turned up, I was so happy.

When I left that day, I asked Michael to call me if there was ever a staff vacancy I could fill. It wouldn't be long before I heard from him again.

Unchain my heart

Round about the same time, I met Frankie Savage at another favourite hangout, El Sombrero in Kensington, a gay club situated underneath a restaurant sporting a neon Mexican hat. Sombrero was popular with a very hip fashion, film and music crowd that included Ossie Clark and Celia Birtwell, Angie and David Bowie, Mick and Bianca Jagger, Elton John, Queen, Dusty Springfield and Derek Jarman. It was owned by Amadeo, a regular at SEX, along with DJ Rudi. This was the first disco in London to have coloured underfloor neon lighting flashing beneath its star-shaped glass dancefloor. A raised section overlooking it could be reserved by ordering champagne, though to comply with the dreaded licensing laws all customers were given a paper plate with a few limp lettuce leaves on it – every bit as classy as Tricky Dicky's gay disco in Brighton.

Frankie Savage was a sight to behold: an Italian New Yorker with a mid-to-short Afro who dressed entirely in black leather with an NYPD set of handcuffs hanging alluringly from his belt. He had a boutique called Ian's, named after his Afghan hound, in Bleecker Street, Manhattan, and he was over in London looking for interesting items to sell. According to David Ireland, who worked with Frankie at the time, Ian's was the first place in New York to move away from glam and into rubberwear and shoes from SEX. We both think it's highly probable Lou Reed bought one of Vivienne's vinyl and mohair tops from there.

Like me, Frankie had a penchant for lovely 1950s clothes, the tailored suits, silk scarves and stilettos, so after we had spent the night doing the 'hustle' on that star-shaped dancefloor, I took him to Portobello Road where there were plenty of such treasures to be found. We also paid a visit to SEX. Michael Collins remembers I was wearing manacles on my ankles – Frankie had cinched me into them.[1]

But he wasn't always so handy with his hardware. He lost the key to those police handcuffs one Saturday night that turned into a very sobering Sunday morning, when, literally still locked in each other's arms, we had to find a working phone box on Wandsworth Bridge Road, where he was staying, to try and locate anywhere that might be open on a Sunday. Then we had to get on the Tube all the way to Shepherd's Bush, where the one locksmith that could oblige finally hacksawed us apart.

But there is a strange link between that incident and one I heard about later, from Vivienne's son, Ben Westwood. His mother used to wear a padlock and chain around her lovely hoof-shaped boots[2] that she once did up so tightly, it stopped the circulation to her feet and she had to have the chain hacksawed off.

It wasn't long after that visit with Frankie that the communal phone rang in the hallway of my flat in Draycott Place. It was Michael Collins, telling me I could start work at SEX immediately. Now I was exactly where I wanted to be.

Out on the floor

So I began work in the shop, getting into the routine of the place, with all its different customers and assistants, and met Vivienne and Malcolm properly for the first time.

VIVIENNE WESTWOOD: You were very noticeable when you came in. You were like a little icon. You had your hair in this sort of blonde quiff, and you were wearing some sort of mac or coat with a belt on it, in black. It was a very clear, special look.

---

[1] Frankie Savage also pierced my ears for the first time, with the aid of a cork and a sewing needle – I had the black cotton still running through my lobes to keep the hole open.

[2] The same boots she is wearing in the famous *Forum* photograph where Vivienne, Chrissie Hynde and I have 'SEX' spelled out across our bums.

When I first worked at the shop, I didn't buy anything from it. I already had my own identity, and it was little ballet skirts and stilettos and big 1950s plastic belts with the big bow on the front. I had a Teddy Tinling tennis skirt, which I loved and would wear the first time I met Andy Warhol – it had little tennis racquets on the zips, in green and white enamel. I brought my own style to that place, because that was how I wanted it; that's how I felt comfortable. But in those days, you'd never see anyone walking down the road in just a pair of tights like I did.

Nor did SEX look like any other shop that had ever existed. Beyond the rubber letters that hung over the pale pink-painted front door were slogans sprayed from aerosol cans in orange, purple and yellow paint, passages taken from Situationist texts and the sadomasochistic novels of the Scottish writer Alexander Trocchi, including this, which made its way onto one of Vivienne's T-shirts:

> I groaned with pain as he eased the pressure removing his thing which had split me... his huge hands grasping me at the hips... my blonde hair forming a pool on the dark wood beneath his feet... he raised me to doting love... soothing the bleeding lips and causing the tearing commotion at my loins to subside in soft corrosion...

There were leftovers of Let It Rock and Too Fast To Live Too Young To Die stuff still in there; it was a mish mash of wonderful things. Screen-printed T-shirts and angora sweaters mingled with studded and zipped masks and leather crotch pouches, whips and ciré pants. Malcolm and Vivienne's discoveries in fetish-land were of both the hard and smooth varieties. Black vinyl trousers and rubberised canvas raincoats in pastel, ice-cream shades, like pretty flashers' macs. There was a shoe display with some fifties waspie belts surrounding them – the shoes were still the best-selling items in the shop and very beauteous they were, too. As well as the patent stilettos, they stocked plastic shoes with peep toes and pillar-box-red soles. At one point, we had an arresting piece of fetish sculpture on display there: a nail-studded leg by Lawrence Daniels, who would later become a multi millionaire by patenting the holograms used on credit cards.

The books of Cain

The Scottish-Italian Alexander Trocchi (1925–84) was a major figure of influence on the 1960s counter-culture whose resonance was keenly felt by the instigators of punk. The author of key Existentialist novels *Young Adam* (1954) and *Cain's Book* (1960), he spent the early 1950s editing the literary magazine *Merlin* from Paris, where, in an atmosphere free from the censorship that plagued the US and UK, he published the likes of Henry Miller, Samuel Beckett and Pablo Neruda, became friends with the influential American writer Terry Southern and developed a heroin habit, partly funded by the stream of erotic novels he wrote for the infamous Olympia Press, from where the 'I groaned with pain'… motif was taken.

Moving to America, he became involved with the Beat writers William S. Burroughs, Allen Ginsberg and Jack Kerouac, and two movements that would go on to influence Malcolm McLaren, the Lettrist International and Situationalist International. In the early 1960s he was living in Ladbroke Grove, where he ran a short-lived jazz record shop with political activist Michael De Freitas (aka Michael X) and then a bookshop, where Beat friends like Burroughs mingled with Barry Miles and the *International Times/Oz* crowd.

Always more influential than successful, after his death his books were resurrected by the Scottish Rebel Inc imprint in the 1990s, and *Young Adam* was turned into a film by David Mackenzie in 2003. He continues to inspire young authors with a taste for the wild side to this day. For a most interesting fictional imagining of Trocchi in his Ladbroke Grove period, see Stewart Home's 2005 *Tainted Love* (Virgin Books).

Set back from the shoes, next to the sheet of rubber that cordoned off the dressing room, was an old metal hospital bed with a rubber sheet, where Michael had been perched the first time I met him. It saw a lot of action of one sort and another, that bed.

Above it was an alcove that stocked the more esoteric items brought in from specialist manufacturers. Negligees made from yellow latex with purple rubber edging. Aprons, skirts, purple stockings and short, frilly tops, all made of rubber, hanging next to rubber bras and suspender belts. Some of the most eye-catching and unusual items were the T-shirts and turtlenecks in smudgy grey or solid black latex, which felt clingy, stretchy and soft. Perhaps the most notorious was the French Letter Suit, once modelled by Vivienne in a photo showing her posing next to the nail-leg sculpture. The suit made you look like a human condom and came in a fetching shade of what I can only describe as Milky Piss.

The top that I think Lou Reed bought from Ian's was one of Vivienne's inspired designs that wove together two fabrics that really didn't belong together: vinyl and interface lining, something you weren't supposed to make garments out of. She sewed vinyl gloves to the end of the sleeves that were far too heavy for the material they were attached to. Those things were so fragile, you could put your finger through them and destroy them in seconds; like the worst pair of tights a woman could ever buy. You had to put them on so carefully, threading your hands inside them. They were one of my favourite things. I had several of them: a long-sleeved one and a short-sleeved one. I found them again, when I auctioned all my clothes in 2015, in the bottom of the wardrobe in the spare room, looking very poorly. All that vinyl had stuck on itself. If it fell to bits, there was nothing you could have done to preserve it. Funnily enough, the zip was perfect, as if it was sewn in yesterday. And the garment was in one piece, which is something, considering it could have not been in one piece the moment after I bought it.

Other things that remained from the shop's previous incarnations were the fifties fridge from Paradise Garage and the jukebox that had once blasted out Billy Fury and Buddy Holly to the Ted faithful, who continued to wander in, bewildered by the change in the place. We still sold them their creepers and fifties ties, but now they were hidden by off-white, floor-to-ceiling drapes. That surplus of T-shirts from the rock'n'roll show at Wembley had been turned into knickers – these were among my favourite items of Vivienne and Malcolm's ingenious recycling. The ties would come in for further alterations in future days.

ROGER K. BURTON: I got a load of fabric when we were clearing out the shop, tie fabric, forties, fifties tie fabric. It ended up in Seditionaries, where Vivienne would make them into little cropped ties with 'LESBIAN' printed on them.

A lot of those clothes were outsourced – you can't just go out and make rubber and leather outfits, you've got to find out who can do it. It's a specialist thing. The shop soon drew in new aficionados who had, until then, used the same small ads Malcolm had raided to source their favourite leisurewear. I developed a nose for this kind of customer quite quickly. Like the fabrics they favoured, leather people were hard, whereas rubber people were soft. You had to be diplomatic with the rubber people. A lot of people didn't let on what they were really after when they first came in, but I could always tell. I'd ask them "Aren't you into the rubberwear?" and that usually put them at their ease.

The rubber men were a mixed bunch. We had regular customers who would have things made to order for them, whole rubber suits, which were terribly expensive. The first thing you learned was that they didn't mind being told what you thought. That's why they came back; if something looked terrible on someone, you said so. But you do have to have an instinct for that; it's not something that can be taught.

MICHAEL COSTIFF: I remember you telling me the story of the rubber men. In Antiquarius there were a few of that sort who came in. There was the satin man, who used to come round and rub all the satin, there was a velvet man and a corduroy man and a fur man... It's always something from their childhood; if you'd sniffed your mother's satin... Everything's man-made now, so you probably don't get them any more.

I have always started by thinking the best of people, and then it goes downhill from there. But the way I looked, that façade of the face, always weeded people out. It was a great leveller; the way I looked and how people reacted told me a lot about their own characters. They had to be pretty tough to stay in the shop. A lot of people would just flick through the rails, pretending to look – but they weren't actually looking at the clothes, they were looking at me. Michael Collins has an interesting take on what I brought to the shop that enhanced what Malcolm and Vivienne were already doing.

MICHAEL COLLINS: People liked to say Malcolm was so arch, but he was very easily influenced. Both he and Vivienne were quite unworldly and I

79

think a lot of their business was to live vicariously through other people. I do think they had some great things to say and they knew a lot of people, but there was a side of life that they really hadn't visited. Whereas you had the look that was beyond some of the things that Malcolm and Vivienne had come up with. Just the way it was put together. Like that really lovely turquoise mohair sweater you had with the pads, that made you look like Chesty Morgan and her deadly weapons. And those white stiletto pixie boots, they were the only pair of white fixed stilettos, and you were size three, it was like you were standing on skyscrapers. I always thought you could get away with it, partly because you wanted to, and partly because you was so short-sighted you couldn't see half the people staring at you.

That was the great thing when I started working there: you could go out and not see anyone wearing the same outfit. There were still a lot of drapes, a few lamé things, creepers, penny loafers. But, thanks to the influence of the shop, the vinyl, rubber and leather got mixed up into that. Different eras as well as fetishes collided at 430 King's Road, possibly for the first time ever. In an article for the adult magazine *Gallery*, journalist David Mays presciently described Malcolm, standing on the threshold of his latest enterprise, as: "A psychotic visionary in the ephemeral sub-culture of the fashion underworld."

Many others of my generation would find an outlet for their own talents at no. 430, and were attracted precisely because of this vision.

Dandies in the underworld

Another new SEX employee who started at around the same time as me was Alan Jones, a young gay man from Southsea, who came down to London to train as a manager for Sainsbury's and quickly defected to The Great Gear Trading Company on Carnaby Street. Following his brief but memorable spell at SEX, he went on to work for the Portobello Hotel, where film and rock royalty mingled with punks, prostitutes and other denizens of London's nightworld in the late 1970s.

It was incredible just who you could meet in that hotel. For example, I can remember going to see Alan one night and being called over into the bar area by an American man who told me how great he thought I looked. It turned out to be the science fiction author Harlan Ellison, who had written one of my favourite *Star Trek* episodes, 'City on the Edge of Forever' (1967), with Joan Collins. It was one of those astounding moments, like meeting Sir Frederick Ashton.

Alan has long since gone on to make a career as a successful film writer specialising in fantasy, horror and science fiction – possibly SEX was a good place to start.

ALAN JONES: We were coming out of glam rock and I looked like a dead ringer for Mick Ronson. At the time of Let It Rock, I was living round the corner from the shop, working for David Bowie's fan club and hanging around with him and Angie a lot, so it was all in my little area. The clothes were the way in for me, 'cos we all wanted to look different. The first time I went to New York, I wore Vivienne's stuff and I got picked up like crazy. The Let It Rock shirt with the plastic pockets with the nudie cutie cards inside. I went with one of the Warhol Factory people, Tony Ingrassia, to see *Chicago* on Broadway, when it was Liza Minnelli and Chita Rivera. One of the chorus boys stared at me all the way through the performance and sent me a note asking me to meet him backstage.

Alan was very into his clothes and Vivienne would even make up items to his specifications. One particularly eye-catching T-shirt had the word 'PERV' spelled out across the front in chicken bones that she had boiled clean and affixed with chains. Sadly, it is no more:

ALAN JONES: The last time I went to look for that, the bones had all shattered and everything had more or less turned to dust, which was a shame because it was a really good one. I used to wear that all the time.

One of my abiding memories of us working together was we'd go out on the street outside the shop and every time a bus came by there'd be people staring at us. We were so blasé, walking down the street in all this stuff, with people screaming at us. Not that I took a blind bit of notice.

Like me, Alan posed for photographs when *Forum*'s Len Richmond followed *Gallery* inside the doors of no. 430 and David Dagley took shots of myself, Alan, Chrissie Hynde and Vivienne with the shop's name spelled out across our bare behinds. Though I was wary of being forced into presenting a certain image of the shop in these shots, I think the end result is iconic. Some of us evinced more enthusiasm for this task than others – I think you can see who are the naturals.

ALAN JONES: Look at us, you've got your tits out and I've got my flies open! I always remember the photographer saying: "I don't want you in here, 'cos you're older than the rest." But I didn't care. I never liked Chrissie, though. I always saw her as a real opportunist, only around because she wanted to be part of the whole scene. But just about every two weeks I'm told by somebody that photo has reappeared somewhere in the world. I wear it as a badge of honour.

Chrissie Hynde, a legend herself now as singer for The Pretenders, worked at no. 430 before me, but a jealous boyfriend, *NME* writer Nick Kent, had convinced himself she was seeing one of the customers and came in to belt her. She maintains that Malcolm hid under the counter, but she was then dismissed.[3] Chrissie briefly moved to Paris after that, but came back to London in early 1976, when the *Forum* shots were taken, drawn by stories of what was going on in the shop.

Some of the stories involved those two lads from Shepherd's Bush, Paul Cook and Steve Jones (who, by his own admission, came into the shop to steal anything he could lay his wandering hands on...).

Steve had left his unhappy home at the age of 15 and, with his head turned by The Faces the same way mine had been, formed a group with his schoolfriends Paul and Wally Nightingale in the winter of 1972–3. A dextrous thief, who believed he had a cloak of invisibility,[4] Steve was adept at crashing gigs and dressing rooms, and the fledgling band's equipment came courtesy of those light fingers. Things were always taken from bands he admired, as if, by osmosis, they would confer on him and his friends some magical musical powers. He took a tuner from a Roxy Music gig, two guitars (including a genuine Les Paul) from Rod Stewart's mansion in Windsor and, in his greatest coup, David Bowie's entire PA from the final Ziggy Stardust gig at Hammersmith Odeon on 3 July 1973. Steve had prepared for this spectacular heist by first hotwiring a van to cart the stuff away.

Calling themselves The Strand – a nod to the opening track on Roxy Music's *For Your Pleasure* – the first incarnation of the group was Steve singing, Paul on drums, Wally on guitar, Jimmy Mackin on organ and Steve Hayes on bass. They rehearsed at the Furniture Cave in the World's End, doing covers of Faces and Rod songs. It didn't last long. Within a few months, it was back to the nucleus of Steve, Paul and Wally.

---

[3] As told to Jon Savage in *England's Dreaming*, p. 68.
[4] See Steve's marvellous, poignant and very self-deprecating memoir *Lonely Boy* (with Ben Thompson, William Heinemann, 2016) for more on this.

Steve thought Malcolm was the obvious person to help with the band. Malcolm saw something in this young Artful Dodger and offered him a sheltering wing. He and Vivienne often put him up at their Art Deco council flat in Nightingale Lane, Clapham, where he shared bunk beds with Ben Westwood and Vivienne and Malcolm's son, Joe Corré.

PAUL COOK: Steve was lost. He had no place to live, really. Malcolm and Vivienne kind of looked after him. I went round their place in Clapham a few times, just to discuss band stuff and that. Malcolm was like the fifth member, or father figure if you like. He was ten years older than us, which seemed like a lot then.

Steve persisted, trying to talk him into a managerial position until, in the summer of 1974, Malcolm paid to get them a rehearsal room in the Covent Garden Community Centre and came down to hear them. It was pretty much a shambles – but Malcolm liked the roguish, mad element of what he saw. Impressed by his Faces knowledge, they drafted in the shop's Saturday boy Glen Matlock, an ex-Saint Martin's College of Art student, as bass player.

PAUL COOK: It was all too good to be true, the way it all fell into place. I remember Steve coming back saying: "Oh, I've found a bass player. Glen, he works in the shop. He plays bass. That's handy, isn't it?" He could play 'Three Button Hand Me Down'. Steve said: "That's it. If you can play, you're in!" Not that we could play anything. We were still learning.

Steve was the real instigator of the Pistols really. He'd be hanging about down the King's Road getting up to all sorts of mischief. That was what was good about the band, us lot, these working-class boys; we didn't feel uncomfortable in that environment. We was looking for something. We wanted to get in a band and go somewhere and we just slotted into the King's Road's very trendy, middle-class situation straight away. The Roebuck, that was our social scene, that's where we drank. Malcolm introduced us to his arty crowd. I think he enjoyed it because he ended up with his little gang, didn't he? He was trying to create a scene. Not exactly the Factory, it wasn't as druggy and decadent as that. Malcolm was just trying to stir it up. He had this idea of Steve being the little urchin, Artful

Dodger, going round cat burgling – he loved that, Malcolm; he loved all that imagery. Us as a gang of ragamuffins and you as the modern-day Nancy. Him being the modern-day Fagin, of course. It's such a cliché, but he *was* a Fagin and we were his gang of urchins. He saw something in us that no one else did, that was for sure.

Whose side are you on?

The full list of 'blasted' (with original spellings) reads:

Television (not the group)/Mick Jagger/The Liberal Party/John Betjamin/ George Melly/Kenny & Cash/Michael Caine/Charles Forte/Sat nights in Oxford Street/SECURICOR impotence or complacency (slogan & Robert Carr)/Parking tickets/19, Honey, Harpers, Vogue in fact all magazines that treat their readers as idiots/Bryan Ferry/Salvador Dali/A Touch of Class/ BRUT – for who cares?/Peregrine Worsthorne, Monty Modlyn, John Braine/ Hughie Greene/The Presidents Men/Lord Carrington/The Playboy Club/Alan Brien/Anthony Haden-Guest, Bif Lownes, to be avoided first thing in the morning/ANTIQUARIOUS and all it stands for/Michael Roberts/POP STARS who are thick and useless/YES/Leo Sayer/David Essex/Top Of The Pops/ Rod Stewart oh for money and an audience/Elton John – quote in NME 25 Sept re birthday spending/West End shopping/Stirling Cooper, Jean Junction, BROWNS, Take Six, C&A/Mars bars/Good Fun entertainment when it's really not good or not funny/Bernard Delfont a passive audience/arse lickers/John Osborne Harry Pinter Max Bygraves Melvyn Bragg Philip Jenkinson the ICA and its symposiums John Schlesinger Andre Previn David Frost Peter Bogdanovich/Capital Radio/The Village Trousershop (sorry bookshop)/The narrow monopoly of media causing harmless creativity to appear subervise/ THE ARTS COUNCIL/Head of the Metropolitan Police/Synthetic foods/Tate & Lyle/Corrupt councilors/G.K.N./Grey skies/Dirty boots that aren't all that dirty/ Andy Warhol/Nigel Waymouth David Hockney and Victorianism/The Stock Exchange/Ossie Clark/The Rag Tade/E.L.P/Antiques of any sort/Housing Trusts who profit by bad housing/Bianca Jagger/Fellini/John Dunbar/J. Arthur's/Tramps/Dingwalls without H/Busby Berkeley MOVIES/Sir Keith Joseph and his sensational speeches/National Front/W.H. Smith Censorship/ Chris Welch and his lost Melody Makers/Clockwork soul routines/Bob Harris (or the sniffling Whistler as we know him)/Job you hate but are too scared to pack in/Interview magazine-Peter Lester/rich boys dressed as poor boys/ Chelita Secunda, Nicky Weymouth, June Bolan, Pauline Fordham halitosis/

Rose & Anne Lambton Chinless people/Antonia Frazer/Derek Marlow/Anne Scott-James/Sydney Edwards/Christoper Logue/Osbert Lancaster/Shaw Taylor whispering grass/The Archers/BIBAS/Old clothes old ideas and all this resting in the country business/The suburbs/The Divine Light Mission/All those fucking saints.

The full list of 'blessed' reads:

Eddie Cochran/Christine Keeler/Susan 602 2509/My monster in black tights/ Raw Power Society For Cutting Up Men/RUBBER Robin Hood Ronnie Biggs BRAZIL/Bamboo Records/Coffee bars that sell whiskey under the counter/THE SCENE – Ham Yard/Point Blank/Monica the girl who stole those paintings/ Legal Aid – when you can get it/Pat Arrowsmith/Valeire Solanis/The Price Sisters/Mervin Jones article The Challenge to Capitalism in New Statesman 4th Oct. 74/Buenoventura Durutti The Black Hand Gang/Archie Shepp Muhammed Ali Bob Marley Jimi Hendrix Sam Cooke/Kutie Jones and his SEX PISTOLS/This country is run by a group of fascists so said Gene Vincent in a 1955 US radio interview/Seven Days with Alexander Cockburn/Olympia Press/ Strange Death of Liberal England – Dangerfied/Mrs Scilly love goddess from Shepherds Bush her house slaves and Search magazine/Labour Exchanges as your local/FREE RADIO stations/A chance to do it for more than a month without being ripped off/The Anarchist Spray Ballet/Lenny Bruce/Joe Orton/ Ed Albee/Paustovsky/Iggy Pop/John Coltrane/Spunky James Brown/Dewey Redman/KING TUBBY'S SOUND system/Zoot suits and dreadlocks/Kilburn & the High Roads/Four Aces Dalston/Limbo 90-Wolfe/Tiger Tiger-Bester/Bizarre Humphries/Woolf-Wavee/Walt Whitman poet/Exupery, Simone de Beauvoir, Dashiell Hammett, Dave Cooper, Nick Kent, Carl Gayle writers/Mel Ramons painter/David Holmes the newsman/Mal Dean cartoonist/Guy Stevens records/ Mal Huff funny stories/D.H./Valve amps/Art Pricne/Marianne Faithfull/Jim Morrison/Alex Trocchi – Young Adam/Patrick Heron v. The Tate Gallery and all those American businesslike painters/Lady Sinthia 908 5569/Experiment with Time – Dunne/John Lacey and his boiled book v. St Martin's Art School experiment to be seen in New York. Imagination…

Only, by the autumn, Malcolm had had enough of the shop and taken a flight to New York in search of further adventures, leaving his friend Bernard Rhodes – who also had a stall in Antiquarius, selling his own screen-printed merchandise – to help Vivienne with T-shirts and "look after Steve". Bernard, or Bernie as he was known in those days, duly took over as the band's mentor.

Before Malcolm left in November 1974, he, Bernie and Vivienne collaborated on what was effectively their first punk manifesto. Called *You're gonna wake up one morning and know what side of the bed you've been lying on!*, it took the form of a tightly worded T-shirt that separated the dead culture of the 1970s, and its hippy end-of-the-1960s antecedents, and pointed the way into the future with two lists of those 'blessed' and 'blasted' by its creators. On it, the newly christened 'Kutie Jones and his SEX PISTOLS' made their first public appearance.

> **PETER YORK:** Oh, it's wonderful. So funny. I think it's a work of genius. So much so that I put it into a little plastic case and kept it. I never wore it, because I was never a T-shirt sort of person, but I've got it, as is.

I had a few troubles of my own by then, too. I had lost the flat in Draycott Place and been forced to move back home to Seaford, from where I commuted to work every day, dressed in my favourite clothes. Which didn't always go down well with my fellow commuters…

6

INDECENT EXPOSURE

Rubber Ducks meet the Dyke from the Deep (1975)

The red shoes

I had many strange experiences on the train from Seaford to London. Sometimes, when I got into the carriage, everybody else would leave. Once, when my outfit comprised a see-through bra and knickers with customised fishnet stockings – I would make patterns by burning holes into them with cigarettes – the police threatened to arrest me. On other occasions, the British Rail guard would move me into First Class to separate me from the rest of the passengers. When that happened, I would be sitting alone and then suddenly, in the blink of an eye, find myself surrounded by besuited businessmen, all pretending to read *The Times*.

It became common in Seaford for people to say: "That bloody weirdo was on the train again today." My parents heard this on many an occasion, much to my mother's chagrin, since she hadn't exactly welcomed me home with open arms.

My reputation was growing at both ends of the line.

LESLEY FOSTER: My brother Colin remembers going up to London on the train with all the suits glancing over the top of their newspapers while you and Colin were in deep conversation. He got some funny looks for actually daring to sit opposite you.

One of those suits had a proposition to make. Mr Hawkins was an old man – in his late seventies, pushing 80, to my 20 – who used to do the same journey from Seaford to London that I did every day. He was the director of a listed company on the Stock Exchange and he lived down in Sussex. I noticed him looking at me on the train a lot – but not necessarily at what I was wearing, despite it being so provocative. Mr Hawkins was looking at my feet the whole time.

One day, when I was wearing some of Vivienne's round-toed, red patent stilettos, he followed me from the train across the concourse of Victoria station and stopped me to say how much he loved my shoes. Then he asked, very politely: "Could you perhaps come and visit me at the place where I work?"

I did feel that I would be safe with him, so I told him: "Look, this is the place where I work. Perhaps you'd like to come and visit me there first, at the shop?"

So he came down the King's Road. He said he had a flat in London and then reeled off the usual "My wife doesn't understand me…" line and asked me if I would visit him in his pad. But I still wasn't quite sure what he was into; whether he just wanted to look at women wearing stilettos, or what? I told him I'd think about it.

There was one person I could turn to for advice: Linda Ashby, a *maîtresse* who bought clothes and accoutrements for her work from SEX. Linda's flat at 1016 King's House, St James Hotel, and her regular nightclub, Louise's in Poland Street, would soon become an epicentre for the shop's employees and our friends, and I would end up living at King's House between 1976 and 1978. She was the one person I knew who would have experienced the likes of Mr Hawkins and would know how to play this situation.

"What do I do?" I asked her. "I don't want to go there on my own."

Always up for an adventure, Linda said she'd come with me.

Mr Hawkins's business flat was very old-fashioned, stuffed full of antique mahogany. He greeted Linda and me with glasses of champagne before disappearing into another room. When he came back out, he was wearing a full negligee, with a little pair of pants on underneath and a pair of patent stilettos – he was probably about a size 12 shoe. It turned out that he just wanted to walk around in them in front of an audience – and he was so pleased to get one.

After that first visit, he said he wanted it to be a regular thing, and offered to buy me a gift in return. I said: "Oh, I don't think so, don't worry about that." But he was insistent: "Oh no, I'd really like to buy you something; I know a really nice jeweller's in Kensington, I'll meet you outside there and you can pick what you like."

I didn't want to take Mr Hawkins for a ride or lead him down a road he couldn't find fulfilling. If I had wanted to watch him wearing those clothes and shoes, I would have done it without being paid. It seemed a bit tawdry and demeaning. So I never turned up. But I was grateful to Linda for coming with me. Despite all the experience I had to draw from at SEX, I wouldn't have gone there on my own.

I've had people who wanted to be my slave. I had a very serious letter where one person said he'd do anything and, the more I wanted him to do, the better it would be. He would clean for me; do anything for me. These days I think – why didn't I get him? He could have done all my washing and everything.

Mr Hawkins's fetish was quite a common one, compared to some of Linda's clients, who had very specialised tastes. She used to have this one trick who would be sitting there naked with a balloon on his lap, which she would have to bounce up and down on until she popped it. That's what he paid for.

Another thing she had to do was poo on a glass table with a bloke underneath, which is quite a common fetish, and they pay a lot for it. The difficulty is that you have to make sure you can do it. It's not easy. She had to be careful not to go to the loo for two or three days because you've got to be ready. There was another bloke who liked to cover his armpits with jam and flap his arms up and down.

As Michael Costiff noted in the previous chapter, the stimulus for all these fetishes is that they're going back to scenes from their childhood.

91

Brief encounter

My first sexual encounter actually came as a result of the strangers-on-a-train scenario, a couple of years before Mr Hawkins, in 1973. His name was Jeff and he worked for a daily newspaper. He was a bit older than me, maybe 22, 23, very bright to be a Fleet Street journalist at that age. He saw me on the train and really fancied me, so he got off at the station before mine and ran after the train blowing me kisses and mouthing: "Can I have your number?"

It was really romantic. And he had a really big cock. We went out several times before he unleashed it and, if I remember rightly, the prelude to our night of love was him telling me how the astronomer Patrick Moore had lured him into his observatory in Chichester on the promise of watching a comet called Kohoutek, a big event in the astral calendar, and then proceeded to chase him around the darkened room like Uncle Monty in *Withnail and I*. My own first close encounter with Jeff caused me quite a bit of physical damage, because he was really big and I was a virgin.

We could have gone on to be proper lovers. But there's something interesting here about psychology. Not a lot of men have taken me on, because I am very strong and witty and a lot of men don't like to be matched. That was exactly what happened with Jeff and me. He didn't like it that I was quicker and wittier. I could see it all coming, the end of it. We'd have a screaming evening, really laughing, really good fun, lots of jokes, lots of chit-chat and I could tell he wasn't comfortable with it. Which is sad. I always wondered what happened to Jeff.

But a lot of straight men don't relate to strong women. That's why gay men are our natural allies. I have to be with someone who will allow me to be me. Most of my years working at the shop and in the music business were spent with men who were totally and utterly shit-scared of me. I heard it all in the years that followed, people saying how much they wanted to approach me and daren't. Actually they wanted it to be like that: they wanted to be nearly approaching me – but stopping.

The secret life of the suburbs

What is so interesting, looking back, is how the worlds of fetish and popular culture came together so seamlessly in SEX, in the way that they wouldn't really do again until the early 1980s at *Skin Two*.[1] What amazed me was that the very specialist types were quite happy to be in that shop, when it had all the other things in it. They certainly weren't angry, like we were taking their space or their limelight. They had a very different mentality to the music-orientated customers.

MARCO PIRRONI: It was unbelievably suburban, the fetish world. There was no crossover into any sort of rebellion. They must have kept it secret from the neighbours because the neighbours wouldn't have got it. I didn't get it, either. But another thing about the shop, a reason that people remember it, was that it had a lot of elements to it, it had all these smells. Smells of the rubber curtains, which you can't really say about any other shop. What did any other shop smell like? I can't really say what Acme Attractions smelled like, or Johnson's.

You can see the two sides to this very clearly in John Sampson's 1977 documentary *Dressing for Pleasure*, half of which was filmed at SEX on the hottest day of the summer in 1976.[2] Part of the alchemy of the shop was the way Michael and I ran things. We made it easy for people to just hang out, and it became a social hub. Obviously the main day was Saturday, when Vivienne would come in and Glen Matlock would be there with the two of us. It was a real party atmosphere. As Michael remembers, the fetish people would always talk to me first, because I could relate to them in a way he couldn't. I was wearing the same clothing as them for a start, but he also thinks they wanted to capture something of the way I presented myself.

Through stocking their preferred clothing, we got to meet the Wigan Society and the Rubber Duck Club, which was wonderful.

---

[1] *Skin Two*, a name referring to rubber or leather as a second skin, is a magazine and shop founded by publisher Tim Woodward and photographer Grace Lau in 1983. See SkinTwo.co.uk

[2] You can see the whole of *Dressing for Pleasure* at www.youtube.com/watch?v=8k8uHcc3I-Y

The Rubber Duck Club, as Marco suggests, had certain people in it that you could just picture leaning over their garden fence, chatting to their next-door neighbour, like Les Dawson's Cissie and Ada but in rubber, or Peter Cook's E. L. Wisty wearing latex.

The Wigans were these lovely macs Malcolm got in, Wigan itself being a particular canvas with bonded latex on top of it. The Wigan Society are the people who go for long walks on muddy moors and marshland to splosh about in these macs; they like a bit of wet. I had a beautiful bright royal blue Wigan, lined with rubber, with lovely epaulettes and lapels and a nice thick belt. The only drawback was, because the rubber was a bit fine on top of the canvas, it did crack after a few years, where the sleeve bent. But it did also once help to save my life, as we shall see.

The tactile nature of rubber was always very important to me; I thought it made great clothes. But I wouldn't think that everybody would look great or feel great in it. The rubberwear wasn't just meant to shock. It was ready to wear. Only, you wouldn't want to wear it unless you were really committed to it and felt happy in it. It was difficult to put on, it didn't last, the number of rubber stockings I got through... The really important thing is that I wanted to appreciate the beauty of rubber and leather, not keep it behind closed doors. I wanted to treat it as normal, not a perversion – just an appreciation of the fabric itself. They were clothes to wear to the office, so I would get up in Seaford, put my rubber on and go. And, as with any office situation, there could be some unforeseen comedy moments...

MICHAEL COLLINS: Vivienne would turn up every Saturday morning in a black cab with at least ten bin bags full of mohair sweaters. She had all these old ladies knitting them for her in Bromley and places and they'd come up loaded on the train and meet Vivienne at Victoria. When she arrived, we would be expected to brush the mohairs up, as they got quite flat in transit. Our technique was to get drunk and take loads of speed – and you had the fitness of a shrew. But one particular Saturday, you had a big load on your plate. An abundance of mohair sweaters had come in and you had been told to brush these up and sew labels on them.

Then this couple came in. We knew the chap very well, he was very upper-class English, and he'd been keen on the idea of us visiting his stately home to ride motorbikes in rubber. Very keen. He was introducing his partner to the delights of rubber and they were quite new on the scene, so Vivienne was trying to explain that it's best to use French chalk, which has got no additives, instead of talcum powder, because that rots rubber. There was these very complicated bondage outfits that you had to put on behind this rubber screen which, if you were looking at the shoes at the end of the shop, you could just turn round and see people in states of undress. I have, I did, and I saw them all. It cost me thousands in analysis to get rid of these images.

It was a particularly hot summer's day, so of course it was very easy to perspire. This poor woman was trying on a rubber skirt and she had to pull it up – all we could hear was this terrible slapping because she couldn't pull it up over the sweat on her legs. So he went in to help out, and then we heard even more slapping, real big buttock slapping, until finally the screen fell over on top of you and your pile of mohair sweaters! It was like a French farce – there was a man in a full rubber outfit, a woman half-clothed trying to put on a rubber outfit now caught short and crouching on the floor, Vivienne being really earnest, and a shop full of punks, Rastas, rockabillies and Teddy boys, probably all stoned as well, thinking: What's going on?

Bear in mind that we had to try and keep a straight face with the rubber people, because they were completely earnest. They wouldn't have come back to us if we'd taken the piss out of them. Which I didn't want to do anyway. But that moment was like *Carry on up the Rubber Tree*.

One of our favourite customers was the newsreader Reginald Bosanquet – the respectable face of ITV's *News at Ten* from 1967 to 1979. Except, beneath that stern, patriarchal exterior, he wasn't all that proper. It was his habit to take long lunches at Osteria, the restaurant next door; then, when suitably refreshed, roll out of there with a model on his arm and make a beeline for me to show him all the wares. He used to bring me beautiful bouquets of flowers from the florist's nearby to show his appreciation. Then he'd give me a knowing wink that night when he was on camera to let me know he was wearing his special underwear beneath that grey three-piece suit. Reggie B. was a big fan of rubber pants.

The Dyke from the Deep

One of our customers told us about the *Evening Standard*'s Headdress and Make-up competition at the Burlesque Club on Brewer Street and Michael thought I should go in for it. So, back in Seaford, I picked up a plastic lobster and some real seaweed and shells from the beach to make into a headdress – cockle shells, whelk shells and more winkles than the rest of my competitors put together. Using skills I'd learned at the shop, I varnished these items until they looked how you'd see them in a fishmonger's window, fixed everything to a collar and reinforced all the ends of it with fish hooks – so, if you got too close, that would be the end of you. The clothes were all rubber: a basque, leggings, mini-skirt with a great big fishtail coming off it and a pair of gloves, and my headdress was finished off with a fishing net. Calling myself the Dyke from the Deep, I swished into the London night.

> **MICHAEL COLLINS:** It was like a work of art – you'd get the Turner Prize for it nowadays. When we got into the club, the real drag queens had taken it all really seriously, and there was you upstaging them all. Do you remember that dance you did? All the pole dancers and strippers of today would like to see that dance. They would learn lessons they'd never been shown before.

By the time I went on, I'd ripped everyone else's costume to bits with my fish hooks. There was one guy called the White Knight, who looked like some Bacofoil nightmare. I turned around and took off his entire headdress without him even noticing. All three judges, including the fashion designer Zandra Rhodes, marked me first and I got a cheque for quite a lot of money – and an orb and a silver-coated banana, obviously meant for a man. But, as the party came to a close, Michael realised that the rubber strap I had employed to keep my headdress in place was starting to cut off my circulation and took it off for me. It was very caring of him to notice – another lesson learned from fetish-land.

Dance to a different tune

Though there was never such a thing as a normal day at the office, what I didn't expect was that one of my childhood heroes might appear without any warning, as was the case when Rudolf Nureyev stepped over the threshold one day while I was in conversation with Marco. The man who had partnered my childhood heroine Margot Fonteyn! At the time, he was still dancing for the Royal Ballet, and he socialised quite a lot at places like Sombrero's, often in the company of Freddie Mercury and Mick Jagger,[3] but this was the first time I had ever been able to have a conversation with him about ballet. He was someone who had such a formative influence on my life. Marco, I'm afraid, was not so impressed by his appearance.

MARCO PIRRONI: He was wearing the worst clothes I have ever seen in my life. It was a khaki safari suit, with a kind of crushed, wet-look maroon plastic hat, like a Donny Osmond peaked cap, and some really horrible, big, clunky brown platforms. The flares on his safari suit weren't quite big enough to cover the front of his shoes. I did recognise him and I didn't expect him to be dressed head to foot in SEX or anything – but I did expect it to be better than that.

MICHAEL COLLINS: I used to know him quite well; he went out with a friend of mine. He used to come to the shop, and he was at Sombrero's a lot. When you've been a ballet dancer, your legs are huge, you can't wear normal trousers any more and your feet are fucked. So that explains the outfit.

---

[3] Nureyev stayed with the Royal Ballet until 1982, when he took over as Director of the Paris Opera Ballet, where he worked until 1989. He danced with Margot Fonteyn for the last time on 16 September 1989 in *Baroque Pas de Trois* – she was 69, he was 50. Nureyev had tested positive for HIV in 1984 but carried on as if nothing was wrong until 1991, when the disease started to catch up with him. He died on 6 January 1993.

We were also visited by the famous American heir and kidnap victim, John Paul Getty III, who had his ear cut off by the Mafia in an extortion attempt on his oil baron grandpa.[4] Not only was he into the shop, he came to a lot of the early Sex Pistols gigs, where people were fascinated both by his presence and by his missing ear, which remained well hidden under his long, curly locks. We had quite a few theatrical types: fittingly, the star of *The Leather Boys*, the late actor Dudley Sutton (later to find household fame as Tinker in the 1980s sitcom *Lovejoy*) and, on the lookout for a fine pair of heels, the genuinely lovely Helen Mirren, who had perfect arches.

Another customer, Jerry Hall, along with rising stars Jessica Lange and Grace Jones, were part of a Parisian set that revolved around the French fashion designer, artist and motorbike aficionado Jean-Charles de Castelbajac, who had first sent Malcolm and Vivienne a letter congratulating them on their customised T-shirts from Too Fast To Live Too Young To Die in 1972. Malcolm called on him the next time he was in Paris and a lasting friendship was sealed over a bottle of Johnnie Walker. De Castelbajac enjoyed the fact that Malcolm called him 'Charlie' – no one else had ever dared.

Mad, bad and dangerous to know

But, although no. 430 could be a portal of delight, you could also be confronted with sudden danger, in all its different forms. We had to deal with a lot of shoplifters – Michael would chase them all around Chelsea and Fulham on his bike. Once, a bloke took an entire outfit, leaving his old clothes, his razor and his discharge papers in the changing room. I ran after him all the way to Fulham Road, in

---

[4] John Paul Getty III (1956–2011) was the grandson of oil tycoon John Paul Getty I. He grew up in Rome, and spent a lot of time in London in the 1960s. He was kidnapped at the age of 16 from the Piazza Farnese in Rome at 3 a.m. on 10 July 1973. A ransom note demanding $17 million was sent to his billionaire grandpa, but he refused to meet the demands. Four months later, in November 1973, a note was delivered to an Italian daily newspaper containing a human ear. It demanded $3.2 million to avoid the rest of him being sent back in similar-sized pieces. JPG I negotiated a deal to get his grandson back for $2.2 million and the unfortunate teenager was left in a petrol station in the province of Potenza on 15 December 1973. JPG III was badly affected by his ordeal, and the rest of his life was painful. He took an overdose in 1981 that left him quadriplegic and was only 54 when he died on 5 February 2011.

bondage trousers. I don't have a wide stride but, even so, that was going some. Then suddenly, as I was closing in on him, I thought: What am I going to do if I catch him? He's just come out of jail, he'll probably knock me out. So I let that one get away.

Shoplifting is an equal-opportunity sport, and if you were so bad at doing it that you were unlucky enough to get caught by Michael, then fame was no balm to his wrath.

MICHAEL COLLINS: I caught Johnny Thunders in Seditionaries with a pair of trousers. He was behind the black fur curtain for ages and there were some very suspicious noises, but I knew it wasn't rubber. He was really wasted to start with and when he came out there was just this one clothes hanger left in the changing room, he'd got them wrapped round his waist like a python. So I made him strip off in the shop in front of everyone. That was really quite cruel. But he tried to rip me off. If he'd just asked me for money, I would have given it to him. Steve Strange I did the same to, and I took real pleasure in that. There was a big party in the shop one night, I think you were in New York at the time, and he had some leather trousers away. There wasn't really any kind of excuse for that. He never came in the shop again, I barred him for life. And after that, I was at some place rollerskating and I lifted this pint of beer off a table and, as I went past him, I poured it all over his head.

We had the Road Rats from Lots Road, a gang of self-styled outlaw bikers who would come in with guns and leave them lying casually on the counter; and Lemmy from Motörhead, who was then living in the strange squatting community around Maida Vale and Warwick Avenue known as Frestonia. Lemmy was not bad company: he was always on speed and he loved talking to me. 'The Dangers of Drugs' was the best lecture I got from him. I couldn't stop laughing. "It's you that's telling me this?" But he said: "It's *hard* drugs, Jordan." He was into psychedelic drugs and speed, but never, ever, heroin. A lot of his friends had died from it. Initially, I didn't know what he was talking about.

Because there was a psychiatric hospital just around the corner, we also got our share of passing lunatics, including Mad John and Jock the Tramp. Jock was an alcoholic, but Mad John was really

Passport to Frestonia

Lemmy and Joe Strummer were just two of the notable characters who took up residence in and around the squatter suburb bordered by Freston Road, Bramley Road and Shalfleet Drive, W10, in the area of London where Maida Vale meets Queen's Park. The properties were owned by the Greater London Council (GLC) but had fallen into such a state of disrepair that residents were rehoused in neighbouring tower blocks. As they left, a bohemian mixture of artists, musicians, drug dealers, bikers and politicos moved into the abandoned properties. When the GLC made a move to try and evict them in 1977, residents led by actor Michael Rappaport, playwright Heathcote Williams and social activist Nicholas Albery took inspiration from the 1949 Ealing comedy classic *Passport to Pimlico* and moved to secede from the United Kingdom and declare themselves the 'Free and Independent Republic of Frestonia'. They submitted a request to the United Nations, and issued their own postage stamps and visas. These actions forced the GLC into negotiations, and the Bramleys Housing Co-operative was formed as a result. Though the UN never responded to the application, the notion to form a breakaway republic was never formally dismissed.

For an idea of how the neighbourhood looked at the time, David Hemmings's directorial debut *The 14*, made in 1973 and starring June 'Dot Cotton' Brown and Jack 'Artful Dodger' Wild, was shot right in the middle of the area condemned by the GLC. I like to think the prominent 'ROXY MUSIC' graffiti might have been the work of our very own Artful Dodger, Steve Jones.

The Frestonian National Archive can be visited at http://www.frestonia.org/

mad – there is a difference. Mad John used to come in the shop and talk mad, while we would stand there nodding. Vivienne would have long conversations with him. She thought he was Sane John. Worse still was Mad Phyllis, who Michael remembers as being a former consort of Nick Kent – "They were attractive, in a London Dungeon sort of way." She was really skinny and did these mad dances, singing 'Bony Moronie' the whole time. Unfortunately, Mad Phyllis would be the one who first brought the drugs Lemmy warned me about into the shop.

At one stage there were loads of black guys coming in, led by Derek and Eric, the twins. We had a pontoon school in there, so people would come in and gamble. In an echo of my dad in his army days, I used to beat the pants off them and they would get so pissed off with me for taking all their money. But they still came back for more.

> **MICHAEL COLLINS:** We had a mix of every person – old, young, white, black, religious, non-religious – 'cos I had all my Rasta friends coming in and we were wearing hardly any clothes and they'd be standing there with their rod of correction.

One of the saddest stories is of the four Venezuelan brothers who came over to work in England: Antonio, Gonzalo, Manuelo and Gustavo. Gustavo worked in the theatre and I used to go out to parties with him; Antonio was a hairdresser and very, very handsome. All of them, but him particularly, were the sweetest people.

We were in the shop one day waiting for Gustavo and Antonio to turn up. Then I got a phone call from Gustavo saying there'd been an accident. He was hysterical. Antonio had on this pair of pale pink loafers, just slip-ons with a leather sole, and he slipped over in the road in Clapham and a great big truck ran over him. Michael Collins and I arranged his funeral at Brompton Oratory, and a lot of friends from the King's Road came to pay their respects, including Michael Costiff, who still remembers how moving the occasion was:

> **MICHAEL COSTIFF:** We all learned something from you that day and it stuck with both Gerlinde and me. There was a big funeral at Brompton Oratory and you said: "We really want to do this so his parents in Venezuela don't think he came to London and died alone. We just want to show them how many friends he had and how much he was loved."

When Antonio was killed, Gustavo wanted me to have something of his to keep. He gave me two things: a Perspex heart pendant with a gold rim and a diamond in the middle, which I wore for years and years and in many photos; I hardly ever took it off. The other thing, really rather upsettingly, was a £5 note that had been in Antonio's pocket when he was run over and was covered in his blood. I kept that for years, too. I don't know why. Gustavo had an unusual sense of humour and thought that Antonio would find that funny. So I kept it.

Secrets of the craft

Other regular faces at no. 430 were the pattern cutter Mark Tarbard, a friend of Michael's who ended up working for Vivienne; Andy Czezowski, the future manager of The Roxy, who at the time did Vivienne's books; and Ozzie, a displaced road rat from Australia. Her four brothers were in prison back home; they were all in the same biker clan. She had bleached blonde hair in plaits at the side, but a face that looked a hundred years old because she'd been out in the sun all her life. She worked as a cleaner in Sloane Square for some rich old dear and she used to bring her desserts up for us, because she didn't like sweet things. This supplemented our usual diet of a good tinned pilchard, tinned macaroni cheese with Worcester sauce and creamed mushrooms. Ozzie was always finding money on the floor. Michael and I loved her.

As well as her army of knitting ladies, Vivienne was assisted by a Greek tailor called Mr Mintos, who had a workshop off Camden Road and would help her to fashion the bondage trousers later sold at Seditionaries; and Mr Nicoli, a Turkish shoemaker from Archway, who taught her the secrets of his craft, including fashioning a shoe around a last. When you see how shoes are made, when you see the effort that goes into designing and making a lasting artefact, what the shoe is built on, how many times it has to be tweaked and changed in order to become a really good shoe, then you can immediately spot a bad shoe at a hundred metres. And it's all because it's not actually made properly to fit a foot. When I saw the original lasts that came into the shop and how a proper shoemaker works, it's such an important thing. All your weight is on that shoe.

And occasionally, those lasts could come in useful for hand-to-hand combat, as we shall see...

102

Signs and portents

While this was all going on in Chelsea, over in the suburb of Finchley, another dominatrix was flexing her wrist in preparation for taking the country sternly in hand. By 1975, Britain had started to pay the price for two decades of prosperity, with the worst levels of unemployment since the Second World War. The three-day week, the oil crisis and a sustained campaign of IRA violence all played their part in the downfall of Edward Heath's Tory government.[5] In February 1975, Margaret Thatcher swept Heath out from under her and became the leader of the Conservatives. Her developing ideology of individualism would run in parallel with the equally radical ideas that fuelled punk.

Someone who seemed to be able to divine the darkening turn of events was the filmmaker Derek Jarman, who was at the time putting together his first feature, *Sebastiane*, about the martyred saint. Derek had played a hesitant part in the Gay Liberation Front since its inception and was troubled by its growing militancy. He had other ideas for getting his message across, and, while he was in the process of editing his debut film, he began working on another script.

The Angelic Conversion of John Dee took for its main character Elizabeth I's alchemist, astrologer and secret agent Dr John Dee, who claimed to be able to talk to angels and speak their language, Enochian.[6] Derek saw Dr Dee as the inspiration for Prospero from Shakespeare's *The Tempest*, another project he wanted to film, to compare and contrast the two Elizabethan eras. The screenplay he was working on began towards the end of the first, when Derek imagined a dialogue between Elizabeth I and her alchemist in which Dr Dee unfolds the secrets of the universe with the help of the Angel Ariel.

---

[5] Heath's Conservatives were ousted in February 1974. Thatcher's policies were developed under the influence of Sir Keith Joseph and the Centre for Policy Studies, based on the ideas of US free-market economist Milton Friedman.

[6] According to some, Dr Dee was behind Ian Fleming's decision to give James Bond the number 007. Supporters of this theory think the '00' part symbolises Dee's eyes, or is itself a code meaning 'for your eyes only'. The '7' is a sacred number for Dee, who was fascinated by numerology. In his 1968 book *John Dee*, author Richard Deacon, a friend of Ian Fleming, called his subject "a roving James Bond of Tudor times".

Then, like Mr Hawkins before him, Derek had his own alchemical intervention, coming down the concourse of Victoria station one morning. He wrote up the vision he beheld in his diary: "White patent boots clattering down the platform, transparent plastic miniskirt revealing a hazy pudenda. Venus T-shirt. Smudged black eye paint, covered with a flaming blond beehive… the face that launched a thousand tabloids… art history as makeup."[7]

That was me, on my way to work, in one of only two of those Venus T-shirts Vivienne ever made. I had no idea I had caught his eye. But it wouldn't be long before I was introduced to another secret world on Butler's Wharf, where Derek and his friends Andrew Logan[8] and Duggie Fields had made their homes in abandoned

[7] From Derek Jarman's papers, published in *Derek Jarman* by Tony Peake (Little, Brown, 1999).

[8] Andrew Logan (b. 1945) is a sculptor, jewellery maker and performance artist. The Alternative Miss World competition was inspired by Crufts Dog Show, in that the criteria for judging would be on poise, personality and originality. The first competition was held at Logan's flat in Hackney in 1972 and attended by Derek Jarman, David Hockney and Keith from Smile. It was won by Patrick Steed as Miss Yorkshire and filmed by Jack Hazan for his film about Hockney, *A Bigger Splash* (1973). The 1975 event was attended by myself, Malcolm, Vivienne and the actress Fenella 'Mind if I Smoke?' Fielding. It was won by Derek as Miss Crêpe Suzette (a nod to Colin MacInnes's 1958 classic novel *Absolute Beginners*).

warehouses. Here they could film, make their jewellery and artworks and hold outlandish parties, including the annual Alternative Miss World competition that Andrew had started in 1972, far from the eyes and ears of the authorities.

All of that was to come, when Malcolm returned to London in May 1975. He brought with him a new momentum to push his vision to the limits – and things happened quickly around him as a result. Punk's blue touch paper was about to ignite.

7

MANUFACTURING OUTRAGE

Malcolm returns with a plan (1975)

A Dolls' house

Restless with what he had been achieving in the shop, Malcolm had gone to New York, ostensibly to sell clothes. But he hadn't been there long before he bumped into an old friend: New York Dolls guitarist Sylvain Sylvain. This band, which Malcolm and Vivienne both adored, was now on a downward spiral in a story already beset by chaos and tragedy. Sylvain remembers that meeting Malcolm again gave him hope.

Sylvain, an Egyptian refugee whose family had come to America via Paris in 1961, had also been involved in the rag trade, initially running a shop of his own designs in Woodstock, before the hippy festival changed the nature of that town forever; then, in Manhattan, designing the knitwear range Truth and Soul. He recalls first meeting Malcolm and Vivienne at an NYC Boutique show in 1971, before they even had the shop and when the first line-up of the Dolls had only just taken shape.

SYLVAIN SYLVAIN: It was at the MacAlpin Hotel, which is now the Sheridan, Sixth Avenue, right across the street from Macy's. I was there with Truth and Soul and I went to lunch one day, about four o'clock, to just walk round and check out everybody else's clothes. This is the end of the hippy time, 1971. So I'm walking down the hallway, and all the way at the very end, I see this really cool guy. He's wearing this baby blue drape jacket with the black trims, winklepickers, that whole Teddy boy thing, and on top of the door it says 'Let It Rock'. He sees me and I guess I look pretty cool, and he says: "Hey, young man! Come into my shop!" So I saw the stuff, and Vivienne, I remember her talking to me for a while. She was looking like a rockabilly chick, not so much with the poodle skirts, she's cooler than poodle. That was a Saturday and Sunday was the last day of the trade show. So I called up Johnny Thunders – or Giovanni Genzale, as he still was then, a nice little Italian boy from Queens – David Johansen and Billy Murcia, and they sold their samples to us. I still have the tie, with a snow scene on it, very 1940s-looking and it says on the back 'Let It Rock'; and this kind of see-through turquoise accordion knit, with a collar and three buttons down. It was really cool. It showed your nipples and everything.

Impressed by their looks and savvy knowledge of street style, Sylvain visited Malcolm and Vivienne again in London in November 1972, when Let It Rock was up and running and the Dolls were due to play some important dates. Their manager, Marty Thau, had arranged for them to open for Lou Reed on his UK tour, but he cancelled them at the last minute. Sylvain speculates that this was down to "rivalry, jealousy, fear and politics".[1] Instead, they opened for acts as diverse as Kevin Ayres, Roxy Music and Status Quo, in the lead-up to a massive support slot for The Faces at Wembley Arena on 29 October – which, incidentally, was where Glen Matlock and skiving schoolboys Steve Jones and Paul Cook saw the Dolls for the first time.

The excitement generated by the Dolls' visit stirred record company interest – Thau was courted by Richard Branson, but turned down his $4,000 offer before Mike Oldfield's *Tubular Bells* put the young impresario in a considerably better financial position. But their

---

[1] For the full scoop on Sylvain Sylvain and his related stories, see *There's No Bones in Ice Cream: Sylvain Sylvain's Story of the New York Dolls* by Sylvain Sylvain and Dave Thompson (Omnibus Press, 2018).

momentum was abruptly curtailed by the untimely death of drummer Billy Murcia, just one week after that Faces gig.

On the morning of 6 November, Billy had argued with David Johansen and walked out of the band's hotel. Sylvain, his childhood friend with whom he had first started the band that turned into the Dolls, tried to calm him down and bring him back.

> **SYLVAIN SYLVAIN:** We would be invited to all these parties where they were like throwing shit at us, drugs and everything else. And the day that Billy Murcia passed away, I saw him in the dining room that morning in the hotel. We had just come from parties the night before and he said: "Sylvain, I almost died last night. Man, all these people giving me Mandies – but I only took a half." And he pulled out a whole bunch of Mandrax[2] that he'd broken in half. I said: "Be careful, man." 'Cos that stuff, you would take one and it would knock you out.

Billy went on to a party on Cromwell Road, Earl's Court, where he started choking and passed out. The people he was with tried to revive him, but they couldn't – Sylvain maintains it was a terrible accident. Thau sent the rest of the band back home before police officers could pose any awkward questions.

Although the Dolls, especially Sylvain, were shocked to the core by these events, their momentum was such that the show did go on. Back in New York, Jerry Nolan – up until then one of the band's biggest fans – took over on drums and the band continued their rock'n'roll quest, playing more gigs at their spiritual home, the Mercer Arts Center, before the year was out. Although the bidding war Thau had been negotiating evaporated in the wake of Billy's death, and the dark aura of drug abuse that hung over it, he secured them a £25,000 two-album deal from Mercury.

Their eponymous debut was delivered in July 1973, produced by Todd Rundgren and featuring such classics as 'Personality Crisis',

---

[2] Billy Murcia's autopsy listed Mandrax in the contents of his stomach. This was the brand name for methaquolone, a sedative sold as Quaaludes in the USA and prescribed to treat insomnia and anxiety and which became popular with musicians for the powerful high it engendered. It has been banned since 1984.

'Looking for a Kiss' and their perfect cover of Bo Diddley's 'Pills'. The Mercury deal was completed with *Too Much Too Soon* in May 1974, this time helmed by veteran producer George 'Shadow' Morton (The Shangri-Las), who came out of retirement because, he said, "The Dolls had energy, sort of a disciplined weirdness. I took them into the room as a challenge. I was bored with the music and the business. The Dolls can certainly snap you out of boredom."[3]

Malcolm and Vivienne caught up with them in August 1973, when Let It Rock were asked to show their designs at the National Boutique Show in the MacAlpin Hotel. The band encouraged Malcolm, Vivienne and their then business partner Gerry Goldstein[4] to relocate to the Chelsea Hotel, where they met Alice Cooper and were invited over to Andy Warhol's *Interview* magazine. Malcolm and Vivienne sold little else on that trip, but enjoyed hanging out with the Dolls at Max's Kansas City – though their first experience of the Chelsea now seems unnervingly prophetic.

VIVIENNE WESTWOOD: That's how I got to really know the Dolls, after we hung out all week at Max's. It's funny because, when we went to New York – and I never took drugs knowingly; seriously, I wouldn't – people were giving me stuff and I didn't realise, I just remember being in a party in New York and suddenly hallucinating. I don't know what I'd had. We stayed in the Chelsea Hotel, and one morning there were chalk marks on the floor near the front door, where there had been a murder.

When the Dolls returned to London in November 1973, their friendship reignited. Vivienne has strong memories of seeing their show at Biba's legendary Rainbow Room restaurant on 26 November, and how impressed she was by Johnny Thunders.

---

[3] Shadow Morton, quoted in *1001 Songs: The Great Songs of All Time and the Artists, Stories, and Secrets Behind Them* by Toby Creswell (Hardie Grant, 2005).

[4] Gerry Goldstein, a Jewish autodidact from Stoke Newington, was a close friend of David Litvinoff, who, together with the gallery owner and art dealer Robert Fraser, connected virtually everyone from the Francis Bacon/Reggie and Ronnie Kray set of the 1950s to the pop artists and swingers of the 1960s and the punk prodigies of the 1970s. For a full account, Keiron Pim's book *Jumpin' Jack Flash* (Jonathan Cape, 2016) is highly recommended. Sadly, Gerry died after a short illness in December 2017.

VIVIENNE WESTWOOD: We hurried up to the Biba building, thinking we would be late for the gig, and they weren't there. So we rushed back to their hotel and David Johansen was still in bed! They got dressed and put these bits of marabou round them and we went with them to this gig, very much later than it was supposed to be when they started playing. David was great on the stage, they all were – but Johnny Thunders had a child's tailcoat and a pair of turquoise blue tights on and a pink-and-white shirt with some frills on it. The way he moved around onstage was like some kind of frog. He looked just like Jeremy Fisher. It was so amazing.

Perhaps the band were taking it easy, because earlier in the day Arthur Kane had nearly been arrested for trying to steal a jacket from the Biba boutique…

SYLVAIN SYLVAIN: People think we were such rich rock stars, but we were on $75 a week – even back then, you're not too rich. So after soundcheck we went downstairs and he was switching price tags. It's that jacket with the leopard collar, it's a girl's thing but he wears it, and it made the BBC news! We played Biba's for two, three nights and we sold out. You had Paul McCartney in the audience – we were like huge at that moment. And Arthur was busted for shoplifting!

A day later, the Dolls would film their legendary *Old Grey Whistle Test* performance, which was dubbed by toothsome presenter, future Sid-Vicious-bait and all-round enemy-of-the-kids 'Whispering' Bob Harris as: "mock rock". Malcolm and Vivienne followed them from London to more gigs at Paris Olympia and the Bataclan that winter.

SYLVAIN SYLVAIN: We became really good friends after that. I had a nice thing with Vivienne, much more so than the other guys. I remember we were all sitting together at Jean-Charles de Castelbajac's party, where they made pizza for us, and spaghetti for Johnny. She asked me how come I was so happy. I said it was because this was the best part of my life. And it was, I think.

Seeing the band in action implanted in Malcolm the notion that he needed to break with the nostalgic past of the rocking 1950s and do something new. This initiated the transition of Let It Rock into Too Fast To Live Too Young To Die and, ultimately, the idea that he needed an actual band to realise the fullness of his ambitions.

Seeing red

When Malcolm arrived in New York in November 1974, Marty Thau had just about given up on his protégés. Living up to the title of their second album, Johnny Thunders and Jerry Nolan had both developed heroin habits, while Arthur Kane's alcoholism was becoming a real problem. Malcolm got Arthur into rehab, while, back in London, Vivienne started sewing and made a whole new look for the band. Sylvain says it was the band's idea to dress in red, to go with a song they had been working on called 'Red Patent Leather'. Vivienne recalls events differently:

VIVIENNE WESTWOOD: Malcolm had the idea of provoking people into getting loads of press coverage by saying they were the representatives of Chairman Mao in China. David Johansen said to them: "Look, it's just a publicity stunt, don't worry." But when they asked Johnny Thunders what he thought, he said: "D'you want to make something of it?" Malcolm told me the reaction of the one he didn't respect [David] and the one he did respect [Johnny].

The Dolls' new look comprised red vinyl trousers, red ciré T-shirts, high-heeled boots and a massive hammer and sickle flag to perform in front of, which they did for the first time at the New York Hippodrome on 28 February. Malcolm produced a manifesto to announce the gig, headlined 'What Are the Politics of Boredom?' in which he informed the public that the Dolls had: "assumed the role of the People's Information Collective in association with the Red Guard". The show did not go down well, but, undaunted, Malcolm booked a tour of Florida that April.

It ended in disaster. Arthur was too sick to play and Johnny and Jerry deserted and flew back to New York to score. There, they ended up forming the first incarnation of The Heartbreakers with Richard Hell, who had just walked off the Television set. Sylvain and Malcolm went on a recuperative road trip to New Orleans, where

Sylvain showed Malcolm his favourite T-shirt design and Malcolm told Sylvain about this group he was getting together in London that he wanted him to join…

> **SYLVAIN SYLVAIN:** Malcolm was incredible. He calls up Alain Toussaint and tells him I'm gonna be the next big thing in England, he's selling me to him and Alain Toussaint thinks Malcolm is Brian Epstein, 'cos he believes in what he's saying. So we're running around those shops on Bourbon Street, tourist souvenir shops that sold a white T-shirt with this picture of a pair of tits going right across it. I bought one for Malcolm, it was like five bucks. Then he brought it home. I think the next day he wandered down that same place and bought a couple more and gave them to Vivienne…

When he came back, Malcolm brought another totem with him – Sylvain's white Les Paul Custom guitar, taken on the understanding its owner would soon be reunited with it. He went to see what Steve Jones and his bunch of reprobates had been getting up to.

The band had continued rehearsing under Bernie Rhodes guidance and even played one gig – described as a "nightmare" by Steve – at Salter's Café on the King's Road. At Riverside Studios, Malcolm was quite impressed by what he saw. But he pinpointed problems with both Wally and Steve. Steve wasn't a good enough singer and Wally wasn't a good enough guitarist. Malcolm gave Steve the white Les Paul – and told him that his schoolfriend had to go.

It was time for them to find a singer.

Something in the air

As if it had been prophesied by its appearance on the 'You're gonna wake up one morning…' T-shirt, the changing of the fashion guard was marked when the Biba superstore in Kensington closed down in November 1975. A full-on revolt into street style had begun and the area around the top of the King's Road was no longer just Malcolm and Vivienne's domain; other upstarts were moving into the markets the pair had untapped. As well as Bernie Rhodes' outlet, Lloyd Johnson had started selling Mod clothes, and Acme Attractions, run by John Krivine, Don Letts and Jeanette Lee, a cheaper, imitation SEX shop,

113

attracted the musically minded with Don's aural diet of dub. Although Malcolm and Vivienne did end up selling them patterns, I thought I would be tainted if I went in there, so I never set foot inside the place.

ROGER K. BURTON: I think everybody tried to jump on the bandwagon – even we did, because we just couldn't sell vintage any more, nobody wanted it. We used to have these clients coming in from Japan every couple of weeks to buy vanloads of stuff. We'd park outside Beaufort Street Market, open the doors and they'd take everything we had. Then all of a sudden it was no more. Everybody wants black, it's all got to be zips and straps and so on. It was an interesting time, from my perspective anyway, how punk clothing started appearing here and there. There was so much intrigue going on in SEX. Because I was dealing with all those other shops, selling them dead stock, and they were all: "What's going on down the road?" All these rumours like: "Malcolm's had a sex change!" It was rife!

I'm not sure if Malcolm really had a sex to change.

Labourers and lumberjacks

Touko Valio Laaksonen (1920–91), best known as Tom of Finland, was an artist known for his fetishistic depictions of very macho gay men, idealised versions of the labourers, lumberjacks and military officers who had inspired him throughout his closeted existence as a young man in Finland and during his service as an anti-aircraft officer in the Finnish army during the Second World War. "The whole Nazi philosophy, the racism and all that, is hateful to me, but of course, I drew them anyway. They had the sexiest uniforms," he is quoted as saying in *His Life and Times* by F. Valentine Hooven (St Martin's Press, 1994). In 1957, his work was first published in the American magazine *Physique Pictorial* under the Tom of Finland pseudonym invented for him by editor Bob Mizer, launching him to a global audience, who liked what they saw. As US censorship restrictions relaxed at the end of the 1960s and into the 1970s, his drawings became more explicit, featuring the kind of exaggerated appendages that appear on the Westwood McLaren Cowboys T-shirt. *Tom of Finland,* the biopic directed by fellow Finn Dome Karukoski, was released in 2017.

Another person who had begun to hang around at World's End was a Law student called Jon Savage, who was about to have his life transformed by the unfolding events of punk, which would lead to him starting his own fanzine and then becoming a music journalist for *Sounds*. He remembers first stepping over the threshold of SEX in 1975.

JON SAVAGE: I would do the King's Road strip – and it was a strip. You'd start off with the market and then it would start to get popcultural. I'd go into Acme Attractions and buy sixties-type round-collared shirts, which I loved. Don played dub reggae, which was a very different vibe. But SEX was threatening – and that got my interest more. I remember being very impressed by the intimidating atmosphere. I actually thought: They

should just beat people up when they go in there. Malcolm was in tune, he had good antennae about society. He found his time in the 1970s, and with you he found his first Sex Pistol.

The shop acted as an information bureau for its clientele, with the new records Malcolm had brought back from America a focus point. Marco remembers a pivotal Saturday afternoon that demonstrates the devotion this could inspire.

MARCO PIRRONI: I went to the shop one Saturday afternoon, and Malcolm said: "You've got to hear this record I brought back from New York, 'Roadrunner' by Jonathan Richman." I listened to it and I thought it was so fucking brilliant I had to go and phone a friend, Jay Strongman, who lived in Reading. I said: "You've got to get down here now and listen to this." This was four o'clock in the afternoon, so he just managed to get on a train and all the way up King's Road...

Offensive weapons

With Malcolm back, the designs generated from SEX became more provocative. The Gay Cowboys T-shirt, featuring a Tom-of-Finland-style cartoon of two well-endowed men, naked from the waist down but for their boots, went into production, as did an eye-catching design of naked women's breasts at exact breast height. Another depicted the mask worn by the Cambridge Rapist,[5] a dangerous, all-

---

[5] Peter Samuel Cook (1929–2004) was a serial rapist who targeted students at the University of Cambridge between October 1974 and his capture in June 1975. During his attacks, he wore a full-face leather bondage mask with a zipper mouth, on which he had painted a pair of eyes and the words 'RAPIST', as well as attaching lengths of black curly hair, to give his victims a false impression about his appearance (his own hair was cropped). Coupled with his terrifying appearance, the frequency and increasing brutality of his attacks sparked one of Britain's biggest manhunts and Cook was captured cycling away from the scene of his final crime wearing a blonde wig and women's clothing. He turned out to be a 47-year-old delivery driver with multiple previous convictions for theft and burglary. He was tried at Norwich Crown Court on 3 October 1975 and pleaded guilty to seven charges of rape, two of wounding and one of gross indecency. He was given two life sentences, and died in HMP Winchester at the age of 75.

too-real predator who had been terrorising the student population of the university city since the previous autumn.

Michael Collins and I suspected one of our customers of being the guilty party, because he'd bought this mask from us that sounded exactly the same as the description the police were giving of the one worn by the Cambridge Rapist. He used to come in with a very thick, made-to-measure rubber band round his neck, so the veins in his neck were always standing out and he was very flushed in the face, like he'd drop dead at any minute. Then we saw a little bit of his rubber one day, which was obviously restricting his breathing. He used to wear it all day at work.

Michael and I put our heads together and decided that, if this could possibly be the same person, then we had a duty to share our suspicions with the police. First, Michael phoned Malcolm to ask his advice on our dilemma.

MICHAEL COLLINS: Malcolm immediately saw a story. He said: "Don't say anything." By the Saturday he'd had the T-shirt made, and linked it to Brian Epstein's S&M activities. And then I phoned the police.

The worst trouble I got into was wearing the Cambridge Rapist T-shirt, because it was so current. They were searching for this guy and people were verbally attacking me for wearing it. The customer, as it turned out, was completely exonerated and the police finally did get their man, who turned out to be even more of a bizarre character than our masked man. Malcolm the provocateur had the bit firmly between his teeth now.

While he hunted for a new singer, Kutie Jones's boys were transitioned into The Sex Pistols via a T-shirt designed to promote both the shop and the band as a package deal. The provocative image of a naked 12-year-old boy smoking had come from a small paedophile magazine called *Boys Express*, which Malcolm had somehow managed to lay his hands on. Some of his designs also had Glen Matlock's guitar and the band name printed on them. But Bernie Rhodes refused to screen-print the central image, so, despite his own misgivings, Glen was talked into making the first limited-edition run using the facilities at Saint Martin's.

That T-shirt still retains its shock value today. When you see the pictures of Paul Cook wearing it, you think: Crikey, he's the quiet one, he's not doing this to be notorious or anything. It's very hard-hitting, especially for a man to wear.

PAUL COOK: You had to be careful wearing that stuff. It was quite a statement at the time. You would get verbally and sometimes physically assaulted in the street.

Unluckiest of all was Alan Jones. He picked up a Cowboys T-shirt, put it on and promptly got himself arrested in Piccadilly by plain-clothes police. It was a case destined to hit the headlines and stir up a debate that divided the nation.

ALAN JONES: My arrest was the most ridiculous thing. I was at Piccadilly Circus and they pounced on me, thinking I was a rent boy. We went to Vine Street, and they were being really nasty. I was with my best friend at the time, who was a Norwegian guy, and he was so scared that he was going to be thrown out of the country because he was with me, he kept going: "Tell them I'm Danish, tell them I'm Danish, tell them I'm Danish!" So I had that going on and then I had the police saying: "What are you doing, why are you wearing this?" I was shocked that I'd even ended up in the police station. You don't expect to be arrested for fashion – not the Fashion Police!

The incident made the front page of the *Guardian* on 2 August, linked to a television exposé about teenage boy prostitution at Piccadilly Circus that had been screened on 22 July, four nights before Alan's arrest. Directed and produced by John Willis, Yorkshire Television's *Johnny Go Home* was an investigative documentary shown in two parts, owing to a murder that took place in one of the hostels while filming was taking place. The first part, *The End of the Line*, shown before the 9 p.m. watershed, followed the stories of a homeless 12-year-old Scottish boy trying to make his way in London and a 17-year-old girl already hardened to life on the streets. The second part, shown after the ten o'clock news, was *The Murder of Billy Two-Tone*, an examination of the crime that focused on the hostel's owner, who ran a housing empire based on sexual exploitation and financial corruption that went unchecked largely because of the ineptitude of social services – a story still horribly resonant today.

> **ALAN JONES:** Back then in Piccadilly, people would just lean on the railings; that was where all the rent boys were. I was only ever a rent boy for one day. I was sharing my apartment with a hooker when I worked at the Portobello on night shifts – she was using it to bring her customers home and she split the cash with me. All along Notting Hill, Queensway and Lancaster Gate was where people would trawl for prostitutes, and I was in Clanricarde Gardens, which was in the centre of all that. She got me out on the game one night... and I didn't like it. If it was a sexy man, it would have been all right, but it was an old man. It was horrible.

Thanks to the efforts of journalist Nicholas de Jongh, the case became the focus of a further series of articles in the *Guardian*, stimulating more debate in the letters pages, where the point was made that the whole function of youth is to rebel. The Labour MP Colin Phipps was spurred into writing to Home Secretary Roy Jenkins to ask him to review the legislation Alan had been charged under, the 1824 Vagrancy Act.

The upshot for the shop was that SEX was raided, eighteen of the offending T-shirts were seized and, on 7 August, Malcolm and Vivienne were charged with 'exposing to public view an indecent exhibition'. Malcolm was quickly on the phone, in search of character witnesses. It was then he decided that a young social anthropologist, who had recently called into the shop on behalf of the Institute of Contemporary Art (ICA) and been given short shrift, could actually be of some use after all.

I fought the law

New Jersey-born Ted Polhemus had been studying at University College London under Professor Mary Douglas when the ICA asked her to contribute to a programme they were running called *The Body Is a Medium of Expression*. She suggested they take Ted on instead, and he ended up initiating a series called *Fashion Forum*, for which he interviewed established designers like Zandra Rhodes and Ossie Clark, and which proved extremely popular. Wanting to find some up-and-coming designers for his next event, he took a trip up to the World's End.

TED POLHEMUS: SEX was a formidable place. It took me a long, long time – about an hour – to work up the nerve to go in. And the only person in there was Malcolm. I introduced myself, saying that I worked for the ICA, and Malcolm said: "Oh, we hate the ICA – fuck off!" But I left him my card and, a couple of weeks later, he phoned me. He said: "I want to do a deal with you. Vivienne and Jordan will appear at the ICA at your *Fashion Forum* if you will appear as a character witness at our trial."

It was really interesting: it must have been the first time in centuries that an item of clothing had caused a court case. Because there used to be all these sartorial laws that said commoners couldn't wear purple, and stuff like that. But that was in Elizabethan times and they couldn't really enforce those laws even then.

By the time the case came to court at the end of November, the police had taken action against the social ills with which the shop had been linked and cleared the Dilly of under age rent boys. As I was going to be called as a witness, I picked out an outfit that wasn't quite what I would normally wear for work: a beautiful black vintage fifties pencil skirt suit with a little cinched-in waist, a sweetheart collar and little faceted buttons, all in black shot silk, worn with my big white bouffant and black eyes, black stilettos and fishnets. In the end, I was never asked to take the stand. But, as Ted recalls, the trial proved an interesting study in police methodology of the mid-1970s, when the defence attempted to ascertain where the material likely to corrupt and deprave had actually been found.

TED POLHEMUS: The different police officers that had raided the shop were all questioned by Malcolm's solicitor. Every time he asked them "Now, did you take it out of the window?" each of them would reply: "No, no, that was someone else." None of them would own up to actually taking the T-shirt out of the window – and that was a key element of the prosecution's case. They were saying that little old ladies could be walking down the King's Road and be needlessly offended. But you had to go into this formidable shop in order to see it. Someone walking down the street in this T-shirt is another story, but the ones on sale in the shop could not be seen from the outside. My memory is that there was only a tiny window and I don't recall the T-shirt being in there.

I'd never been in a British court before, but I did what I had to do: I said that Malcolm and Vivienne were serious and important fashion designers. When it came to the Cowboys T-shirt, it got even more bizarre. The prosecution alleged that the penises were touching each other and the defence leaped up and said: "No they're not!" And then someone had to fetch a ruler...

Malcolm and Vivienne got off with a fine, but, without the solicitor Malcolm had promised to represent him, Alan ended up pleading guilty, purely because he didn't know what else he could do. The ruler farce was not so funny for him and, to this day, the biggest shocker of all for Alan remains Malcolm's behaviour.

ALAN JONES: That's when I realised what a complete creep Malcolm was, because he promised me a lawyer but he never did anything. My fine was £15, a lot of money in those days. It made me realise *what* he was – and that put me off the whole thing.

After that raid, we started to hide the shirts in the horrible little toilet on the landing above the stairs, between the shop and the flats above it, one of which used to be inhabited by the actress Lesley-Anne Down. The stairs were all broken and really quite dangerous and, although the toilet was locked and you had to get a key to use it, there was always the chance that the stock could get nicked by someone other than the police. But it was better than being raided and losing the whole lot in one go. When we ran out of the ten we had on display, we'd go upstairs and get another ten from the lavs, where there'd be about 150 of them piled up in boxes. The police did come back periodically, but there was never another raid.

Not long after Malcolm had been arraigned to appear in court that August, another momentous meeting occurred. The one that would finally turn the idea of The Sex Pistols into a reality...

8

THIS IS WHAT YOU'LL GET

Becoming a Sex Pistol (1975)

Let the right one in

While Malcolm had been away in the US, a group of four young men, all called John, had started coming into the shop. John Beverley, sometimes known as Sid; John Wardle, later to become Jah Wobble; John Grey; and John Lydon, who stood out by merit of his home-dyed green hair and customised Pink Floyd T-shirt, on which he had scrawled the immortal line 'I HATE' above the band's name in marker pen.

I always got on very well with Lydon, who had seen me wearing one of my dance tops, a royal blue leotard that I'd ripped across the bust until it gaped and then pinned back together with safety pins. I think it might have given him an idea… But Vivienne was more impressed with John Beverley, and when she mentioned to Malcolm that he should consider one of these Johns for his new singer, that was who she actually meant.

VIVIENNE WESTWOOD: Sid was such a lovable person. But he didn't know the difference between right and wrong. He was dangerous, definitely, but so clever, funny and intelligent. And manipulative, I would say. Because he just made you like him. You couldn't help it.

Though it was Sid (John Beverley) who had first found his way to SEX and introduced the others to the shop, he was off working on a stall on Portobello Road when Malcolm first encountered the other three Johns, and it was Lydon who immediately caught his eye. He confronted him with the challenge: "Can you sing?"

Lydon replied disdainfully in the negative. Legend has recorded that his reply was: "No, but I can sing out of tune." But my memory is of him saying: "I can play a violin out of tune."

Whichever it was, Malcolm was as intrigued by this response as he was by Lydon's appearance, and invited him to come and meet the group in the Roebuck at seven that evening, when we had closed the shop.

Steve Jones, Paul Cook and Glen Matlock awaited him apprehensively, and with good reason. Malcolm and Bernie Rhodes had previously approached Midge Ure as a potential lead singer: in true Larry Parnes fashion, Malcolm started looking towards Scotland following the phenomenal success of the Bay City Rollers. Ure, whose band Slik had just been signed by the Rollers' label Bell, thankfully wasn't interested.

PAUL COOK: I don't know what that was all about. Malcolm had gone up to Scotland to see him, but that was nothing to do with us. There was no way we'd have had Midge Ure as our singer. It would never have worked with him.

The band had held their own auditions, but hadn't found anyone who really clicked, either. When Lydon turned up, bringing John Grey for moral support, he was surly and abrasive, an attitude that Steve Jones in particular took umbrage with. Malcolm, who liked what he saw, suggested they hold an impromptu audition back at the shop. The candidate was duly placed in front of the jukebox, with a shower attachment standing in for a microphone, and told to sing along to Alice Cooper's 'I'm Eighteen'.

PAUL COOK: He turned up all bolshie, down the pub. Had a few drinks, went back to the jukebox. What a place to do an audition: "Go on, sing along to this!" And he just did, like *that* he went straight into his Johnny

124

Rotten, mad, in front of the jukebox. He was desperate to be in a band and be part of it. It was hilarious, he was brilliant. After about ten seconds, we knew we'd found our singer.

With his scowling, spitting, hunched-over performance, inspired by his love of Sir Laurence Olivier's performance as Richard III, Lydon had won over the sceptical nucleus of the band, though, from watching his antics, Steve Jones decided that this new singer needed a new name. Although the idea now seems like a twist on Larry Parnes' stable of Furies and Wilde boys, it was Steve and not Malcolm who rebaptised John 'Rotten', thanks to the state of his teeth.

Their first band rehearsal was not an auspicious one. In fact, it didn't happen at all. Steve, Paul and Glen were told to turn up for rehearsals with Rotten a week later, in a cooperative run by a bunch of squatters from a former granary in Rotherhithe. Malcolm knew some of its residents, the Crunchy Frog animation group. Nobody except Rotten turned up and he was not best pleased to be left wandering the run-down docklands on his own. When – under Malcolm's orders – Glen later phoned to apologise, John threatened to kill him. It was a lesson to the new manager, who decided things needed to be run a little more seriously now.

The gun is loaded

A month after The Sex Pistols' first rehearsal, Glen found an ad for a rehearsal space in *Melody Maker*: an attic over a small ground-floor rehearsal room, reached by a crumbling passage between 6 and 8 Denmark Street. The lease on this former silversmith's workshop was owned by former manager Bill Collins[1] and lay on what had been, in the 1950s, the epicentre of the music business, a road more commonly known to this day as Tin Pan Alley.[2] Needless to say,

---

[1] Bill Collins managed the ill-fated Badfinger and was the father of *Professionals* star Lewis Collins.
[2] Tin Pan Alley – called after the similar street in New York City – was where the first music paper *Melody Maker* was founded in 1926. Music publishers took offices in the street from 1911 onwards, followed by instrument shops, recording studios and clubs. Most of this characterful enclave survives, although Crossrail bulldozers saw off the last music venue, the 12 Bar Club, which closed on 16 January 2015. For more information, see the 2018 documentary *Tales from Tin Pan Alley*.

Malcolm loved this connection to 1950s London and happily took the place over.

Interestingly, before Denmark Street was built, this area of London was the notorious slum, St Giles Rookery, a haven of seventeenth-century punks, villains and thieves, whose world is vividly depicted in the etchings of William Hogarth. 'Punk' in those days meant 'prostitute' and this was the definition that travelled to America, where it still causes confusion to this day.

Despite having Sylvain's guitar,[3] Steve's playing was not considered up to scratch yet, so an ad was placed in *Melody Maker* looking for a "WHIZZ KIDD GUITARIST" with the specification that applicants must be 20 years old or younger and "not worse looking than Johnny Thunders". With nowhere else to call his home, Steve moved into the attic above the rehearsal space in September 1975 and commenced his Les Paul studies in earnest, taking black bombers and playing along to Stooges and New York Dolls records all night. He upped his game at exactly the right moment, as the hopeful recruits answering Malcolm's ad – including one Fabian Quest – were all so awful that it was decided he could do the job better after all.

PAUL COOK: We did audition other guitarists and that was really my doing. I thought we needed another guitarist. But all these weirdos turned up. Steve New turned up, from The Rich Kids, but we thought it was a waste of time. He was a good guitarist, but we knocked that idea on the head pretty quickly because Steve progressed so much as a guitarist. He was like to the manner born, amazing. He never found himself good at anything until he picked up a guitar and then he was a total natural. None of us started learning until we was about 17, 18, really. By the time we made *Never Mind the Bollocks*, we'd only been playing about two years. Denmark Street was a big turning point. We realised how serious Malcolm was when he got us the premises. Because I had a job at the time, I had an apprenticeship and everything. I was in a dilemma, really, thinking: What

---

[3] Sylvain says that Malcolm shipped over his Les Paul Custom guitar and Fender Rhodes piano with the promise that a plane ticket would follow. Instead, he gave Steve the guitar and sold the piano to pay for the lease on Denmark Street. See *There's No Bones in Ice Cream: Sylvain Sylvain's Story of the New York Dolls* by Sylvain Sylvain and Dave Thompson (Omnibus Press, 2018).

am I going to do here? Lucky I made the right decision. 'Cos I was the only one working properly out of the band. John wasn't, Steve obviously wasn't. Glen was at art school. I was the only one who had a job. I don't think we took ourselves too seriously until then. It was brilliant – what a move.

Now able to rehearse every day, the band worked their way through covers of bands they admired, such as The Stooges' 'No Fun', The Count Five's 'Psychotic Reaction', The Small Faces' 'Whatcha Gonna Do About It' and The Who's 'Substitute', along with songs Rotten managed to turn on their head with his unique vocal delivery – Dave Berry's 'Don't Gimme No Lip, Child' and The Monkees' 'I'm Not Your Stepping Stone'. This rapidly progressed into writing their own material.

Until Rotten came along, the band only had two original numbers, 'Did You No Wrong' and 'Seventeen'/'Lazy Sod', both written by Steve. John now started writing new lyrics for these and, while he was getting his creative juices flowing, began decorating the walls with graffiti and cartoons of the targets of his bile, such as the TV presenter and tub-thumping Christian Malcolm Muggeridge, who clearly represented all the respectable Middle England values he was aiming at. Thankfully for future students of satire, these artworks were saved for the nation in 2017, when the rehearsal space became a Grade 2* listed building because of its association with The Sex Pistols. Astonishingly, it was the Conservative Party who so decreed it.[4]

The first song to emerge from these intense sessions was 'Pretty Vacant', written by Glen, the most technically proficient musician in

---

[4] The Denmark Street rehearsal space was given its Grade 2* listed status on the fortieth anniversary of 1977. The campaign to save the building from demolition was led by local artist and historian Jane Palm-Gold, together with Henry Scott-Irvine from the Save Tin Pan Alley campaign. She says: "I'd never done anything like that before in my life but I was fucked if I was going to let that little building fall. The developers were furious. Glen Matlock lived there back in the 1980s and he put corkboard over the walls to preserve the graffiti..." On the day their status was made official, Tory Heritage Minister David Evennett said: "These seventeenth-century townhouses not only exhibit well-preserved architectural detail but helped nurture Soho's influence on the global music industry during the 1960s and 1970s. As we celebrate forty years of punk, I'm delighted to be granting further protection to these buildings which acted as a home and studio to The Sex Pistols."

the band, and wordsmith Rotten. The relationship between this pair was always antagonistic, but at this point it only added to the vital spark of the music they were creating.

PAUL COOK: They all came together so quick, the songs. It was amazing. Because we had so much energy and John had so much to say. We were there every night, hanging out, writing songs and playing, crashing through stuff.

They were on a roll and ideas were flying, not always in the direction intended. When Malcolm suggested they write a song called 'Submission' about sadomasochism, John turned out a lyric about going on a submarine mission. I used to really love it when the band came into the shop when the very first new stuff hit the rails; Malcolm would pick out what he wanted them to wear. But The Sex Pistols were never very easily directed. At times the whole lot of them would tell him: "I'm not wearing this! What's this piece of rubbish?"

PAUL COOK: Well, we did feel like we was being used a little bit, as his clothes horses. We did like the stuff, but we didn't want to be seen as showcasing his shop, so there was that conflict going on. We did wear the things we liked and we weren't forced. It was a very interesting dynamic what was going on then. A bunch of misfits, basically. There wasn't that many of us around at the time.

In a way, we were isolated. There is a picture of me walking up the King's Road, looking very much like I did when Derek Jarman first saw me, with that see-through net skirt on, and what is interesting to look at now is what's going on in the background – it's really grey, with corrugated iron, almost like a bomb site – and that was me walking on my own like that. We were very much on our own to start with.

But Malcolm was intent on changing that situation by booking some gigs.

By the autumn of 1975, bands like Kilburn and the High Roads and Canvey Island's Dr Feelgood had opened up a circuit of more intimate pub gigs to a younger generation alienated by the stadium gigs of rock royalty. Other players on this scene were The Stranglers from Guildford,

Eddie and the Hot Rods from Southend, and Joe Strummer's 101ers, then living at 101 Elgin Avenue, neighbouring Frestonia.

But Malcolm wanted nothing to do with any of that. Drawing on what he had learned in his art-school past and using those same facilities that had got his merchandise screen-printed, he got Glen to secure The Sex Pistols their first gig at Saint Martin's College of Art.

Love at first bite

It was a month of financial black clouds and murdered children's TV presenters: Chancellor Denis Healey announced £3 billion spending cuts and *Record Breakers*' Ross McWhirter was shot

on his doorstep by members of the Provisional IRA. The day after Bonfire Night, on 6 November 1975, The Sex Pistols walked their equipment over from Denmark Street to the small upstairs room Glen's art college had arranged for the gig on their Charing Cross Road campus. Me, Malcolm, Vivienne, Michael Collins and Andy Czezowski came with them and formed a sort of punk Praetorian Guard around the front of the stage. Malcolm was insistent that I should stand on the side of the stage with the band and people have often asked me if I was ever considered to actually be the singer. When I put this to Paul Cook, he was refreshingly honest on why this could never have happened:

PAUL COOK: No, no women. The punk scene blew the doors wide open as far as women were concerned in music, but we were too blokey to have a girl in the band, being honest. Groupies were scared to talk to us, anyway, 'cos of how John was and Jonesy being a nymphomaniac. I kid you not.

Steve had put on his Cloak of Invisibility and liberated a hundred-watt twin-reverb Marshall amp especially for the occasion. To calm his nerves, he had taken a Mandrax. John, dressed in baggy pinstriped trousers, braces and his customised Pink Floyd T-shirt, had dosed himself on Strepsils, which he chewed on-stage and spat at the audience. Steve's amp cranked the Pistols sound up so loud that the plug got pulled on their debut after only five songs and fifteen minutes – but what a fifteen minutes. After debuting their unique take on 'Substitute' and 'Whatcha Gonna Do About It', with the lyrics altered to: 'I want you to know that I *hate* you, baby...', the set ended in a fight when Rotten called the headline band a bunch of cunts.

That band was a 1950s revival act called Bazooka Joe. Their lead singer, Danny Kleinman, took umbrage and jumped up onstage to pin Rotten up against the wall and demand that he apologise. However, their bass player had a different reaction. Stuart Goddard was so impressed by what he had seen that he stayed where he was in the audience. Feeling that the ground had shifted beneath his feet, he left Bazooka Joe the next day to form his own band and write original material, which he would do under a different, transformative name: Adam Ant.

It was the first time he had ever clapped eyes on me, too, and apparently he liked what he saw; my pointed white beehive and black zig zag make-up held his attention as strongly as the band's performance. Not long after this first encounter, I started receiving anonymous admiring letters at the shop. Could the two things have possibly been connected?

Looking back on that first gig now, Paul Cook reflects that the seeds of the Pistols' destruction were probably sown right at that very moment.

PAUL COOK: Once he saw the band, Malcolm wanted to be John, I think, and that's why he and John had a big conflict. As we know, Malcolm went on to make records himself. So that was the start of that, I think.

Another gig had been arranged for the next day, at the Central School of Art, where the band played with a mirror in front of them and their confrontational attitude caught the imagination of the audience. The Pistols were channelling the smell of cordite in the air and Malcolm capitalised on their momentum by getting them as many gigs – and in as unorthodox a way – as possible.

For the next nine months they would tour the country, recruiting the dispossessed youth of Britain along the way to form their own bands in reaction. One of Malcolm's best ideas was to turn up with the band at gigs when they weren't actually booked and just blag his way in, claiming some kind of managerial mix-up. The trick was not to let on to any of the Pistols that this was what he was up to, so that they acted naturally. I can just see him rubbing his hands and saying: "Now, where shall I get them in tonight?" Paul Cook remembers that one of these gigs was at a school in Turnham Green that his daughter Hollie would one day attend, for some sort of summer fête.

Playing at art colleges instead of pubs also helped attract an audience of like-minded people – although there might only be one person in the crowd who immediately got it. One of the gigs that Malcolm blagged was at Ravensbourne College of Art on 9 December 1975. In the audience was Simon Barker, who, having paid his 30p entrance fee, remembers being one of only about ten people in the audience. He was the only one clapping and not shouting abuse at the band.

> **SIMON BARKER:** It was just a case of right time, right place. Obviously we didn't go to see the headline act Fogg, and no one knew then of The Sex Pistols or knew they would be playing. I don't know why but, for some unknown reason, I was the only one there when they played – and, as I remember, the only one applauding. When the others arrived, I told them everything, of course, and we talked with Malcolm and the band. I can still vividly picture Malcolm standing at the back of the hall in his black-with-silver lurex-flecked fake fur coat, looking to all the world a big-time manager. Only the cigar was missing...

Simon hailed from the heart of Vivienne's Knitting Country: the Kentish suburb of Bromley, a place where, beyond the clack of the needles, the twitching of the curtains and the distant, slapping sound of rubber on flesh, rebellion was already fermenting. As a student at Bromley Technical High, Simon had made friends with Steve Bailey (later known as Steve Severin), then Billy Broad (later Billy Idol), who was a student at Ravensbourne. They went on to encounter the future Siouxsie Sioux at a Roxy Music gig. All of them shared a passion for Roxy, Bowie and Stanley Kubrick's stunning, futuristic 1971 screen adaptation of Anthony Burgess's cult novel *A Clockwork Orange*, which by then was already a banned film. Simon had already made the pilgrimage up to 430 King's Road, so we knew each other, although we wouldn't become really close friends until I moved into the St James Hotel flat.

The erstwhile Susan Janet Ballion, aka Siouxsie Sioux, was brought up in neighbouring Chislehurst, loathing her environment with a passion. Her sister was a go-go dancer and Sioux would follow her up town to dates at the Gilded Cage and the Trafalgar, a half-gay, half-straight environment where Disco Tex, Bowie, Roxy and Barry White ruled the airwaves. Like Simon, Sioux had been to SEX before she saw the band, bringing her friend, Bertie 'Berlin' Marshall, another Bromley resident with a head full of *Cabaret* and Bowie, with her on an eye-opening trip to buy fishnet stockings from the shop. Bertie's recollection, similar to Ted Polhemus's in the last

132

Play your fuzzy warbles

A Clockwork Orange was pulled from UK circulation by Stanley Kubrick himself in 1973, after a spate of 'copycat' rapes and violence reported by a hostile press. Police officers turned up at Kubrick's home and convinced him that his stylish rendering of Anthony Burgess's dystopian vision had become a template for evil. Certainly in the early 1970s there were gangs of 'Droogs' reported across the country, dressing like the film's delinquents, led by Malcolm McDowell as Alex, a bowler-hatted, false-eyelash-sporting lover of "the old ultra-violence". There were also gangs of 'Ziggy Boys' dressing like Bowie's alter ego, and the two would clash. The director aimed to put an end to this – until his death in 1999, the only way you could see the film in Britain was on a dodgy video obtained from somewhere on the Continent, or at an illicit screening. But it never lost its power. In 2010, the *Guardian* voted it the "Best Arthouse Film of All Time".

There is a King's Road connection, too: the sequence in which Alex goes into the Musik Bootick record shop and picks up Gillian (*Beat Girl*) Hills and Gaye (*Rocky Horror Show*) Brown was filmed at the Chelsea Drugstore, a purpose-built hipster hangout at 49 King's Road on the corner of Royal Avenue that opened in 1969, was namechecked by The Rolling Stones in 'You Can't Always Get What You Want' and was finally taken over in the 1980s by McDonald's. Later on in the film, Alex returns to the environs of the King's Road and is given a beating on the Chelsea Embankment by the tramps he attacks at the beginning of the film.

For an astonishingly detailed breakdown of the record shop scenes, see www.johncoulthart.com/feuilleton/2006/04/13/alex-in-the-chelsea-drug-store/

chapter, gives you an idea what a rite of passage it was to actually enter the shop.

BERTIE MARSHALL: I had gone up there before, but I didn't go in. I went all the way from Bromley to the door and, seeing that blacked-out door and the sign and the torso in the window, I just couldn't go through it. Because you couldn't see in – unlike any other shop – and you didn't know what was going to be in there. I had no idea; I was a 15-year-old boy on my own. But it was literally the next Saturday that Siouxsie said we'd go together. That's when I would have seen you for the first time, at the far end, by the jukebox. Siouxsie was quite outgoing; she was talking and I was just standing there, observing. And you didn't say anything – no "Hello" or "Can I help you?" It was great – all the expectations of a shop had been turned on their head. You couldn't see in the window; once you got in there, the person who was working there didn't engage with you on any level! I don't know if you were purposefully intimidating, but when you encounter someone who is really themselves and they're not making any adjustment, it's quite scary. That was part of your mystique and the experience of going in the shop. You didn't make any compromise. You were just totally in your look and in your thing, like Simon, Steve and Siouxsie were. It was very, very powerful.

After Simon had told his close-knit group of friends about the Pistols, they fell in love with Rotten's hate songs, and from then on bolstered the ranks of the Pistols' Praetorian Guard at every gig they could get to.

SIMON BARKER: I'd never seen a band who were that in-your-face before. And the gigs were so remote, you had to phone the shop to find out when they were playing next. We went to just about all of them: St Albans, Manchester, Paris and, of course, London.

This added to the exclusive feeling around the band; that you were part of something very special; that only the select few, bold and stylish enough to be accepted, were being let in on the act.

PAUL COOK: It was kind of secret. You knew who you would meet at gigs, there was a little gang who you knew would be there and hook up. It was very exciting. We definitely tapped into something, a feeling of unrest somewhere along the line. They were turbulent times. People were pissed off and angry and we were their focus.

While the Pistols' base was growing, Bernie Rhodes, up to then Malcolm's ally, decided he wanted a band of his own. Like the

134

good Jewish boy he was, he turned his attentions to a band calling themselves the London SS – then numbering one Mick Jones from Ladbroke Grove and Tony James from Shepherd's Bush. Two distinct factions would form: one around the Pistols nucleus on the King's Road; the other Bernie's protégés and their friend Don Letts from Ladbroke Grove.

It was as if a big portal had opened in some sort of science fiction film – and everyone that was on the edge of that portal went straight through it.

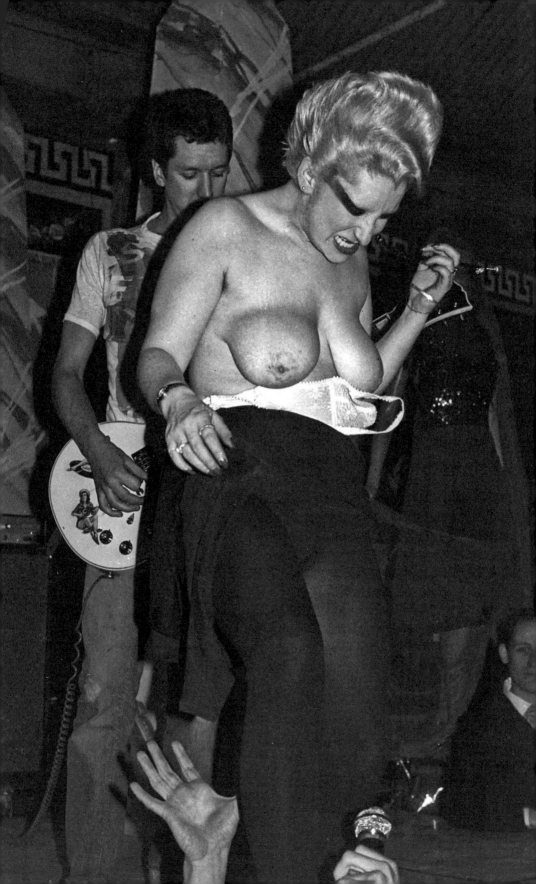

9

YOU WANNA BE ME

The horror horde take London (January–April 1976)

Don't dream it, be it

I hated *The Rocky Horror Show*. Absolutely loathed it and still do. It's another King's Road-based production that is often cited as a precursor to punk, and I suppose the parable of prim, straight-laced Brad and Janet who wander by mistake into a world of cross-dressing deviance at the Transylvanian-style castle-cum-laboratory of the crazed Doctor Frank N. Furter does have some similarities with what was going on at no. 430. But, to me, it's more like Walt Disney. The brainchild of New Zealand-born actor Richard O'Brien and Australian theatre director Jim Sharman, it debuted Upstairs at the Royal Court Theatre in Sloane Square in June 1973, starring Tim Curry as Frank-N-Furter, Patricia Quinn as Magenta the maid, O'Brien himself as butler Riff Raff and fellow Antipodean 'Little' Nell Campbell as groupie Columbia.

Not everyone agreed with my opinion: the show was a hit. Needing a bigger venue, it transferred within a month to the Chelsea Classic Cinema, where it stayed for three months until finding a semi-permanent home at the 500-seater King's Road Theatre, where it remained until 31 March 1979. It was made into the movie *The Rocky Horror Picture Show* in 1975.[1]

I did know virtually everybody who was in it. I witnessed Jim Sharman's flat – he had a waterbed, which was the thing that you had to go and see, almost with a little arrow above it. My Venezuelan friend Manuelo worked on the King's Road Theatre production and both Nell and Pat Quinn would soon be appearing alongside me in another controversial celluloid adventure, thanks to the fact that many of the original cast were also friends of Derek Jarman, Andrew Logan and Duggie Fields.

In November 1975, Derek asked me to appear in the opening scenes of *Sebastiane*, which he was shooting right at the end of his schedule. These would be the establishing shots of an orgy at the Roman Emperor Diocletian's palace – which was in fact a set inside Andrew Logan's warehouse space in Butler's Wharf. Typically ingenious with a lack of real budget, this regal pleasure dome had been constructed from items salvaged from the children's department of the now-defunct Biba superstore, to which Derek's artist friends had added a Pompeiian-style frieze and a pink marble-washed floor. While Lindsay Kemp and his troupe, all sporting gigantic papier mâché dildos, danced a priapic ballet that culminated in the mass squirting of yoghurt and wallpaper paste all over their leader, I joined the Emperor's guests lounging around on cushions and eating grapes. I played a prostitute, Mammea Morgana, and the man you can see stroking my leg is Peter Hinwood, the original Rocky Horror himself. Nell and Pat Quinn can also be glimpsed circling around the Emperor, played imperiously by the artist and theatre designer Robert Medley. Derek told me to come in my office clothes – so, unlike the rest of the cast, who are wearing togas, I'm the one wearing black rubber in ancient Rome. As far as Derek was concerned, this was

---

[1] *The Rocky Horror Picture Show* was shot at Bray Studios and on location at Oakley Court, an old country estate best known for its appearance in so many Hammer films. Richard O'Brien adapted the musical with director Jim Sharman, and starred alongside original cast members Tim Curry, Pat Quinn, Nell Campbell and Peter Hinwood, with Susan Sarandon as Janet and veteran Hammer actor Charles Gray as the Criminologist who narrates the tale. The tank used for Rocky's birth also comes from a previous Hammer production, *The Revenge of Frankenstein* (1958).

just a reflection of how much contemporary London resembled the decadence of AD 303.

DEREK JARMAN: I know it was supposed to be Rome, but Rome was supposed to be like modern London in its own way. They were all playing themselves. All the original dialogue was like modern chit-chat – "God, London was so boring, I'm glad to be back in Rome". The word 'boring' was in the original script. That was in '75. Pretty vacant, and all of that.[2]

Derek's set, and the people he assembled there, reflected the merging of social circles that went on at the ICA for the Fashion Forum talks organised by Ted Polhemus and his wife Lynn Procter, as well as the mixing up of different eras and elements of style – gay, straight and fetish cultures with vaudeville, pantomime and England's historic use of theatrical codes in clothing. Looking back on this now, Ted considers it was a pivotal moment that could only have happened in London.

TED POLHEMUS: It was about taking all these different elements and whacking them all together in a most surprising, covert and powerful way. Some anthropologists subscribe to the theory that something doesn't exist until it has a name, but what was the essence of punk and the energy of punk was there before it had a name. Punk was always a sampling and mixing, not just of different styles but different meanings and connotations. Playing with the masculine/feminine, the extra-terrestrial. The British have a long tradition of sartorial eccentricity. Every little village had its own crazy person who dressed in a strange way and the village would be accepting of that.

On 4 February 1976 Vivienne and I kept Malcolm's part of the bargain he'd made with Ted and appeared at his latest 'Fashion Forum – New Designers at the ICA', along with upcoming designers Swanky Modes and Miss Mouse.

Swanky Modes was the brainchild of Saint Martin's graduates Esme Young and Willie Walters, who opened their first shop in Camden in 1972. They were joined a year later by Royal College of Art graduate

---

[2] Derek Jarman, courtesy of Jon Savage.

Judy Dewsbury and in 1974 moved to 106 Camden Road, where they stayed for the next seventeen years. Willie now teaches at her alma mater, where she is course leader of the BA in Fashion.

Rae Spencer Cullen was the designer of Miss Mouse, who also tapped into the 1950s revival of the early 1970s. Top Shop stocked her line and, in the words of her friend Duggie Fields: "Every office girl in the country had one of her print dresses." She went over to New York in 1977, but, despite the success of her initial collection, Terminal Chic, things did not go well for her there. Duggie Fields picks up the story:

> **DUGGIE FIELDS:** She left London on a high. She was recycling period dead stock, all these 1960s men's jackets and men's underwear from the 1940s, which she'd make into women's tops and styled them so they looked just fabulous. She accessorised them with foam tits hanging from suspenders in a homage to Man Ray. She also did tops with four arms that had hands with fingernails hanging off them so you could wear whichever arm you liked. She did bras as outerwear before Gaultier or Westwood. It was a very creative collection. She came up with the concept of the Fashion Police and wrote a whole manifesto about them in 1978, way before anyone else had used that expression. One of the rules of the Fashion Police was that you had to be cruel to your wardrobe before it was cruel to you.
>
> But things went downhill in New York. She got physically ill, then she got emotionally ill and ended up homeless... I'm not sure how old she was when she died, but I think early fifties.

Though you could say the occasion at the ICA was a raging success, it didn't go exactly as Ted had intended. When we reminisced about it as we were doing the interview for this book, I let him in on a little secret he had never suspected me of before.

> **TED POLHEMUS:** When finally you and Vivienne appeared at the ICA, someone let the fire alarms off. Was it you? But how could you do that? You were in front of the audience!
>
> I heard this alarm in the distance, so technically I suppose I should have evacuated the building. But it seemed like it was far away. Then about

140

ten minutes later – and there was about 200 people there, and we were talking about rubberwear and rubber fetishism – the back door opens and these firemen come in wearing bright orange rubberwear, as if they were coming down a catwalk! You couldn't make it up. I always thought that was one of Malcolm's great Situationist art pranks…

It was John Rotten who set it off, but it was me who egged him on to do it. Though I must admit, those firemen's outfits were an added bonus I hadn't foreseen.

This is one of many examples of people thinking Malcolm masterminded a great outrage that in fact he had nothing to do with. That prank was entirely down to John and me. However, Malcolm did have plenty of his own tricks up his sleeve, and we were only just getting started at the ICA. The events of February 1976 would see the flames of outrage fanned higher and higher.

It's behind you!

On 12 February, the Pistols supported Eddie and the Hot Rods at the Marquee – a gig that demonstrated the difference between them and the headlining pub rockers right in the Wardour Street heartland of the old, sweaty, beery order. What happened that night was an extreme reaction John Rotten had to himself, as he walked off the stage into the audience. From this new vantage point he could hear himself coming through the monitors for the first time and the way he sounded came as such a shock to him that he sent everything flying – chairs, people, and even, like a mad ballet we were choreographing on the spot, hurling me across the floor. Climbing back on the stage, he finished the set by smashing up the monitors. And all because he didn't like the sound of his own voice – an opinion that would soon be shared by many others.

Up until then, Eddie and the Hot Rods had been written about in the press as if they were the future of rock'n'roll. Though not for this Marquee audience member:

MARCO PIRRONI: Those people weren't special. They were just ordinary people doing OK stuff. There was a difference between them and us, the

141

people who had grown up with Bowie and Roxy. We have to do something special, we can't just knock out anything. You want to change something; do something that people hadn't done before.

Neil Spencer of the *NME* thought he was seeing something a bit above the average, too. He interviewed the band before they played and published his subsequent review under the headline 'Don't look over your shoulder but the Sex Pistols are coming', in which he astutely compared the band to The Stooges. The most brilliant line in it came from Steve: "Actually, we're not into music. We're into chaos."

Spencer's review didn't mention Eddie and the Hot Rods.

My Bloody Valentine

On 14 February, we were all invited to Andrew Logan's Valentine's Ball, which was taking place at Butler's Wharf on the set where Derek had shot the *Sebastiane* Roman orgy. Logan's parties brought together an artistic, bohemian community that were as concerned with style outrage as Vivienne and Malcolm were. A lot of them were SEX customers. Writing in *Harpers & Queen* in October 1976, Peter York would define the sort of people who had gathered for the Ball as 'Them', a tongue-in-cheek reference to the 1954 science fiction monster movie: "A mysterious aesthetic conspiracy, a new breed, the creators of the dominant high-style aesthetic of the seventies." That night, he was to witness 'Us' – the fruition of Malcolm's aesthetic movement for the first time – and it would be more horror show than any of 'Them' could have imagined. Peter recalls the atmosphere:

PETER YORK: The thing was, they were people who had known each other for quite a long time already. Duggie Fields and Andrew Logan had known each other about ten years by then, and they were about ten years older than the punks. So it was a funny tension. The punks quite liked the attention of these smart, sort of wacky older people, but at the same time didn't want to be too much associated with them because it all looked rather bourgeois.

My dad the Commando and my mum the beauty, with their little son, Michael,
who sadly died of scarlet fever, 1943.

Spot the gonk.

Unrepentant hairstyle.   **Things are stirring.**

He nearly kicked the bucket. [Sheila Rock]

"Get those trousers off, Jords, someone wants to by 'em." [Mirrorpix]

The world is smooth and shiny. [Jane England]

Candid camera. [Harri Peccinotti]

Send a letter to Jordan.

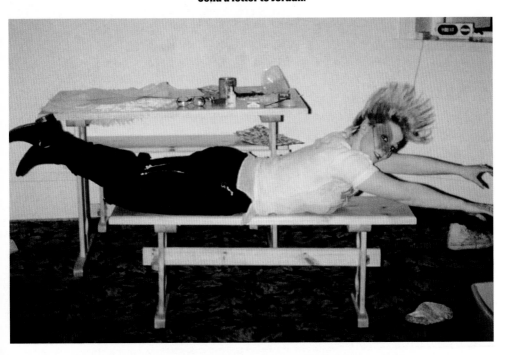

Jubilee tutu adaptations turn into 2 a.m. Aqua Marina impersonations,
egged on by **Simon Barker.** [Simon Barker]

The world looks clear to me. [Harri Peccinotti]

I've still got my mink earrings. [Chris Moorhouse/Stringer/Getty]

We still didn't wanna do it, Simon! [Mirrorpix]

Ooh, matron! With David Bowie at the Cannes Film Festival, 1978. [Kypros/Getty]

I wanted to defy gravity. A still from *Jubilee*. [TCD/Prod.DB/Alamy]

In fact, the events of the evening would fracture friendships as the generations split along the lines foreseen in the 'You're gonna wake up…' T-shirt. For a start, when he agreed to the Pistols appearing, Andrew Logan didn't realise how many people Malcolm would actually invite; most of them were pissed and had no regard for Logan's sculptures that were all housed inside the building. So, for a long time, a crowd that included John Rotten was shut outside the converted warehouse. Then, by the time Vivienne finally persuaded the men on the door to let him in, all the drink had gone. John's reaction to that news was a bit extreme, too – he gave Vivienne a black eye.

DUGGIE FIELDS: Malcolm seemed to have invited half of London and Andrew wasn't prepared for that at all; it was supposed to be a much smaller, private party. I don't think he'd seen The Sex Pistols at this point and didn't know what he was getting involved with.

Malcolm, on the other hand, was really excited because Nick Kent was in attendance. He rushed up to me, saying: "The *NME* are here! Do something, Jords! Take your clothes off, girl!"

I responded in the negative but he was not to be overruled.

"Go on!" he urged. "We haven't got much time!"

I said to Malcolm that I would not do it unless John took control of the situation; otherwise it would just reduce it to me being like a stripper. I wanted to push John into acting what he was singing in words, to be forceful within himself and for me to rebuke him, so a scene was set out where he had to react, to push himself and do something with his hands to somebody else onstage. I would have walked off if he hadn't played his part in this or understood what I meant: I wanted him to react. And he got me pinned to the floor with my arm right behind my back; he actually pushed me over. To this day, people don't know which way that photo's supposed to be, because you can turn it through ninety degrees and it looks like I'm standing up. But I'm actually on the floor, squashed on the floor with my bosoms out and he's got my arm twisted right behind my back but I'm not showing any expression. I'm not reacting. Which is my sort of feminism. Do your worst but do something; don't just stand

143

there and pose. What I'm trying to get at is that the woman can come out on top in that situation.

They are quite disturbing photos in a way, I think. But they were used everywhere.

The warehouse had a metal roof like an aircraft hangar, so the sound coming off the stage was intense. That, coupled with the cold, meant that Logan and his friends took refuge in the Gold Room, a greenhouse covered in foil, in the centre of the space. Derek, on the other hand, filmed everything. The first live footage of the Pistols that he shot that night would later find its way, via a tortuously convoluted route, into *The Great Rock 'n' Roll Swindle*. He later recorded the events of the evening in his diary: "Sex Pistols were playing on Andrew's stage for a slightly bemused audience of glitterati while Jordan and [Vivienne] threw themselves around with bacchic abandon, hurling insults at the

band and the audience. John Rotten turned his back on us and sang to the Roman frescoes, while the drummer, Paul, picked his nose. Christopher [Hobbs], who guarded me and the camera from all the pushing and shoving, said when it was all over – 'Thank God that's finished and we'll never hear of them again.'"[3]

For Derek, this was a turning point. 'Them' had been usurped, the rug pulled out from under them by "a gang of King's Road fashion anarchists". For someone who had felt like an outsider all his life, Derek's sympathies lay with the confrontational punks rather than his older friends, and especially with me. I think what he saw in me was someone who had defied all the old gender stereotypes and made my own transformation into the person I wanted to be. Which is why, not long afterwards, he asked me to begin collaborating with him on what was to become the film *Jubilee*.

DEREK JARMAN: Obviously there has been some sort of protest running through my whole life, against my bourgeois background, against the way homosexuals are treated, and so forth, and seeing people protesting about these things, one felt... kinship.[4]

I personally didn't see that there should be any barriers between what was happening at the shop and what Derek, Andrew and Duggie were doing, and I never treated anyone differently, I got on with all of them. But there are others who were there at the time who think Malcolm's calculating treatment of his former friends at this party was exploitative.

SIMON BARKER: All that crowd loved Vivienne and Malcolm for what they were doing, and Malcolm used that, got them to play at Andrew Logan's party and then invited everyone. I don't think Andrew Logan did any more parties after that because he got scared.

JON SAVAGE: I thought Malcolm was very cruel to Andrew and Duggie, who were fantastic people. And it stuck to them, because in many

---

[3] From Derek Jarman's papers, published in *Derek Jarman* by Tony Peake (Little, Brown, 1999).
[4] Derek Jarman, courtesy of Jon Savage.

ways, they haven't been taken seriously ever since.[5] I can understand
why Malcolm and Vivienne did it, because it was a mixture of their
personalities – Malcolm had the Aquarian detachment and cruelty, and
without cruelty, there is no feast. That's the side of it I don't like, because
it imprinted itself on the whole period. They were very successful in doing
that. There was a lot of cruelty in punk.

Night of the vampire

It certainly wouldn't be the last time there'd be a blow-up between
'Them' and 'Us', and the next incident would be caused directly by
Jubilee when Derek incurred the not inconsiderable wrath of Vivienne. In
the meantime, Peter York coined another new term for how he saw us:
"The people who run the Sex clothing store at the World's End represent
an extreme ideological wing of the Peculiars," he wrote in *Harpers &
Queen*. "The Sex shop people, untypically, have political views, of a kind
which they describe as anarchistic… Their associated pop group the
Sex Pistols are alleged to cause trouble wherever they go."

After Neil Spencer's review of the Marquee gig, the music press –
notably Jonh Ingham of *Sounds* and Caroline Coon of *Melody Maker*
– started taking note.

JONH INGHAM: It was that last line of the *NME* review: "We're not into
music, we're into chaos." I'd been trying to find something new for at
least a year – it was so dull out there. I had no idea what something new
was, but I was out every night seeing lots of new bands. And the name
alone – The Sex Pistols. That was the best name I'd ever heard or seen, it
looked so bizarre, it just crashed through everything. But I couldn't ring
up Neil Spencer and say: "How do I get hold of the band?" We all felt we
were in competition, so you couldn't. So I hadn't a clue how to find them
and I was kind of poking around and then Malcolm called the office and

---

[5] Actually, at the time of writing, Duggie Fields (b. 1945) is having a renaissance. The Glasgow
International 2018 staged a recreation of the artist's Earl's Court flat, where he has lived for the past fifty
years. The show featured Field's post-Pop, maximalist work collaged with earlier paintings, video and
sound pieces, all hung around his leopard prints, cushions, mannequins and mirrors. For more on what
Duggie is doing now, please go to duggiefields.com

146

Vivien Goldman answered the phone and I heard her say: "The band's called what?" And I just took the phone off her: "You won't like them."

The same *NME* review sent two lads from the Bolton Institute of Technology down to London in search of the Pistols – Howard Trafford (soon to become Devoto) and Peter McNeish (Shelley). Howard's former schoolfriend Richard Boon, who had settled by then in London, led them to SEX to get details of their next gigs at High Wycombe and Welwyn Garden City on 20 and 21 February.

At High Wycombe, the band supported Screaming Lord Sutch and the Savages, who, sixteen years before them, had been making audiences scream with their mix of horror vaudeville visuals and trashy rockabilly sounds.[6] Now it was the turn of their fans to take umbrage at John, who, in a manner not dissimilar to the 1960s incarnation of the Screaming Lord, crept along the front of the stage, reaching out to tousle people's hair, and then smashed his microphone to bits when it stopped working – provocations enough to start a fight between the rival factions in the audience.

Howard, Pete and Richard were inspired, and Howard invited the band to play at their Bolton college, a gig he promised to organise for them and an important opportunity to reach like minds beyond the capital. Someone else who had been standing alongside his old friend Lord Sutch and watching John's antics with amusement was 100 Club manager Ron Watts. He also stepped forward to offer them a gig.

Soho confidential

The 100 Club was – and, against all odds, still is – a basement club tucked beneath the Tottenham Court Road end of Oxford Street, with a strange arrangement of pillars that obscure the view of the

---

[6] Screaming Lord Sutch (1940–99) used to stare down from the walls of Let It Rock with his trademark madcap grin, and in many ways can be seen as one of the Godfathers of Punk. He was known for leaping out of coffins and driving round the East End in a hearse chauffeured by his producer, Joe Meek. Sutch first stood for Parliament in 1963, representing the Teenage Party. But it was the coming of Margaret Thatcher that inspired him to rebrand his political pranksterism The Monster Raving Loony Party and he became a regular thorn in the establishment's side at elections until his suicide in 1999. Many of the demands he stood for in 1963, including a lowering of the voting age to 18, have since come into law.

stage from almost every angle. Nonetheless, it had a pedigree for encouraging new talent that stretched back to the early 1960s, when the skiffle, trad and Beat boom spawned the likes of Lord Sutch in the first place, an era with many parallels to punk. Despite this link though, it didn't seem like an illustrious beginning when the Pistols first arrived there on 30 March 1976. For a start, there was a funny smell…

PAUL COOK: It stunk of horrible Chinese food, 'cos they had a restaurant in there, plus a bit of bleach slung in, that horrible thing of trying to cover it up.

Then the gig was a fiasco – John had an argument with Glen about the order that his words were supposed to be coming in and stormed off-stage in the middle of a song. He made it as far as the bus stop outside before Malcolm ordered him back onstage again. The band only narrowly managed to avoid splitting up and got through the rest of their set. You have to remember, they were rehearsing more or less on the spot. So what you were seeing was them trying things out. It was from the heart, that was what that anger was all about. It was not rehearsed. It's very hard to do that over and over again.

MARCO PIRRONI: They just walked on, and before they'd even played I just knew. The first thing I heard was the guitar riff from 'Did You No Wrong' and I thought: Yeah, this is brilliant. I could have walked out and gone home then and they would have been my favourite band. Because that attitude had never existed before, Rotten's attitude.

BERTIE MARSHALL: The gig itself was like a mess, it just seemed to fall apart. There was that rage, it's above anger, it's screaming rage… That's not what you expect when you go to see David Bowie. There was an idea of a show and the Pistols wasn't about that at all. It was like an anti-show, basically. It all fell apart around you. You see someone on a stage who's screaming and spitting and walking off, and just the sound of noise – I wouldn't call them songs at that stage at all.

My memory is of Siouxsie standing behind me and shaking me and then she used my shoulders to push down and jump up, and then when she came up again she took me again. So we did this thing of just moving around shaking each other. Jumping up and down. Supposedly that was the pogo – but who knows and who cares?

You were with Paul Getty III, because I remember looking round thinking: Who's the hippy? He was quite nice-looking. I was trying to see the ear. Or the lack of it.

So, as well as being the birthplace of the pogo, the 100 Club would stay true to its history and play an important part in the story of punk. As did another, very different venue, which also had long roots in Soho and catered for a crowd that didn't want to go with the flow.

Every little breeze seems to whisper Louise...

Louise's was a lesbian club situated at 61 Poland Street – the same address where once my grandad had worked as a leather gilder. In true Soho style, the red-painted door had a brass nameplate and a small spyhole where guests were scrutinised before being admitted. Madame Louise herself ran the door: a very chic, older French woman in a black dress and jewellery with Marcel-waved grey hair and heavy eyeliner, who often wore a grey fur coat to protect her from the cold wind whistling under the ill-fitting portal. You entered her domain through a small foyer, where Madame Louise sat at a low desk, protected by Michael, the American doorman. Bertie Marshall can remember exactly how the place looked the first time he went down there, as clearly as Alice falling down a rabbit hole:

BERTIE MARSHALL: That first time we went down there, Siouxsie talked us in. We had to join as members, which was a huge amount of money. I think it was £3, which was a lot in 1976. They had to do it by law, and that's why all the drinks were served with food. In Louise's, it was literally a basket with a yucky bit of spam flung in there and a Ritz cracker. I don't think they went as far as a salad.

The foyer led to the dimly lit bar, decorated in black and red with long mirrors, a long black leatherette banquette, black chairs, red carpet and small drinks tables with red tablecloths. The bartender's name was Tony and the head waiter was 'Ballerina John', also known

149

as Seamus, an Irish queen. A spiral staircase led to the basement, a small dancefloor surrounded by low tables. DJ Caroline, with cropped, dyed hair, drainpipes and heels, played Motown and soul, Roxy, Supremes, and a lot of old 1930s Dietrich, 1950s Doris Day and 'Love Hangover' by Diana Ross.

BERTIE MARSHALL: We got downstairs and it was very, very tiny. It was painted black and red, black and red side tables all around us, mirrors on all the walls and a staircase that was metal, so that you could see people's feet coming down. That was when I realised that the older man, with his glamorous 1940s bird, slightly Rita Hayworth with a cocktail dress on, wasn't a man… One was very defined butch and the other was very defined femme. So they looked like a straight couple, that was what they were doing. It wasn't two butch dykes, it was that kind of contrast. We were like foreigners there, really.

The customers were mainly middle-aged, middle-class lesbians, playing roles in men's suits or as gangster's molls. One regular was Butch Joe, a black woman with a shaved head and no front teeth, who wore a beige Burton's suit and used to say, while speeding the night away: "Strap a dick to me, dear!" and "I want my tits cut off."

Not everyone there who saw the sexually ambiguous, androgynous collection of Bromley punks, whose number that night also included Simon Barker and Steve Severin, liked them at first sight. But one very important person did.

As if by magic, Linda Ashby appeared.

BERTIE MARSHALL: She said: "I've been looking at you lot and you look great; let me buy you a drink." She was quite famous in that club and on that scene. So she became the bridge between ourselves and Louise's.

SIMON BARKER: We were quite naive, being from Bromley. I couldn't believe there were all these tennis players from Wimbledon dancing together; I had no idea that so many women tennis players were lesbians. It was so weird. When you're from the suburbs, you're green, really. You think you're causing ripples with people from Bromley, but then you come up to London and there's Billie Jean King dancing with Margaret Court…

150

This charming man

Nils Stevenson (1953–2002) was introduced to Malcolm by Alan Jones. Brought up in Dalston, he was a Barnet Art School drop out who had ended up working for Richard Buckle, ballet critic at the *Observer*. It was Nils who introduced Malcolm and Vivienne to the Andrew Logan set and, once Malcolm had got the Pistols together, it wasn't long before he invited Nils to be part of the band's infrastructure.

Nils brought in his older brother Ray, a veteran photographer who had cut his teeth on Glam superstars Bowie and Bolan, to take the first pictures of the band. Because money was so tight for all of them, he also moved in with Steve Jones to the flat above the rehearsal studios in Denmark Street. I'll leave it to you to imagine what these two Casanovas got up to in there – and on a diet of stolen baked beans and all. After the hard graft of driving the Pistols round the north in a Transit van for their first tour, Nils got fed up with Malcolm's tight-fisted ways and defected to tour-managing The Heartbreakers, then became the first manager of Siouxsie and the Banshees. He was fast and effective in getting them a deal and worked with the band until 1982, when heroin took over everything. He would later say that Steve Jones saved his life by dragging him to Narcotics Anonymous. In 2002, Nils produced the book *Vacant: A Diary of the Punk Years* (Thames & Hudson) with Ray. His death from a heart attack on 20 September 2002 came as a total shock. He was only 49.

Billy Chainsaw worked for Nils running the Banshees' fan club from 1979 onwards, later becoming PA to the band. He offered the following memories of his friend: "On 1 September 1979 I quit my shiftwork job at the Bakelite factory, left my parents' home in Birmingham and moved into a squat in north London. That same month, after a record store signing of their just released album *Join Hands* in Aberdeen, Banshees guitarist John McKay and drummer Kenny Morris walked out of the band, to be temporarily replaced by support band The Cure's Robert Smith on guitar and Lol Tolhurst on drums. I was called into the office for an audience with Nils, who said, 'So we won't be needing a fan club now.' Thinking on my feet, I answered, 'Unless that's the end of The Banshees, they'll still need a fan club, won't they?' Nils simply smiled and said, 'I guess you're right.' No questions asked, no more mention of the matter, I was in for the long run – a full sixteen years of it. The incident proved to me that

> if Nils saw potential in people he was always prepared to give them a shot… Long after he'd stopped working with The Banshees, I ran into Nils at the private view/launch of Dennis Morris' *Destroy* book of Sex Pistols photos. We spent a lot of time catching up and when I told him that I'd moved on from The Banshees and was working for the King of Soho, Paul Raymond, on a couple of his top shelf titles he laughed, congratulated me with a huge hug, and said: 'I taught you well.'"

Louise's was a godsend. It was one of the very, very few places that I used to want to stay longer. When they used to play 'Every Little Breeze Seems to Whisper Louise' at the end of the night I would think: Oh no! Come on! Another hour! Because it was so good there; it was a great, great mixture of people.

The club would soon become the centre of our social life and, not long after that first meeting, Simon Barker moved into Linda's flat in Buckingham Gate, in April 1976.

That was the same month that the first Ramones album was released on the Sire label, the band signed by its influential founder Seymour Stein. This was a watershed moment for the bunch of misfit pretend brothers from Queens, New York – and, in comparison, the Pistols still had nothing. It was time to up the ante. Newly promoted to tour manager, Alan Jones's friend Nils Stevenson and his photographer brother Ray, assigned to capture the band's image on film, set out with Malcolm to scour Soho for a venue in which to host a Sex Pistols happening that would really get the record companies going.

What they found was as close to heaven as Soho is ever going to get…

BOTH ENDS BURNING

Louise's and Sombrero's were two of the most important nightclubs in the punk story, but there were many others we frequented that have earned their place in history. Here are some notable quotes from those that frequented those illicit dark spaces between the bright lights from where it all began…

The Masquerade, Earls Court Road

This club was situated in the basement of a launderette in the 1970s gay ghetto.

ALAN JONES: The Masquerade was drag-queenie, everyone was dressed up there to the nines. You couldn't walk through the place without smelling Habit Rouge, which was the big perfume at the time.

MICHAEL COLLINS: Bowie and Bryan Ferry used to go to Masquerade, that's why we used to go there. It was more a sort of male escort club; you got a lot of wealthy men going there. That's where they used to put poppers in the air system so everyone was on a permanent high. It was mirrored, with a really small dancefloor. People used to go there to see if you could pick up someone with money and then go to Sombrero's to spend it all. In those days, there was no real places in the whole of the UK where drag queens went. So they came to London. There was certain areas, like Earl's Court, Philbeach Gardens and that Wimpy bar there, that were just full of Scottish drag queens.

I got barred from that Wimpy bar – for throwing a chair through the window.

The Catacombs, Finborough Road, Earl's Court

Scenes of epic debauchery are recalled at Derek Jarman's favourite nightspot.

DEREK DUNBAR: Down the Catacombs club there'd be priests dancing with young rent boys. I went down there with Derek Jarman

– I think he used the place in *Jubilee*. Priests in frocks dancing with rent boys! And I'd just come from my grandmother's!

SIMON BARKER: It doesn't really exist now and everything's very segregated – for fat boys, for hairy boys...

DEREK DUNBAR: Where have all those rent boys gone?

SIMON BARKER: They're all on Grindr. The other thing was, when I came up to London and met all these queens and they were all loving Sioux, they would introduce themselves as: "Hi, I'm Gerry Paris." And I'd think: God! Why do I have such a boring name? I actually believed that was his real name! That's how naive I was.

Maunkbury's, Jermyn Street, W1

One of the most exclusive nightspots of the early 1970s, this tiny basement club is one where you really had to look right to get through the door.

MICHAEL COLLINS: Maunkbury's, Saturday nights. Trevor Shakes was DJ. It was a posh club that we took over, just next to Tramp. On Saturday it was full-on – we'd go there about one o'clock in the morning.

PETER YORK: I can remember being in Maunkbury's and in came David Bowie and Marc Bolan, not very long before the latter stopped being alive. They were obviously very old mates and I was excited beyond measure that these two very important cultural people were there, just like ordinary people.

The Regency Club, Great Newport Street, W1

The Regency Club in the West End, up the stairs through a little doorway, was somewhere where Danny La Rue might go. It looked like it was still the 1950s, with the tiny lamps on the walls that were completely original, not put there to be ironic or anything.

SIMON BARKER: The Regency Club was all drag and rent boys and gangsters and there was a guy with a tattoo on his head and somebody nudged me and said: "You know who that is? That's Kendo Nagasaki." At that time, his mask hadn't been revealed. I don't actually know if it was him or not, but it was such an obscure thing to say, I believed it. And that doesn't happen now. Also, they didn't care about age things in those days. You'd see some little camp queen about 14 or 15 and then you'd see some gangster muscle man.

The Gateways, Bramerton Street, Chelsea

This is the infamous lesbian club with the green door, captured forever in *The Killing of Sister George* (Robert Aldrich, 1968), although it was actually a mixed club until 1967, when Gina Cerrato, whose husband Ted had won the club in a poker game in 1943, took over the running of the place with her American lover, Smithy. I went to the Gateways with Linda and I was wearing a chiffon, polka-dot 1950s sticky-out dress with petticoats underneath, low cut, with a little chiffon bolero that went with it and my hair all up, my blonde beehive. And I absolutely got smacked to pieces. People were bumping into me deliberately, treading on my feet. I got such a bloody going-over. And it was packed, 'cos it was just a box with a bar at the end. They just did it through body language, nudging you, knocking you. And in the end, I said: "What the fuck do you think you're doing?" And they just looked at me. I suppose they thought I was just there as a voyeur. Which I wasn't. I had high heels on as well. But that was the one place in the whole world that I've ever been where I stuck out more than anyone else. It just tells you what everyone else was like.

BERTIE MARSHALL: Linda took me there. It was a Sunday lunchtime and Linda used to go to the stables in Hyde Park and ride a horse across the park. She came back and wanted to go to Gateways. Gateways' policy was very strict: no men whatsoever. But she had the Devil in her and said: "I'm going to take you to Gateways." She told me to go and put my make-up on and keep my mouth shut. I had black tights and these black leatherette lace-up knee boots and a black V-neck cashmere and a white shirt, black tie. And she said:

"You mustn't talk, because if they hear your voice... I'll introduce you as my bird and you keep dumb." It was Sunday lunchtime and it was packed to the rafters with those cross-dressing dykes. They were more like 1950s rocker types, that sort of look. And Linda was very well known on that scene, very popular. So everyone kept coming up to talk to her and she would introduce me as her bird and say I was too shy to speak. It was so dangerous of her to do that because if she'd have got found out... Who knows? They were really tough. They would have beaten her up at the very least. And she would have been persona non grata on that dyke scene forever...

The Rollerdisco, Dunstable

There used to be a coach trip from the Fulham Road down to the Rollerdisco in Dunstable every Tuesday night. I'd go with Michael Collins, Mark Tarbard and a whole gang of others – even including the Pistols.

MICHAEL COLLINS: You couldn't skate very well, I think you had the ability to be pushed and stay upright for a little while. But there was one time, you'd gone down a whole flight of stairs without actually touching any of them, like Yoda in *Star Wars*. You managed to get all the way, straight onto the rollerskating floor and you skimmed across that like rocks on water, except you was on your arse, right across the floor.

But I didn't spill any drink, though. I had a tray of drinks; it cost me a lot of money. There was a little turn just at the end of the stairs and I was looking at

156

the glasses, which is why I slipped. It was a big round. And afterwards I was left with a bruise on my arse that Michael said looked like a map of the world!

The Embassy Club, Old Bond Street, W1

At the same time as Studio 54 in New York, this tiny West End club attracted the same calibre of celebrity, from European royals to transsexual vamps. On Sunday night it was £7 to get in, which was a lot in those days, but you then got free drink all night. We went there about half past seven and just drank solidly. Once Michael Collins and I came off the coach from the Rollerdisco and went down the Embassy Club and Michael had kept on his roller boots. I let go of his arm and he shot past me straight into the Embassy and just knocked the whole dancefloor over like skittles. Everyone went.

MICHAEL COLLINS: I would go down on my own sometimes to meet loads of people and I would order a tray of drinks for about twenty people and then I would secrete them around the club like squirrels store nuts. Behind pot plants – checking that someone hadn't been sick in them first. But give me another hour...

I remember Donna Summer's 'MacArthur Park' – you had a certain shimmy to that, you couldn't stop once you'd started. You were a goner. They had these really shit-kicking girl dancers there too, but you out danced all of them. In your pixie boots. Remember that dance when you used to leap up in the air, shaking and gyrating at the same time? And land on your heels. It was quite a look.

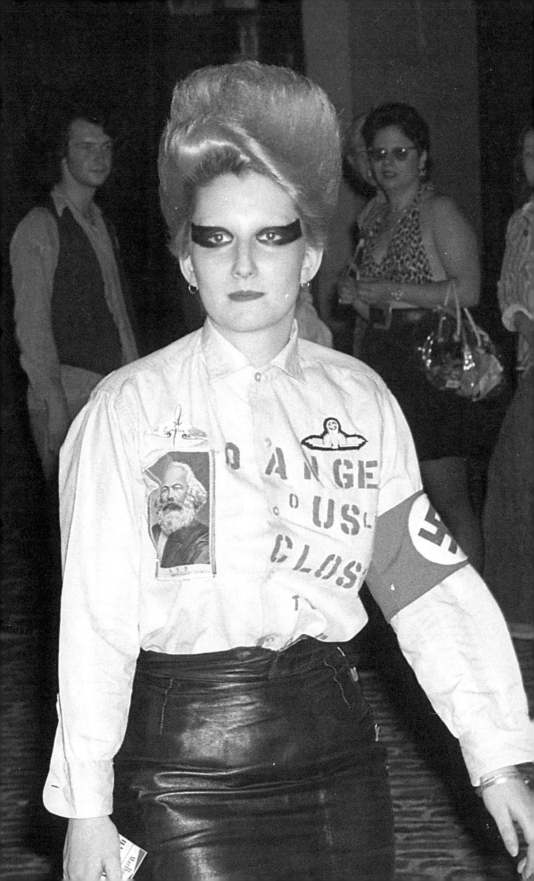

10

HOT UNDER THE COLLAR

Summer of anarchy (April–July 1976)

Halfway to Paradise

The venue that Nils Stevenson found in Brewer Street was a strip club called El Paradiso. It was another portal back to the post-war Soho that Malcolm so fetishised, as it was run by authentic Maltese gangsters and was the sort of strip club where girls just walked out and took their tops off and then couldn't move, couldn't do anything – that was the law in those days. I can clearly remember seeing the signs backstage giving instructions to the strippers: 'Don't move, hands to your sides'. And you had to keep certain garments on; you weren't allowed to strip totally.

This club only had a licence to serve 2 per cent alcohol. It smelled horrible and the stage was only just big enough to fit the band and all their equipment, with a ceiling low enough to seriously crack your head.

For Malcolm, it was the Promised Land. He had Nils track down the owners and hired the venue for the Pistols to play on 4 April 1976. He printed up a load of leaflets promoting it, and some further dates he'd managed to book at the Nashville, a pub that looked out onto the start of the M4 motorway in West Kensington, which sought to unite the capital's youth with the words 'Teenagers from London's Shepherd's Bush and Finsbury Park: "We hate everything".'

As usual, he managed to rope us all into his plans, persuading Alan Jones to DJ and Michael Collins and me to run the bar, ordering us to be really discreet because of the liquor licence. We filled a big dustbin up with one of Michael's trademark punches, which he christened 'fruit cup'. It was so potent that by the end of the night people didn't even know their own names. Including us! As well as doshing this out to all and sundry, we were also supposed to be selling T-shirts – the first ever pop-up shop, you might say. Ted Polhemus remembers me giving him one of the 'Little Boy Smoking' T-shirts for his wife Lynn. Michael remembers throwing all of his in the bin. There was so much spillage from our punchbowl, we were sloshing around in liquor.

El Paradiso was one of the best nights ever.

ALAN JONES: That's burnished on my memory because I had to do so many things – I was the DJ; we had to clean up the floor afterwards; then I took the money on the door; and then Malcolm came over, got it all from us, fucked off and there was no money to pay the Mafia!

SIMON BARKER: It was so glamorous. It wasn't called El Strip or anything seedy, it was called El Paradiso. It wasn't a rough, sawdust shithole, it was faded glamour, which is always the best kind. And of course, being in there, we felt glamorous, the whole thing was glamorous. There was you behind the bar with Michael, this good-looking guy with cropped blond hair and capped T-shirt and tight jeans on, which people didn't wear then. The two of you together looked so good. I was so excited; I was at the bar waiting to get a drink and John Paul Getty III was there on one side of me – he was really quite handsome and he had these blond curls and I was trying to see his ear, and thinking: How did he get here? He'd only just been released by his kidnappers.

Then the other side was these three guys from America, really awful guys in leather jackets and jeans. They were the group The Arrows. No one can remember The Arrows, they were awful, but they wrote 'I Love Rock'n'Roll'.

ALAN JONES: John Paul Getty III was there, because I asked him to come. He was one of the guests at the Portobello Hotel and he came to the shop, too. He came to the Hotel just after the whole kidnap thing, that's how I met him. There were also people there who thought they were going to see a strip show. And Malcolm wouldn't let them get their money back. It was 50p to get in.

SIMON BARKER: I can remember the strippers turning up, and it was the time when you weren't allowed to move, so they would stand there and pose, and then the curtains would close. Then about thirty seconds later they would open again and something would be missing. A glove, it always started with a glove. It was fantastic. Can you imagine, this keeps on happening until the strippers are down to their undies and then the curtain closes again. And next time it opens, The Sex Pistols are standing there. And it's not professional rock lighting, the shadows are all along the walls and John Rotten is just looming out at you – standing there all hunched with funny lighting on him. It was unbelievable.

BERTIE MARSHALL: It was a bit like a David Lynch moment. Then Steve Jones rammed his guitar at somebody and was threatening someone. Then somebody had a knife out. It was all "Ooooooooohhhhh! Time to go!" I probably went to Louise's afterwards. I mean, it was a mess, but it was fabulous. That threat of violence was always around. That rage coming from the stage amphetamine-fuelled rage.

Following his phone call from Malcolm, this was the first time Jonh Ingham had seen the band, and he was joined by his friend Caroline Coon, who was writing a piece on The Arrows for rival music paper *Melody Maker*. The band he was pinning his hopes on more than lived up to his expectations.

JONH INGHAM: John just didn't look like anything you had ever seen. He had this tiny kid's sweater on that must have been two or three sizes too small for him, it was all ripped up the side so he could get it on and it's got holes in it and he can't sing or anything, but he's absolutely compelling. People say they couldn't play but that's bollocks; right from the very beginning it was obvious they had a great rhythm section, you

161

knew that was good. You could tell Steve was learning to play because he didn't do solos; he got to the middle eight and then he did something else. But you could see it was a good idea. John's going, "You better clap or I'm wasting my time," and there was like one person clapping. It was really funny. But the thing that struck me was that he didn't want to be liked. And everyone wants to be liked who gets up on-stage, they're all in it for the glory, and he was actively pushing it away, which fascinated me and I did think: I've found the future.

Any violence projecting from onstage was nothing compared to what could have come our way if the Maltesers had found out about the punch we were serving. And they nearly did. There was a knock at the door and Malcolm lifted up the shutters on this big, heavy metal sliding door – and you could just see these pairs of shoes, highly shined pairs of hand-tooled brogues – and they said something to him through the crack of the door.

He said: "Yeah, everything's fine." And he was absolutely bricking it, everyone was bricking it, because if they'd asked to come in and check out what was going on in there, everyone would have been in the shit. But they were just talking through this gap at the bottom of the door. "No, everything's fine! Won't be long, be out soon!"

Then Malcolm eased the door down, in a natural manner, concerned that they might twig, and he came over to us and said: "I think we'd better wrap this up." So Michael and I shouted out: "Drink all the evidence!" And everybody just downed what we had left. It was sloshing around at the back of that bar area; it was like being in some sort of bilge pump. I don't know how Malcolm didn't get his legs broken – or worse.

SIMON BARKER: He was quite mouthy then. He used to say things and then just disappear. He instigated these situations, I mean, anyone else wouldn't have dealt with the Maltese Mafia.

MICHAEL COLLINS: And when we left, we saw that very eccentric man who was always in the West End, whirling around with his umbrella. The Twirling Man, I used to call him, he used to twirl around in circles all around the West End. I thought it was a good omen.

162

Later that month, the band played two nights at the Nashville on 23 and 29 April. The first of those dates was supporting The 101ers, Joe Strummer's band of pub rock squatters. Like Adam Ant at the first Pistols gig at Saint Martin's, Joe realised he was witnessing the future the moment the Pistols started playing, too.

PAUL COOK: See, we didn't know we was having this effect on people. Bit like Joe Strummer and The 101ers. We supported him one day and he left The 101ers the next day. Obviously we wanted to shake things up and do something different, but we really didn't realise how much we was going to do.

After that, Joe started hanging out at the 100 Club, where he met Bernie Rhodes, who suggested that he should give him a call. Jonh Ingham and Caroline Coon were both in attendance. Jonh arranged to interview the band straight after El Paradiso.

JONH INGHAM: That was a Sunday, and I went into *Sounds* and my editor, Alan Lewis, asked: "How was it?" And I told him, and he kept getting this weird look on his face, and after a while he said: "I want you to do a story on them." And I said: "No, no, it's much too early for that." And he said: "Go and interview them. You've been talking about them for fifteen minutes."

Malcolm said: "Meet me at Denmark Street at 12.30." So I showed up dead on time and he said: "Where were you? You're late. The band all got really bored, they left." Then he set a new time to meet, seven o'clock in Denmark Street. So I came half an hour early and they were all standing there. And Malcolm said: "You're late again!" And I said: "Fuck off Malcolm!" and they all laughed. We all went down to the Cambridge Arms and they were really nice guys, somewhat naive, it seemed, just spouting Malcolm's manifesto at me and Steve was sitting next to me saying: "We don't take drugs." And I thought: Yeah, let's see how long that lasts. The first part of the interview was with Steve, Paul and Glen, and they were talking about John and the audition in front of the jukebox, and somewhere around that point John walked in with two women. They sat down about ten feet away and they were just talking away, he was ignoring us, looking kind of bored by the whole thing. Meanwhile, the others were still talking about him in the third person while he was in front of us, which I thought was really odd. I still wasn't really sure what to make of him. So I said: "John,

163

they've been telling me about who you are, what do you think?" And John just went wham into: "I hate this, I hate that." It was like a machine gun going off, it was really fast. And this would have been his first interview so he'd have no idea of how to work the press. And he was doing that laser glare and he really meant it, it wasn't put on, that was the other thing. I could sense Malcolm over to one side, staring at me, and the other guys staring at me, seeing what I was going to do. Then he stopped and I just burst out laughing. 'Cos it was funny. On top of all the intimidation, it was funny. I was sold; it was just too good.

Alan Jones remembers bringing Caroline Coon to the first Nashville gig.

ALAN JONES: I was still sleeping with girls then and Caroline Coon was one of the last ones. She embarrassed me that night. I'll never forget it. She turned up and she had a tie and she'd put safety pins all down it. And I said: "You can take that off, for a start." You know. "I'm not walking in with you like that." It was really embarrassing. And that's when she started writing about it. So I played my own part in the history there. 'Cos if I hadn't, she wouldn't have written about it and it wouldn't have exploded the way it did. That was still my favourite night, the Nashville night. I loved it.

It was Caroline Coon who coined both the terms 'punk' and 'the Bromley Contingent', neither of which went down entirely well at the time but have passed into legend now. I've even been labelled as Bromley Contingent, so it's morphed into anyone who was around at that time. Even if you are from Seaford.

BERTIE MARSHALL: I don't think any of us would have liked a label, then, now or forever more. What was worse was she then said in the paper that we and the Pistols went to Louise's – and that ruined it. Madame Louise made a lot of money, but it went from a place to sit and drink with friends to just another fucking punk club.

Two days after Jonh Ingham's *Sounds* feature came out, the Pistols played their second gig at the Nashville. This time, the audience included Tony James, Mick Jones, Adam Ant, Vic Godard and Dave

Vanian – the bare bones of The Clash, The Ants, Subway Sect and The Damned all in one small room.

JONH INGHAM: It was put on the front cover on the Tuesday and the Nashville was on the Friday. The place was packed, because it was The 101ers headlining. But you also got the sense that a lot of people were there because of the story. It was a front cover and two pages inside, and for a band that small it was just crazy.

In the middle of 'Pretty Vacant' Vivienne started a fight, which turned into a mass-participation rumble, with John throwing punches from the stage and Steve trying to pull people off each other. The incident was caught on camera by Kate Simon and Joe Stevens and ended up in all three music papers and across the front of one of them.

SIMON BARKER: When the scene was happening, Vivienne was very rarely there. I can think of only maybe four times out of all the gigs we went to that Vivienne was there, and every time she had to cause a to-do. Every time she had to start a fight to prove she was there. At the Nashville she caused a fight that went on the front cover of *Melody Maker*, at Andrew Logan's party she got punched by John Rotten – she loved it, actually. She got so drunk and so obnoxious, it was almost retarded behaviour.

VIVIENNE WESTWOOD: It was my fault, I did start it. I didn't start it on purpose, but this bloke told me to get off his seat, he'd gone to the bar and I'd sat down on his seat and he'd come back from the bar and I'd thought: Come on, this is punk, I don't get up off my seat for you, it's all part of the Establishment. I wouldn't get up and this man tried to lift the chair and tip me over, and as soon as he did that the band were there. Steve Jones stopped playing in order to protect me, and Sid, who was in the audience, took his belt off and hit this man round the head. It was dreadful.

Hissing Sid

Sid was like a snake with that belt. I saw him do that trick more than once, and the next time he would be aiming it at Nick Kent in their infamous altercation at the 100 Club on 25 May, when his belt did connect with Kent's face and spilled quite a lot of claret – Ron Watts had to get Sid off that time.

Sid's personality was changing fast. As well as attending all the Pistols gigs, he had started working at the shop, standing in if someone was on holiday. Not that he did anything other than the standing. He was an expert at doing absolutely fuck all. If somebody wanted to know what size something was, he'd say: "Doesn't it tell you that on the label?" Or how much it was? "I dunno. Don't ask me." He was there for decorative purposes, let's say. And he liked a natter. He was a difficult person on his own, but he was much better in company. I think he was quite an introverted person.

The thing to remember about Sid was that he was pretty conservative when I first met him. He worried about getting his exams; things you probably wouldn't believe now. The day before the first Ramones gig in London, on 3 July, we'd gone down to Hastings Pier to see the Pistols supporting Budgie – that's Budgie the Welsh heavy metal band, by the way, not the future drummer of The Slits and The Banshees.

It was so funny. The audience was just a load of tourists, on a day trip from I don't know where – France, probably. They were like rabbits in the headlights, they'd no idea what they'd got in front of them. They'd only gone there to play slot machines! Sid and I walked in and they just looked at us. Poly Styrene was also in the audience, but we didn't know her then. We must have been the only people in there who knew what was going on; everybody else had stumbled to the end of the pier by accident. They probably didn't understand a single word. They didn't play a very long set, either, only about five or six songs.

But my sister Sally can remember meeting me and Sid for dinner in London one evening and being really intimidated by him, just sitting there in silence too mortified to speak, because she found him so intense. This is weird, because it's the opposite of how I remember him behaving back then. I just remember him laughing and joking.

By then, Sid had formed his own band, The Flowers of Romance, with his then girlfriend Viv Albertine and Sarah 'Palmolive' Hall, both of whom would go on to form The Slits and were also regular customers at SEX. Sid was a pretty useless shop assistant but he was very inventive. He would wear garters over his jeans or a padlock over his crotch, for instance. John would need someone to tell him what to do half the time, but Sid was already there when it came to style, which was why he had taken Vivienne's eye. Unlike Steve, I don't think either of those two were sexually mature. Sid had more of a physical presence than John, who, I suppose, didn't want the trappings of a normal person. But being near, and then in, The Sex Pistols changed Sid dramatically.

The sound of the suburbs

Another two new shop assistants who would became enduring icons were friends Tracie O'Keefe and Debbi Wilson, the latter of whom was not from a certain Kentish suburb either – but you'll always find them labelled as Bromley Contingent. As events hotted up along with the weather in the summer of 1976, so did life at no. 430. Actress Candy Clark, who had been Oscar-nominated for her role in 1973's *American Graffiti* and was currently David Bowie's co-star in *The Man Who Fell to Earth*, came into the shop and bought a load of stuff. She was in London filming Michael Winner's version of Raymond Chandler's *The Big Sleep* with Robert Mitchum – an interesting story that we shall come back to.

Meanwhile, the Pistols set off to tour the north of England. Having returned from High Wycombe to form Buzzcocks, Howard Devoto and Pete Shelley made good on their promise of a gig, although when their college declined the booking Howard was forced to play promoter and booked them in at Manchester's Lesser Free Trade Hall on 4 June. It was a gamble that paid off. Like the last gig at the Nashville, it was attended by an array of budding musical talent, this time including Peter Hook and Bernard Sumner, Morrissey and, most importantly for the band, Tony Wilson, host of the influential weekly Granada music show *So It Goes*.

As well as playing, the band were writing more songs and, while what would become 'Anarchy in the UK' took shape, Vivienne introduced the Anarchy shirt to the shop. This was one of her

The terrible twins

Tracie O'Keefe (1960–78) and Debbi Wilson (aka Little Debs, aka Debbie Juvenile, 1960–2011) were two teenagers who wanted to get away from their backgrounds in Bromley and Burnt Oak respectively. They appeared at the Pistols' earliest gigs and clubs like Sombrero's and Louise's and went on all the dates of the first 'Anarchy' tour. When we moved into Buckingham Gate, they got involved in Linda's world of prostitution, although, as Debbi told Jon Savage: "Park Lane was the campest, most outrageous place in the world. None of it was serious, it was completely mental. The early days for me were camping it up and down Park Lane with a gang of trannies."

Bertie Marshall remembers them always being together: "They were like the terrible twins."

Debbi and Tracie spent the most time in the shop when it became Seditionaries in January 1977. The classic photographs of them with the Bromley Contingent were taken by Ray Stevenson at Buckingham Gate for Malcolm's *Anarchy in the UK* paper, which they sold on the Pistols' tours. But their time in the glare of the lens of notoriety proved shockingly short.

Tracie fell seriously ill in 1978 and died in May of that year from leukaemia, at the age of 18. Malcolm sent a wreath of flowers to her funeral that read 'NEVER MIND THE BOLLOCKS TRACIE' and had her funeral filmed for use in *The Great Rock 'n' Roll Swindle*. It caused more media outrage, but Simon Barker thinks that Tracie would have loved that her last act was to be in the Sex Pistols movie.

Debbi lived with John Rotten for a while when he bought his house in Gunter Grove. But, with Tracie's death and the end of the Pistols, there came too many dark clouds. She told Jon Savage: "Everyone around that scene was slowly falling apart really, 'cos when you've been in a close-knit thing and suddenly you're all just pushed away into your own direction, there's a sort of aftermath, it was like the death of something."

She was working in the film world, firstly for director Alex Cox on the script for his 1986 film *Sid and Nancy* or *Love Kills*, as it was originally called, then with production designer James Merifield, when she also died suddenly, in 2011, from cancer. Says Merifield: "Debs worked with me on *Little Dorrit* as my set decorator, for which she won an Emmy in 2008. She had such a great eye for detail. I guess this stemmed from her earlier life when she was surrounded by groundbreaking talent and ingenuity. Mind you, she never spoke of her former life – she was too busy getting on with the present… There isn't a day I don't think of her and miss her friendship."

masterpieces, made from the surplus of 1960s fine-striped pin-through round-collar shirts that Roger K. Burton had seen Malcolm buying in great numbers in 1973, dyed in stripes of red, black or brown and stencilled with slogans such as 'ONLY ANARCHISTS ARE PRETTY'. More slogans, hand-painted on silk or muslin, with explicit references to anarchist heroes and the events of the pivotal Paris May uprising in 1968,[1] were stitched on the side of the chest, and above the pocket on the collar was an inverted swastika. The whole thing was finished off with an armband that read 'CHAOS' and also featured a swastika.

Vivienne's line, which she would repeat to anyone who came in and tried to buy one of these shirts, or any other of her creations that were adorned with the most potent symbol of the Second World War, was that she was trying to demystify the icons used by tyrants. This didn't always go down so well with the man on the street. Or even in the music press.

JONH INGHAM: I don't entirely buy that. When the swastika showed up for the first time, I was fairly horrified by it. 'Cos I'm older, I was 24 going on 25 then, Caroline's even older and certainly in our household, I was brought up in Australia, even from that distance that was a symbol of evil. So when you saw it, and then you talked to someone like Siouxsie about it, she had no idea about what it meant. In that sense, it was consciousness-raising. But, as it rolled on towards the end of 1976, it looked more and more like Dada, they were just ripping everything down. Then, when The Clash came along with Bernie's whole manifesto stuff, that seemed more like Surrealism. They were trying to build something new, go in a direction that was positive. But that whole political slant that Malcolm brought in, the anarchy symbols, no one ever made a critique of that at the time. Anarchy was just another word.

---

[1] The events of May 1968 almost brought about another French revolution. It began with a series of student protests against capitalism and American imperialism in Vietnam and spread to disgruntled factory workers, with 11 million downing tools for France's largest ever general strike. There were street fights between students and the police, and Charles de Gaulle fled Paris, with a crowd of 500,000 singing him goodbye. But, once the police had restored the status quo, de Gaulle called a general election and then won the biggest parliamentary victory in French history.

ALAN JONES: My famous story was when I went to see *A Chorus Line* and the manager of the Drury Lane Theatre tried to throw me out because I was wearing the armband. And I was oblivious, just blithely walking along. If anybody challenged me, I just paraphrased what Vivienne always said. Not that I ever understood what she was talking about, because it was just fashion to me, it wasn't a manifesto. But I'd say we were trying to demystify them.

I had a big fight in Louise's with the DJ, Caroline, because I wore my Anarchy shirt down there with the swastika armband. Caroline was Jewish and she came up to me looking to punch my lights out, talking about the war and Belsen and tattoos on people's arms. It was a tirade of anger out of the blue; I had no preparation for it.

I just said: "Well, you're making a mystery out of this all over again and another drama, and this is to make people remember it." It got really close to a full-on fight and I didn't know what to do. I just said from my heart that this is so people won't forget and it demystifies the whole symbol of it. This isn't a glorification of it, and I pointed my finger at Karl Marx, who was on my bosom. But it was a really serious moment. People just didn't understand it. My dad didn't; he was a commando. Can you imagine me walking into my house wearing that, when my dad had fought in the Second World War?

BERTIE MARSHALL: Caroline did that to Siouxsie as well, when she had her armband on. I was there when she said it. Siouxsie went off to the toilet and drew little swastika beauty spots on her face. Caroline hated us, because she blamed us for breaking her and Linda up. When Linda met everyone else, she decided Caroline was boring.

You could never just buy anything in the shop. It was always *why* are you buying it? Vivienne could always rationalise what she was doing, she could always make it into some political statement about the world today. Michael and I just sold the clothes; the customers don't want to know about that. But Tracie and Debbi, being younger, they were the perfect age to absorb her schoolteacher lectures and take it all to heart.

BERTIE MARSHALL: Tracie and I shared a room at 19 Oakley Street, two doors down from David Bowie and Simon Turner. Tracie had her bed in one corner and I had mine in the other, under the window, under the tree. I loved it, because I could end up calling it 'The Four Sordid Rooms' in Chelsea, which is from *Cabaret*, 'The Two Sordid Rooms'. Tracie was involved with Steve Jones and Debbi with Nils, and the two of them were very, very close. I didn't see much of Tracie, as she was very much involved with the shop and with Steve, and really suffering from being with him and not getting what she wanted. But she was one of the people who I think embodied the spirit of punk, meaning that she was prepared to chain herself to Chelsea Town Hall and blow herself up for the cause. She meant it. Everything Malcolm and Vivienne did was right, there was no question about it. She was the embodiment of that.

Be reasonable, demand the impossible

Part of the input for the Anarchy shirt, as well as the new flyers Malcolm was making, came from Jamie Reid, whom Malcolm had first met at Croydon art college in 1967. Born into a family of activists – his grandfather, George Watson MacGregor Reid, was head of the Druid Order and stood for Parliament just before the First World War – he and Malcolm, with fellow student Robin Scott,[2] tried to stoke their own revolution in the summer of 1968. Inspired by events in Paris in May of that year, they staged a sit-in, which gained enough attention for a piece in *The Times*, as well as hassle from the local police and more sinister threats from the Board of Governors of the college to have Malcolm committed to an asylum.[3]

After leaving college, Reid founded a local printing company called the Suburban Press in Thornton Heath in 1970. It was because of his printing expertise that Malcolm brought Jamie back in to help him, but the events that brought them together in the first place would now impact clearly on the Pistols' visual image. I found Jamie to be a very

---

[2] Robin Scott went on to start his own record company, Do It, which would release some of the earliest Adam and the Ants records, as we shall see. His most famous fifteen minutes came with M, the band he fronted, recorded and produced, with the 1979 hit single 'Pop Muzik'. Find him at facebook.com/robinscottuk/

[3] Jamie Reid, quoted in Jon Savage, *England's Dreaming*, p. 29.

retiring person who was deeply into art and didn't want the limelight. Very political, but part of the beauty of the Situationist philosophy as I see it is that there's no concrete rules to it, it's just what you feel – you pick and choose the bits you like.[4] Which is much like punk.

On 4 July, The Ramones played their first ever London gig, at the Roundhouse in Camden, supporting The Flaming Groovies. For me, this was a big, big moment. When I heard their first album, it was like: What the fuck? Where have you come from? I just couldn't believe what I was hearing.

In return, they were equally blown away by London, Dee Dee in particular. He was very quick to recognise the unusual and interesting, and he just took one look at me, backstage at the Roundhouse, and that was it. They had not seen anything like it. They walked in with their uniform, for want of a better word, which was great and it really suited them. Then they saw this sea of people who looked so bizarre to them but were such huge fans of theirs already. After that gig, London became the centre of their universe.

I so believe in England as being a real hub for fashion, music, art, acceptance of new things – unlike some places in America. There shouldn't be a 'We did it first, they did it first,' kind of thing, but there often is, with New York and here. But I don't think Americans would have accepted what we looked like.

TED POLHEMUS: That's the difference between the American and the British thing. American punk was like a kind of post modern pastiche on the 1950s. The Ramones are like a 1970s vision of 1950s juvenile delinquency. British punks would go into charity shops and wear something from their grandad's generation, whacked together with something that looked like it came from outer space. Playing with the unexpected. You'll see people in America who get dressed up for one gig – like, say, David Bowie – the way they would get dressed up for a fancy dress party. But you don't wear that 24/7. Only the British do that.

David Ireland, at that time still working for Frankie Savage in Ian's, New York City, and living in the Ramones' home suburb of Queens,

---

[4] Find the Situationist International texts at: cddc.vt.edu/sionline/si/beginning.html

notes that the relative lack of choice in the UK compared to America actually made us more inventive:

DAVID IRELAND: You only had the three TV stations, and there was only John Peel on the radio. So there was this huge focus, everybody was listening to John Peel. Then you'd go down the pub after work and everybody would be talking about it. Whereas in the States you had thirteen TV channels and numerous radio stations, which were much more heavily promoted, they dictated what you heard.

For all the wildness of New York, it could be very conservative. I used to get such abuse when I walked down the street. If you wear your heart on your sleeve here, people will look but they don't say anything. In New York, people come up to you and call you 'Ice Cream Cone Head' or 'Freak', and there have been times when everybody is shouting at you. It's a very macho culture, and you had to have a certain something to cope. I used to use speed to cope with it. It wasn't easy. Sitting on the subway going home in the rush hour, two black girls standing over me, one saying: "Don't stare at him, it's not nice." And the other one's saying: "Well, look at him,

he wants to be stared at." It was funny on one hand, but when you're 17 and a bit sensitive...

It's the buzz, cock

On 20 July, the Pistols returned to Manchester to play another gig at the Lesser Free Trade Hall. A like-minded community had emerged in that city, and Buzzcocks, who supported them that night, were at the forefront. As well as being another meeting of the tribes, the gig led to the Pistols being booked to go on Tony Wilson's *So It Goes* on 4 September. Perhaps their finest ever televisual hour awaited.

But, first, the Pistols recorded seven tracks with Dave Goodman, who had been renting them their PA and working as their sound man on the four-track machine at Denmark Street: 'Anarchy in the UK', 'Pretty Vacant', 'Seventeen', 'Satellite', 'Problems', 'I Wanna Be Me' and 'Submission'. This was their second demo: they had previously recorded 'Pretty Vacant', 'Problems' and 'No Feelings' (which would become 'God Save the Queen') with The Sharks' guitarist Chris Spedding, who was the first person to show Steve and Paul the basics of using a studio.

PAUL COOK: We did do a few demos here and there to see what they sounded like. We done the first demo with Chris Spedding – again, a connection with the shop. Chris Spedding used to come in and again Malcolm asked him: "I've got this band, could you produce a couple of tracks for us?" And he did. Which shows you how important the shop was to everything. He was a well-respected guitarist, and I took notice of every little thing he did, how to play things. He got into a different era of rock'n'roll, but he didn't mind hanging out with us lot.

Chris was a great improviser on the guitar; he always kept his mind open. I think that's what his mental make-up was; he didn't mind what genre he was in or who he hung out with. He wasn't precious. But those first three tracks hadn't captured enough depth of the Pistols' live sound for Malcolm to be happy sending them out to A&R men. Dave Goodman recorded four or five more takes of each song and then added overdubs in an eight-track at Riverside Studios.

174

Armed with what became known as 'the Spunk Tapes', Malcolm began his assault on the record companies. With the Nick Kent incident adding another big tremor to the palpitations already resounding through a wary music business, he decided he needed another big event to sound his attack. This time, it would be cinematic in its scope.

11

IN THE HEART OF THE ESTABLISHMENT

Under the nose of Buckingham Palace (April–October 1976)

The goods from the Gate

Simon Barker and Derek Dunbar were the first to move into apartment 1016 King's House, St James Hotel, Buckingham Gate, London SW1.[1] A room became available in April 1976 when 'Little Helen' Wellington-Lloyd, a Goldsmiths contemporary of Malcolm's and one of the most recognisable faces of punk, moved out. The red-brick Victorian building where Linda Ashby ran her business stood right in the heart of the British Establishment, surrounded by Buckingham Palace, the Wellington Army Barracks, the Home Office, New Scotland Yard and Westminster Cathedral. The IRA's ongoing campaign of bombing in the capital made the area even more of

---

[1] For a vivid snapshot of life in Buckingham Gate, Simon Barker's *Punk's Dead* (Divus, 2016) is essential, bringing together all his photographs, painstakingly restored from original negatives taken on his pocket camera, of us living there between 1976 and 1978. See www.six.cz and www.divus.cz for more.

a high-security operation, although shades of an older London, terrorised in Georgian times by rogue buttock-stabber the London Monster,[2] lived on in such surrounding street names as Perkin's Rents and Old Pye Street.

DEREK DUNBAR: We'd come out and Prince Philip would be going past in his car – he used to go to all those pubs around the Home Office. If we went to Sainsbury's to get a couple of potatoes and a carrot, the police would stop us and say: "What you got in that bag?" And you would walk out every morning in your Let It Rock knickers, high heels and stockings. Off to work! The police used to stop us all the time and the way they could tell you was gay was if you had a packet of KY in your back pocket. It was illegal to be gay until you were 21 in those days.

SIMON BARKER: This guardsman outside Buckingham Palace came up and started talking to me one night. He said: "Do you ever have a problem with those Teddy boys beating you up?" And I said: "Well, I haven't, but I do go up the King's Road a lot." I was *so* innocent. He said: "Yeah, 'cos a few of my mates have had a Teddy boy, but no one's had a punk yet." Oh my God, he's chatting me up!

Linda's business was discreet. Simon can remember only a few regular punters: one who always used to arrive with a big bottle of vodka; and 'Dick the Trick', who she made carry all her shopping up the stairs, even though there was a perfectly serviceable lift, but that was part of the kink. Linda used to shout to him from her bedroom – "Dick!" And he couldn't hear her. "Dick!" He'd go: "Yes?" She'd say: "Could you come and help me move the wardrobe, please?" And we all used to laugh, because she had fitted wardrobes. It was a code for: "I'm ready for you." She'd got all her clobber on in the bedroom.

---

[2] Predating Jack the Ripper by 100 years, the London Monster stalked the streets around St James between 1788 and 1790, brandishing a posy of flowers and wearing a blade on his knees with which he would boot his female victims up the behind – after flicking them with the concealed blade in his floral lure first. Ladies took to wearing copper petticoats to protect themselves from his sudden advances, as recorded by artists James Gillray and William Hogarth. Eventually, a florist named Rhynwick Williams was arrested, but he could only be charged with the crime of defacing another person's clothing and got six years in Newgate. See Jan Bondeson's *The London Monster* (Tempus, 2004).

The misfits

Helen Wellington-Lloyd (b. 1954, aka Helen Miniberg, aka Helen of Troy) first met Malcolm at Goldsmiths art college in 1968. The child of rich South African parents, she had come over to London to study film and photography – and any other excitements the capital could offer. A highly visible misfit herself, as a dwarf, she was drawn to the equally exotic world of gay subculture, became an expert in Polari and a friend, sometime lover and muse for Malcolm, with whom she collaborated on his major Goldsmiths project, the *Oxford Street* film, along with Patrick Casey and Jamie Reid. This Situationist-inspired psychogeography illustrated Malcolm's fascination with London's lowlife history, and eventually came to a kind of fruition in his 1991 TV movie *The Ghosts of Oxford Street*.

Helen returned to South Africa after graduating, but came back in 1975, when she and Malcolm briefly lived together in Bell Street, off the Edgware Road, and she met the Pistols for the first time. She was often involved in helping Malcolm fashion both their image and that of the shop – you can see her helping me to pick out my rubberwear in *Dressing for Pleasure* (John Sampson, 1977), and Malcolm credited her for inventing the 'ransom-note' lettering cut out from newspapers that was used on the flyer to advertise the El Paradiso gig and would go on to be a defining part of Pistols imagery. Bertie Marshall has fond memories of meeting her at Buckingham Gate: "Little Helen was always around. I had to share a bed with her once, which was quite funny. She didn't take up very much space! I could never understand much of what she was saying, because she'd be talking in Polari. But she was lovely."

Helen also appears with me in *Jubilee* (Derek Jarman, 1978), *The Tempest* (Derek Jarman, 1979), *Punk Can Take It* (Julien Temple, 1979) and as Malcolm's constant companion in *The Great Rock 'n' Roll Swindle* (Julien Temple, 1980). The last time I saw Helen was at the premiere for *The Filth and the Fury* (Julien Temple, 2000), where I had such a good time talking to her, Simon Barker and Steve Jones in the pub over the road beforehand that we almost missed the beginning of the film.

Though friends tried to keep in touch with her, she seemed to disappear into the ether after selling her collection of punk memorabilia, which included the earliest surviving Sex Pistols poster and some of the Let It Rock knickers, at Sotheby's on 20 September 2001.

Linda's style was very 1970s New York-Halston-Warhol. It was all Heal's sofas, and shagpile carpet so thick that you could hardly open the door in her all-pink bedroom, which Bertie Marshall imaginatively described as "glowing like a big cunt" – not something I think he'd know from experience. We had a Sony Trinitron, which was the top-of-the-range TV in those days – and very thick damask curtains, naturally.

But it was so easy-going that the key dangled on a string behind the letterbox and sometimes Simon's Burmese cat would climb up the string and poke her head through the letterbox to see who was there. The Hotel comprised several different houses, with a connecting gateway that they used to keep shut, so we had to walk through the hotel to get to the flat all the time. Just opposite was the Salvation Army, who used to feed all the homeless from around Buckingham Palace – and us.

> **DEREK DUNBAR:** You used to get a three-course meal – soup, your main meal, vegetables and chicken or whatever and then a good pudding like apple crumble with custard – all-inclusive for 50p. In old 1940s/50s cups and crockery.

> **SIMON BARKER:** There'd be tables of old tramps and me, Derek, you and Siouxsie sitting among them! They got used to us in the end.

At the time, Derek was working for Martin Samuels, who famously styled David Bowie's hair in *The Man Who Fell to Earth*, at Crimpers, London's first unisex hair salon, in Baker Street. He was also my official hair-dyer.

> **DEREK DUNBAR:** Your hair was never white enough. It had to be pure white – 60 per cent peroxide I used on your hair for forty minutes. That's the maximum your head can take and I said, "You can't get any whiter than that." But you wouldn't listen. You sat in a cold bath and did it twice and your head broke out in heat sores. You were screaming: "Wash it off, wash it off!" And when I started to wash it off you screamed: "Stop!" Because the hot water had opened the pores on your scalp.

180

My whole head turned into a giant scab – not a pleasant experience. But Buckingham Gate was where I did all my experimenting with hair and make-up, spending days and sometimes weeks perfecting new looks. There was never any shortage of inspiration around the place.

Little black books

One of the people who used to come around was the influential art dealer Robert Fraser, who at one time had represented all the British and American Pop artists and brought them to the attention of the music elite of the 1960s. At the same time, he inhabited the illicit 1950s gay/gambling underworld where David Litvinoff, the Kray twins, Francis Bacon and Lucien Freud met, leading Mick Jagger to memorably describe him as a man "bridging two worlds... that was his blaze, his quick swathe through London".[3] We only knew of him from the famous photo where he's been handcuffed to Jagger following the infamous drugs (and rugs) bust at Keith Richards' country house Redlands on 12 February 1967. No wonder Malcolm was keen to make friends with him.

Fraser, who would buy Sex Pistols posters from Simon for £10 and then sell them on for £1,000, took a massive shine to Derek, who was given a vivid glimpse into the darker side of his nature.

> **DEREK DUNBAR:** He was living in Cecil Beaton's apartment in Leicester Square when he was introduced to me by Derek Jarman, and he became a bit of a stalker. He had a black book full of famous people that he showed to me; now I know who they are. At the time, I didn't, I was just a 16-year-old kid, but now I've put it all together. When he died, it went missing.

Another person who liked to keep inadvisable records was Vicky de Lambray, a transvestite prostitute who was having affairs with people in high places and put it about that she was keeping a book

---

[3] For the full lowdown on Robert Fraser (1937–1986), Harriet Vyner's *Groovy Bob* (republished by Heni in 2016) is a superb oral history of how he affected pop culture from the 1950s to the 1980s, with quotes from everyone from Malcolm to Mick Jagger. Fraser served time in Wormwood Scrubs for being in possession of heroin. He re-emerged in the 1980s, promoting Jean-Michel Basquiat and Keith Haring, but died of AIDS in January 1986.

with all her clients' names in it. She used to drive around Shepherd's Market in a Rolls-Royce with 'VICKY DE LAMBRAY ENTERTAINER' written across the back window. She got a bad name from trying to sell stories to the newspapers that were not exactly true, although she did service a lot of very rich clients; the champagne was always flowing around Vicky. Strangely, she wasn't even that attractive; she had a fat face with a kind of side-parted boy's hairstyle, so who knows what her specialities were. Her story ended in 1986, when she called the police saying someone had shot her up with a fatal dose of heroin. They went round to her flat in Stockwell about half an hour later and she was dead, though no puncture marks were found on the body and no cause of death has been established to this day. Nor has her book been recovered, if it existed.

The other of Linda's notable friends was Lindi St Clair, aka Miss Whiplash,[4] who claimed to have administered her corrective services to upstanding members on both sides of the House. I can remember her calling us very early one morning, in a really hard voice, saying: "I need to speak to Linda, quickly." And the message was: "Just get out of there now, leave whatever you're doing." So obviously we were going to get busted. They came at five o'clock in the morning thinking they'd catch us out, but we used to stay up to four o'clock in the morning to wait for the bread delivery to the hotel and nick all their bread rolls. So when they came at five, we were having tea and toast, all dressed, with a game of Scrabble on the floor. I greeted the officers with a cheery "I'm doing toast, anybody want some?"

By the end of 1976, both John Rotten and myself were living at Buckingham Gate. Linda had taken a shine to us, but a lot of the people in her world thought we had changed her and hated us for it. Especially her former girlfriend Caroline, the DJ at Louise's who went off at me about the Anarchy shirt. That probably wasn't the only thing

---

[4] Lindi St Clair (b. 1952) became infamous in January 1993 when, facing bankruptcy, she staged a vanishing act, leaving her car at Beachy Head. She had sent a letter to *Sun* editor Kelvin MacKenzie offering to name 252 MPs who had paid for her services. After a police hunt, she was found on a cruise liner off the coast of Australia. In 1993, Lindi launched the Corrective Party and stood in eleven elections, sharing an agent with Screaming Lord Sutch. But after another dramatic interlude, when her jeep ran off the road into a stream and left her trapped for twenty-four hours, she underwent a religious conversion. She has now legally reverted to her birth name.

she didn't like – Linda really fancied me and always wanted me to stay in her room. It was really difficult when I had to say "I don't want to do this any more, actually". I did sleep with Linda a few times.

SIMON BARKER: She was so lovely to us and we took over that flat. Linda would come in and just go to her bedroom and close the door because we controlled the lounge and we controlled the kitchen, we were really selfish without thinking. You know when you're young, you just don't think. We took over the kitchen completely when you made the outfit for *Jubilee*, the ballet outfit. There was glue and feathers all over the place. And Linda would just sneak in, make a little cup of tea and sneak out again. We never once asked her if it was OK.

The worst thing is, I think Linda was in the shop with me when she met Nancy Spungen, and that's how Nancy ended up back there – which was a disaster we shall come to all too soon. Before then, she had us so well trained, she had even got me and Sid into her favourite leisure pursuit: an early morning ride across Hyde Park.

Can you imagine? There was this whip-cracking woman at the stables, terribly sensible, and we turned up early one morning when the stables had just opened. She took one look at us and said: "Well, you'll have to wear a helmet." I pointed to my hair and said: "I'm not spoiling that," and Sid said: "I'm not, either." We stood our ground and in the end, she said: "Oh, all right then, get on." We didn't know how to get on a horse! I remember her getting out this wooden block for me to stand on.

There was a guardsman riding his horse, all decked out in his uniform, riding along Rotten Row, and he hit this branch and fell off his horse looking at us. We nearly fell off our horses laughing at him falling off his horse. But this is the backdrop from which The Sex Pistols were launched on the Establishment – the very heart of it.

Baldy old Sheila

It was their televisual broadcast debut and nothing could possibly demonstrate better the need for The Sex Pistols to intervene in British musical entertainment than the *So It Goes* show broadcast

183

from Manchester's Granada Studios on 28 August 1976. The whole thing was unbelievable. Malcolm asked me to go up to the recording of the show to add, in his words, "a bit of ambience", so, wearing an Anarchy shirt with swastika armband, I took the train up from London with the band. I think we even travelled first class – maybe the Manchester branch had been having a word with the British Rail staff in Seaford.

PAUL COOK: It must have looked like such a sight to all the commuters, all of us turning up in the morning to get on the train to Manchester. 'Cos it was all very straight at the time.

From the off, my appearance caused ructions. Almost as soon as we got there, I was asked to remove the armband and, when I refused, I was taken downstairs into the bowels of Granada TV to discuss it – my memory is that all happened in the *Coronation Street* dressing room, with all their outfits on rails around us. I wouldn't take the armband off; Malcolm wouldn't let me take the armband off; and the Pistols wouldn't go on-stage unless I was there. So there was a total impasse for a couple of hours. My argument was that it was part of the make-up of the shirt: 'We don't need your symbolism' is what it means. But it was very touch-and-go that they would allow me onstage. Three hours later, we were still in negotiations.

There were three bands on that day. The others were Gentlemen, in their blue satin suits, playing 'My Ego's Killing Me', which was apparently inspired by an advert for girdles; and, coming on just before the Pistols, the light jazz sounds of The Bowles Brothers Band performing 'Charlie's Nuts'. There was John and I, sitting in the dressing room listening to them playing a double bass and talking about Joni Mitchell. We just looked at each other. What have we got ourselves into here? We'd already taken as much piss out of Tony Wilson as we could. I actually really liked him, but he had a very bad pair of shoes on and I couldn't let it go. And long hair, curly hair. And he was wearing a denim jacket. John was like: "Fucking hippy!" and I was like: "Look at his shoes!" Within seconds, we'd eyed him up and that was it. But he turned out to be a really great bloke.

184

The other guests were Clive James and, one of Rotten's heroes, Peter Cook, who knew all about annoying his betters, being the first person to dare to mock a prime minister in public and running his own nightclub called the Establishment in Greek Street, Soho, from 1961 to 1964. The *Derek and Clive (Live)* album was just about to come out and Cook was being interviewed by James as his alter ego, Clive – the ideological doppelgänger of Steve Jones. The reactions of these two elder satirists towards the Pistols couldn't have been more different.

Peter Cook was a saving grace. He was so funny, really clever and quick, even when he was drunk – and he was getting steadily more so all day. He even gave us a packet of his fags when we ran out. But Clive James didn't get the Pistols, and he didn't get what Peter Cook was saying, either. It took him years to get over the swastika armband. He was vile to me on that programme, which is why I called him a baldy old Sheila. Afterwards, he did a column in the *Observer* and he was still talking about it, I should think about two years later. How obscene it was and how much he disliked me for doing it.[5]

Eventually a compromise was reached – the show's producers put some sticky tape over the offending symbol. In his link, Tony Wilson helpfully pointed out there was a warning on the *Derek and Clive (Live)* LP and noted: "Our final live band tonight also have a warning on them. One of the most reviewed and most reviled rock phenomena of recent weeks, we got a few votes, Sex Pistols, you can hear them warming up in the background."

The camera panned into my smiling face. "The Sex Pistols", I informed the viewing public, "are, if possible, even better than the lovely Joni Mitchell." That was for The Bowles Brothers, and you can hear John laughing in the background.

"Get off your arse!" Rotten, a vision in a pale pink ripped dinner jacket adorned with safety pins and iron crosses, razor blades dangling from his earlobes, yelled into the microphone. Glen, on his right, also wearing an Anarchy shirt, Steve to his left in pink shirt and red trousers and Paul behind in John's personally customised I HATE PINK FLOYD T-shirt pumped out the opening rumble of

---

[5] Clive James wrote up the appearance in the *Observer*, describing Rotten as "a foul-mouthed ball of acne calling himself something like Kenny Frightful".

'Anarchy in the UK'. I stood at the side of the stage, throwing chairs and whatever else came to hand towards the stupefied studio audience, who just sat there – like those strippers at El Paradiso. They absolutely didn't want to move in case John or I jumped down off the stage and got them. I was interviewed afterwards and I think I said at the time that they looked like people on Death Row waiting to be executed.

I still think that was the best performance John ever did. He always rose to the bait, which was great, and when you've got an audience like the one on *So It Goes* they're just feeding him the venom he needs to survive on. He was great at that, feeding off adversity. But never mind the sticky tape, I actually lost a few buttons off my shirt throwing that chair.

Vision on

The next day, 29 August, via his old art college friend Roger Austin, who was now managing an art-house cinema in Islington, Malcolm had set up a gig at the Screen on the Green, advertised via the first flyer to be designed by Jamie Reid. The 'Midnight Special' brought together the Pistols, The Clash and Buzzcocks with the cinematic treats of Kenneth Anger's lushly provocative films *Kustom Kar Kommandos* (1965) and *Scorpio Rising* (1964) in a line-up tailored to attract the A&R men Malcolm needed for the next stage of the game. Not that the close friends of the Pistols let this night of divine decadence pass unmemorably: Siouxsie, in her half-cup bra and swastika armband, attracted most of the photographers' attention, while Alan Jones was already tripping.

ALAN JONES: I loved that night. I was on acid. I'd taken it with this guy and we'd come out of this wild sex orgy and ended up at the Screen on the Green. That's why I had a fabulous time.

JONH INGHAM: When you were on *So It Goes* and the camera pulled back and there you were in your brown shirt... You did look amazing with your hair and those black eyes, like a Marvel superhero. It always looked like an image of strength, which I think was really interesting and

186

important. Then watching these women come out: Siouxsie and Debbi and that whole family of women, and how you all looked and thought was very appealing. Siouxsie's outfit at Screen on the Green, one fishnet stocking, one rubber stocking and she's virtually naked from the waist up. Then she gets up on the stage and dances. You can just think: Well, everybody's an exhibitionist...

Under the strict guidance of Bernie Rhodes, The Clash were being just as carefully groomed as the Pistols. The original line-up of Joe Strummer, guitarists Mick Jones and Keith Levene, bassist Paul Simenon and drummer Terry Chimes had just played their first, invitation-only gig at their Camden rehearsal rooms before the Screen on the Green introduced them to the public. They were so secretive they even got changed into their paint-splattered outfits in the alleyway outside.

PAUL COOK: The Clash looked much more manufactured than we did, with their slogans and their leather jackets, collars up and all that.

SIMON BARKER: People think The Clash were working-class heroes, but they had Jasper Conran doing their clothes and Sebastian Conran was their roadie.

PETER YORK: Clash-land was subtly different to Pistols-land – and there was a lot of jealousy between them. Bernie Rhodes was tremendously jealous of Malcolm.

I had a problem with The Clash in that they looked so nostalgic. The clothes with the slogans on them, Bernie's boiler suits and Jackson Pollocks – they all looked like painters and decorators. There are a few songs I liked, but a lot of it I didn't. 'White Riot' is good, a couple of others. But it wasn't just that Pistols and Clash thing, it wasn't a rivalry thing, it's to do with them being totally different styles.

Watching the Pistols play for the first time was Simon Fisher Turner, the young actor and musician who was, at the time, also a live-in child minder to David and Angie Bowie's young son Zowie, at Oakley Street in Chelsea.

SIMON FISHER TURNER: I saw The Sex Pistols at the Screen on the Green. I really was there, and all my friends were there too. I used to go there to see late-night films, when it was called the Roxy before it was the Screen on the Green. But that night was the first time I ever saw a mohair jumper! Johnny Rotten, I remember, he'd broken a tooth or something; he came on the left side of the stage and he was so rude it was fantastic. I had never seen an audience looking like this before, it was so awfully brilliant. I thought it was amazing.

I have to admit, my own memories are not quite so clear. Roger Austin, who is a very dear man who played a much larger part in all of this than he would ever take credit for, has an abiding memory of why. I took so much speed that I was feeling really ill. He found me sitting outside on the step with my head hanging; my head was bursting. And he came out with a cup of tea in a little china cup and saucer and saved my life.

Oooh la la!

A week later, on 4 September 1976, the band flew to Paris to play the opening night of a disco in the Bois de Boulogne, called the Chalet du Lac, that had been set up with the help of Jean Charles de Castelbajac and also featured The Damned, The Pink Fairies and Roogalator, demonstrating a sort of evolutionary scale of counter-culture from hippies to punks. Simon Barker went over with Siouxsie, Debbi and Steve Severin, in a van driven by Billy Idol, who would soon be forming a band of his own.

PETER YORK: I remember meeting Billy Idol. He explained to me the idea that punks would so annoy the Establishment that they would destroy them and the triumph of the proletariat would follow. And I remember saying: "Well, what is it that you do, Mr Idol?" He said he was a van driver. Of course, whatever van driving he had done had been very temporary, because he had been a student of Philosophy at Sussex University. I thought he was very entertaining, because he talked such nonsense.

This time, Siouxie's topless outfit, a mirror image of the one she'd worn to the Screen on the Green, didn't go down so well. Simon remembers her being molested and punched by the locals, and the situation got so bad that the Pistols' entourage had to be moved to another part of the club for their own protection, staying in the dressing room until the promoter said it was safe to come out. Meanwhile, I had also made a bit of a perilous crossing in the company of Vivienne.

The night before, I was staying with her at her place in Clapham; we had to get the flight the next day from Gatwick to Paris to meet Jean-Charles de Castelbajac. I was lying in bed with her, in her and Malcolm's bed in Nightingale Lane, when she asked me: "Jordan, have you ever been with a lady?"

I said: "Well, actually, I have." I've had relationships with women, but nothing long-term. And she said: "Oooh, what's it like?" I thought that might be an opening, and I thought: No! You can't imagine Vivienne having sex, but I think she sort of half propositioned me that night.

Maybe she was feeling frisky, because that Paris gig was also the debut of her latest design masterstroke – the Bondage suit.

Rotten debuted the look – with all its zips, straps between the legs and pièce de résistance towelling bum flap – at the airport, to the bemusement of his fellow passengers, and then on-stage, to the toast of Paris's artistic elite. Malcolm and Vivienne were hailed as *Couturiers Situationnistes* by the influential Michael Esteban, owner of *Rock News* magazine.

All they needed now was a recording contract…

All that glitters…

A couple of London-based labels had started up off the impetus of punk. Former market stallholder Ted Carroll and his business partner Roger Armstrong had expanded out from their Rock On outlets in Golborne Road and Camden to form the label Chiswick, while Dave Robinson and Jake Rivera started Stiff in July 1976, making the first punk signing with The Damned, whose 'New Rose' single would come out in September. But, like the pub rock circuit that had helped to bring these ideas to life, Malcolm wanted nothing to do with anything indie. He set his sights on wooing the major labels and began gathering people around him who could help him in his quest. Sophie Richmond, who had worked with Jamie Reid at the Suburban Press, became his secretary; Stephen Fisher, his solicitor and co-director; while Jamie Reid was to provide all the artwork. He called his management company Glitterbest and took an office in Dryden Chambers, near Oxford Circus. He took on Simon Barker to book gigs for him.

SIMON BARKER: Dryden Chambers doesn't exist any more, but the ground-floor offices was where Barry Foster's tie killing in Hitchcock's *Frenzy* took place.[6] That's typical Malcolm: he found things that had these links, he was so knowledgeable. When he was in that office, he'd often arrange to do something and then change his mind about doing it,

---

[6] Alfred Hitchcock's 1972 film *Frenzy* was based on the 1966 novel *Goodbye Piccadilly, Farewell Leicester Square* by Arthur La Bern, who had covered the trials of Acid Bath Murderer John George Haigh and killer conman Neville Heath, a couple of smooth-talking spivs who haunted post-war London and on whom Barry Foster's necktie-wielding charmer is based. The film is a lot more low-down and dirty than Hitchcock's usual, mainly thanks to Foster's mesmerising performance.

and so people would be banging on the office door. Malcolm would put a finger to his lips and we would just sit there until they went away. The office that we had was on the fifth floor with no lift, so of course they were puffed out and they wouldn't come back.

The Hot 100

Inspired by the event at the Chalet du Lac, Glitterbest's first venture was to stage a Punk Festival at the 100 Club. The idea was for it to run over two nights. On 20 September, the Pistols, Subway Sect, the newly formed Siouxsie and Stinky Toys (a French band who didn't end up doing the gig) were booked. On 21 September, The Vibrators, Buzzcocks and The Damned completed the line-up. Prior to their appearance, earlier that day the individual Pistols signed a management contract with Glitterbest which awarded Malcolm 25 per cent of their earnings and 50 per cent of their merchandising rights. Glen Matlock wanted to get a lawyer to take a look at it first; the others overruled him.

Malcolm was keen that the 100 Club should be packed with good-looking punks, and had me phoning round my friends.

ANTON BINDER: I can remember you calling me up and saying: "We want people who are the right kind of people to come." So at the 100 Club I was on Malcolm McLaren's guest list. Though no one believes me!

Not that Malcolm needed to be worried about a shortage of takers. Walking up Oxford Street towards Tottenham Court Road, Paul Cook remembers feeling disbelief at the scene outside the 100 Club.

PAUL COOK: That's when I realised something was really happening, 'cos we turned up for soundcheck and there was a massive queue around the block. We thought: What's this for? They was all waiting to see us; queuing up at six o'clock outside the 100 Club. So we knew we was on the right track. That's the main thing I remember.

The Banshees had been hastily conceived after a night at Louise's. With Siouxsie as singer, Sid Vicious on drums, Marco Pirroni on

191

guitar and Steve Severin on bass, they took their name from the 1970 Gordon Hessler horror flick *The Cry of the Banshee*.

> **MARCO PIRRONI:** It was a real spur-of-the-moment, let's-do-this thing. There was no reason to do it; it wasn't a great career move or anything. But what do you know? I was 17. It was just the thing to do. The fact that it did actually do us all good wasn't anything we anticipated at that time. We didn't think it would get us good profile or get us into other bands, or make us famous or anything like that. It was just the urge. The subconscious urge that you had to do something.

The song that they played that night has passed into legend. It was an extended, improvised version of the Lord's Prayer that segued into The Velvet Underground's 'Sister Ray' (which the band members loved) and Bob Dylan's 'Knocking on Heaven's Door', The Beatles' 'She Loves You' and the Bay City Rollers' 'Young Love' (all of which they hated). Marco still seems bemused by it.

> **MARCO PIRRONI:** Well, I hadn't really discussed it with the others. I just thought we were doing 'Sister Ray' and that made sense to me. We were all influenced by The Velvet Underground but I didn't know that Sid, Siouxsie and Steve were all as in love with them as I was. I could have guessed, probably. We just knew, whatever it is that you've got, we don't want it. Like Groucho Marx: whatever it is, I'm against it.

But all of us had supreme confidence in ourselves and our own bodies and our own minds; we wanted to go out and try and make a mark, or just be out there.

> **ANTON BINDER:** Inspired by Richard Hell, a couple of friends and me had already started putting little rips into T-shirts and seeing what people said about that down the gay clubs, because it had been all about looking as smart as you could. Then it started being about, not as scruffy as you could, but as odd or oddly wrong as you could. I was really into Warhol, so I'd made this T-shirt with a lot of Warhol quotes written in felt pen and ripped, and I remember you introducing me to John Rotten and him reading my T-shirt. I think it said: "I want to be plastic." I got a paragraph

written about me in *NME*. It said: "Why even Anton looks blank. Anton is a David Bowie lookalike and as doppelgängers go, he gängs more doppel than most."

Bang to rights

The Pistols that night were phenomenal. It was the next night that rivalry between them and The Damned flared into actual violence. When they started playing a version of The Stooges' '1970', someone threw a beer glass at the stage – Sid is in the frame for this incident. Some people think he was aiming it at Dave Vanian; others, at Captain Sensible. Whoever the intended victim was, the glass hit one of the pillars in front of the stage, shattered and showered glass over the audience, hitting a girl in the eye. An ambulance was called and the police followed it to the scene in short order.

MARCO PIRRONI: I didn't actually see it happen; I was there but I wasn't looking in that direction at the time. It was aimed at Ray Burns [Captain Sensible], not Dave Vanian, because he was wearing big white flares, and who can blame Sid for that? So he hit one of the pillars and this bit of glass went into this girl's eye. I didn't know who she was, but I heard she was one of the people from Smile. I don't even know what happened to her, she's never resurfaced to tell her side of the story. I think it was me and Steve Severin who went to phone Malcolm and Vivienne, who were at home, to tell them Sid had been arrested. Malcolm answered and said: "Yes, I'm going to do everything I can to get him out." Then, obviously, he just went back to sleep and forgot all about it.

Jonh Ingham was standing next to Sid and Mick Jones of The Clash when the arrest was made and, to this day, he considers Sid was not only innocent of throwing the glass but was also set up by plain-clothes police already at the gig.

JONH INGHAM: The Damned stopped playing and Dave Vanian said: "Somebody just threw a glass and there's a girl here with blood all down her face." So Ron rang 999 and that's why the police showed up. Everything was stopped. This girl was lying on the floor, there was people helping her, the cops all came. I could see them coming down the stairs and talking to Ron. They come towards us and grabbed Sid. He was standing next to me and they just grabbed him without saying a word, five guys picked him up – his feet weren't even touching the ground. Caroline was the first to react, sprinting up the stairs after him and going to the Commanding Officer: "What's the charge?" I could hear her screaming all the way down the hall. He just ignored her completely. So she grabbed him by the shoulder and said: "What the fuck is going on?" And he said: "All right, you too." Picks her up and throws her in the back of the van, too. Then this other guy is thrown in with them, this dude in a T-shirt, jeans, spiky hair and he starts acting like he was in with the audience. But she sniffs him out in a second. Then it became apparent that they had been down there, tracking the whole thing.

Sid and Caroline were taken to West End Central police station at Savile Row for questioning. The 100 Club closed and everyone left. Jonh waited for Caroline back at her house in Ladbroke Grove.

JONH INGHAM: She came back about an hour and a half later and she said they'd both been in the same room but there was a divider down the middle, so she could hear them but she couldn't see them. The cops were going: "Don't think you're so tough now, do you?" And she could hear this noise, like they were bashing his head on the table. And he'd come back up and go: "Fuck you!" And they'd bash his head again, and he'd come back up and go: "Fuck you!"

This went on for quite a while, but he wouldn't give in – he kept mouthing back at them and they kept hitting his head. So she got onto one of her lawyers and Sid was arraigned the next morning at Great Marlborough Street court, which was full of black kids all on sus arrest, just one right after the other. You saw the British Establishment at its purest right there. Pushing kids back down who didn't know their place. And Sid came in with his entire face one purple bruise and dressed in the same clothes he'd had on for the Punk Festival, something like the Cowboys T-shirt with his ripped jeans and brothel creepers – he had a condom tied to one of his belt loops, but that had gone, he wasn't entirely stupid. There was something about Sid; it always struck me that he was a really smart guy, but he chose to behave like a moron and I could never figure out why. It didn't seem like something I could ask him. He donned these clown's clothes because they got him attention.

Sid was subsequently sent to Ashford Remand Centre. To help with his rehabilitation, Vivienne gave Sid a book about Charles Manson to read.

JONH INGHAM: They remanded him on £10,000 bail, about a year's wages. I owned a house and I was separated from my wife, so without telling her, I put up the house as surety on his bail. And that changed my relationship with Sid completely. Because I'd stood up for him, that really had an effect on him. When there was no one else around and it was just the two of us, he was a very different person, and extremely thankful.

The Pistols were banned from the 100 Club, Ron Watts feeling unable to carry on staging gigs that could have his club closed down. But its part in punk's legend was already sealed. The A&R men present at the Punk Festival and at the Screen on the Green had liked what they had seen. Chris Parry at Polydor wanted to sign the Pistols but was having trouble convincing his superiors. Mike Thorne from EMI had already been at the Screen on the Green gig and pestered his senior, Nick Mobbs, to catch the Pistols on tour in Doncaster on 27 September, where Malcolm convinced him he would be saving the music industry by signing his band.

On 12 October, the Pistols signed a two-year contract to EMI Publishing for a non-returnable advance of £40,000. EMI wanted 'Pretty Vacant' as the first single, but Malcolm insisted 'Anarchy in the UK' went first – the Pistols' manifesto in a nutshell.

Both Caroline Coon and Jonh Ingham wrote positive reviews of the Punk Festival, which piqued the interest of the tabloids. Their reports were not initially hostile – even in the *Sun*. But all that was about to change.

12

THE FILTH AND THE FURY

Punk hits the headlines (April–December 1976)

Sealed with a kiss

Sometime in the spring of 1976, I started getting letters addressed to me via SEX, signed with lipstick, sealed with a kiss. Michael Collins immediately started trying to work out who the author was by looking at the lips of everyone who came in. It was excruciating, because it was in the time when there were two posts each day, and we'd be looking at the postmark, looking at the writing. He finally narrowed it down to a man called Adam who had just started coming into the shop. Then he started making really big hints about letters when Adam was standing there.

"Do you come from Wood Green?" he would ask.

MICHAEL COLLINS: I think I asked him to write something down for me to check out the writing. Adam was quite sweet. He cracked in the end. He had the hots, big time – and I had him bang to rights.

He had spent weeks and weeks and weeks writing those letters. I can see that sexual magnetism, because at a distance I was

197

his ideal, I was totally the woman of Adam's dreams. Everything he'd seen, all those lovely dominatrix books that he really liked by Eric Stanton and Allan Jones.[1] I didn't know about any of that, at the time. I hadn't modelled myself on any of those things – I just was. Wearing rubber every day was something I really did and it's a heavenly thing when you see that, I guess. Sometimes it's far more exciting to look at that from afar, almost as if I was in a book. I was hard. Which made a lot of people fancy me even more. People were afraid of me. The slave thing, you know, people saw me as being a living embodiment of what their fantasies were. Adam introduced me to all those lovely dominatrix images, the ones with the really high heels. I've still got the original badges of some of those – the one with the metal mask. But he never wanted me to do any of it in real life. All that side was very much in his imagination, rather than reality.

Adam Adamant

I was unaware that, at that point in his life, Adam had also undergone a major transformation, which had been triggered by the first Sex Pistols gig. In 1973, Stuart Goddard, as his parents named him, had begun studying Art at Hornsey Art College. He was taught by Peter Webb, author of *The Erotic Arts* and friend of Allan Jones, whose bondage-themed work would become a major influence on the Ants and whose look Adam swiftly emulated. Here he joined the rockin' revival band Bazooka Joe, fronted by fellow student Danny Kleinman. Adam played bass and, as well as learning and

---

[1] Allan Jones (b. 1937) is a British Pop artist who, like Adam, began his studies at Hornsey College of Art in London before transferring to the Royal College of Art in 1959, where he studied with David Hockney and Derek Boshier but was expelled in 1960 at the end of his first year. Despite this, his work was displayed in the Young Contemporaries exhibition in 1961 that launched British Pop art. Jones moved to New York in 1964, where he began to immerse himself in the transgressive, fetish underground that would become his hallmark. Back in the UK a few years later, he began incorporating more sculpture into his work: his fibreglass *Chair* (1969) began a series of life-sized images of women as furniture with S&M overtones that continued with *Hatstand* and *Table* in 1970. These works, referenced by Kubrick in *A Clockwork Orange* (1971), provoked huge controversy. Jones was elected as a Royal Academician in 1986.

contributing to the band's 1950s-themed material, became well versed in covers such as The Shadows' 'Apache' and 'Walk Don't Run', which he credits with saving him from the worst excesses of the Teds-versus-punks rumbles on the King's Road that in 1976 were just on the horizon.

At Hornsey, he met and married a fellow art student, Carol, in 1975, moving into her parents' house with her in Wood Green. She switched colleges to Saint Martin's, scene of that revelatory Pistols debut when they supported Bazooka Joe. This was also the first time he'd seen me. After witnessing the Pistols' twenty-minute set, Adam left Bazooka Joe, convinced he needed to pursue the anger and energy he had witnessed that night and make his own kind of music. He started a band called The B-Sides, the idea being to cover the B-sides of 1960s singles that hadn't been hits, with Lester Square (aka Tom Hardy, later of The Monochrome Set) and bassist Andy Warren. They described themselves as 'losers'.

Adam started writing his own songs, which would later become Ant singles 'Fat Fun', 'B-Side Baby', 'Fall In' and 'Puerto Rican'. But he also began to suffer from hallucinations, which had plagued him as a child. This time they were a result of the claustrophobia he felt sharing a house with Carol and his in-laws. He took an overdose, telling Carol that he couldn't go on like this any more. He was rushed to Friern Barnet hospital and, when he came round, he shed his former identity as Stuart Goddard and renamed himself Adam Ant. He left Carol's parents' house and went to live with his father Les and his stepmother Doreen in St John's Wood, in streets not far from where he had spent his childhood. Distraught at this turn of events, Carol renamed herself Eve.

The Band With No Name

In a complex series of musical shuffles, The B-Sides would eventually replace Adam with singer Bid and become The Monochrome Set. I first met some of the embryonic Ants, including drummer Dorothy Max Prior, who was then also doing part time work with Ted Polhemus and Lynn Procter at the ICA, when the Pistols played the Babalou Disco on the Finchley Road on 5 May 1976.

DOROTHY MAX PRIOR: I was in the first line-up of what would become the Ants, a sort of Band With No Name that became the Ants and The Monochrome Set. I met Andy [Warren] when he came round this house I was living in in Exhibition Road. I was just sleeping on the floor of this flat with this girl called German Monica, who was one of two singers in this band; the other one was Bid. Then this person called Stuart reappeared, who'd previously been in The B-Sides with Andy, and then mysteriously disappeared. I know now, which I didn't know at the time, that he was having a lot of medical problems. He had anorexia, which was very unusual in a teenage boy, and depression and various other things. He would disappear and Andy would say: "Oh, he had to go to hospital for something." Then he'd be gone for two months and none of us would know what was going on.

When Stuart, as he was then, suddenly reappeared, this band now had three singers, so Monica was out and I was the drummer. Andy just decided that I would be a drummer and that I would be called Max. I thought afterwards, Velvet Underground, Mo Tucker, female drummer, one syllable beginning with M – why not? Or it could possibly be the connection with *The Night Porter*,[2] 'cos Adam and Andy really loved that film, they loved Dirk Bogarde, and the main character was called Max. So, I was told I was the drummer. I'd never played drums before and I didn't own a drum kit. Never mind, who cares? So we rehearse. We had one song called 'Fat Fun, Flash Trash' and one called 'Dirk Wears White Sox' and nobody could come in on time. Normally, the easy way to come in is with the drummer going one-two on the bass drum, but I didn't have a drum kit so I picked up a tambourine and I went [mimics hitting instrument]: "Dirk wears white sox!" And that's how that song started... Stuart and Bid were about as diametrically opposed in their songwriting and their styles of singing as

---

[2] Dirk Bogarde (1921–99) has cast a long shadow over British pop culture since he appeared as the juvenile killer in Basil Dearden's *The Blue Lamp* (1950). The Italian psychological drama *The Night Porter* (Liliana Cavana, 1974) starred Dirk as a former Nazi SS officer, alongside Charlotte Rampling as a Holocaust survivor. The pair have a highly charged and ambiguous S&M relationship in a concentration camp that is viewed in flashback when they accidentally meet again in 1957 in Vienna, in a hotel where he is working as a night porter. Bogarde, who served in the British Army during the war, was present at the liberation of the Bergen-Belsen concentration camp in April 1945: "The gates were opened and then I realised I was looking at Dante's *Inferno*... Nothing could be as bad as the war or the things I saw in the war." He said the experience had left him fearless, and he never shied away from a difficult role.

it's possible to be. Everything about them together was just wrong. So Stuart disappeared again for a while and I did some rehearsing with the rest of them, now with an actual drum kit... The band still had no name.

Adam was very determined about his reinvention when he sought me out, and those letters would eventually turn into the Ants' song 'Jordan (Send a Letter To)'. He became a regular fixture at Buckingham Gate, as did Dorothy Max.

DOROTHY MAX PRIOR: I remember hearing about Linda's customers, that she had all these powerful men, and being a little bit in awe of her because there were so many people pretend doing it, but she was for real. She really *was* thrashing the arses off judges and headmasters. Plus, it was such a grown-up address, St James. So select... [Adam] asked a lot about what these people were like and I said it's like the most elegant cocktail party; everyone has respect for each other and everyone's so refined. It was an idea that Adam really took to: the thought of these City gents with their immaculate pinstriped suits and bowler hats and underneath there's a pair of rubber knickers.

COUM as you are

The general public were not so taken with the exploration of sexual taboos staged, with the help of Dorothy Max, Ted and Lynn at the ICA on 19 October, by COUM Transmissions, art activists from Hull who were about to mutate into the band Throbbing Gristle. The show was an archive of Cosey Fanni Tutti's work as a porn model, stripper and performer, with framed and dated photographs of her in her working clothes, plus a piece titled *Tampax Romana* that consisted of four boxes containing her used tampons in gradual states of decay. The show was called *Prostitution*, and the opening night on 18 December was a chaotic clash of punks, provocateurs and the press, which signalled the dark turn events were about to take. The *Daily Mail* the next day had a picture of Siouxsie, Severin and Debbi with the headline 'THESE PEOPLE ARE THE WRECKERS OF CIVILISATION'.

The *Daily Mail* wouldn't have to wait long to get even more outraged on society's behalf. Malcolm and EMI were by now putting the final touches to their advance.

Your future dream is a shopping scheme

Now they were finally equipped with a contract, the Pistols went into the studio in early October 1976 to record 'Anarchy in the UK' in Wessex Studio in Highbury, with Chris Thomas, producer of the first Roxy Music album, which had been pivotal to the band's history. Steve was delighted to be working with him and they began to perfect the 'wall of sound' guitar effect that would become their hallmark.

EMI's TV plugger Eric Hall was keen to get as much pre-release coverage as possible, and so on 12 November the band appeared on *Nationwide*, where they were described by the seemingly astonished long-haired presenter Lionel Morton (formerly of *Play School*) as "leaders of a whole new teenage cult that seems to be on the way to being as big as mods and rockers were in the sixties". Much was made of the 100 Club ban on punks and the threat of violence that followed the band around.

"You have to destroy in order to create" was Malcolm's rebuke to that.

'Anarchy in the UK' was unleashed on 26 November. Jamie Reid designed a striking front cover – a plain, shiny black bag – and, for the poster, he tore up and reassembled a Union Jack flag with safety pins. The song and these graphics perfectly echoed the state of the country, which had been at boiling point over the long, hot summer and now seemed on the verge of financial collapse, with youth unemployment at a high and Chancellor Denis Healey locked in talks with the International Monetary Fund (IMF) to try and stave off the collapse of the pound.[3]

JON SAVAGE: Between October and November 1976, that was when the whole thing hit warp speed. I saw The Clash at the Royal College of Art, which was the famous fight with Joe Strummer, Sid and Paul Simenon – that was extraordinary. Then I saw the Pistols at Notre Dame Hall, which was

---

[3] When James Callaghan took over the Labour Party from Harold Wilson in 1976, investors became convinced that the pound was over valued and a large-scale sale of sterling began. By June 1976, the pound had reached a record low against the dollar and, by September, it became clear that the government would have to ask the IMF for assistance to save sterling from collapse. Chancellor Denis Healey's request for a $3.9 billion loan was the largest ever, and in return the IMF demanded heavy budget cuts. Old Labour and the policies of post-war Britain unravelled in unison, setting the scene for Thatcher's victory.

very theatrical, very Warholian, because it was quite a small room; there was television cameras there. What interests me about The Sex Pistols and why I ended up writing a book about them was that when I saw The Clash, I got it immediately. I could understand it and I liked the fact that they were hurt boys, like The Who or The Kinks but ten years later. They were assimilable – whereas The Sex Pistols weren't. My reaction to them was a mixture of intense interest and attraction, I was riveted, but also there was something scary about them, something repulsive about them. There was a challenge and I accepted it. Punk made the time lag between thinking about something and doing it telescope. I met Poly Styrene; she and I went to see The Clash in October 1976, and within six weeks of seeing that I had started my first fanzine and she was putting X-Ray Spex together.

Two days later, the Pistols appeared on the *London Weekend Show*, presented by Janet Street-Porter, along with Sid, Siouxsie and Bertie Marshall. The programme had footage of the infamous Notre Dame Hall gig Jon mentions, which took place in a Roman Catholic church on the corner of Leicester Square on 15 November. The band performed under a fountain of gob from the audience. and Vivienne, making one of her rare gig appearances, danced on the edge of the stage.

VIVIENNE WESTWOOD: I did that to give support to them, that's why I went on-stage dancing. I knew that was going to give The Sex Pistols support and these were the greatest band ever.

Janet Street-Porter's interviews with the Pistols, Banshees and various others were more of a confrontation – and she was more than up for the task.

BERTIE MARSHALL: Sid had a tampon on his lapel as a badge and Janet Street-Porter was sitting there with her clipboard asking questions. Sid just kept acting up, interrupting her when she was trying to be professional, and she kept saying: "Shut up, shut up, you cunt!" He threw this tampon at her and she just went off. She was not scared, was Janet.

I had a moment with Janet Street-Porter myself. She wanted to do an interview with me for *Gay News*. And I reluctantly did it, but I did think that quite a lot of gay women dress in uniforms and probably gay people are the last people in the world who want a uniform. So I was quite argumentative with her. She came round to Buckingham Gate and I had a little bowl of toffees. I offered her a toffee and it was a joke toffee, a mustard toffee. But, in retrospect, she did stand her ground.

Another iconic image was recorded at this time by Ray Stevenson, in Linda's kitchen, for *Anarchy in the UK*, the music paper Malcolm made to promote the band on tour. It's the one that's always referred to as 'the Bromley Contingent', although a usurping Philip Sallon is edging Bertie out of the frame.

BERTIE MARSHALL: Siouxsie and Philip knew each other from the gay clubs, and he would know of parties, he was like a connector. He's just out there, totally, to this day. Last time I saw him he was in a full RAF uniform. The time before, he was in Safeway's on Tottenham Court Road in a pink crochet top and pedal pushers. But in terms of punk and how he's in that

Bromley Contingent photograph, that was all so annoying. We all made it really clear not to invite him when Ray Stevenson said he was going to take the shots in Linda's kitchen, and to this day we don't know how he found out about it. But he turned up and I got pushed to the edge, literally, and for years they'd crop me and him out! He did ruin that picture.

You dirty rotter

While Glitterbest was busy booking a nationwide tour with The Clash, The Damned and inviting the second incarnation of The Heartbreakers over from America to join them, Eric Hall struck again. One of EMI's biggest acts, Queen, pulled out of an appearance on Thames Television's early evening magazine programme, *Today*, presented by Bill Grundy. Hall suggested the Pistols as replacement. I was feeling poorly and couldn't join the band and friends Siouxsie, Simone, Severin and Simon Barker, but I gave Simon the Anarchy shirt Clive James liked so much to wear.

I should have known it would end badly, as I'd already had a run-in of my own with Grundy, when I appeared on his show with Duggie Fields, Andrew Logan and others from the Alternative Miss World orbit. He looked everybody up and down and said: "I don't want you in the front, or you or you or you." Then he pointed to me and said: "I want you in the front." I had those Vive Le Rock knickers on over the top of my tights and I turned round and went: "Vive Le Cock! Which is exactly what you are."

He was so rude and disrespectful.

SIMON BARKER: I was working for Malcolm at the time, with Sophie Richmond, booking the tour, and it was all very last-minute. Suddenly the PR from EMI told Thames: "Oh, there's this great band from London that everyone loves – they're called The Sex Pistols." So Malcolm said: "Get everybody, whoever you can get." It had to be people who were in London that afternoon. That was why it just happened. I don't know why you weren't there, Bertie wasn't there. Little Helen wasn't on it.

I was in hospital, but I got the shirt to him somehow. Vivienne had altered it; the original armband was taken away, she wanted to take that off and keep it. I think she took the Karl Marx badge off, as well. But, although a swastika was clearly visible, it wasn't the symbols on the shirt that anyone was going to be upset by this time.

The band and friends were taken by EMI limo to the studios, where they were offered drinks in the green room. Grundy was already in his cups and, two bottles of Blue Nun later, Steve quickly caught up with him. The exchange that followed between them when the cameras rolled would go down in legend.

PAUL COOK: You should have been there. I just remember Steve getting really pissed and me sitting there, really nervous, not knowing what to say. Then, all of a sudden, all hell broke loose. Grundy was a patronising, sneering old git. His attitude was: "Oh look at this lot..." He was drunk all the time, but he met his match with Jonesy, who was even more pissed than he was. His timing was fantastic, spot on. "You dirty fucker. What a fucking rotter." It's still brilliant now, still fantastic. But life was never the same after that.

SIMON BARKER: When you look back, there was no fuss about the swastika that was blatantly on display and going out at six in the evening. It was all about the swearing. People now would be outraged by the swastika and the swearing wouldn't be so important. But think about it: at the time, Spike Milligan used to do this joke with a traffic warden who was Adolf Hitler, Freddie Starr used to do it, and Blakey from *On the Buses* had a Hitler moustache. In Europe you're not allowed to show a swastika, they're hypersensitive about it. But I think we had a better way, because we ridiculed it, we laughed at it. We had no respect for anything. But the thing about the swearing was, that really was how Steve spoke. He really was a council-estate wide boy. The phrases he came out with could not have been scripted better. But all these things didn't suit Malcolm; that wasn't one of his plans. All the things Malcolm *did* plan were a damp squib.

Heartbreak Hotel

At the same time that all this was happening, The Heartbreakers, which now comprised Johnny Thunders, Jerry Nolan, vocalist/

What a clever boy! The Grundy transcript

GRUNDY: I'm told that the group have received £40,000 from a record company. Doesn't that seem, er, slightly opposed to their anti-materialistic way of life?

GLEN: No, the more the merrier.

GRUNDY: Really?

GLEN: Oh yeah.

GRUNDY: Well, tell me more, then.

STEVE: We've fucking spent it, ain't we?

GRUNDY: I don't know. Have you?

GLEN: Yeah. It's all gone.

GRUNDY: Really? Good Lord! Now, I want to know one thing…

GLEN: What?

GRUNDY: Are you serious or are you just making me, trying to make me laugh?

GLEN: No, it's all gone. Gone.

GRUNDY: Really?

GLEN: Yeah.

GRUNDY: No, but I mean about what you're doing.

GLEN: Oh yeah.

GRUNDY: You are serious?

GLEN: Mmmmm…

GRUNDY: Beethoven, Mozart, Bach and Brahms have all died…

JOHN: They're heroes of ours, ain't they?

GRUNDY: Really? What? What were you saying, sir?

JOHN: They're *wonderful* people.

GRUNDY: Are they?

JOHN: Oh yes. They really turn us on.

GRUNDY: But suppose they turn other people on?

JOHN: [whispered] Well, that's just their tough shit.

GRUNDY: It's what?

JOHN: Nothing. A rude word. Next question.

GRUNDY: No, no, what was the rude word?

JOHN: Shit.

GRUNDY: Was it really? Good heavens. You frighten me to death.

JOHN: Oh, all right, Siegfried…

GRUNDY: What about you girls behind?

GLEN: He's like your dad, in't he, this geezer? Or your granddad.

GRUNDY: Are you worried or are you just enjoying yourself?

SIOUXSIE: Enjoying myself.

GRUNDY: Are you?

SIOUXSIE: Yeah.

GRUNDY: Ah, that's what I thought you were doing.

SIOUXSIE: I've always wanted to meet you.

GRUNDY: Did you really?

SIOUXSIE: Yeah.

GRUNDY: We'll meet afterwards, shall we?

STEVE: You dirty sod. You dirty old man.

GRUNDY: Well, keep going chief, keep going. Go on, you've got another five seconds. Say something outrageous.

STEVE: You dirty bastard.

GRUNDY: Go on, again.

STEVE: You dirty fucker!

GRUNDY: What a clever boy!

STEVE: What a fucking rotter!

GRUNDY: Well, that's it for tonight. The other rocker, Eamonn, and I'm saying nothing else about him, will be back tomorrow. I'll be seeing you soon. [To the band] I hope I'll not be seeing you again. From me, though, good night.

It was goodnight from Grundy, too. He was sacked the next day for "a gross error of judgement".

guitarist Walter Lure and singer Billy Rath – recruited when Thunders fell out with Richard Hell earlier in the year – along with their manager, Leee Black Childers, had arrived in London. They were met in another EMI limo by a visibly shaken Malcolm, Nils and Sophie, who had just caught the first barrage of flak from the foul-mouthed fusillade on TV. The phones were ringing before they had even left the Thames studio in their limo that was to take them directly to their rehearsal rooms in Harlesden. The police arrived at Thames just as they were burning rubber in the opposite direction.

The tour had been scheduled to begin on 3 December, but, when the Pistols were splashed all over the front covers of the newspapers the next day, promoters rapidly started cancelling. This hadn't been in any of Malcolm's plans and he was in a panic when he billeted Johnny and Jerry at Buckingham Gate. They had to sleep on the floor.

SIMON BARKER: I was so excited. Malcolm said: "Can you put up a couple of The Heartbreakers?" And I was like: Please let it be Johnny Thunders and Jerry Nolan, not these other ones that I don't know. And it was Johnny Thunders and Jerry Nolan, we did get The New York Dolls.

DEREK DUNBAR: And they were so quiet, they slept all the way through it. Because the smack was ten times stronger in London than it was in New York.

Hacked off

Just after Grundy, I came back from London to find my mum saying that the *People* newspaper had been camped out in my street in Seaford, wanting the low down on Bill Grundy because I'd done that show previously. She didn't know what to say, it was really difficult for her. They wouldn't go away, so I just did an interview and told them what I thought of Bill Grundy. They printed it. In those days, TV companies would willingly get you really drunk before you went on air. That's what the green room thing was all about: let's get them drunk.

PAUL COOK: It was the same for my mum. The press turned up on our doorstep, 'cos it was such big news, nothing had happened like that since The Rolling Stones' drug bust. This was pop culture exploding again, all over the national papers. The horrible youth of the punks! But she'd make up all these stories when the press come round, she was so funny, my mum. She'd go: "Yeah, that Johnny Rotten was round here once and he's a real bastard. When I was looking for some safety pins for my old man's winkles, he'd nicked them all! He took all my safety pins and the old man couldn't get his winkles out!"

In the immediate aftermath of Grundy, EMI production workers at the pressing plant in Hayes went on strike, refusing to sleeve 'Anarchy'. Leslie Hill, who had signed the band, was in the firing line from Thames TV, who owned half his parent company, and then the hostile press were incensed by his seeming lack of contrition. His house was soon surrounded by the morality squad of the *Daily Mail.*

PAUL COOK: Then we had the press following us around, wanting us to cause a scene wherever we went. Which we did, just to get the story, any old story. You'd be in a restaurant, a hotel bar or something, and the press would be there. "Go on, Steve – throw that flower pot over there!" He'd go: "All right, here you are!" – and it would be in the paper the next day: 'PISTOLS DESTROY POT! WHOOPS! THERE GOES ANOTHER!' Anything like that, that's all they wanted. That's when it got like a cartoon. That's when it stopped being fun, really, as well. It got serious after that. Getting bashed up and smashed. Teds and punks wanting to kill each other.

The opening night of the Anarchy tour in the University of East Anglia in Norwich was cancelled by the vice-chancellor, prompting a sit-in by enraged students. The bands moved on to Derby – The Damned in their own tour bus; The Clash, Heartbreakers and Pistols in another bus together; the atmosphere fractious. When they arrived at King's Hall, they were told that the Derby Leisure Committee would only agree to the gig going ahead if all the bands auditioned to prove their respectability. The Pistols refused and the roadshow moved on without playing a note – or getting any money. Only when they reached Leeds on 6 December did the first show go ahead, preceded by an appearance on Yorkshire Television in which Malcolm was restored to his role of provocateur, replying to a question about people being sick on the stage: "Well people are sick everywhere. People are sick and tired of this country telling them what to do."

After the Leeds gig, The Damned were sacked, apparently because their road manager had said they would have played in Derby without showing solidarity to the Pistols. It came as a blow to them, but the next day's gig in Bournemouth was also pulled. 'Anarchy' had just reached no. 43 in the charts, selling between 1,500 and 2,000 copies a day, although only John Peel was still playing it at the BBC and the smaller shops who could have sold bigger quantities couldn't get enough stock. At the same time, at EMI's Annual General Meeting, the board – including Shadow Chancellor Sir Geoffrey Howe and Chairman Sir John Read – moved to terminate the group's contract, a situation that the latter discussed with his friends in the press. The *Daily Mail* dutifully reported the band's response to that: "Tell him to fuck off."

The writing was on the wall. Out of twenty-two booked gigs, the bands played a meagre seven. By the final date, on 22 December at Plymouth, 'Anarchy' was no. 27 in the charts and EMI were still fighting about the group's future.

JONH INGHAM: I was on the last night of the tour. It was depressing. There was nobody there, for a start – about ten people, if that. The Heartbreakers were a very divisive group and the Pistols were just very down. It was freezing cold and it felt like they were under attack the whole time. Back in their hotel, there was a really depressing after-party with Debbi and Tracie – they were just destroying their rooms. Meanwhile, the press were raving. I remember Phil Collins saying: "I could play better than them with one hand tied behind my back." You're missing the point, Phil. That's exactly why they're here. Yes, you can play better than them, and we're all bored of it.

There was an element of that with those established bands. I tried to have an argument with Freddie Mercury over what he had said about the Pistols in the music press. They felt very, very threatened that their whole era was over and everything they'd had all this time was going to disappear. David Bowie wouldn't have been like that; he would be like Malcolm and take something from it. But people like Freddie were desperately worried that they were suddenly looking out of date and irrelevant. He said the most scathing things about the Pistols, which is what caused me to approach him at Sombrero's. His bouncer saw me coming across the dancefloor and he took him and ran! I felt cheated. Really cheated. I was only going to take him on verbally.

Roxy music

Over in Covent Garden, something else was stirring. Vivienne's former book keeper Andy Czezowski, his partner Susan Carrington and business partner Barry Jones were nosing about an abandoned nightclub in Neal Street, on the corner of the old fruit market. After a brief dalliance as The Damned's manager, Andy had been asked by Billy Idol, Tony James, John Towe and Gene October to manage their band Chelsea. Andy agreed, on condition they got rid of Gene and made Billy the lead singer. Then, rather than go through the trouble he'd seen Malcolm going through getting gigs, he hit on the idea of opening his own punk club instead.

The small, dark, dingy room, replete with red lights and leatherette, had formerly been the amusingly named gay club Chaugerama's (say it out loud), another favourite nightspot of ours, which was about to lose its licence.

Andy initially booked the venue for two nights in December for the princely sum of £50. Providing all the staff and even the beer, he hired a PA system and put the newly rechristened Generation X on top of the bill. The Roxy was born, and for the next five months would become the agar plate that incubated the punk virus.

Retreating from cancelled Scottish dates on the Anarchy tour, The Heartbreakers were broke. Andy saw them hanging around outside the Ship in Wardour Street at a loose end and he booked them for another two nights on 15 and 16 December. Leee Black Childers, who already had plenty of friends in London, decided that when the tour was over they were staying put.[4]

---

[4] Leee Black Childers first came to London as the stage manager of Andy Warhol's only play, *Pork*, at the Roundhouse, Camden, in 1971. It featured Wayne County as Vulva Lips and Superstar Cherry Vanilla as Amanda Pork. David and Angie Bowie saw the show several times. *Pork* actor Tony Zanetta ended up working for Bowie, and Leee became the vice-president of his management company, MainMan, which was established in 1972. According to County: "if it hadn't been for Andy Warhol's *Pork* there wouldn't have been a MainMan, or for that matter a Ziggy Stardust" (see www.warholstars.org/pork-3.html).

SIMON FISHER TURNER: This is a funny thing. Christmas 1976, The Heartbreakers in England. On Christmas Day, Leee came to my mum's for Christmas lunch with, I think, Paul Cook, Steve Jones and a couple of others – and my mum just took it all on board.

Andy Czezowski made a regular deal with the club's owner to hire the Roxy, and launched it as a permanent nightspot on New Year's Eve 1976, with The Clash, who chose the midnight hour to premiere their latest song. Marco Pirroni remembers how 1977 began for him:

MARCO PIRRONI: I went to the Roxy to see The Clash on New Year's Eve 1976-7 and they did '1977' at midnight and it was brilliant. I thought: Fucking hell, this is just an absolutely amazing moment. Then halfway through the song I thought: Oh God, there's this horrible feeling of togetherness forming here. I don't want that. I'm not together with you.

13

YOUR PRETTY FACE IS GOING TO HELL

Sedition, swindles and syringes (January–March 1977)

No future

While Malcolm was busy with the Pistols, Vivienne had been just as industrious. Reinventing again, she began to create what she called 'confrontation clothing', including the Bondage trousers that Rotten had premiered in Paris; the Destroy shirt, printed with swastikas and the broken head of the Queen on long-sleeved muslin; and a jacket made out of parachute silk, hung with four straps attached to D-rings that met in the middle of the breastbone and were initially held together by a plastic Hoover ring.

These new lines were for a reinvention of the shop itself. SEX closed its doors for the last time in December 1976 and reopened in January 1977 as Seditionaries. While it was being refitted, Vivienne used all her resourcefulness to get the new lines ready. The Bondage trousers were made up for her by Mr Mintos in his Camden workshop, in black shiny cotton, although she would later reproduce them in pinstripe and tartan, inspired by a tartan miniskirt I had been wearing. The parachute silk shirts had three different elements to them: a quote from Italian anarchist José Buenaventura Durruti,[1] stencilled onto one side of the chest; a portrait of Karl Marx; or the slogan 'ONLY ANARCHISTS ARE PRETTY' written across the breast pocket. These jackets were fiendish to construct – and I know, because she made me sew them for her. The worst mistake I ever made was telling her I could sew.

My workshop was a tiny cubicle with a bare light-bulb, a sewing machine and a pile of things that needed sewing. Parachute jackets were really difficult with the buckles; you couldn't get underneath them to sew them very easily and you were putting a buckle onto something that you could hardly get a needle into. Then there were all the clips, the D-rings, and it's all French-seamed – you sew it on the right side and then you have to turn it back on itself. I had hundreds of these things, in all different colours. Just because I could sew doesn't mean that I wanted to. But she needed me to do it, because two or three of her outworkers couldn't get it done in time. She even roped Sally into the gruelling task of unpicking mohairs, which she stood for about a day before fleeing for the hills.

SALLY REID: SEX was being turned into Seditionaries, so we were in her flat and not at the shop, and she gave us all these mohair numbers to be unpicked. It was a nightmare. You could have spent an hour just doing five or six rows... I was traumatised.

I got to dread going round there so much that I turned up later and later, until the day came when there was just a note on the door saying: 'Fuck off, you're fired!' So I put underneath: 'I've fucked off'. But what she was saying was, I was sacked. So I took it up with her

---

[1] "We are not in the least afraid of ruins" is one of the quotes Vivienne favoured. José Buenaventura Durruti (1896–1936), considered a hero in the anarchist movement, played a crucial role in the run-up to the Spanish Civil War. On 24 July 1936, he led a 3,000-strong force, later known as the Durruti Column (and taken, wrongly spelled, as a band name, The Durutti Column, by Vini Reilly in 1978), across the country from Barcelona to Madrid, where he was shot dead in disputed circumstances. See https://theanarchistlibrary.org/library/joe-king-buenaventura-durruti

and she said: "You've got to understand, Jordan, that you're on my bandwagon."

You could knock somebody out by saying that, couldn't you? I'd been the spokesman for that shop for so long. I'd been the frontman when she wasn't able to speak succinctly to the press; it was me that they always came to. I wasn't going to leave. We had tea at this little teashop across the road from the shop and I refused to be sacked. "You can fuck off if you think I'm going to fuck off," I said. And she said: "Yeah, all right, I can quite see what you mean."

Now, I look back in pride on that time, when both Malcolm and Vivienne refused to say: "It can't be done." That runs through all of their lives, that great fortitude. They weren't going to take no for an answer. That showed in the designs. The buckles – where do you get those made? The buttons – where do you get those made? Well, I don't know, but we're going to find somebody.

BERTIE MARSHALL: I remember the anticipation of those clothes coming in, and getting the money together to buy the black cotton Bondage trousers and the black parachute shirt. The whole thing about how you wore them, you put them on and they were hanging off the hip, they're very low, and then you've got the zip going round and up. Then the bondage thing between your legs, so you go to take a step and you can't – so suddenly, you have to really think about what you're wearing. You have to adjust the strap so you can move your leg, tighten it, unzip it; you had to work out how to wear them. And then the shirt and I got the beautiful suede slingbacks, and those checked boots with the chisel toe. Spiderman boots. That was such a great look.

We can be heroes

It was the same with the new look of Seditionaries. All that remained from SEX was the gym bars on the wall, which had been polished and moved to the centre. On the walls were huge photographs, hung upside down, of the bombing of Dresden during the Second World War. Malcolm smashed a hole in the ceiling to add to that 'just air-raided' effect. According to Vivienne, the first person they asked to do the redesign got as far as designing the blown handkerchief on the front door before disappearing into the ether.

VIVIENNE WESTWOOD: ...there was a man called Andrew who was going to help us carry out the design of this change in the shop, this SEX change. So he did that door handle, like a blown handkerchief on the door, and I don't think he managed to do any other of the designs, 'cos he paid the people to do it and they ran off with the money. But the architect billed us the money and they split, so we didn't have any money whatsoever.

Instead, the couple turned to Ben Kelly, who would later design the Hacienda in Manchester, and David Connor, who built a table with a live rat in a cage. The front-of-house glass was milked, so you couldn't look in. Outside was a fluorescent light and a brass plaque screwed to the glass with the shop's name engraved on it.

VIVIENNE WESTWOOD: Under 'Seditionaries' I also put a sort of subtitle: 'Clothes for Heroes'. Nobody's ever thought of the idea that we were heroes and let's call ourselves heroes, and then you just got it everywhere. I've been responsible for lots of things where, if I hadn't said it, other people would never have said it.

Inside was a rugged grey industrial carpet and Futurist 1960s chairs in fluorescent orange. A label with black letters on white showed the Anarchy symbol and the legend: 'For soldiers prostitutes dykes and punks'.

ROGER K. BURTON: The whole idea of it being like an army was really appealing – to a guy, anyway. But the way they'd fucked with it completely, this army of outsiders, it was so, so inspiring. And no wonder everyone was intrigued by what was going on in there. You couldn't see in the window, could you?

MICHAEL COLLINS: I missed the fact there were no windows in Seditionaries. We used to love doing the windows. Malcolm used to really look forward to doing them, as well. Like to celebrate Guy Fawkes, I'd have bondage masks with big dildos sticking out of their mouths.

218

The flowers of romance

To go with it, I designed a radical new look for myself – the geometric, pink-and-black, Mondrian-inspired make-up took several weeks to get right and Simon Barker took some wonderful photos of me experimenting with that, like an artist with canvas. It's knowing when to stop with art, the moment when it looks right. It took a long time to work out what was right for my face and for it to be at one with me.

Bertie Marshall remembers being terrified by this new look.

BERTIE MARSHALL: I think it was to do with that you went away and came back looking completely different. I heard about it from Simon and it was by accident that I was coming out of Sombrero's and you were coming in, and the last time I'd seen you was with the beehive. And I don't think it was the finished version, either. I think it was a work in progress, which I found very disturbing. How did you do it – did you have a ruler?

No, it was just by hand – with the help of vodka and orange, probably. I didn't have a ruler, I just did it by sight. I used a good eye pencil, Christian Dior and Alexandra de Markoff for the lipstick and blusher, high-end make-up. Nothing from Woolworth's.

Out went the beehive at the same time. My new idea for my hair was that I wanted it to look like daffodils growing out of a lawn. So you have a flower spike, but around it the lawn is short, everything was cut round. Robert Lobetta did that hairstyle for me at Ricci Burns' salon on the King's Road.[2] He would take areas of my hair, twist them and make them small and then cut around, crop around them all, so they were isolated like flowers coming out of a lawn. It's just so different from taking lumps of hair and trying to make a spike, because you have isolated the spike. You've made it stand up, but the shortness around it was the base of keeping the spike up. Between us, Robert and I worked it out.

---

[2] Robert Lobetta is still working in his salon in London (see robertlobetta.com). In a recent interview with infringe.com, he looked back on my daffodil hairstyle: "We ended up with a style which now, looking back, really represented punk at that moment in time. At first I sort of hated it because it was the antithesis of everything I'd been taught about cutting hair. But it was a tremendous learning curve in understanding how punk could make you think differently. It taught me to look at hair in a different way."

For people discovering the shop for the first time in the wake of the Pistols' newfound notoriety, crossing the threshold remained a daunting experience, in many ways a trial. That's how the (then) 17-year-old Richard Cabut, who was just on the verge of a journalistic career that would see him writing as Richard North for *NME*, sees it.

RICHARD CABUT: When I went to Seditionaries for the first time, it was scary as fuck. It caused you to momentarily take a look at your inner self as well as your outer self. Before you went into the shop, you thought to yourself: Do I come from a place where I have that moral quality to go into this shop? Do I have that revolutionary spirit? I think I do. So I walked in and there was you – and you weren't very welcoming. This is part of the performance art side of it – it was more like an installation than a shop and it was valuable because it raised questions in people. Without you being there, it would not have been so important and I don't think I would be the same person I am now if I hadn't had the experience of going in there. I'm sure it was the same for other punks who went in there in those days. Also, there was often hardly anybody in there, there wasn't twenty people looking at clothes, there was just you. Jordan's looking at me and she's not looking at me, and she's on the phone and I'm trying to listen in, hear where she's going later, something's happening tonight!

When I met you years later at the 2016 British Library *Punk 1976–1978* exhibition, I said that story to you and I expected you to say: "Oh no, there was no need to worry." But you said: "Actually you are right to worry about coming into that shop, because I only wanted people in there who had that attitude."

It should have been a challenge to go in there. The verbal quizzing of why you would want to wear something leads on to one of the biggest questions I'm always asked: Why was it so expensive? But you do not give away works of art for nothing. And you have to be a genius to make those clothes. It's inverted snobbery, that kind of thing, and it means whoever asks doesn't get it. You should save up for things that are important and it will mean so much more to you if you do. You've got to understand the value of things. Buy less and make it last longer.

People came to Seditionaries from far and wide. Holly Johnson, along with the friends that would become Frankie Goes to Hollywood, made the trip from Liverpool.

HOLLY JOHNSON: I went a couple of times, with Paul Rutherford and another time with Ged Parker, trips to London from Liverpool specifically for that reason. Paul charmed money out of his mother and Ged worked hard to buy his first black glazed cotton Bondage trousers, because he loved the shape of them. He had no intention of wearing the strap, which Paul and Pete [Burns] were wearing around town. Simon Barker started questioning me and Ged about our leather clothing – he thought we might have been Scandinavian. At the time I was interested in leather and the drawings of Tom of Finland. I wore some clothes made by Walter Wright, a leatherman in Liverpool. Muir cap, trousers and a waistcoat, a leather tie, leather jacket, and so on.

Another couple of young visitors who would go on to shape 1980s pop history were already regular customers.

MICHAEL COLLINS: Boy George used to come and sit in the shop, him and Jeremy Healy, still in their school uniforms. Remember the Spiderman boots? The printing didn't come out and I had to sit there painting it on with silver paint. Boy George bought a pair when he was at school and he sat there and waited a whole afternoon while I painted this really intricate design on. George waited, him and Jeremy Healy were kissing on those big seats we had. You could fit two people on them.

George was the only person who ever got my make-up right. He turned up dressed as me at a fancy dress competition where you had to come as your hero and I was one of the judges. It was the *Jubilee* me, and he must have worked hours on it. His friend Marilyn was also quite adept at copying my *Jubilee* hairstyle. Pete Burns, on the other hand, was my biggest groupie. Anything I was wearing, the next second he'd have it on. I wasn't very nice to him, but he got on my nerves more than anyone else, ever.

Blow up

Michael and I had our biggest punch-up ever in Seditionaries. Michael started it by throwing a clothes hanger at me that hit me just above the eye. I had been asked to dance later on that night, by Derek Jarman – I was doing the Trout Dance at the Alternative Miss World he was hosting at his place on Butler's Wharf.

Vivienne turned up at the point we were smashing each other's faces in. Michael was trying to bang my head off those gym bars and I was hitting him with a shoe last. At least, I remember it being a shoe last, but he's got another version of it.

MICHAEL COLLINS: You know that big cabinet we used to have all the rubberwear in? There were three big drawers at the bottom of it and we used to keep things in that people had ordered. Somebody had phoned me about an order and I knew I'd put it away and then I found it was gone. So I asked you if you'd seen it, and you said: "I don't know, I've not dealt with it, you deal with it." You got quite shirty with me. And I thought: OK, so this is how we're going to play this one. I was really controlling; I liked everything to be a certain way and because I didn't know where this thing was, I went completely berserk. I was shouting at you, you were shouting back at me – this is in a shop full of people on a Saturday. Then it came to blows, and I just threw this hanger. I didn't even think; it was beyond thought, I was so frustrated. And that was it. You were kicking me, I had big bruises down my legs. It was like trying to pull a goat around who was kicking me with these goat hooves. Then Vivienne walked in and she just couldn't make head nor tail of it.

She told me: "Go outside, just go outside." We were like kids and she had to separate us. I started trying to argue and she was like: "No, go outside." So I had to stand outside, I didn't know what to do. And she had a talk with me and a talk with Michael. Then we made up and I went on to dance the Trout Dance with the biggest bruise ever on my face.

There was another time when I fell asleep in the shop and had all my jewels taken off me. Rings, everything, even a big sod-off wedding ring that Adam had given me – everything on my hand was missing. Someone had walked in and taken it all.

When the two sevens clash

The Pistols could have seen in 1977 at the Roxy, but Malcolm wouldn't allow it. After The Clash and The Heartbreakers played instead, a permanent Saturday night fixture was established in the Neal Street club that would be punk's real testing ground. The Damned played the first Monday of every month in lieu of their management fees and went on to build up their following there, as did newly formed bands Wire, The Adverts and Marco Pirroni, who hadn't joined either The Banshees or Sid's mooted Flowers of Romance, but instead got together his own group called The Beastly Cads. All the A&R men had to do was turn up.

The last vestiges of an accord between the Pistols, Clash and Heartbreakers ended after a meeting on 18 January. An attempt to set up an umbrella punk organisation instead led to Malcolm, Rhodes and Childers all going their separate ways.

After a lot of wrangling, on 6 January, EMI brought out a press release announcing that the company and The Sex Pistols had "mutually agreed to terminate their record contract". The deal Malcolm made meant they got to keep everything they'd so far received: the £20,000 balance of the record advance and £10,000 from EMI Publishing. He was already talking to more record companies, including A&M and Polydor, whose Chris Parry would lose out yet again, but end up signing The Banshees instead.

Enter Sid

More recriminations between Rotten and Glen Matlock led to the latter leaving the Pistols at the end of January 1977, to be replaced by Sid Vicious at John's insistence. Only, thanks to Sid's ineptitude at bass playing, Glen did actually end up staying on until 3 March to do an audition session for A&M, after which he was paid a £2,966.68 severance fee.

PAUL COOK: Sid just joined the band and wanted to be as outrageous as possible, more than anyone else. That's what fucked it up. It was John who got him in, so he had his mate in the band, and then Sid totally took over and the chaos took over. He and John fell out straight away, really. Sid thought John weren't outrageous enough, that he was the king punk rocker who should go around causing chaos. And that's not what we wanted at the time. The last thing we wanted, really.

Malcolm also wanted Sid; he could see the commercial value in him. Me and Steve were like, he looks great but he can't play the fucking bass, what's he going to bring to the table? But we were coerced into it. That was the only time that Malcolm and John connived together, to get Glen out of the band and Sid in. There was this campaign by them two to diss Glen all the time, and they was always having a go at us until, eventually, they got their way.

I think Paul Simenon should have been stolen from The Clash at that point – though a few years later, Paul and Steve would get to play with him as fictitious band The Looters in the film *Ladies and Gentlemen, The Fabulous Stains* with Ray Winstone as their lead singer.[3] At the same time as Glen was forced out, Nils Stevenson also left Glitterbest in a dispute over money, and went on to manage The Banshees, along with his brother Ray. He was replaced as the Pistols road manager by John Tiberi (aka Boogie), who had previously worked with Joe Strummer's 101ers.

JOHN TIBERI: My thing was the theatre of it all. Up until then I was working with Joe, and then Bernie. I fell out with Bernie, but it doesn't make much difference if you fall in or fall out with Bernie. It was usually both states at once. He actually is a kind of opposite to Malcolm: he will try and give you all the information, whereas I know at certain points Malcolm deliberately wanted to confuse you. They were very close but they were opposites... They connected with the politics, they connected with the theatre. I was really taken with that.

Enter the Dragon

Leee Black Childers had seen enough over the Christmas period of what was happening in London to not only tell The Heartbreakers to

---

[3] *Ladies and Gentlemen, The Fabulous Stains* (Lou Adler, 1982) also starred Diane Lane as the leader of the all-girl band of the title, who go on tour with ageing US rockers The Metal Corpses and upstart UK punks The Looters (guess who?). Paul Cook: "It was a quirky film. We thought it was a load of crap at the time but it's got a cult following since."

stick around but also call up his old friends from Andy Warhol's *Pork*, Cherry Vanilla and Wayne County, and tell them to get over from New York to London fast.[4]

Accompanying them was Miles Copeland, the son of a former CIA chief and now scouting for new musical talent to record, whose label BTM had recently folded and who was looking for a way back in to the music business. He also saw London as the land of opportunity and paid for their flights, setting up showcase gigs at the Roxy that also acted as a promotion for his brother Stewart's new band, The Police, on 2 and 3 March.

Although so sophisticated in many ways, Childers found himself slightly out of his depth in London, and accepted a deal from Track Records, founded in 1966 by The Who's managers Kit Lambert and Chris Stamp.[5] This outfit had been a leading British independent, with The Who, Jimi Hendrix, Arthur Brown and Thunderclap Newman on their books in the late 1960s. But, despite the outward appearance of riches, after The Who broke with them in 1974, Track as a business was floundering.

"I was dealing with madmen," Childers later recalled.[6]

SIMON FISHER TURNER: Track Records was in Carnaby Street; there was Chris Stamp and Kit Lambert, and Andy Newman from Thunderclap Newman. Leee signed The Heartbreakers and, at the same time, Angie Bowie, now David's ex, also put out a single and Roy Martin, an actor who was a friend of Heathcote Williams, became Angie's lover and lived in

---

[4] Wayne County (b. 1947) became Jayne County, one of the most outrageous and groundbreaking performers to come out of the New York Max's Kansas City/CBGBs scene. Born Wayne Rogers in Dallas, she moved to New York in 1968, where she became a regular at Stonewall, taking part in the historic riots of 28 June 1969. She wrote the play *World – Birth of a Nation (The Castration of Man)* in which she played both Florence Nitingale [her spelling] and her sister Ethel, alongside Cherry Vanilla as nurse Tilly Tons. In 1974 she formed Wayne County and the Backstreet Boys, playing regularly at Max's and CBGBs, where she was also a DJ. She was cast, at my insistence, in *Jubilee* (see next chapter). It is well worth seeking out her audacious memoir *Man Enough to Be a Woman* (with Rupert Smith, Serpent's Tail, 1996) for more tales of outrage. She is currently living, as Jayne Rogers, in Atlanta, Georgia.

[5] Track Records ceased business in 1978, but was revived in 1999, by former Stranglers' manager Ian Grant, who has released records by Hugh Cornwell, Big Country and Larry Parnes's former protégé, Joe Brown. Kit Lambert died in 1981.

[6] Leee Black Childers to Jon Savage, *England's Dreaming*, p. 303.

Oakley Street. Somehow, through Chris Stamp, who ran the artistic side of Track, Leee got a deal.

The Heartbreakers were given a £50,000 deal and temporary housing in Denbigh Street, Pimlico. They recorded demos for 'Let's Go', 'Chinese Rocks', 'Born to Lose' and 'All by Myself', the first mixes of which I got to hear – they were amazing. But it was kind of a disaster, that whole thing with The Heartbreakers. There was a lot of drinking and an awful lot of drugs at that time. People don't realise, they think it was just Special Brew and pogoing, with a bit of speed for a chaser.

PAUL COOK: Everyone's in charge of their own destiny, as far as drugs are concerned. Sulphate was the drug of choice with the punks: speed. I never took it before we played, that's why our songs are a bit slower than all the other punk bands.

SYLVAIN SYLVAIN: I dabbled with heroin myself, everybody in the Dolls fucked around, baby. It's just unfortunate that Johnny and Jerry liked it so much, heroin had them by the balls. Me, I'd smoke a joint and I'd cool off, and that was that. But with Johnny... The first time me and Billy Murcia turned him on to a joint, he called me up the next day and said: "Sylvain, I bought a whole pound of pot!" A whole pound! He'd never even smoked a joint before yesterday.

It's The Heartbreakers who are always blamed for bringing heroin over to the UK punk scene, but it didn't arrive from New York with them. Heedless of Lemmy's advice, I had already begun to dabble and it was because of a related problem that I was recovering in hospital when I got a surprise visit from my two favourite Heartbreakers as they were recording their Track sessions.

I was in bed with all my make-up on – I put it on every morning, even there – and in walked Johnny and Jerry, with Thai orchids, which were really rare in those days, purple and spiky, lots of blooms in each stalk. I started singing 'Pills' by the Dolls, the line about the rock'n'roll nurse. It was a very bizarre moment, as I am sure you can imagine. The nurses were already freaked out with me as it was.

226

Enter Nancy

But one thing you can perhaps blame on The Heartbreakers is Nancy Spungen. It was The New York Dolls who first brought her from Philadelphia to New York in the back of their tour van, at the end of 1974. She later said she had sex with all the Dolls except Arthur Kane on the way and, according to Sylvain: "She may well have been correct, as well."

It was Jerry Nolan who inadvertently summoned her to London, when he called his girlfriend, Phyllis Stein, in New York and asked her to come over to see him. Nancy, who was ostensibly friendly with Phyllis while stalking Jerry, went ballistic when she heard the news. She let everyone in New York know she intended to follow her over.

Death on two legs

According to the account of her mother Deborah in her book *And I Don't Want to Live This Life* (Penguin, 1996), Nancy was pretty much uncontrollable from birth. She was first taken to see a psychiatrist at the age of 3 to try and overcome her rages, and by the age of 11 she was undergoing intensive therapy. She ran away from home, in suburban Philadelphia, several times in her teens and twice tried to commit suicide. When she got in the back of the Dolls tour van at the age of 17, other than demands for money, that was the last her parents ever heard from her. Ensconced in NYC, she had brief affairs with Richard Hell and Joey Ramone, among others on the scene, using heroin as a bargaining chip for sexual favours. As Sylvain notes: "She was definitely a troubled person. I don't think she was happy to be alive."

I have this memory of her with a big photo album that she lugged around all over the place like a security blanket. There were pictures of her with bands and singers, but there were also loads of photos missing. She'd make up stories about who the people in the missing photos were. I don't think she was a bad person at all, but she was really bad news for Sid. They were star-crossed lovers.

Nancy arrived in Carnaby Street on 15 March, carrying a Fender Stratocaster Jerry had hocked in New York before leaving for London. She found Track records and Leee – horrified, he told Nancy he would let her see Jerry over his dead body. Nancy shrugged it off and found him anyway. But Jerry had a reprieve: Sid.

Nancy had a plan. Most groupies, like her, had a very clear plan – it's a job, in a way. She'd already had Jerry and Johnny in New York prior to all of this and came over here wanting John Rotten. She ended up in Buckingham Gate with Sid.

Everything seems to become clearer as the years go by. I did actually see a postcard that she sent to a friend back in New York that was left on our ironing board in that kitchen. It said: 'I've got a Sex Pistol. It wasn't John, which is what I wanted, but I've got Sid'. It was in her handwriting and she showed it to everybody.

> **PAUL COOK:** At first, Sid really wanted to be in the band and was trying hard, but that went out of the window pretty quickly when Nancy turned up. Then we had her tagging along to deal with as well. Total fucking nightmare. You got Sid, you got Nancy as well.

Not with a bang, but a Whisper(ing Bob)

Derek Green, the director of A&M Records in Britain, was very excited with the demos the Pistols recorded for him, which included Chris Thomas's production of 'No Future', retitled 'God Save the Queen'. Jamie Reid had drawn up a startling image to go on the sleeve of what both Malcolm and his new suitors wanted as their first release: the Queen with a safety pin through her nose. On 10 March, the band signed a two-year deal with A&M for a yearly advance of £75,000 to cover eighteen recorded tracks, not including publishing. It was Malcolm's idea for the ceremony to take place outside Buckingham Palace. The whole thing quickly turned into a farce.

> **PAUL COOK:** The best fight we ever had in the band was when we signed for A&M; we done that big press conference at nine in the morning at that big hotel in Piccadilly, I forget what it's called, some old dive [the Ritz].

We'd all started drinking early, Sid was on the vodka and then we went from there to A&M Records and that's when it all blew up and that's why we got the sack 'cos of what went on there. But on the way there, I had an argument with John and we started having a fight – as much as you can with four people in the back of a car. Sid had his legs up on the seat, it was so funny, his skinny little legs, and then Steve got involved and fell on Sid's legs and he couldn't move! And we ended up, no one could move, "Aw, me fucking hand!" "Aw, me legs!" We was all entangled, it was just like a fucking joke. I ended up with a cut eye, it was pathetic really. We was all drunk, four drunken blokes in the back of a limousine having a dust-up! Then we went off to A&M and got kicked off the label the next day. So that was that!

The larks went on at the record company's offices. Sid passed out in the Promotions Office, while Steve disappeared upstairs. Brought round by one of his bandmates throwing wine in his face, Sid looked down at the injuries sustained in the limo and saw that his foot was bleeding. He ran into the toilet, broke the toilet bowl and then the window in his attempts to wash off the claret. Meanwhile, in the ladies' toilet, Steve was getting familiar with a female member of staff.

Horrified, Bob Green rushed them out of the offices, but nonetheless, he sent 'God Save the Queen' to press at the end of the week, on the same day that Rotten had a date with Marlborough Street Magistrates Court for possession of amphetamine sulphate. John was fined £40 and, in the company of Sid and Jah Wobble, went straight out of the court into the pub and then on to the Speakeasy, a club on Margaret Street, Fitzrovia, that was the watering hole of choice for most of the recording industry's Establishment figures, including *Old Grey Whistle Test* host 'Whispering' Bob Harris. After some initial taunting of the 'mock rock' presenter, things started to turn ugly and Sid got pushed around. He went for Harris with his beer glass in his hand, threatening to kill him.

By the Monday morning, A&M had a letter from Harris's lawyers. At 2 p.m. on 16 March, Bob Green called Malcolm into the premises of A&M's lawyers and told him the band was dropped and the 25,000 newly pressed singles and their master tapes would be destroyed. The Pistols had earned £75,000 in just one week, but this really wasn't the result Malcolm was hoping for. With the Silver Jubilee only months away, he was desperate to release 'God Save the Queen'.

It was going to be a long, hot summer…

14

POTENTIAL H-BOMB

The Jubilee summer (April–June 1977)

You think you're a man...

As usual, it didn't take long for Malcolm and Vivienne's copyists to react to what was going on at Seditionaries. By the end of March, John Krivine's Acme Attractions had become BOY, selling T-shirts painted in dried animal blood, jewellery made out of syringes and mocked-up death pictures of Gary Gilmore, the American murderer whose execution in 1977 also inspired The Adverts' single 'Gary Gilmore's Eyes'. Their window displays, made by Peter 'Sleazy' Christopherson, of Throbbing Gristle,[1] and featuring forensic cultures and simulated burns, looked so realistic they ended up impounded by the police.

---

[1] Peter Martin Christopherson, aka Sleazy (1955–2010), was a founder member of Throbbing Gristle, along with Genesis P-Orridge, Cosey Fanni Tutti and Chris Carter. He was a commercial artist, designer and photographer who made record sleeves for Pink Floyd's design team Hipgnosis at the same time as his inflammatory BOY window displays. He once did a shoot of The Sex Pistols posing as rent boys in the YMCA toilets that even Malcolm found a little strong for his taste, shown here on p.235. He took part in a successful Throbbing Gristle reunion from 2004 to 2009. At the time of his death, he was working on the last Throbbing Gristle project, a complete reworking of Nico's 1970 *Desertshore* album. For more about his work and related bands, David Keenan's *England's Hidden Reverse* (Strange Attractor, 2015) is highly recommended.

At the same time, Beaufort Street Market, a clothes market just around the corner from Seditionaries, had become a hub for new designers, including Poly Styrene, who was on the verge of starting her own band, X-Ray Spex. Poly had also been in the audience at the Sex Pistols end-of-the-pier gig in Hastings that I went to with Sid, which took place on her nineteenth birthday. The daughter of a Somali father and an English mother, she had previously worked in the fashion industry, dropped out and followed the hippy trail, then put out one single under her birth name, Mari Elliot. Always ahead of her time, Poly was selling things that appealed to her taste for kitsch: plastic latticed handbags with plastic flowers attached to them and see-through Mary Quant shoes from the King's Road's previous Pop art era.

From the perspective of someone who was selling a lot of vintage dead stock to everyone in the area, the buzz was getting louder…

ROGER K. BURTON: I used to sell a lot to Beaufort Street Market. There was a T-shirt stall in there called Fifth Column, and a guy called Nigel Pugsley who had a little shop doing more sort of faux Seditionaries. It was an interesting time, how punk clothing started appearing everywhere. BOY saw themselves as complete rivals and they hated the fact that I could move between these worlds and go into Seditionaries and they couldn't. Although, Vivienne and Malcolm sold them some of the patterns, as they were always pleading poverty. BOY bought the screens for a lot of their T-shirts and sold them cheaper than the originals.

JON SAVAGE: Everything about punk had to be new. And one of the very interesting things in terms of things being new was the very different way in which women asserted themselves. It was a fantastic time for women to explode and do things that they'd never done before, like you did, and obviously Poly Styrene, Siouxsie, The Slits, Gaye Advert, Pauline Murray. That was so important. Gay politics was way, way behind feminism. I was very interested in gender politics in general, and the way it would be expressed would be more in supporting women than dealing with gay topics, because the gay stuff was still quite underground, especially in the music business. It was possible for women to make great strides in that time, but not for gays. The gay explosion came half a decade later.

234

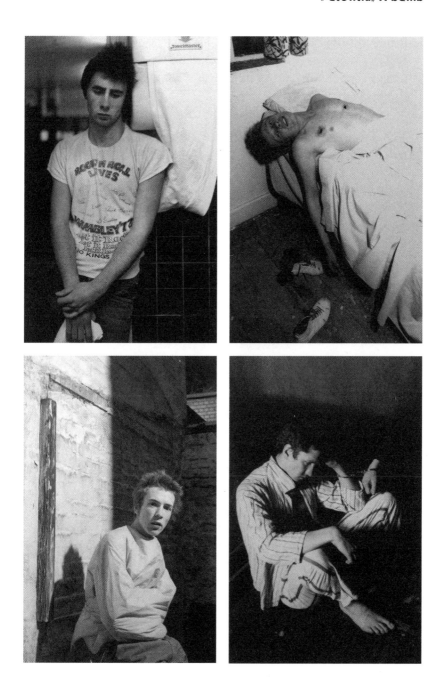

HOLLY JOHNSON: But it created a scene across the country where anything was possible. Overnight people on the street stopped calling me a queer and shouted "punk" at me instead. Which was an interesting shift in perception.

One of the most beautiful photo sessions I did at that time was with Simon Barker, in the middle of a building site. We didn't want to do it, because of the location and the fact that we had to get changed into about four different outfits out there. The photographer had that tabloid sense about him; we both hated him and were on the verge of walking off. It was a really cold day and he wanted this image to fit the story he was concocting. He kept asking us: "Spit, can you spit?" Luckily we had all those clothes from Seditionaries to wear; otherwise, he would probably have asked us to wear a bin bag – which would have been more than rubbish.

Honeymoon in red

That young couple in love, Sid and Nancy, had moved into Buckingham Gate, where they lived in a pile of clothes on a mattress under the kitchen table, ensuring that a lively time was never far away. To try and fund their habits, Nancy got work as an escort. I found out about her success rate at this when there came a battering on the door one night and I opened it to find Nancy with one shoe on and one shoe in her hand with the heel broken off.

She banged the door behind her, she was really puffed out and her tights were all ripped. I asked her what had happened and she went: "Fuuuuck, I can't believe it, I fuuckin' sat all night in this place and made no money and then I had to run off from the taxi…"

So she was working in this escort place where you sat in the window and nobody picked her. Nobody fancied her, only Sid. Funny that. So she'd had no money to pay the taxi, she'd had to run away from it, and what really annoyed her was she'd broken her shoe in the process; she was down on the price of a pair of shoes for the evening. And at that moment, I did feel a tad sorry for her. I thought: Nobody's picked her. Can you imagine sitting there and everyone else is being taken away and you're left sitting there on your own, the last turkey at Christmas?

What was her allure for Sid? He was enormously sexually naive. He once asked me to have a relationship with him, and I said: "Oh stop mucking about, you stupid bloke." Years later, I wondered: Oh God, if he'd had somebody that could have maybe fulfilled that side for him... But could it, or was he too damaged to start with, having a junkie for a mother who moved him around from pillar to post for all his young life? Nancy thrust herself at him but, whatever you may say, he did love her. He thought she was great.

You never have a normal relationship on heroin, of course – you never can. Because nothing is clear, everything is shrouded and clouded. Half your life on heroin will be sleeping; it stifles people's imagination. It's a poor drug in all ways. It doesn't make you get up and do anything. Even if people are over stimulated by some drugs, at least some of them make you a bit more productive. But I think heroin takes all your energy away.

The other thing that Nancy brought to the flat was her own sea life centre. Bertie Marshall says he got crabs just from sleeping on the floor next to her.

BERTIE MARSHALL: It was down to: "The only place you can sleep is *there*." Next to where she lay, under a big pile of coats, passed out. She was so toxic that she was someone I started to blank out on, even though I caught crabs off her. It was her constant whining and neediness and hysteria. And being terrified of the idea that Sid... would come back and think I was *sharing* the bed in the kitchen with her. Sid was the most dangerous person, that's what he felt like to me. He seemed different towards Siouxsie and Linda and you – he seemed to have a different way with women. I think he was homophobic.

Banned from the Roxy

The Roxy came to a premature end on the night of 23 April 1977. There was another problem with the lease, probably because the club was now doing so well that its owners thought they could sell it to someone with more money than Andy Czezowski. Andy was not even allowed entrance to his own place for the final gig, headlined by The Banshees, now comprising Siouxsie, Severin, drummer Kenny Morris and guitarist Pete Fenton.

But as he stood on the pavement outside, Andy was approached by Adam, who asked if he'd be interested in managing his band. Andy said maybe. Adam – who didn't actually have a permanent line-up at the time – quickly put one together: himself singing, Lester Square (who he renamed Thomas da Vinci) on guitar, Andy Warren on bass and Paul Flanagan on drums. They premiered their skills at Eve's room in her parents' house, an event that was also witnessed by Poly Styrene, who had by now assembled X-Ray Spex with 16-year-old saxophonist Lora Logic, and her manager Falcon Stuart, who was also interested in looking after Adam in a managerial role.

Adam showcased for Andy Czezowski at Scarf Studios on 6 May, then for Falcon Stuart at Alaska Studios on 7 May. Neither went very well and, two days after the latter, Lester Square quit. Adam quickly recruited Mark 'The Kid' Ryan (real name Mark Gaumont) to play guitar. They had to work fast, because Adam had wangled a gig at the café in the ICA theatre only three days later, claiming to be a folk band.

DOROTHY MAX PRIOR: Andy and I go down the Roxy and Stuart [Adam] has turned up in a leather jacket, so he's back on the scene but he doesn't come back into rehearsals with us. What he does instead is to regale me with the idea of this band he wants to form, and he already knows what he wants to call it, The Ants, and he wants to call himself Adam and have all the little girls screaming for him. And I'm like: "Yeah, yeah. I don't think so." Because, to me, he was a self-effacing boy in a lumberjack shirt and a pair of glasses. He was working on Andy, trying to get him to leave Bid and form this new venture, and then he was working on me to work on Andy, and by this time Andy and I were living together in Exhibition Road. The Band With No Name now decided to call itself The Shades and we booked a gig. I was still sort of working at the ICA, enough to persuade the café manager to let us play. Although he did say: "It's very quiet here, we only want singer-songwriter sort of stuff." And I said: "Oh yeah, yeah, of course, we're very quiet."

In the meantime, Stuart, who's now called Adam, has really been working on me and Andy, and eventually Andy and I have a talk and he'd really enjoyed being in The B-Sides, and he didn't know what to do because he'd been at school with Bid – they'd been really close and all the rest of it. But he did eventually say: "I think I need to do this with Adam." So, in the end, it wasn't me and Bid that played that gig, it was Adam and Andy, because they had already rehearsed, they were ready to go, and the rest is history.

On 10 May the Ants went onstage at the ICA café with Adam in his Cambridge Rapist T-shirt, leather trousers, mask and make-up. They played two songs, then launched into 'Beat My Guest' before the manager ran over with his hands over his ears, ordering them to stop.

DOROTHY MAX PRIOR: The café manager was absolutely furious; there was Adam in a gimp mask lying on the floor going: "Beat me! Beat me!" in front of all these people eating their salads and drinking their cappuccinos.

The next night they were booked to support X-Ray Spex at the Man in the Moon pub on the King's Road, which went well enough to earn them a repeat booking the week after. But neither Falcon nor Andy would commit to the manager's role. So Adam had a better idea: he asked me.

MARCO PIRRONI: I came into Seditionaries one Saturday afternoon and you said: "Hello, this is Adam Ant." I started talking to him and he kept going on and on about his band, as he would do. After about five minutes, you think: Yeah, great, that's brilliant. But after six minutes, you think: OK, can you shut up now? After about ten minutes, you think: Look, I really don't give a FUCK about your band! Can you shut up now?

The man in the leather mask

The first time I ever saw Adam play was at the Man in the Moon on 25 May, supporting The Banshees. He opened the gig with his fantasy-made-flesh 'Jordan (Send a Letter To)' wearing a black leather mask with a zip mouth and leather pants over black leather trousers, an idea he said was inspired by The Slits wearing their knickers over their strides. They played this song three times in a row, during which time everything that could go wrong did go wrong, all the equipment failed and, apart from that, the very small audience were shit-scared of him. They just kept moving further and further back, away from the stage. By the end of their set, there was only me, The Banshees and Marco left in the room.

MARCO PIRRONI: I came down to meet you and we walked all the way round to the Man in the Moon, which was like 75 feet away from the shop. It's very hard to explain what I thought, because I thought they were fucking awful, but also thought they were having a bad time. I knew there was something there. [Adam] went so insane, you couldn't understand what was going on. There was no reason to go that insane, because you're not getting across anything but insanity. There's nothing else to focus on.

How good is that – you've got hardly any audience in a really small pub and yet you still want to go for it? It's like an athlete who is last by about ten minutes in a marathon. It takes a lot to carry on. That night I thought: God, he's giving it absolutely everything. So I turned round and said yes to Adam's offer.

ADAM ANT: Jordan created punk rock – she was literally selling it on the front line, she was living it on public transport when other people were just dressing up. There is fashion and there is style, and she is the epitome of style. It was an extremely auspicious start to have somebody looking that good managing us.[2]

---

[2] From Katie Baron, *Music + Fashion: Creatives Shaping Pop Culture* (Laurence King, 2016).

240

Wide-screen thinking

While I was taking my first steps as a manager, Malcolm was wrapping up his quest to get the Pistols signed and 'God Save the Queen' out by Jubilee week. He needed to find a venue for another gig to lure back the A&R men, but the only place that would oblige was the Notre Dame Hall, on the condition that the audience was limited to fifty people. This was to be Sid's onstage debut, and he certainly succeeded in bringing the chaos with him – hundreds of people milled around outside the venue in Leicester Square and it took all Sophie Richmond's diplomacy to wrangle the priests who ran the hall into finally letting 150 of those hopeful punters in.

Although the band had by now received £125,000 in six months, they were all still on salaries of £40 a week. But Malcolm's ambitions were expanding fast. His latest wheeze was to make a film that would document the band and their exploits to full, shocking effect. Julien Temple was asked to combine concert footage he had shot into a short documentary that also featured video and news montages of the sackings from EMI and A&M and scenes from the Grundy programme that Temple reshot from video. Titled *Number 1*, the resulting twenty-five-minute short told the story of these outrages from the group's point of view.[3] Pleased with the results, Malcolm and John Rotten went to visit Peter Cook to ask him if he would be interested in writing a screenplay for a possible feature film.[4] Malcolm also put Gerry Goldstein on a salary to develop the idea with his own film contacts, and had John Tiberi phoning round potential backers.

However, more pressing concerns pushed this onto the back-burner: all the major labels had turned their backs on The Sex

[3] Julien Temple (b. 1952) first developed an interest in film as a student at King's College Cambridge, where he discovered the work of French anarchist director Jean Vigo. He went on to the National Film and Television School, where he encountered another manifestation of anarchy in the form of the Pistols, and his interest in documenting punk led him swiftly to Malcolm's door. Much of his significant output as a director has been entwined with what began with *Number 1*.

[4] Peter Cook dropped out of writing a script for Malcolm's film, to be replaced by Python Graham Chapman and Johnny 'Alf Garnett' Speight. Their screenplay was rejected by Malcolm as being "too documentary".

241

Pistols. Even when Larry Parnes stepped forward with an offer to set up a label purely to accommodate them, Malcolm wasn't interested in his hero's patronage – what he wanted was a huge advance. Roger Austin was called upon once more to host another showcase at the Screen on the Green on 3 April. The group were supported by the rough cut of *Number 1* and the third live appearance of The Slits, the band formed by Viv Albertine and Palmolive with former Castrators singer Ari Up (Ariane Forster) and bassist Tessa Pollitt.

> **MARCO PIRRONI:** That was the first time I'd ever heard 'God Save the Queen', which at the time I thought sounded exactly like 'Cum on Feel the Noize'. Which to me is a compliment. Now I can see it's one of the greatest singles ever made – in fact, perhaps *the* greatest single ever made.

Exit the dragon

The next day, The Sex Pistols were turned down by five record companies and Sid was in hospital with hepatitis. That was the end of Sid and Nancy's stay at Buckingham Gate. They had already been bringing far too much trouble to Linda's door, including a police raid.

> **SIMON BARKER:** That was the last straw with Nancy, the heroin. It was obviously her that brought the police there. Although she was fearless, I was quite scared, there were quite a lot of burly policemen, and Nancy was so New York. "You got a warrant?" Stuff like that, and when they called us poofs, she was right in their faces saying: "You've got no right to say that!" She was on heroin, obviously.

She wanted to keep them away from that pile of clothes in the kitchen where the heroin was. But they didn't go anywhere near it. It had a biohazard warning on it.

There was also an incident where Sid attacked Adam, who was kipping on the mattress in the kitchen, after doing some painting and decorating for Linda. It was because Adam had offered to help him with his bass playing, which went into Sid's brain and came back out

Mr Parnes, Shillings and Pence

Malcolm's hero Larry Parnes (1929–89) was the first major British rock manager, who built up a stable of young, good-looking boys that he mostly scouted from the legendary 2i's coffee bar in Old Compton Street, with the help of a young art student called Lionel Bart, who was very much tuned in to the nascent British Beat boom of the late 1950s/early 1960s. Like Malcolm – and so many other managers who have shaped the course of UK pop history – Larry was Jewish, born to a middle-class family in Willesden, west London, and, like his northern counterpart Brian Epstein, he was also clandestinely gay.

Originally he was destined to go into his family firm – in Larry's case, selling furniture. But in 1956, the year that Elvis Presley had his first hit with 'Heartbreak Hotel', destiny led Larry to the 2i's, where Tommy Hicks was performing. Larry reinvented him as Tommy Steele, Lionel wrote some tunes and a star was born. Bart's next suggestions were Reg Patterson (formerly Smith), who was promptly rechristened Marty Wilde, and the Liverpudlian who actually could rival his rocking American counterparts, Ron Wycherly, who became the sublime Billy Fury. There was also Dickie Pride (Richard Knellar), Duffy Power (Ray Howard) and Georgie Fame (Clive Powell). Only Joe Brown refused to play this game, sensibly opting not to become Elmer Twitch. *Panorama* labelled Larry 'the beat Svengali'; the press called him Mr Parnes, Shillings and Pence. Peter Sellers satirised him as Major Rafe Ralph on the 1959 album *Songs for Swingin' Sellers*, and Laurence Harvey plays a character clearly based on him in the classic Beatsploitation Cliff Richard flick *Expresso Bongo* (1959).

Larry moved into West End theatre, buying the lease to the Cambridge Theatre in 1972, where he staged, among other things, Peter Cook and Dudley Moore's *Behind the Fridge* and Joan Collins's *The Last of Mrs Cheyney*. He retired in 1981 and died from meningitis in his South Kensington penthouse in 1989, aged 59.

Jonh Ingham notes: "Andrew Loog Oldham was also really captivated by all that… You've got to find a group, so he finds the Stones and sets about making them media-savvy… and then you've got a band who's evil and horrible and 'Would you let your daughter go out with a Rolling Stone?' Malcolm updated that template with the Pistols. Before the Anarchy tour, he told me the whole idea was looking at the Larry Parnes package tour… He was almost talking about an alternative, parallel music business in a way, with all these new groups. Then, of course, the second Grundy happened, that all fell to pieces."

again as: "He thinks I'm a shit bass player, so I'm going to get him."
It was all totally skewed.

The worst thing was that Sid came into that room and Adam didn't
have any clothes on – you can't really defend yourself when you're
naked, it's awful. Sid had gone terribly out of control. He used to
turn up at three or four in the morning, banging on the door. He was
uncontrollable – you couldn't do anything with him.

Held to Branson

There was one person who really did want to sign the Pistols: young
entrepreneur Richard Branson, whose Virgin record company and
shops had a massive cash injection following the success of his initial
signing, Mike Oldfield's *Tubular Bells* in 1973. Malcolm was very
wary of this bearded hippy-on-the-make but, unlike him, Branson
had nothing to lose by pursuing the Pistols. He had a vision of the
moment; and, anyway, time was running out for Malcolm's Jubilee
masterplan.

> **JOHN TIBERI:** Malcolm hated Branson. He got right up his nose, because
> Branson was too involved in it; he had to own the film... I'm not really
> privy to all the ins and outs of it, but giving him the money for the
> film wasn't straightforward. Somebody had to blink first, and Branson
> recognised that and played Malcolm on that. Malcolm tried to get the film
> financed directly, rather than using the band's money, which was the way
> it kind of ended up. Branson recognised the vulnerability Malcolm was in.
> Because he was up against the Jubilee opportunity and Branson kind of
> got the better of him, really.

With no other option, on 12 May the Pistols signed to Virgin for
an initial £15,000, to cover the cost of recording an album, and a
further £50,000, paid a month later, for rights to release the record
in all world territories. Sid couldn't sign until 16 May, when he came
out of hospital. There would be no extravagant ceremony this time;
Malcolm and his new benefactor had a better idea in mind.

'God Save the Queen' came out on 27 May, so it stood a chance
of getting into the charts for the forthcoming Jubilee celebrations.

244

The response of the Establishment was phenomenal – the BBC refused to play it, although John Peel defied this dictate and played it twice; Woolworths, Boots and W. H. Smith refused to stock it – but it sold 150,000 copies in five days, enough to get to number eleven in its first week of release. In the end, it was only kept off the number one spot by what many see as an industry conspiracy to protect the dignity of Her Majesty and the ears of her subjects.[5]

Cruising down the river

That was the last thing Malcolm and Virgin had in mind when they cooked up a scheme to have a boat party on the Thames on 7 June, two days before the Queen was due to make her own voyage up the river through the capital, and on the day decreed to hold the National Tea Party. Virgin's John Varnon even managed to hire a boat called *Queen Elizabeth*. At 7.30 p.m. on Jubilee night, it set sail for infamy.

> **PAUL COOK:** Another one of Malcolm's great ideas – let's go down in the boat and let's play 'Anarchy' outside the Houses of Parliament, brilliant. It doesn't get much better than that. Apparently you're not allowed to do that on the River Thames – but no, you *are* actually, it's just because it was us, they knew the Pistols was on the boat and that was it, the police turned up.

The omens were poor. Malcolm started the boat party too early and John was really pissed off, he was ready to walk. I had to spend about two hours talking to him to get him to come on board. Richard Branson nearly missed the boat completely. John and I were looking over the side and we saw him running up the quay in a dreadful pair of suede Earth shoes that looked a bit like desert boots and a knitted jumper. He'd just signed this band, and he was late for his own party,

---

[5] In order to prevent the single from going to the top of the official British Market Research Bureau (BMRB) chart, for one week compilers decreed that "shops which sold their own records could not have those records represented in the charts", thus preventing sales from Branson's Virgin record stores from being counted. Only the *NME* showed the single in the number one position; its name was blanked out from some representations of the charts and Radio 1 DJs refused to mention its title.

running down the gangplank like a loon. John and I were standing on either side by the railings of this boat, looking at each other. And John went: "Let's bang his knuckles."

We tried to knock his hands off the railings when he had to leap for the boat. He was just a couple of feet away and he had to jump. But then we realised – if he had gone into the water, there would have been no one to put the record out. So we relented and helped him onto the *Queen Elizabeth* instead.

> **JON SAVAGE:** I've never been on a boat party since. I remember feeling trapped on this boat and really hating it: you couldn't get off, it was very claustrophobic and the weather was terrible. There were too many people on there and there was a lot of faffing about. A load of speed being lined up in the bar.

By about 9.30 p.m., the Pistols got onto the top deck of the boat. A banner had been unfurled along the side reading: 'QUEEN ELIZABETH, THE NEW SINGLE BY THE SEX PISTOLS "GOD SAVE THE QUEEN"'. They started playing in a hail of feedback; they sounded very raw. The sound was shit, Sid couldn't play, the ceiling was low, so if you wanted to jump you'd knock yourself out. But as we drew up alongside the Houses of Parliament, they launched into their new single.

> **JON SAVAGE:** They did do 'Anarchy in the UK' outside the Houses of Westminster, which was fantastic. That justifies everything.

They played 'No Feelings' and then 'Pretty Vacant' – at which point, two police launches came speeding into view and began to circle the boat. The Pistols responded with 'No Fun' and then everything kicked off.

> **PAUL COOK:** There was some mad people on that boat, there really were. We invited all our mates from round White City and John invited all his lot from north London and they nearly had a fight between them. John was there with all his brothers, who were just trouble as well. They were

eyeing us lot up, but that didn't happen, because they all teamed up and had a go at the police in the end.

Once the police had got onto the boat, they turned the electricity off, so the only person who could carry on playing was Paul. I was sitting on a table just to the left of him, banging the top of it. It went from me to Paul, me to Paul, this little protest, and we stayed there while everyone else was hauled down the gangplank and into the waiting meat wagons – Malcolm, Vivienne and Branson first.

PAUL COOK: I remember the policeman with his hand on my shoulder, saying: "Come on, son." It just shows you how chaotic things were at the time. Too many people on the boat, the police went up beside us on their speedboat: "Pull over, get off the boat now, disembark!" And everyone – Wobble's there and all John's mad mates and all our crew and everything – all pelting the police with bottles, cans of lager and everything. Everyone was off their nut on speed. Eventually, we pulled over and Malcolm got arrested, got himself arrested on purpose, of course, for maximum publicity at the end of the day. We all disappeared like rats off a sinking ship, I tell you, we were. We shot down the backstreets.

ALAN JONES: It was clearly a disaster. As much as it was fun to be there, when we got taken off and everyone was being beaten up... I can still visualise that as if it was yesterday. I can see Vivienne on the floor being kicked by the police, I can see Nils – I can see all of it.

MICHAEL COLLINS: The main thing I remember is trying to get there on time, because I was already out of it, getting on, getting more out of it, and then getting off it and trying to get away from the police. I remember seeing Vivienne leap on someone like a fruit bat; someone was trying to nick Malcolm and she leaped on the policeman's back. I went to the Sombrero. Then I went to work the next day, late. Malcolm and Vivienne were in the nick overnight. I just carried on as normal, did the usual thing. What most people would see as a major crisis, I just saw as business as usual.

I tried to get arrested. I spat in a policeman's face, thinking: That'll do it. But I reckon, by that time, because I stayed back with Paul for so long, by the time I'd gone down the ramp they'd all been arrested and the van was full. I didn't know what to do when I came off the boat. Roger Austin was there and he'd had a bang to his head, and an egg had come up. He said: "Come with me, I'll make sure you're all right." And we walked into the night. But it was very disturbing, it really was. We were in shock, just wandering the streets.

JON SAVAGE: We went to Bow Street, to try and get people out. I went with Tony Parsons and Peter York to Bow Street and then we went to have a drink in Covent Garden and it was really fucking heavy. Because we all looked a bit punky and the looks we got… You're going to pay for this now. You're going to pay for being different.

PETER YORK: At the end, when people were being hauled away, everyone was terribly serious, as if we were living in an oppressive, totalitarian state, that the police had taken these people, hauled them away for playing too loud on a marine vehicle or something – I don't know what the exact charge was – and then, because Vivienne put up a fight, they pulled her out and arrested her. I went with a group of people that included Jon Savage to a pub in lower Covent Garden, when they still had working-class pubs there, and we were convinced that everybody would know we were on the boat and would want to kill us and eat us. And Richard Branson was aboard, which is a good reason to arrest everyone.

While Roger and I were wandering the streets in a state of shock, Dorothy Max and Andy were waiting at the Screen on the Green for the after-party that never was, which the Ants were supposed to be playing. Adam had come with me on the boat, but I must have lost him in the melee.

DOROTHY MAX PRIOR: We didn't know what to do, either. The Ants were supposed to be playing. Everyone was supposed to get off the boat, go to the Screen on the Green and watch the Ants. But Adam was with you, the rest of the band were setting up the equipment, doing the soundcheck and then just waiting… and waiting… and waiting. There were no mobile phones or anything. We just had no idea where you were. Everything just fell apart.

'PUNISH THE PUNKS' ran the *Sunday Mirror* headline the next day – and the public took it upon themselves to do just that.

15

RULE BRITANNIA

The making of Derek Jarman's **Jubilee**
(February 1977–February 1978)

A director calls

While the madness of the summer of 1977 was going on, I was working on the film *Jubilee* with Derek Jarman, who had been just as inspired by the recent turn of history as Malcolm. Derek had been working on his *The Angelic Conversion of John Dee* screenplay, and instead of Doctor Dee and the Angel Ariel showing Elizabeth I the secrets of the universe, he decided that he should instead move them forward in time to the reign of Elizabeth II in her Silver Jubilee year.

Derek first asked me to help him make a Super-8 documentary about the punk scene after the Andrew Logan Valentine's Ball. I took him with me to the Roxy, and to other gigs and nightclubs, where he met a lot of people he brought into the making of *Jubilee*. Derek immersed himself in all the punk fanzines I could get him, as well as the materials that were being pored over and repackaged at 430 King's Road: Valerie Solanas's *SCUM Manifesto*, Erich Fromm's *The Fear of Freedom* and William S. Burroughs' *The Wild Boys* all chimed with Derek's ideas.

DEREK JARMAN: As far as I was concerned, Jordan was the original. Everyone else in the fashion side follows on from Jordan, even

251

> Vivienne and the shop, because without Jordan the shop wouldn't have worked. She was the original Sex Pistol. Everyone else came in and saw Jordan dressed up, and the attitude, and it took off from there. She was the Godfather, the Godmother, if you like... She was the purest example of all.[1]

But when he came back to the shop one day and told me it was now going to be a scripted feature film, I was slightly taken aback.

"Will you act in it?" he asked. He had a part he had specially written for me.

I thought about it for a minute, then said: "Why not?" and just went into it from that moment on. Derek had an approach to filmmaking that I imagine was completely different from most directors. Rather than coaching you, he wanted people who would bring something of themselves into the project – and with me it was my background in ballet, as well as my immersion in punk, that he wanted to bring to the fore.

> **ALAN JONES:** I remember us going on the Tube on the day you got signed for *Jubilee*. The whole rest of the Tube was completely silent; there was just me and you talking about how you were going to be in this movie. I'll never forget looking around and realising everyone was just staring at us and listening to every word we were saying.

Written in blood

Derek had backers, in the form of Howard Marlin and James Whalley, who ran their company Megalovision from a wonderful old Georgian house in Campden Hill Square, Holland Park. Like the shop, this place brought together all sorts of like-minded people and lifelong bonds were forged there during that summer. There were people from very different walks of life. Lots of older male patrons of Derek who chipped in whenever he ran out of money.

---

[1] Derek Jarman quote reproduced by kind permission of Jon Savage.

Unusual people who were right out of the mainstream, but still wanted to contribute.

At the same time that the Ants were taking shape, Adam had been reading about tribal customs and how cutting was a rite of passage for a young warrior. He asked me to carve the word 'FUCK' into his back with a razor blade. It was very spontaneous and he nearly fainted when I'd finished and he got up too quickly. I washed his back and put an old T-shirt over it to soak up the blood. Feeling better, Adam took a walk around the King's Road. He had only gone a few hundred yards when a man ran up to him. "He had short-cropped black hair, piercing eyes and a cut-glass upper-class accent," he later recalled.[2] It was Derek. He thought the word on Adam's back was a tattoo, he hadn't realised it had actually been cut into his skin by me. Inspired, he would later recreate the ritual cutting in a scene in *Jubilee*.

The 'Historian of the Void'

The production was centred at Butler's Wharf and all the principal filming went on in June 1977 around Southwark, Rotherhithe, Victoria Docks and Deptford. Although property developers were already starting to move in – Derek's previous studio, opposite St Paul's, was an early casualty – the footage captures a desolate, run-down capital in the throes of economic breakdown, a place which is now completely lost to us. Derek created a parallel universe, in which a gang of girls wreak havoc across this desolate landscape. One of the first acts of their 'Queen' Bod (short for 'Boudicca', after the ancient British queen of the Iceni, who led an uprising against the invading Romans) is to kill Elizabeth II and steal her crown.

Bod (Jenny Runacre, who also plays Elizabeth I) has five members in her gang. The part that Derek created for me was Amyl Nitrate, in my Mondrian make-up and with a pink twinset and pearls, the 'Historian of the Void'. Little Nell is Crabs, a nymphomaniac; Toyah Willcox is Mad (short for 'Madimi', one of the angels with whom Dr

---

[2] Adam Ant, *Stand & Deliver* (Sidgwick & Jackson, 2006), p. 89. Adam also states that the idea for the cutting came to him after reading *People of Kau* by Leni Riefenstahl, although I remember it being more my idea.

Dee claimed to converse), a pyromaniac; Linda Spurrier is Viv, an artist; and Hermine Demoriane, a friend from Andrew Logan's circle who had crowned Jarman as Alternative Miss World the year before, is Chaos, their mute au pair.

Attached to this group are twin gay brothers, Sphinx (Ian Charleson) and Angel (Karl Johnson), who will end up the dead victims of police brutality. Adam was cast as Kid, a hopeful young musician and, on my recommendation, after seeing The Electric Chairs playing Dingwalls, Wayne County was asked on board to do a star turn as demented transvestite pop star Lounge Lizard. Chelsea's Gene October plays Happy Days, who ends up getting murdered by the insatiable Crabs.

The sinister impresario Borgia Ginz, owner of the world's media, was portrayed by the incredible, blind Jack Birkett;[3] *Rocky Horror Show* creator Richard O'Brien was a shoe-in for Dr Dee; Little Helen Wellington-Lloyd played Elizabeth II's lady-in-waiting and David Haughton, another of Lindsay Kemp's troupe, became Ariel.

'Plastic Surgery' disasters

Derek wanted to record a lot of bands playing live and, of course, the Ants were given a role. Unfortunately for him, Paul Flanagan got bored of the waiting around involved in filming and failed to turn up for their first big scene, playing 'Plastic Surgery'. Kenny Morris stood in for him. As well as playing drums for The Banshees, he was also helping out his friend, film student John Maybury,[4] with

---

[3] Jack Birkett (1934–2010) came from a working-class family in Leeds; his mother was Romany. Like me, he had an early passion for ballet, and trained hard, earning the money for classes by posing as a life model at Bradford College of Art, where he was sketched by both David Hockney and Lindsay Kemp. He moved to London in the 1950s and worked as a dancer and singer in such productions as *Oklahoma!* and *Bye Bye Birdie*. He began to lose his sight at the age of 32, but refused to give up performing, mentally charting all the stage areas he worked in. He was so convincing that, on the set of *Jubilee*, a lot of people didn't realise he couldn't see and that Kevin Luciano was holding his arm for most of the film. He went on to star in more of Derek's films, as Caliban in *The Tempest* (1979), the Pope in *Caravaggio* (1986) and Pontius in *The Garden* (1990). He died in London at the age of 75.

[4] John Maybury (b. 1958) went on to direct iconic pop promos, including Sinéad O'Connor's 'Nothing Compares 2 U' and The Pet Shop Boys' 'West End Girls', before making his first debut feature, the haunting and visually stunning Francis Bacon biopic *Love is the Devil* (1988), with Derek Jacobi as Bacon and Daniel Craig as his ill-fated lover, George Dyer.

some of the punk costumes and the interior to Bod's Southwark HQ, as assistants to set and costume designer Christopher Hobbs – Derek had met them previously at a Banshees gig at the Roxy. Mark Ryan called his friend Dave Barbe, the drummer for Desolation Angels, who had supported the Ants at Hornsey Art College on 2 June.

DAVE BARBE: I remember it being The Kid, Mark Ryan, ringing me and saying: "You know I'm in that punk band, the Ants? Well the drummer can't make it, can you deputise? We're playing in Chelmsford supporting The Slits." To which I replied: "OK", having no idea who Adam was or anything. I'd only ever seen punk rock on telly. Then suddenly there was a knock on my door and there was Adam, Mark and Andy. I got my drums out and we set up and Adam just said to me: "Keep up!" and that was it. Then after the show he said: "Fucking hell, you're good mate! Do you want to be our drummer?" And that was it.

You and Adam were very kind and welcoming to me, as an outsider. I wasn't a punk rocker at all. Adam really thought the world of me. I think I was unusual and unique being coloured in that scene, there weren't a lot of us about. But it felt like an instant family. Because there was a lot of snobbery around it, a lot of peacockery, but you being the queen of it all and the most amazing-looking human being of the lot, cut that right out of it.

He took over three days later and played the first Ants gig at Andy Czezowski's new club, the Vortex in Wardour Street, alongside The Slits and The Banshees. This new line-up would record 'Plastic Surgery' as their debut single on 14 July. For the film, the Ants also recorded 'Deutscher Girls', while The Banshees performed 'Love in a Void', Wayne County 'Paranoia Paradise', and Chelsea 'Right to Work'. There were further cameos by The Slits, who played a gang of street toughs that set upon one of Borgia's escorts, played by the artist Luciana Martinez de la Rosa, who was also doubling as the film's wardrobe mistress. Brian Eno wrote the score.

In an early note on the screenplay, Jarman wrote that the film was dedicated to: "All those who secretly work against the tyranny of Marxists facists trade unionists Maoists capitalists socialists… who have conspired together to destroy the diversity and holiness of each life in the name of materialism… For William Blake."[5]

Becoming Britannia

The most Blakeian moment of the film is the mesmerising sequence 'Jordan's Dance', filmed by Derek himself in Super-8, when I pirouetted around a fire on a disused dock in Deptford, wearing the tutu with ostrich feathers that I had sewn on the night before in Buckingham Gate. That was an act of improvisation. I made it up on the spur of the moment, and Derek often said it was his favourite part of the film. We shot the entire sequence in only two takes.

While I danced, books were thrown onto the bonfire and in the background stand three masked figures, two of which represented Michelangelo's *David* and Death himself. It wasn't the easiest thing to pull off. My legs were burned by the flames, my feet were being crushed on the rubble and concrete – it was a really, really difficult place to dance when you think that ballerinas usually perform on sprung floors. But you get into a zone, it's almost like being out of your body, and you don't worry about those things at the time.

It brought back all the discipline of my serious ballet days, especially the pointe work. It was a huge discipline of pain, when I used to have to soak my tights off my feet because they were stuck there with blood. You couldn't just pull them off, because all the skin would come off with them.

My other big sequence as Amyl Nitrate was an operatic rendering of 'Rule Britannia' (though it's actually sung by the classically trained Suzi Pinns) as a Eurovision entry, filmed on the set of *A Chorus Line* at the Theatre Royal, Drury Lane, which had been lent to Derek between shows and was where most of the band footage was also shot. For this, I donned the helmet and trident of our ancient island queen.

These, I have to point out, were the only elements of all the clothes I wore during the *Jubilee* shoot that were actually supplied by the costume department. Everything else you see me in was my own

---

[5] Tony Peake, *Derek Jarman* (Little, Brown, 1999), p. 246.

clothes: the pink twinset and pearls; the pair of Vivienne's buckle boots that got wrecked; the Bondage trousers and parachute jacket worn by Adam; and the stilettos I wore for the dance. Needless to say, Britannia's helmet didn't fit and it really hurt to wear it – but we improvised a solution to that as well; I put Derek's beret on underneath it. Thanks to the stilettos, my feet were a bloody mess by the end of it, too.

But it's like my favourite line from the film: "I wanted to dance, I wanted to defy gravity." Derek really tapped into the heart of the matter with that one.

Future imperfect

These two set pieces worked perfectly for me – I hate rehearsing and have always been much better at improvising dances on the spot. But lots of times when we were filming I was concerned I could have improved my dialogue or performance and I'd ask to shoot a scene again. Derek didn't want that kind of polished perfection; he wanted imperfection and he made sure all of that stayed in. He'd always tell me, "You were perfect there in that take". so I would have to leave it there. He knew exactly what he wanted. It was such a joy to work with him; he really was a unique man.

Jubilee was made on the hoof. Derek never got official permission to shoot in any of his locations and at one point we nearly got arrested when concerned residents thought the prop guns we were using were real. This heightened the atmosphere, the feeling that we could be shut down at any moment.

Filming *Jubilee* was a harrowing experience for Adam. During the shoot of 'Plastic Surgery' at the Drury Lane Theatre, he dislocated his knee and was unable to walk for a couple of days afterwards; it was an injury that would come back to haunt him. His character, Kid, was involved in two fight scenes, in which he remembers becoming the focus of some real menace.

During the sequence that showed Lindsay Kemp's dance troupe performing in the crypt of Westminster Cathedral – actually the Catacombs club in Earl's Court – American actor Donny Durham, one of the two policemen who kill Adam's character, got very drunk and told Adam that he had been directed by Derek to go after Adam with real violence when it came to filming that scene.[6] "I don't care if you break his leg," he was supposed to have said, "it's got to go on celluloid." But, forearmed with this knowledge, Adam was ready for the two actors playing the cops (Dunham and Barney James) and I had to pull them apart. Everyone thinks I'm pushing Adam onto the chair; it's because he really was going to have a fight with them. He ended up with bruised ribs and wanted to quit, but I persuaded him to finish the film. It was difficult for him, but I knew the importance of what we were doing. It's taken a long time, but I think that's finally becoming more understood.

Giving a rhino the horn

The film ends at Borgia Ginz's mansion, where the cackling impresario is having tea with Adolf Hitler, devouring Kentucky Fried Chicken with wine and uttering the prophetic announcement: "They all sign up in the end!" This was filmed at Longleat in Wiltshire, a massive Elizabethan 'prodigy house' with sweeping steps running up to it, in the personal library and kitchen of its owner, the eccentric Marquis of Bath. As you may recall, the safari park in its grounds was the scene of my teenage near miss with the lions. Now it became the setting for more beast-related terror – this time, with about three tons worth of frisky rhinoceros.

In the original script, the idea was for me to be driven to a field in the safari park where the rhino was waiting. So I was quite nervous. I was wearing a pair of really high stilettos, the ones I did 'Rule Britannia' in, and a Japanese-style silk dress, which again I provided, because it looked pretty straight and I wanted that juxtaposition with my hair and the straight clothes, the same as the twinset and pearls.

I was given a briefing by the staff of the safari park on the correct etiquette before meeting my co-star. I was told not to wear any perfume, because rhinos' noses are extremely sensitive, so I didn't even use any deodorant, nothing.

---

[6] Adam Ant, *Stand & Deliver* (Sidgwick & Jackson, 2006), pp. 111–12.

Mordecai (aka Modi) Schreiber, who worked on the film as production manager, was quite well-moneyed, I think, and he borrowed his dad's Roller for the scene. We drove across this field while the film crew were stationed about 500 metres away with long lenses on their cameras, and a park ranger, a white-hunter-type of bloke, was standing by with a tranquilliser rifle, just in case – God knows, you wouldn't be allowed to do any of that these days. I got out of the car and walked up to the nearest rhino.

This was supposed to be a very simple scene. All I had to do was look at the beast, then there was going to be a sentence that went with it that would be over-dubbed afterwards: "Will you buy me a rhino to ride along the King's Road?" But as I got closer he started huffing and snorting, then his great big fat hoof started scraping on the ground and… I think he might have fancied me, actually. I think I might have given him the horn.

The next thing, there's a message coming over the tannoy from the park ranger: "Walk away from the rhino." I was in the middle of a field, I was wearing stilettos. If he went for me, I was dead – as simple as that. I couldn't dodge him, let alone run away. So I stepped backwards, heart pounding, and walked backwards as slowly as I could towards the Rolls-Royce, opened the door with my hand behind my back, got in and Modi drove off. Meanwhile, this thing's in the field, just standing, staring at me. Actually, he was a handsome beast, incredible to look at – and he had a massive horn.

We had to drive all the way around the perimeter of the rhino enclosure, back to the film unit, where it was explained to me that, out of all the rhinos in that field, I had picked the bull rhino of the herd, who had got his horn underneath a Land Rover the week before and tipped it on its side – the ranger with the rifle was in it at the time.

So, obviously, the line in the film had to change from "rhino" to "tank", because in the end there was no footage of the rhino.

Even funnier, Derek was having palpitations, because, not only did he think I was about be killed, but the loaned Rolls-Royce was also going to get smacked in. On the way out, we went past the Bengal tiger enclosure and Derek said: "You don't fancy getting in with one of them instead, do you?"

Fright night

The film was cut quickly, at cameraman Peter Middleton's house in Ealing, and was ready to open in February 1978 – a year to the day after Derek shot the Pistols footage at Andrew Logan's Valentine's Ball. The British Board of Film Censors (BBFC) were not impressed with the levels of violence in the film, and Derek had to meet with James Ferman and agree to cut some of the Happy Days murder scene before he granted it a certificate – and then it was an X, only to be shown to adults over 18.

Nobody told me that I was going to be on the poster for the film. I was on the Tube to Notting Hill Gate, and while I was still on the train I could see it going by. Then, when I got out, there was this huge poster. I was staring at it and everyone else on the platform was staring at me. It was obvious I looked exactly the same as the poster; it wasn't like I was an actress doing a part. I was it – I was the poster.

ROGER ROOKE: I was working in London when *Jubilee* came out and that was quite something. Getting on the train and seeing your picture, you were the poster girl for that, weren't you? And I wanted to shout out: "That's my sister!" They were good, actually, really well designed.

The premiere took place on 22 February 1978, at Gate Two, a cinema on the east of Russell Square then owned by The Rolling Stones. I made my own outfit for the occasion, taking the lace off Jeannie's first wedding dress and wearing it under my Venus T-shirt with a mink collar around my neck. When she found out about that, years later, Jeannie was not best pleased.

The signs were not auspicious.

A man fainted in front of Derek and his parents; the film was interrupted by shouts of "This isn't punk!" from members of the music press; a section of the audience that was morally offended by the sex and violence stormed out – and some of them were the extras! My parents came up for it, joined by Roger, Linda and Sally. They managed to stay in their seats – but it wasn't a comfortable experience for them, either. Obviously it was quite shocking; there was so much they weren't used to – openly gay people, violence against the police. But when the ballet sequence started, Mum turned round to Sally and said that was the real me. It gave her some solace, I think, because she didn't like the film very much.

Even Derek's good friends in the press felt compelled to voice their doubts to him.

PETER YORK: I thought he'd got it wrong, he didn't get it and saw punk in this rather elaborate, historical, over educated, over worked way. I can remember seeing it in this little cinema in Notting Hill, the Gate, and taking Derek into the coffee bar next door afterwards. I feel quite ashamed about this because I sort of laid into him. I said: "Do you really get what these people are about?" And he looked so crestfallen. I shouldn't have done it. He couldn't help it; he saw it this way because he was this sort of person. But no one will ever forget *Jubilee.*

The titillation of his masochistic tremblings

You can see Vivienne's anti-*Jubilee* T-shirt at http://collections.vam.ac.uk/item/O68609/top-vivienne-westwood/

The full text reads as follows:

Open T shirt to Derek Jarman from Vivienne Westwood JUBILEE I had been to see it once and thought it the most boring and therefore disgusting film I had ever seen. I went to see it again for afterall, hadn't you pointed your nose in the right direction? Rather than I deal with spectacular crap as other film makers do, you had looked at something here & now of absolute relevance to anybody in England with a brain still left let's call it soul. I first tried very hard to listen to every word spoken in the flashbacks to Eliz. I. What were you saying? Eliz: 'This vision exceedeth by far all expectation. Such an abstract never before I spied.' And so she went on – fal de ray la lu lullay the day! And John Dee spoke 'poetry' according to Time Out (those old left overs from a radio programme, involving a panel of precocious Sixth formers, called "Cabbages & Kings", whose maturity concerns being rather left from a position of safety) though even now I can remember no distinguishing phrase from amongst the drone, only the words, 'Down down down' (Right on)! And Ariel who flashed the sun in a mirror, & considered a diamond & had great contact lenses: 'Consider the world's diversity & worship it. By denying its multiplicity you deny your own true nature. Equality prevails not for god but for man's sake.' Consider that! What an insult to my VIRILITY! I am punk man!

And as you use the valves you give to punks as a warning, am I supposed to see old Elizabeth's england as some state of grace? Well, I'd rather consider that all this grand stuff and looking at diamonds is something to do with a gay (which you are) boy's love of dressing up & playing at charades. (Does he have a cock between his legs or doesn't he? Kinda thing)...

As to the parts about the near future there were 2 good lines in it. Adam (kid): I don't care about the money I just don't wanna get ripped off.' (Funny) & Angel or Sphinx to Adam: 'Don't sign up', etc... Life is more exciting on the streets.' Accepted that no one would want any dealings with clichéd figment of your fantasies, Borgia Ginze, what did the streets have to offer? Well, they then pinched a car to go visit a nutter with a garden of plastic flowers. They then went to the roof of a tower block to give out the kind of simplistic spiel Alf Garnet, or rather Mick Jones of the clash gives out. Is that your comment about the street? What Good - the low budget, independent, using friends, none-equity aspect. Good that the none-equity members weren't required to act but allowed P.T.O.' to say their lines as if reading from a little book inside their head, because what happened by result of this acting, as against none acting ability was that the performances depended for strength upon how much humanity the people behind the role possessed. Thus Jordan & Helen were good whereas Jenny Runacre's mediocrity of spirit bludgeoned through. Albeit - these aspects of your approach & style were anarchical, I am not interested in however interestingly you say nothing. [The Rule Britania Eurovision Song Contest was good because you said something - nationalism is vile & Eliz II is a commercial con trick]. Just like E.I.

An anarchist must say, 'Trust yourself'. It's the place to start. But self-indulgence is not the answer. You have to be brave & you are only a little. You have to cut the crap & not the cheese & chuck out - UGH - for instance, those Christian crucifixion fixations (sex is not frightening, honest) – "the pervasive reek of perverse & esoteric artinesss, the delight in degradation & decay simply for its beauties when stylized. An irresponsible movie. Don't remember punk this way" (all quoted from Chris Brazier in M. Maker)

But I ain't insecure enough, nor enough of a voyeur to get off watching a gay boy jerk off through the titillation of his masochistic tremblings. You pointed your nose in the right direction than you wanted. It was even more boring than Uncle Tom Don Letts' even lower budget film.

Getting shirty

The reviews, especially in the music weeklies, were almost all harsh. Still, a month later at the premiere party for *Saturday Night Fever*, the press were fascinated enough by my role in *Jubilee* to try and get me to dance with John Travolta. I did go and say hello to him, but ducked out of asking him for a spin around the dancefloor, though I wish I had done it now, as it would have made a great shot.

But Vivienne's reaction was the most extreme – she had a T-shirt printed with a lengthy diatribe against "the most boring and therefore most disgusting film" she had ever seen.

A lot of people have asked me since what I thought had triggered this. All I can say is, there wasn't a bad scene going on between me and Vivienne at all, and I'm all for free speech, so if that's what she thought at the time, then she had the right to say it. Duggie Fields, who makes a fleeting appearance in the catacombs scene of the film, has an interesting take on it:

DUGGIE FIELDS: Soon after *Jubilee* came out, Vivienne put out a T-shirt attacking Derek Jarman. I had a conversation with her shortly after. Round the corner from the shop there was a café, it might have been Beaufort Market, it was on the second floor somewhere nearby, and it was a chance encounter. I tried to tell her that she and Derek were a lot more alike, that they had a lot in common and that she was wrong in her opinion of him. But Vivienne wasn't prepared to listen, and was very forceful with her criticisms. Then, maybe a decade later, at another random encounter, she said she had to apologise to me. At first I didn't know what for, but it became apparent it was that conversation. She said: "You were right." I'd forgotten about it, and was very impressed that she had rethought and withdrawn the T-shirt, never allowing anyone to reproduce it. I thought the real issue was maybe Vivienne was being possessive about Jordan. Jordan was her star and I thought she just didn't want her taken away to be somebody else's star. But that's insecurity, and she got over that as her self-confidence grew.

Derek always laughed it off, but when, in 1992, Vivienne was awarded the title of Dame Commander of the Most Excellent Order of the British Empire (OBE) for her services to the fashion industry by Queen Elizabeth II, he noted the event in his diary with a touch of irony: "Saturday 20. Vivienne Westwood accepts an OBE, dipsy bitch. The silly season's with us: our punk friends accept their little medals of betrayal, sit in their vacuous salons and destroy the creative – like the woodworm in my dresser, which I will paint with insecticide tomorrow. I would love to place a man-sized insectocutor, lit with royal-blue, to burn up this clothes moth and her like."

264

As Borgia Ginz said: "They all sign up in the end!"[7]

Can the Cannes

However, the French had different ideas, and in May 1978, Derek, myself and Jenny Runacre set off for the Cannes Film Festival, where *Jubilee* had been selected for La Semaine de la Critique (Critics' Week). With Jenny driving, we crossed the Channel and headed first to Paris, where Derek wanted to show us Caravaggio's *The Death of the Virgin* in the Louvre. While we were there, Derek made a Super-8 short of me standing alongside the *Venus de Milo* that he called *Every Woman for Herself and All for Art*. Then we went to see the *Mona Lisa* – and every single Japanese tourist in the room turned their attention away from the great Leonardo and onto me!

The museum staff came and got us, took us away to this basement ticket office and said that we were disturbing the peace, disrupting the gallery. They gave us a ticket called a *laissez-faire*, which I think means 'fuck off' in French, which gave us entry into all the galleries in Paris. So we crept back into the basement to look at all the Egyptian stuff on the same ticket…

Then, when we got to Cannes, our hotel was broken into and the thieves took all of Jenny's clothes – and none of mine. All my clothes were either rubber or net, everything totally inappropriate for the hot weather. But they did take my handbag with my passport in it, which made it very difficult for me to get back home, leaving only a homemade shiv on the radiator in the hotel room in return. Jenny didn't have a stitch to wear; Derek had to go off and buy her a few outfits. She was wearing tuxedos, almost men's clothes really, and they'd had them all away.

The net skirt I'd made did get to have its moment, when I met David Bowie, who was there to promote *Just a Gigolo*, and got my photo taken with him. But my rubber miniskirt totally let the side down when I stood up in a restaurant and it melted off my body. The whole seam just went. It hung on – thank the Lord, because I had no knickers on – by this little waistband that was a separate bit of rubber

---

[7] Tony Peake, *Derek Jarman* (Little, Brown, 1999), p. 25.

that hadn't perished, and I had that to hold it all together, gather it all in and hold it, stretch it over me to get out of the restaurant. Now, who would wear that? No one else would wear rubber to Cannes!

There was also a mini-riot, when Jenny, Derek and I took the stage at the Five Nation televised opening with festival director Louis Malle, between some rival French punks in the audience. Derek absolutely loved that. Controversy followed us all the way out of France. The British Consulate managed to sort me out a temporary passport to fly home with, but the airline staff were about as happy with my appearance as Seaford British Rail. They refused to let me board the plane until chivalrous Derek gave me his mac to wear over my rubber gear. The arguing went on all the way up the runway.

Kind of *Blue*

Derek was a very dear friend to me. I did more work with him over the years, including *The Last of England* (1987), and he even made a film of my wedding. It was thanks to knowing him, the Megalovision boys and all those people who met at their place that I first got to cross paths with Simon Fisher Turner, who began working for Derek in the summer of 1978 and would, for a short and very entertaining time, become the Ants' tour manager. Simon worked on the soundtracks to all Derek's films after *Jubilee*, up until Derek's death in 1994. Brian Eno returned to write the soundtrack of the posthumous cut-up *Glitterbug*, a compilation of Derek's Super-8 films, so that collaboration came full circle too.

The last contribution I ever made was a short piece for *Blue* (1993), the film that he made at the very end of his life. From what I understand, at the end stage of AIDS, if people go blind, all they can see is blue from behind their eyelids. This is why that film is called *Blue*.

PETER YORK: There's a thing that I really feel bad about, and I don't imagine he will have noticed, but the last time I saw Derek he was really ill and had visible lesions. I can remember walking past a café window in Soho and seeing him inside and thinking that nobody knew how AIDS got transferred. I remember thinking, and this is so wrong, I know: Go in,

266

say hello, but DO NOT SHAKE HANDS. On the other hand, I could have not gone in.

Keep your daughter off the stage, Mr Jarman

At the time of writing this book, *Jubilee* has been revived for the stage, with only Toyah, playing the part of Queen Elizabeth I, from the original cast. I was invited to the London premiere at Hammersmith Lyric on 20 February 2018, and right up to the night before I had people on the phone urging me to go. But I'm glad I resisted. A couple of very good friends went to it and one of them said that she wished the interval had gone on for ever.

The film itself has recently been rereleased in a special BFI edition, which includes in the special features a thirty-three-minute interview with yours truly called *Jordan Remembers Jubilee*. It's interesting to see how very differently the film is seen now.

> **JON SAVAGE:** It's not perfect, but what's good about it is that it's a record of London's streets in 1977 and there are not many of those. Derek got it, because he was very sharp, even though he wasn't of that generation. He got a lot about punk.

> **RICHARD CABUT:** That film was like a mixture of bleakness and optimism and poetry and magic. It put the whole idea of magic into the punkosphere. Not just the physical world, it's the spiritual world. *Jubilee* is famous for having "Post-Modern" written on the wall and for me the film itself exposed the workings. The way that you performed was not like a rock performance, it was as a living artwork, which is why it remains so powerful. Questioning authenticity. Not all artwork has to be a statement; it is more of a query, which is as important as a statement.

Derek Jarman was a beautiful man. The way he would throw his head back and laugh, he was wonderful – 'wonderful' being one of his favourite words, as well. I will always miss him.

16

THROUGH A LENS DARKLY

Rise of the Ants, fall of the Pistols
(July–December 1977)

Assailants unknown

After the Jubilee weekend was over, the first casualty of the *Sunday Mirror*'s crusade to 'PUNISH THE PUNKS' was Jamie Reid, who was attacked around the corner from his flat in Borough and had his nose and leg broken by people he had never seen before. The Sunday after that, John Rotten and producer Chris Thomas were attacked close to Wessex Studios, where they had been recording, by a knife-wielding gang who shouted "We love our Queen!" while striping John across his left hand, severing two tendons, and hacking at his leg with a machete – he credited his leather trousers for saving this limb from being severed completely.

As reported in the press, these two assaults were a feud between Teddy boys and punks. By the following afternoon, Paul Cook was pursued up the Goldhawk Road, near his home in Shepherd's Bush, by a gang of Teds, and set upon with some metal piping.

MICHAEL COSTIFF: That whole Punks v Teds thing was completely whipped up by the *Daily Mirror*. They started that and they made a big deal of it. Because, why were punks fighting Teds? All the rest of the population hated those two groups. In a way you could understand it, because Teds were the last ones to get a bit of attention for their looks. It started in the *Daily Mirror*, they stirred the whole thing up from nothing.

Dawn of the Teds

The Ted battles soon spread to the King's Road. This was the worst time to be working in Seditionaries. The Teds had never been happy with Let It Rock's transmogrification into SEX/Seditionaries and now they had the excuse for a full-scale war with the punks that ran the length of King's Road every Saturday. Adam's knowledge of Gene Vincent songs spared him a beating from such a gang; he was also helping me to clean up after attacks on the shop the whole time.

At the same time, we got it in the neck from football hooligans from nearby Chelsea FC. I could hear them coming down the road and had to rush out with those great big grilles and padlock them onto the windows. They would have kicked them in and come in, otherwise.

PAUL COOK: It was a horrible, dark time for football, as well. That was a sign of the times, though; it was a very violent time. The shop was an easy target, 'cos those were the sort of guys who hated punk rock, the football hooligans. That was just another reflection of society. The shop was the epicentre of everything when you get down to it, you was right there in the middle of it all.

Sometimes, when the numbers outside were too great, it was impossible to stop big groups of lairy people from steaming into the shop and taking everything they could lay their hands on. Then, after work, I would be walking down the King's Road with all the cash from the shop in a leather bag that said 'BANK BAG' in big letters on it… I'd have to do the cashing-up from the shop on my own and walk down to the night safe. I don't know how I got away with it.

VIVIENNE WESTWOOD: So many punks came on this pilgrimage [to Seditionaries] that the police used to wait for them at the Tube station in

Sloane Square that was the nearest tube station – round them all up and, when they'd got a certain number, they'd escort them up the King's Road to the shop in a procession of about 200 at a time.

There was this man called Pete the Murderer;[1] he was a little demagogue who said we were capitalists ripping them off and encouraged them all to come in and have a go. Pete the Murderer used to come in my shop with an axe and I'd say: "Oh you fucker, you're tough aren't you?"

[At one point] the shop-front was about to come down, they were all outside and I thought: Well, I've got to stop this. I said to Michael Collins, "Look, I'm going outside to talk to them, you leave the door just a little bit back and I'll go out there." And he did not do that. 'Cos I would have stopped them all. Michael Collins told me afterwards what happened – the reason this [lifts right index] finger is so thick now is because I was holding on to the grille, trying to keep it shut and Michael Collins was trying to open it because he was frightened for me and he just couldn't stand it, he thought that they might kill me or something. I wanted him to shut the door but he didn't. So they all came in and emptied the shop in one go.

Out to lunch

Malcolm was struggling to deal with the post-boat-trip fall out and its effect on the band. At first he installed them in the Portobello Hotel, where Alan Jones was working, but even with a friend on the staff they got thrown out and ended up in an apartment called the Chelsea Cloisters – John, Wobble, John Grey, Nancy and Sid all living together. When they got sick of each other's company, they would go out and get set upon by the public. Paul and Steve, by contrast, spent as much time as they could in the studio, working on the album with Chris Thomas and honing their craft.

Malcolm arranged a tour of Sweden to get the band out of the hostile public glare.

---

[1] Pete the Murderer was a sometime boyfriend of Debbi Wilson. According to Bertie Marshall: "He was kind of handsome, East End or south London gangster type, curly blond hair and very blokey. And he murdered someone! Didn't dare ask who."

JOHN TIBERI: When we went to Sweden, I told Sid that Nancy wasn't coming and he told her. I did impress on him that that wasn't what he was supposed to be doing with this band. That's not what the job description is. It's not the Bay City Rollers with the permanent groupie.

I can remember Nancy's reaction to being told she was not welcome to join them. She had this great trick of having a massive asthma attack whenever she didn't want something to happen. So she started hyperventilating: "Oh Sid, Sid, I'm dying, I'm dying!" He wasn't very impressed with it.

But, with 'God Save the Queen' still in the top 10, Virgin were keen to rush out another single. 'Pretty Vacant' did not have lyrics that anyone thought could be banned, despite the unique way John pronounced the second syllable of the second word in the title. It came out, with a prophetic version of The Stooges' 'No Fun' on the B-side, on 1 July 1977. Two days later, Malcolm was off to Hollywood to see the Pistols' American record company Warner Bros. and start panning for film gold.

Wardour Street Babylon

Without an actual screenwriter, Malcolm had written his own treatment for the film and had managed to coax Russ Meyer on board as a director.

We were all fans of Meyer's absurdist satire of the Californian music business, *Beyond the Valley of the Dolls* (1970), and the director's conditions included that his *Dolls* scriptwriter, the *Chicago Sun Times* film critic Roger Ebert, came on board with him, and that there would be a role for Meyer's girlfriend, Kitten Natividad.

JOHN TIBERI: Meyer was brilliant – he went right back to the old school – and Ebert persuaded him that this was an opportunity for him. There was this idea that Meyer never really wanted to break into the Hollywood mainstream, but actually it's not true: he did want to, on his terms. He wasn't a committed outsider, like arguably John Waters. But the thing that impressed was his credibility, his artistic ability.

The immoral Mr Meyer

Russ Meyer (1922–2004) began his film career in the US army, serving in the 166th Signal Photo Company as a combat photographer during the Second World War, where he was often assigned to General George Patton. He filmed the original 'Dirty Dozen' before they were parachuted into France and E. M. Nathanson's best-selling novel, subsequently made into the film, cites him as its source. "In the real story," Meyer said, "they disappeared and were never heard of again."

The challenge of filming in the heat of battle, with the lack of readily available film stock, made him a genius with his framing and editing techniques, skills he would deploy to great effect on the film that made his name, *Faster, Pussycat! Kill! Kill!* (1965), which followed three go-go dancers led by the black-clad, raven-haired martial artist Tura Satana on a killing spree across the California desert. After the unexpected success of *Easy Rider* in 1969, 20th Century Fox hired him to direct *Beyond the Valley of the Dolls*, which, under the transformative pen of Roger Ebert, would bear no relation to its source material, Jacqueline Susann's *Valley of the Dolls* novel. What it did instead was tell the sex-and-drugs-infused story of girl band The Carrie Nations and their journey through Hollywood society.

After his participation in *Who Killed Bambi?* came to its abrupt end, Meyer retired from filmmaking at the end of the 1970s, and spent his dotage making millions from his sexploitation films on the home video and DVD market. His fans included John Waters, The Cramps and Mudhoney, who took their name from one of his celebrated odes to the female form. Meyer produced his epic autobiography *A Clean Breast* in 2000, before succumbing to dementia. Said Roger Ebert – who also sadly died, in 2013 – in his affectionate obituary in the *Chicago Sun Times*: "He was unique in that the women were always the strong characters, and men were the mindless sex objects." Most of his cinematic oeuvre is available on DVD.

ROGER EBERT: I wrote it in LA with McLaren feeding me background ideas. Then Meyer, McLaren and I flew to London to meet Vicious, Cook and Jones. Meyer was wary of McLaren's Bondage pants, so he insisted on sitting on the aisle. He said: "If we have to evacuate, he'll get those goddamned straps tangled up in the seats!"[2]

---

[2] Roger Ebert quote reproduced by kind permission of Damon Wise.

The film was initially scheduled to begin shooting on Halloween 1977. Russ, Roger and Kitten were given a whirlwind punk tour of London, which included a visit to the Vortex. The plan was to recreate the main incidents of the Pistols' career so far, including the El Paradiso and Nashville gigs, the latter of which was going to be turned into a redneck bar brawl. The working title was *Who Killed Bambi?*, based on a sequence Meyer planned to shoot of a character based on Mick Jagger going out with his chauffeur to shoot a deer on the Queen's reserve. The title is one of the few things from Meyer's initial vision that survives to the finished film.

That summer, the Vortex would play host to an unusual number of American film stars. Arnold Schwarzenegger, then the reigning Mr Universe, had been shooting the film *Pumping Iron*[3] in London when he came down there to see the Ants play on 11 July, with The Banshees and The Slits. It was almost like meeting King Kong! I was with Little Nell and Howard and James from Megalovision, and we were talking, funnily enough, about muscles. I invited Arnie to feel my thighs, and he was impressed by the muscle density I'd achieved through my dancing. But, having said that, he just lifted me up with one hand and put me on the bar – he was as fit as a flea then, just one giant muscle. I think he was after something that night and I could have been that person, but I didn't fancy him – though I think Nell might have done.

Simon Fisher Turner brought Robert Mitchum to see The Banshees, too. He had been shooting Michael Winner's *The Big Sleep* with the Hollywood legend, some of it right outside Buckingham Gate – I walked past the production one morning, and Winner called out to me: "Where are you going, love? Fancy dress party?" Needless to say, I gave the dinner-fixated director a right mouthful in return.

SIMON FISHER TURNER: I was playing this gay man's boyfriend and I wanted to dress like a punk. I wanted to be a young leather boy. And [Winner] would have none of it. They took me off and bought all these Italian clothes in Kensington and Knightsbridge which I felt really uncomfortable in. It was me who took Candy Clark into the shop, and she got all her clothes there. Then I took Robert Mitchum to see Siouxsie and The Banshees at the Vortex and, suddenly, I wasn't Simon Turner, this posh actor who was in *Tom Brown's Schooldays* any more, I was with Leee Black Childers and The Heartbreakers and introducing them all to Robert Mitchum.

---

[3] *Pumping Iron* (director George Butler) was the 1977 docudrama that launched Arnold Schwarzenegger on the world. It focused on his rise to the top of the body building rankings in the 1975 Mr Universe and Mr Olympia competitions, where he outdid the efforts of *Incredible Hulk* star Lou Ferrigno with his personal brand of charm coupled with extreme psychological warfare.

I was also in the Vortex on the night Elvis Presley died, on 16 August 1977, when people started cheering. But when Marc Bolan was killed in a car crash on Barnes Common on 16 September, people started ringing up the shop as if we were bereavement counsellors.

ALAN JONES: When Marc Bolan died we kept getting all these calls from people saying: "Marc Bolan's dead!" And I kept saying: "Well, why are you calling us?" Then you'd put the phone back down, it would ring again and it would be another person saying: "Oh my God, Marc Bolan's dead!" It was like they had to have someone to talk to and we were the only service available!

We've got chicken in the barn

Russ Meyer might have been interested in a film I made around this time, thanks to Ulla Larson-Styles,[4] who also had a part in *Jubilee*. She said that a friend of hers was producing a porno film and she thought immediately of me to be an extra. So I thought: What the hell, it might be a crack – several cracks, in fact. I was auditioned in the toilets of the Roebuck, I had to show Ulla my tits and she said: "Oh yes, these will go down really well, they will like you."

So I was taken to this barn, out in the countryside – I can't remember where now – and I had to take all my clothes off and just stand there, amid all these hay bales. And this bloke came on the set – this skinny little bloke with the hugest cock you've ever seen. I didn't have to do anything, just stand there in the nude, and get bitten by a bloody great horsefly while I was doing it. To my amazement, footage of this has recently resurfaced as an extra 'found footage' feature on a DVD reissue of a 1976 Mondo movie, *Savana Violenta* (*This Violent World*), by Antonio Climati and Mario Morra – hunt it down if you dare, thrill-seekers.

---

[4] Ulla Larson-Styles also had a part in *Love Is the Devil* and the film of the 1980 Alternative Miss World. The last time I saw her was at Vivienne's Retrospective at the V&A in 2004 and suddenly there was this woman shouting out: "Yordan! Yordan! This is the original Yordan and not the Yordan with the big tits!" That was her.

Stockpile electricity

With Dave Barbe now fully ensconced on the Ants' drumming stool, I got the band some much-needed rehearsal time at the Screen on the Green, thanks to the generosity of Roger Austin. I couldn't wait to get my hands on them and see what I could do, so, from June onwards, a punishing schedule of writing and rehearsals began.

DAVE BARBE: I was an assiduous student. I loved playing and I studied it. Adam was a very hard taskmaster, a very studious and exacting musician and that was a good start for me. He was a glorious, scary kind of guy and I wanted to serve, I wanted to do the very best I could, because the rewards were great. Those were seriously amazing gigs. Money couldn't buy the feeling of those gigs.

There was one song that I used to perform with the Ants that was written after Sally and I had gone to see Lou Reed at the New Victoria Theatre in April 1977. It was almost like an argument, that song. Because I hated that one performance he did, it was so awful and I had expected so much. I wrote the whole thing on a napkin on a table in the Roebuck straight afterwards and Adam put it to music. Over the years, people have often misquoted the lyrics, so I think it's worth reproducing them as they are meant to be in full here:

Lou

Lost your unpredictability
They said you were an ageing whore
Stockpile electricity
But now my friend you're out the door

Andy Warhol video
Four quid for a ticket, oh
Pack up your arse and lick it, oh
No tribute to you, Lou

I know you shoot up aspirin
You fell but n-n-n-n-never hurt yourself
You never st-st-st-st-stagger in r-r-r-r-reality
But now my friend you're on the shelf

Andy Warhol video
Four quid for a ticket, oh
Park it up your arse and lick it, oh
No tribute to you, Lou

My vocal on that wasn't really singing, it wasn't ever meant to be, but it was a wonderful thing to be able to walk on-stage with that power, and the fact that I'd written the lyrics, that meant a lot to me. I didn't want to thank the audience; I wanted to look them straight in the eye. It was very empowering and I felt it added a lot to the Ants set. My interaction with Adam on-stage was great too, and a lot of people said they stopped going to see the band after we stopped doing it, that was it for them. We were very in tune with each other. What we've been through together has been groundbreaking times, for both of us.

I remember being backstage at the Nashville Rooms, ready to come on to sing 'Lou' and I completely forgot all my lyrics. Only time it ever happened. I sat there thinking: Shit! All on my own, with the rest of the band onstage, and the intro started… and that night the intro went on for about seven minutes.

MICHAEL COSTIFF: That was so exciting, that intro going on like that. We love a good entrance; you can't top it. Make a fantastic entrance and then get off. You don't want to see through the magic.

Then there was the time, on 1 December, when John Peel's producer John Walters came to see us at the Royal College of Art and the pair of us ended up getting locked in the dressing room after I'd come offstage from doing 'Lou'. Nobody could hear us banging on the door to get out! But it still got the Ants their first Peel session – and John Walters insisted that we couldn't do the session unless we did 'Lou'.

RICHARD CABUT: The Ants wouldn't have got their cult following if there hadn't originally been the association with you. Your participation in SEX and Seditionaries gave that original band their depth and gravitas. The Ants were great, but there were loads of great bands then.

PETER YORK: It was absolutely super and wonderful! Berlin decadence with a little British twist. It was more fun-loving than Berlin and you made a very creditable noise. It wasn't quite singing but it was a very special noise.

Van trouble

On August 1977 we had our first gig outside London, at Rebecca's in Birmingham with The Banshees. Of course, we didn't have any transport, but we borrowed a van from someone's mum for the night. It was gas- and petrol-driven, and neither part of it worked. Near Birmingham it broke down and there was nothing we could do to get it going again. So, thinking on my stilettoed feet, I managed to hitch us a ride.

The band all hid down a gulley, by the side of the hard shoulder, with all their gear, and I stood at the side of the motorway with all my rubber clothes on, those great big articulated lorries whooshing past me at great speed. Then one came juddering to a halt about 100 metres down the road, because that was as quickly as it could stop.

I ran up in my high heels and said: "Can I have a lift?"

The driver leaned out of his cab and said: "Yes of course, darling." I don't think it was only the shoulder that was hard. He thought he was in: This girl's in rubber, on her own, on the hard shoulder – all my dreams have come true! Then I said: "I've got some friends as well…" And they all appeared out of this ditch and ran up the hard shoulder with the drum kit, all their guitars and everything. I thought at this stage the driver was just going to put his foot on the pedal and shoot off. But, fair play to him, he said, "Yes, of course, get in!" and we all got in the front cab of this artic. He said it was the most he'd ever managed to get in, with all the gear as well. He dropped us off somewhere near the Bull Ring, took us all the way there – ten minutes before we were due to soundcheck.

We got a lift home with The Banshees, but the owners of the van were not best pleased to discover it had somehow been left in an underpass on the outskirts of Birmingham. I didn't sort that one out. I was at home with the sheets over my head!

Inside the Antmobile

We needed some help, and Megalovision's Howard and James provided it. Adam kept me as his personal manager but let them take over the running of the band. In September 1977, they bought us a much-needed tour van – a bright orange VW camper with a white lid, some airline seats in the back and enough space to take all the gear. One of the many people I met at their offices in Campden Hill Square was Simon Fisher Turner and, when I found out he had a driving licence, he was immediately hired. His first gig was a trial-by-fire in Bristol.

It was a Saturday, a football day, and the venue was really hard to find. When we finally got there, it was virtually empty. Half an hour before showtime there were still only about twenty people there and the band were getting really spooked. I went to the promoter and asked, "What's going on?" and he said, "There's a pub over the other side of Bristol that does rough cider cheap. They get pissed there first and then take buses back."

Just like he said, they all turned up suddenly, en masse, completely drunk, chanting "Bristol City!" and up for a fight. We had to stop the gig at one point, when I had a pint glass come whizzing past my ear, a proper old pint mug with a handle. I got *covered* in beer. Even Simon got on-stage and started shouting at the audience.

SIMON FISHER TURNER: I'd never done that before. It was something like: "We've driven up from fucking London, excuse me!" That was the only time I've ever lost it like that. But I had to defend our honour.

Then, for some reason, they tried to diddle us out of the money, too. Afterwards, we were holed up in the dressing room, people were banging on the doors and the Antmobile was getting rocked up and down outside, because they were all drunk on their rough cider. And

I still had to get the money. In the end I opened the dressing-room door and just screamed at everybody to get out of the way, got the promoter and demanded our money: "NOW, we've got to get out of here NOW. No more five minutes, nothing. I want the money now." And then we ran for the Antmobile, which was still on four wheels. Just. Can you imagine going through all that shit and going home with no money? People could have got killed that night. I could have got killed. I guess that, if you looked like an ordinary woman, you wouldn't have got your pay at the end of the evening. But I didn't look like an ordinary woman.

> **SIMON FISHER TURNER:** They were hairy days. I remember a couple of things specifically. Driving up the M1 and just going into a service station with you and the band. It was hysterical. I looked like a tramp, none of us had any money – I don't think Howard and James gave us any money. It was a real old vagabond thing. And the fogs on the roads at night – my God. But it was so great to see people's faces when you and the band walked in. It made it all fucking worth it.

By the end of September, Mark Ryan left the Ants to form his own band.[5] It wasn't just because of the van getting ditched in Birmingham, either.

> **DAVE BARBE:** Adam always had trouble getting the right guitar sound, and Mark, bless him, couldn't keep up with playing. It's a very physical job; you have to be very strong, and he wasn't robust enough to keep up with the hurly-burly of those shows. You had to be young and strong when the bottles were flying…
>
> Mark wore thick glasses, black-rimmed – they enlarged the eyes on his small face. His fair hair, even then, was thinning. Although he was frail, he could put away pints of Guinness better than anyone in our group. The 'group' from his school in Wood Green were academic, witty, arty, muso

---

[5] Mark Ryan (1959–2011) then joined Steve Strange's The Photons for a while, before going back to college to study music seriously. Moving to Cardiff, he wrote over twenty plays, from a one-woman study of Dorothy Squires to the acclaimed *The Strange Case of Dr Jekyll and Mr Hyde as Told to Carl Jung by an Inmate of the Broadmoor Asylum.*

sixth-formers. I survived in their company, even though I'd never sat an exam. I loved to read – my education.

Mark was into punk. I knew nothing of it, he spoke of a new way and teenage revolution – he drew me in, I could listen to him for hours. He was a good friend… It was he who asked me to 'dep' for the Ants on the drums and Adam took a shine to me. After Mark got the chop (like many before and after him with Adam), I lost touch; band life shot me into another kind of galaxy.

Many, many years later I heard that he had died due to a drink problem. His work as a composer and academic at the university was displayed and lauded. There were pics of him with Adam and me… *Jubilee* and all that.

Mark was replaced by Dave's friend John Beckett, aka Johnny Bivouac, who made his debut at the Marquee on 4 October. It was the start of an eventful tour, on which we were joined by another member of Howard and James's Campden Hill Square retinue, Don Hawkins, the former drummer in one of Adam's favourite bands, Vince Taylor and The Playboys.[6] He was a very handsome man, was Don. We used to call him Dong, because apparently he had a whopper.

After a twelve-hour B-road journey to Plymouth on 7 October, Adam split his head open on a beam above the stage and me and Dong had to carry him off and take him to A&E. A week later, at Eric's in Liverpool, he did the same thing and split all his stitches open. That gig was the worst. It started with me standing outside while the band was loading in, and someone shouted: "Who do you think you are – Jordan?" Then Johnny Bivouac broke four strings on his guitar, they went one by one, and there was no money in the pot for replacements, so he had to try and play with only two strings. Worse still, I got stuck with Margi Clarke – or Margox as she called herself then.[7] She would not stop talking. But others remember that gig more fondly than I.

---

[6] Vince Taylor (1939–91) and The Playboys were part of the original British Beat boom that came out of the 2i's coffee bar on Old Compton Street. Though more popular in France than his native UK in his heyday, Vince became a bit of a cult hero to the punk generation.

[7] The actress Margi Clarke later married Jamie Reid, but that didn't end well.

HOLLY JOHNSON: It was a very dynamic performance, really exciting. Adam was using a stool or beer crate as a prop. Your appearance from the wings was great. You were a kind of stylistic touchstone. A new sex symbol, who didn't need the theatrical showbiz glamour of Diana Dors, but with a huge impact on our generation. The defiance etched into your face, not another anorexic [role] model but someone who could dress herself and have ideas.

More fun followed in my old stamping grounds at the Brighton Regency. In a new dirty-tricks low, the management tried to charge the band for hiring the microphone. I got into a slanging match with them, which culminated in me pushing the DJ off his stool, grabbing the mic and telling everyone that the band weren't performing and they should ask for their money back because it was the management's fault. The audience – over 200 of them – did just that.

SIMON FISHER TURNER: You were the best – you would always get the money. And also you were very good at telling me: "Stay sober, we've got to get home alive." Because it's very easy to drive to a gig in the afternoon, have a few drinks, then forget about the journey home...

A load of Bollocks

While the Ants were out building up their following, the Pistols, having enjoyed a controversy-free interlude in Sweden, were on their Nowhere Bus, on their cloak-and-dagger SPOTS (Sex Pistols On Tour Secretly) tour, aimed at getting round the many bans that had been enforced on them by local councils on the Anarchy tour. Sid's playing had improved while he'd been away from Nancy in Sweden, but he had not enjoyed the experience. I was getting calls from him while he was out there, saying how bad he was feeling, and you couldn't just jump on the plane in those days, so what I used to do was just try and talk him through it, make him feel better. It was the start of the downtime for him, although he was OK on-stage, I think.

By October, filming had begun on *Who Killed Bambi?* Sets had been built at the home of Hammer Horror, Bray Studios, including

283

a recreation of the Nashville. But the whole thing collapsed within weeks and Meyer and his entourage went back to the States, never to be seen again. Many reasons have been posited for this, including that one of the backers, 20th Century Fox, pulled out because of angry letters from shareholders, including Grace Kelly, or that there had been an ego clash between Malcolm and Meyer. John Tiberi has a different take.

JOHN TIBERI: Malcolm pulled the plug. Malcolm didn't think he was going to be able to control it enough. Malcolm had only one person he did counsel with, and that was Vivienne. Of course he had his partner, Stephen Fisher, his lawyer who would talk about contracts. But with Vivienne it would be expressed wholly in artistic terms, which would be: he didn't want to perpetuate the myth of the rock star. Which didn't really explain a lot, really. To some extent he always had to have chaos around him. When it got on the page, Ebert made sure that every revision went through the Screen Writers Guild. There were about seven reprints. At that point, you could say Malcolm had a film ready to go. But he was really very fickle. And that's the only explanation I can give you. There's never been a better one. Meyer's been quoted as giving a very short explanation – "It was that idiot McLaren." But that is expressing the surprise that it was [pulled] at the last minute. It's not that there was anything unamicable between them.

Meanwhile, and despite having recorded many different versions of nearly every track, the band had not settled on what they should use for their coming album. Only the title had been agreed on: *Never Mind the Bollocks*, supplied by Steve Jones. The next single, 'Holidays in the Sun' – inspired by 'Wanted' posters Rotten had seen for the Baader-Meinhof Gang in Berlin – came out on 20 October, seven days after most of the militant terror cell were killed in a shootout with West German commandos.

Disputes over the album tracks created a tension between Virgin and Malcolm, which the latter happily exploited by putting out his own bootleg, 'No Future UK', under the name of Spunk, from the Dave Goodman tapes recorded in July 1976 and January 1977. When Richard Branson learned of this wheeze, he ordered that the album proper be rush-released on 28 October.

PAUL COOK: You know what: he was too cunning for Malcolm. Branson won that battle of wits, I tell you. 'Cos Malcolm tried to wind him up so much into getting him to drop us again and he wasn't having any of it. He could see what was going on. We was still on Virgin when we split up. And the *Rock 'n' Roll Swindle* Branson got as well, so he won the battle at the end of the day, as far as Malcolm was concerned. [Malcolm] met his match, didn't he?

The album was immediately banned by Boots, Woolworths and W. H. Smith, because of its title, the inclusion of 'God Save the Queen' and the new track, 'Bodies', with its "four-letter storm" of lyrics, as the *Sun* put it. However, advance orders of 150,000 meant the album went straight in the charts at number one. Which was more than the Establishment could stand.

In the second week of November, plain-clothes police visited London branches of Virgin and Small Wonder and advised staff they faced prosecution under the 1899 Indecent Advertisements Act for displaying the album, then seized all the copies in the window and on the racks. When the manager of the Virgin shop, Chris Searle, replaced the window display, he was arrested. Branson consulted the veteran barrister and *Rumpole of the Bailey* author John Mortimer, who had represented him before, and hired him to act for the Pistols in the action due on 29 November.

Mortimer brought in some expert witnesses, including James Kingsley, Professor of English Studies at Nottingham University, who asserted the proud history of 'bollocks' as a good, upstanding Anglo-Saxon word, used in records from the year 1000 and quoted in Eric Partridge's definitive *Dictionary of Slang*: "I would take the title to mean 'Never mind the nonsense, here's The Sex Pistols'."

The case was dismissed. Said the chairman of the jury: "Much as my colleagues and I wholeheartedly deplore the vulgar exploitation of the worst instincts of human nature... we must reluctantly find you not guilty..." The *Sun*'s front cover the next day reacted: "Astonishing! That gives Johnny Rotten and his foul-mouthed Sex Pistols the chance to put up two fingers to the world!"

Said Rotten, simply: "Bollocks!"

Bad moon rising

With Sid and Nancy reunited after the SPOTS tour, it didn't take long for the couple to get back to their old ways, making the front cover of the *Sun* in early December for smashing up a hotel room. Malcolm decided the only way to deal with the situation was to send Nancy back to America with some money and a one-way ticket – but they didn't even get as far as Heathrow.

JOHN TIBERI: It was daft, but we were that desperate to try and persuade her she was not wanted. It was a half-baked idea. Me and Sophie were supposed to get her to the airport and put her on the plane – as if anybody was going to fall for that. She just said no. The only thing that would have worked was to get her deported. Which meant you would have to grass her up [for heroin], and that meant that Sid could be involved, too – and I wasn't going to do that. Actually, we should have moved to the next base, which was basically get another bass player. I don't know why we didn't.

Trying to separate them another way, Malcolm organised another short tour. In a rare interlude of peace and goodwill, the Pistols played Ivanhoe's Club in Huddersfield on the afternoon of Christmas Day 1977, for the benefit of 500 children of striking firemen, laid-off workers and one-parent families of children under 14.[8]

JOHN TIBERI: That was when Nancy turned up on Christmas Day. I suppose it was a bit romantic. She got a taxi all the way to Huddersfield, a black cab she'd taken all the way from London – on the Glitterbest account.

On 29 December, on the eve of their first US tour, the band were refused visas into the States due to their various previous petty criminal convictions – Rotten for amphetamine possession, Steve

---

[8] The BBC Four documentary *Christmas with the Sex Pistols* was directed by Julien Temple, with footage shot by him and contemporary news coverage of this touching lost moment before everything went pear-shaped for the Pistols. It was first screened in December 2013 and, at time of writing, can be easily accessed on YouTube.

and Paul for theft, Sid for various assaults. The Warner Bros. attorney got to work and the band were allowed in on 31 December, providing their record company provided a surety of $1 million.

I didn't want Sid to go. The violent outbursts were a problem and that's what I thought would be his ending. I told him that – if you do something like pull a knife on someone or whip your belt off your trousers and smack someone round the face with it, someone will come back at you.

I thought he'd probably get knifed, and said so. We were outside Finsbury Park, I remember exactly where we were standing, the day before he was going to America. I said to him: "If you go to New York and you do what you're doing here, which is just exploding at people with a knife, they won't put up with it. You'll die." And he was just doing all that tossing hair, rolling eyes, saying, "It'll be all right," and I said: "It won't be. This is a different world."

17

SOME NEW KIND OF KICK

Crawling out from the wreckage of punk
(December 1977 – October 1978)

Behind the yellow curtain

Christmas 1977 was a good one for the Ants. Although very little attention was being paid to them in the mainstream music press, crucial fanzines like Richard Cabut's *Kick*, Tom Vague's *Vague* and Tony Drayton's *Ripped & Torn* were keenly following their progress, and the band had built up a big live following who enjoyed the exclusivity of a band that wasn't being shared with the mass market. As Adam said: "You love or hate the Ant sound. You love to hate the Ants. There can be no neutrality."

We ended the year with a residency at the Marquee and an invitation to play Andrew Logan's Christmas party at Butler's Wharf. Like all Andrew's parties, it was another memorable occasion, and important, I think, that the Ants were the first band to play at one of these gatherings since the Pistols at the Valentine's Ball.

DAVE BARBE: I remember it, I've got pictures of it. It wasn't a stage, we just set up on the floor. It was all full of electric egos – a very significant party, wasn't it? Max was there, wearing something translucent.

DOROTHY MAX PRIOR: But people remember things differently at different times. It was a funny, half-made room, wasn't it, full of cubicles and things? There was a toilet up on a plinth and you had to tiptoe up, you knew that everyone was looking at you, this toilet in the middle of a huge space with a little curtain around it. What colour were the curtains around the toilet? In my head they're yellow.

I can still feel the embarrassment of that night when somebody pulled down the curtain while I was sitting on the throne. There were hundreds of people in this place and there was I, just sitting there, not yelling loud enough to be heard over the music. Whoever did it wasn't coming to my aid, so I think I actually got up off the toilet myself to put the curtains back up. The culprit of that crime has never confessed and is still at large. The Phantom Curtain Puller of Olde Butler's Wharf!

The Ants continued their Marquee residency into the New Year. Adam and I used to go into Soho to watch porno films after the soundcheck and before the show. Can you imagine, just me and him walking into a porno, dressed in what we would be wearing on-stage later that evening? I had a lovely pair of evening gloves, kid leather with little tiny pearl buttons that he used to spend ages getting me into with a hook and eye, then tying a ribbon around the top so they'd stay up. They had come from Big Biba's; I must have found them on the floor there once, because I certainly couldn't have afforded the £45 price tag.

I did try a lot of different outfits out at those gigs and a lot of new make-up ideas. Sometimes I was wearing rubber, sometimes I was wearing a man's shirt with a tie, a leather pencil skirt…

BERTIE MARSHALL: That's what I saw, a twinset and pearls with a brown rubber A-line skirt. And you could see the gob running down your skirt, it was flying through the air, it was disgusting. There was some guy at the front who was doing it over and over again and you picked up the microphone, twirled it around and SMASHED HIM down to the floor. He had that coming.

Serves him right for being too close. If he's in gobbing distance, he's in smacking distance. I did warn him: "You spit at me one more time, I'm going to smash your face in." And he spat.

290

Pus in boots

The Ants' following was very loyal. They would injure themselves, but they would never go home. They painted their own clothes with pictures of us – there was one really great one with Adam on one sleeve and me on the other. They would jump onstage and leap into the audience with no fear at all.

DAVE BARBE: They were amazing: Duncan Greig, Jon Srobat and Martin Pope. They were really tough boys. They used to go down Rotherhithe and have punch-ups with skinheads. They were working-class boys whose dads were firemen and builders, classic punk rock boys.

One of them came to a gig with a terrible septic hand. It was Justin Time, another member of the gang. He was looking really ill when he turned up, all white and sweaty, and he showed me his bad hand. The night before we'd played and he'd jumped on the stage, jumped off the stage, and the whole of his hand had gone across the floor. He had poison going up to his elbow and all of his hand was pus. I said: "OK, right, you can watch the gig and you come to me straight after, or I'll find you if you don't." Then I took him to hospital. I mean, he had fucking septicaemia coming on. He wasn't going to miss the gig, though. That would have been a headline: 'MAN DIES OF SEPTIC HAND AT ANTS GIG'.

RICHARD CABUT: The Ants had a very violent following of their own. They had all those people like Duncan and Martin: they were young and they wouldn't take shit. In those days when punks were being picked on by skinheads, that didn't happen with the Ants, or in any area where the Ants were playing because the Ants crowd were tougher and more psychotic than anything or anyone. They kind of mirrored Adam's manic-ness with this hardcore element.

Quatermass and the Peel session

Also in January, John Walters made good on the promise he had made behind the locked dressing-room door and invited us to Maida Vale Studios to record the songs 'Puerto Rican', 'Deutscher Girls', 'It

Doesn't Matter' and 'Lou' for the first Ants Peel session. We were totally unprepared for the situation; we had never even heard of a parabolic microphone before, let alone encountered a room full of them.

But I did find the door to the Radiophonic Workshop.[1] I was so excited. I opened it up and thought there were going to be Cybermen and Daleks and everything flying around like that scene in *Poltergeist*. Instead, it was a dusty old room with a box of sand and a pair of pretend shoes used to make walking sounds. Not even a man in a lab coat. It must have been his day off.

When *Jubilee* came out in February, the soundtrack LP contained the first Ants recordings of 'Plastic Surgery' and 'Deustcher Girls'. Adam and Dave had also backed up Toyah as The Maneaters, on a song called 'Nine to Five', which she performs in the film. Adam had been very pleased with the German translation that he sang in 'Deustcher Girls' – until James Whalley got to hear it.

DAVE BARBE: James Whalley was like something out of Oscar Wilde and Adam was in awe of him – he had style, panache, he was very classy and erudite. I can remember when Adam did 'Deutscher Girls' when he sung in German, he'd got it translated. James turned round and said: "Sounds fucking Dutch." Adam was shattered.

House of Whiplash

Back in December, after Russ Meyer and Roger Ebert had departed, Malcolm cast around for replacements. He turned to our in-house exploitation cinema expert for advice, and between them they came

---

[1] The BBC Radiophonic Workshop is a sound-effects unit, set up in 1958 to create incidental or 'foley' sounds and new music for radio and then television productions. It was originally based at Delaware Road, Maida Vale, where the Peel sessions were recorded, and is most famous for creating the effects for the classic sci-fi series *Quatermass and the Pit* and, of course, the *Doctor Who* theme. Two women were significant in pioneering the electronic music created there. Co-founder Daphne Oram (1925–2003) was the first female ever to direct an electronic music studio, set up a personal studio, and design and construct an electronic musical instrument. Delia Derbyshire (1937–2001) created the electronic arrangement of the *Doctor Who* theme from a score by Ron Grainer in 1963. Another girl, another planet, indeed.

up with independent horror-meister Pete Walker and screenwriter Michael Armstrong.

> **ALAN JONES:** After Russ left the project, I did discuss Pete Walker with Malcolm because he asked me who was big in UK exploitation at the time. I loved Walker's *House of Whipcord*, *Frightmare* and *House of Mortal Sin*. The screenwriter David McGillivray was a good friend of mine at the time, but Malcolm didn't want David, he wanted Michael Armstrong, who wrote and starred in *Eskimo Nell*, one of the best Brit sex films of the decade. That was Malcolm all over: he asked for info, used it, never gave you any credit.

Walker and Armstrong were courted with a trip to see the Pistols play live, material that Armstrong would make good use of in his screenplay.[2] He had already produced some masterful scripts for *Mark of the Devil* (1970), *Eskimo Nell* (1975) and the hugely controversial *The Black Panther* (1977), and had a clear vision of how to present the story: he planned to use all the tricks of 1950s Tin Pan Alley, when plenty of music movies had used the device of the film industry, completely misunderstanding the rebel set they sought to exploit.

The vision he wrote for Malcolm is littered with details that suggest Armstrong had a crystal ball: Rotten's mother is a dominatrix called Miss Whiplash, a virtual stand-in for Linda and Buckingham Gate; Sid's relationship with his mother is uncomfortable to the point of actual incest.[3] But the most uncanny act of precognition is the name he gave it: *A Star Is Dead*.

Armstrong handed the finished draft to Malcolm in January 1978 and didn't hear from him again for seven years. In 1985, out of the blue, Malcolm got back in touch and invited the seemingly forgotten scriptwriter out to dinner in Los Angeles, where he gave his version

---

[2] See *A Star Is Dead: The Screenplays* by Michael Armstrong (Paper Dragon Productions, 2017), in which Armstrong recounts his and Walker's hair-raising introduction to the Pistols in hilarious detail, as well as his subsequent, revealing meeting with Malcolm in Hollywood in 1985, in which Malcolm explained that "the whole thing had been nothing more than a gigantic scam perpetuated to try and make himself a millionaire" (p. 36).

[3] Marianne Faithfull was at one point slated to play Sid's mother, when Russ Meyer and Roger Ebert were still on board. John Tiberi: "That was really the big one because they had to have a sex scene together. I don't know if Sid would have ever done that, though. He was quite prudish."

of what happened next. In view of what had occurred between the original commission and then, perhaps Malcolm could not be entirely blamed for explaining his tardiness away as "Events, dear boy, events."

Beers, steers and queers

The Pistols' tour of America was a disaster. Wanting to avoid Los Angeles and New York, Malcolm had booked dates across the Deep South, the very place where the band were least likely to be understood or accepted.

> **JONH INGHAM:** That was where Malcolm really screwed up. He thought he could duplicate England, forgetting that America is a huge country.

At the beginning of the tour, the plane Warner had laid on for them was hit by lightning. They reverted to travelling by bus instead, covering endless miles across a hostile winter landscape, which didn't add much to the general bonhomie. The tour managers employed by their American record company to go over the heads of ostensible tour managers John Tiberi and Sophie Richmond did everything they could to prevent Sid from going AWOL and scoring, including beating him up. But he didn't let that stop him.

> **VIVIENNE WESTWOOD:** Malcolm told my son Ben that, when they were touring America, The Sex Pistols were in some redneck diner and there were these blokes sitting there, looking them up and down, waiting for them to have something to eat. And Sid got up, went over to this table where they were and cut his wrist on the bloke's steak. They just sat there while he did it and he walked back again. They thought they were going to be waiting for them outside, but the blokes just got up and went; they didn't hang around. I mean. He was very crazy.

They were pelted by bottles of Jack Daniel's in San Antonio, where the audience erupted in a seething mass of fighting good ol' boys who did not appreciate the Cowboys T-shirt Rotten was wearing any more than the Old Bill in Piccadilly Circus had enjoyed seeing Alan Jones in the same design. In Baton Rouge, Sid started having sex on-stage with a willing blonde. This time, the audience showed their appreciation the same way as football hooligans back home – by raining their small change down on the Pistols' heads.

JOHN TIBERI: It's not as if there's a line you must not cross, but not even since Charlie Manson or Altamont has anyone ever done theatre in rock'n'roll in America the way the Pistols did it. It isn't a death wish or an outlaw thing; it was just a rock gig, and people were throwing themselves in the way of the bass guitar more than they were getting hit by it. It was nuts. It was too nuts. We were opening up the floodgates to insanity.

After this gig, Steve refused to go back on the bus with Sid and John; he and Paul started flying to their next venues instead. The group was fragmenting, but Malcolm continued to ignore what was in front of his face and come up with new ideas for the film instead. By the time they got to San Francisco on 13 January, he had made plans to meet up with Great Train Robber Ronnie Biggs in Rio next.[4]

John was not going to have anything to do with this. At San Francisco Winterland on 14 January, after an epic encore of 'No Fun', he asked the crowd: "Ever got the feeling you've been cheated?" before dropping his mic and walking out of the Pistols.

JONH INGHAM: I went to Winterland and they were fantastic. When John said: "Have you ever got the feeling you've been cheated?" that was just incredible. You could see that they were just letting out all that frustration, the way things had been going, the bad ride they'd had in the media and everyone hating them with no context whatsoever for anyone to be understood, Sid out of control – the band were really falling apart. You could tell because there was the Paul and Steve faction, Sid being

---

[4] Ronnie Biggs was one of the Great Train Robbers who held up the mail train from Glasgow in the early hours of 8 August 1963, his own 34th birthday. The gang got away with £2.6 million in untraceable bank-notes (the equivalent of £50 million today). He was arrested three weeks later, along with eleven other members of the gang, and was jailed in 1964 for a thirty-year term. Biggs served only fifteen months before scaling the wall of Wandsworth Prison and absconding, first to Australia and then to Brazil. He eventually returned to the UK in 2001 and was immediately imprisoned. Suffering from poor health, he was released on compassionate grounds in 2009 and died in 2013, aged 84. An honour guard of Hells Angels escorted his hearse to the crematorium.

Sid and John out front on his own – the focus is all on John. And he was just phenomenal. I was standing towards the back on the main floor and everyone around me was just going mental.

PAUL COOK: Looking back at it now, even Malcolm underestimated the crowds we got there. Sid nearly did die in San Francisco. He OD'd after our last show. I found him on the floor of some shithole somewhere in the middle of nowhere. So the writing was on the wall, really.

The next day, John flew to New York and then back to London. Sophie Richmond took the deathly ill Sid to Los Angeles for a night to try and recover. They flew on to New York the next day with John Tiberi, and couldn't rouse Sid when they arrived. He was in a drug-induced coma and had to be rushed to the nearest hospital – in the middle of a blizzard. Still following Malcolm's plan, Paul and Steve decamped to sunnier climes with Julien Temple, to meet Ronnie Biggs in Brazil. Dazed by the rapid unfurling of events, they still hadn't come to terms with what had happened.

PAUL COOK: I thought we'd split up for a little while, everybody would have a break and we'd get back together. I thought we'd have a few months for everyone to calm down a little bit – but that took twenty-five years. Everything was so fucked up. We were stuck in Brazil for six weeks and we ended up getting into all sorts of chaos there with Ronnie Biggs. We did have a great time, though.

And now, the end is near...

The *Sun* was the first paper to announce the break up of their most hated band, all across its front cover on 19 January. Nonetheless, Malcolm still seemed to think he could put things back on track. But, by the end of January, when he, Rotten and Sid were all back in London and he had record companies and disgruntled former colleagues breathing down his neck, it became very evident there was no way back. On 3 February, Richard Branson paid for John, now using his real surname, to go over to Jamaica, ostensibly as an A&R consultant for Virgin's new reggae signings. Malcolm sent John

Tiberi after him to try and find out what was really going on and shoot some footage that might be usable in the film. Neither plan worked.

JOHN TIBERI: In my experience, Malcolm was always picking on John. It wasn't a negative picking on him; he responded to it and they worked together. But, after September 1977, that was completely lacking. Malcolm wasn't doing that any more, all he was interested in was the film. John was quite troubled by that. He wouldn't say as much, but he didn't understand the way it was going to work, that it was really only a vehicle. He was suspicious of this – and the nature of film is that you have to trust a lot… Nobody explained. Like the band breaking up, that's never really been explained. The film may be similar. What I'm hinting at is that it's Malcolm. That's the explanation. In both cases.

PAUL COOK: John had had enough and we'd had enough of John. Everyone had had enough of everyone. No one could handle it. John always thought everything was about him. A difficult, complex character. When we first got together, I really made the effort to connect with him. I used to go with John to his place, stay with him and we'd go out together drinking. I really made an effort to bond and I think that he appreciated that. I was still at home then, and he used to come round and stay at my mum and dad's place. Mum asked me once: "What's up with him? He looks a bit depressed?" Well, he might well be.

VIVIENNE WESTWOOD: Malcolm was this sort of demagogue who wanted to be important, and this is what was similar to Johnny Rotten. Johnny Rotten would be really nice – but as soon as you got close to him, he'd do something really horrible to push you away. I call it jiving they try and keep you on a string all the time. In the case of Malcolm, it was self-preservation, absolutely. They are the same in this thing of self-preservation and being horrible to people. It kind of works together.

Prole art threat

In the wake of *Jubilee*'s release on 22 February, I had the misfortune of being interviewed by the so-called *enfants terribles* of the *NME*,

Julie Burchill and Tony Parsons, in a piece published on 15 April 1978. The only issue I've ever had with any journalist in my whole time with punk is with those two. The whole thing felt like a set-up, them trying to bully me into a corner.

Their analysis of *Jubilee* was that it was the product of middle-class people desperate to return to the 1960s and remake *Blow-Up* and contained none of the truth of punk's strictly proletarian roots. Which was more of a leap than I could ever have made, even at the height of my ballet powers. They were remarkably ignorant about where Malcolm, Vivienne and I had all come from.

I should have walked out, but I didn't want to give them the satisfaction of saying that I had walked out on them; that would have been just what they wanted. They both went at me, calling me middle class, because I came from Sussex and had recently appeared on the front cover of *Ritz* magazine in a shoot by David Bailey. Burchill also came out with the statement that Adam sang Nazi songs. I'm not violent, particularly, but I came very close to knocking her block off that day.

Between working on the publicity for *Jubilee* and working at the shop, everything got too much for me to continue being in the Ants. It was pressure of work, it was Derek Jarman telling me to pop up to Liverpool and do an opening and a talk, and there might be an Ants gig on that night and I couldn't do both. There was no falling out. I don't think I've ever had a bad word with Adam in my life.

My final gig with the Ants was at Camden Roundhouse, with X-Ray Spex, on 14 May 1978. It was Johnny Bivouac's last stand, too. Things were drawing to an end for the original group of people who had met at 430 King's Road. From the house he had recently bought in Gunter Grove, John was formulating what would become Public Image Ltd with Wobble and Keith Levene. Tracie O'Keefe had suddenly fallen ill and, at the end of May, she died. Not long afterwards, Poly Styrene suffered a breakdown while on the road with X-Ray Spex, who by now had cracked the charts with 'The Day the World Turned Day-Glo'. She left her band and her punk identity behind at the age of 21 in June 1978.

Catch a falling star

Adam had been approached in May by a subsidiary of Virgin called EG, set up by David Enthoven and John Gaydon to release Brian Eno's ambient albums. They offered to sign him on the understanding that he would ditch the Ants and go solo. This didn't happen. Instead, Johnny Bivouac was replaced by the charismatic Matthew Ashman.

DAVE BARBE: Matthew Ashman worked brilliantly, but he and Adam never got on. He walked into the rehearsal room with a guitar without a case, going, "Which one's Adam? Fucking cunt this and cunt that," and spit, spit, spit... Adam looked at me aghast. But he hammered the audition, he was brilliant, and then he left and Adam turned round to me and went: "He hasn't even got his own gear!" And for the rest of the time I was in the Ants I was trying to bridge the gap between them.

299

The cheeky chappie at the bar

Matthew Ashman (1960–95), with his Travis Bickle hairstyle and incisive guitar style, cut a distinctive and influential figure throughout his musical career, which was tragically cut short from complications arising from diabetes when he was only 35. After his time in the Ants and Bow Wow Wow, he formed The Chiefs of Relief with Dave, Leigh Gorman on bass and former premier Ant fan Duncan Greig on keyboards. Paul Cook also played in a later version of the band.

In the later 1980s he became a session guitarist, playing with Oui 3 and Wendy James, and in early 1990 made one record with my former husband, Kevin Mooney. His final project, Agent Provocateur, released two singles on the influential Wall of Sound dance label before getting picked up by Epic, for whom they intended to record an album with Black Grape's producer Danny Sabre. *Where the Wild Things Are* was finally released two years after Matthew's untimely death.

Dave Barbe writes: "He was beautiful and stroppy. An archetypal 'Sid' style punk. He and Adam shared the same birthday. They never got on. Adam would take the piss, calling him the 'Norman Wisdom' of punk, 'Mr Grimsdale!' But however Adam derided him, he knew he couldn't get a better, more passionate guitarist. Adam was the god, but Matthew always had his little retinue down the front: the tough Ant fans. They migrated to Bow Wow Wow after the split . . .

"Matthew always thought he'd be a star in his own right, but never quite had that very special thing that someone like Adam has. He was my best mate: eight years sharing rooms in the Ants and Bow Wow Wow, travelling all over the world . . . Wot fun we had. But he always had that thing for drugs and drink, and he was a man who could not put limits on his tastes. He was darkly humorous with that charming smile and gobby snarl. Stylish and delicate . . . I still miss him."

For a fictional rendering of Dave and Matthew's adventures, Dave's own brilliant novel *Mud Sharks* (as Dave Barbarossa, Ignite, 2013) is highly recommended.

RICHARD CABUT: Adam was so threatened by Matthew Ashman, man of the people. Because everyone loved Matthew. We all went to see the Ants, but Adam was not really approachable, was he? Whereas Matthew was the cheerful, cheeky chappie at the bar.

The first three Ants gigs with the 17-year-old Matthew were a debutante's ball at the Hard Rock Café in June 1978, attended by Formula 1 Champion James Hunt; and two Rock Against Racism (RAR) benefits, at Ealing Technical College on 10 June and then South Bank Polytechnic on 17 June.[5]

The first RAR gig passed off peacefully, but the second came close to a riot when skinheads wrecked the changing rooms and someone set fire to the PA in the middle of the Ants' set. Undeterred, Adam and his men played on and managed to end the evening peacefully, despite, as Dave remembers, being hit over the head by flying bottles. Watching in the audience, an impressed Decca A&R Mike Reid stepped forward to offer them a deal, which they signed a month later. Meanwhile, they recorded a second Peel session of 'Physical', 'Xerox', 'Friends' and 'Cleopatra'. It seemed that the Ants were properly on their way.

Beneath the pavements, Sid

Coming back from Jamaica empty-handed, John Tiberi had thought of another idea. He and Julien Temple scouted the perfect venue and shot footage of Sid in an empty theatre inside an eighteenth-century hotel on the rue de Rivoli, Paris. On a set built for Serge Gainsbourg, Sid interpreted the Frank Sinatra classic 'My Way' as only he could. This was probably the best moment of the entire *Rock 'n' Roll Swindle*.

The recording, produced by Steve Jones in his first ever credit, was released as the new Sex Pistols 45 at the end of June, with one of two tracks recorded in Rio by Steve, Paul and Ronnie Biggs, 'A Punk Prayer', as the B-side. Ironically, this would prove to be their best selling single. Eager to tell the story of the Pistols entirely from his point of view, Malcolm now transformed all the footage Julien Temple and John Tiberi had accumulated into what would become

---

[5] RAR had been formed in 1976 as a confrontational counterpoint to the National Front, who were gaining increasing numbers of recruits, large numbers of whom had started infiltrating punk gigs. They started organising gigs across the country in early 1977 and staged their biggest event in April 1978, with a march from Trafalgar Square to Victoria Park in Hackney where 100,000 people watched X-Ray Spex, Steel Pulse and The Clash. Daniel Rachel's epic oral history *Walls Come Tumbling Down* (Picador, 2016) tells the story of RAR, 2 Tone and Red Wedge in detail, featuring the voices of all involved.

The Great Rock 'n' Roll Swindle, presenting it as a ten-point plan to do over the music business while embezzling as much money as possible along the way.

Malcolm's ten-point plan was as follows:
- Lesson One: How to manufacture your group
- Lesson Two: Establish the name Sex Pistols
- Lesson Three: How to sell the swindle
- Lesson Four: Don't play, don't give the game away
- Lesson Five: Steal as much money as possible from the record company of your choice
- Lesson Six: How to become the world's number one tourist atttaction
- Lesson Seven: Cultivate hatred, it is your greatest asset
- Lesson Eight: How to diversify your business
- Lesson Nine: Taking civilisation to the barbarians – USA
- Lesson Ten: Who killed Bambi?

Shooting began in August, with Eddie Tenpole Tudor filming the track that was the sole link to the original script, *Who Killed Bambi?* Malcolm was auditioning him for the role of new Pistols singer.

People have asked me lots of times over the years, why I wasn't in it. Well, there was a clip of me from *So It Goes* in there. But I really, really didn't want to be involved. Early on, I heard the rumblings of it when it was starting to be filmed and it was obviously going to be really shit. There was no way I wanted to be in it.

PAUL COOK: The band had split up and Malcolm was on this quest to make a film and obviously he couldn't get John involved, 'cos he'd left the band, so me and Steve were coerced into doing it, Steve being the main one because Malcolm had that influence on Steve and he was really into it. I didn't really want to do it. It was such a mish-mash. They had to make up cartoons – and this is when Malcolm started going on his trip, he actually believed the story. The only important bit about it is the story about conning your way to the top of the music business in ten easy steps – I kind of think that Malcolm thought that was his idea to start with and it wasn't. Nothing was contrived, it all happened naturally. But I think by then Malcolm believed that he'd come up with this masterplan... It's him being Fagin, basically. It wasn't a good period.

They called me up from the studios and said could I come, because everyone was really down. Everybody, the crew, actors, everybody – and would I jolly things up and make things better? As if I'd come down and tell some jokes and it would all be all right again. I said: "No, fuck off."

There were so many opportunities to make a good film, but I think, truthfully, that Malcolm didn't want to hand the reins over to someone who knew what they were doing. He wanted complete control over it.

PAUL COOK: You're right there, he wanted to create his own myth. This is when the Malcolm McLaren show started to roll into full force. To be fair, he did have a vision, but it was all so mixed up, there was so much madness going on all the time.

Sid, having performed his final works as a Sex Pistol by recording versions of two Eddie Cochran songs, 'C'mon Everybody' and 'Something Else', also washed his hands of Malcolm. He had, of course, been reunited with Nancy by now. They were sharing a flat in Pindock Mews, Maida Vale – which at the time was heroin central. Things got so bad there that one of their friends overdosed and died while lying on their bed and they were so stoned they didn't realise. This temporarily shocked them into taking the methadone cure, which only succeeded in getting them onto an even more addictive opiate. Then Nancy had a better idea – to go back to New York. To get the money for their fare, they played a final gig at the Electric Ballroom in Camden as The Vicious White Kids with Rat Scabies, Steve New and – irony of ironies – Glen Matlock. In the last week of August, they got on the plane. Their first stop was the Chelsea Hotel.

18

CRISIS, WHAT CRISIS?

The Winter of Discontent
(September 1978–May 1979)

Chelsea girl

The Chelsea Hotel, at 222 West 23rd Street between Seventh and Eight Avenues, has been a designated New York City landmark since 1966 and was placed on the US National Register of Historic Places in 1977.[1] The twelve-storey redbrick building has housed many famous residents, from Mark Twain to William Burroughs, Jimi Hendrix to Patti Smith and Robert Mapplethorpe, while Iggy Pop, Dee Dee Ramone and Johnny Thunders have all passed through its portals. Leonard Cohen penned two songs about his affair with Janis Joplin conducted between his room 424 and her room 411 in 1968; and Arthur C. Clarke wrote *2001: A Space Odyssey* during his tenure there in 1964, when he and Stanley Kubrick were in collaboration on

---

[1] In August 2011, the Chelsea stopped taking reservations in order to undergo renovations. Although long-term residents stayed put, by November the *New York Times* was reporting that all the hotel's famous artworks had been taken off the walls, supposedly for their own protection, but this was perceived by the residents as a bad omen. The building got a new owner in 2013, but plans to turn it into a boutique hotel were halted in 2016 by a further legal clash with residents. At the time of writing, it was scheduled to reopen in 2018, but had yet to do so.

the movie. Andy Warhol, of course, filmed *Chelsea Girls* inside the building in 1966 and it was the last place Dylan Thomas ever checked into, passing through its doors and into infinity on 9 November 1953, after, legend has it, consuming eighteen whiskies in a row.

There is something very gothic and forbidding about the appearance of the Chelsea. Not for nothing is this the location where PI Harry Angel (Mickey Rourke) meets his sinister employer Louis Cyphre (Robert De Niro) in *Angel Heart*, Alan Parker's 1987 supernatural noir that was based on William Hjorstberg's novel *Falling Angel* and the author's memories of sinister feelings stirred by the old hotel. It's really not hard to imagine the Devil taking a suite there.

Perhaps he might have been in residence when by far the most notorious incident in the hotel's history occurred on 11 October 1978, in room 100, where, in the early hours of the morning, Nancy Spungen was found stabbed to death.

As I had already discovered when I made my own first visit to New York in 1976, at this point in its history the Chelsea's fortunes were in decline, its main attractions for Sid and Nancy having been cheap rent and the fact that, as *Rolling Stone* magazine would put it when reporting on her death, the first three floors had been pretty much "reserved for junkies and other low-life types".

The dream had been that, from this base, Nancy would manage Sid to fame and fortune. They quickly put together a band, enlisting old friends Jerry Nolan and Arthur Kane, and played a gig at Max's Kansas City on 7 September. The New York music industry was not unduly impressed, either by Sid's performance or Nancy's attempts at public relations when dealing with a crowd of people who had already seen it all. Thanks to their habits, neither of them was in strong physical shape: Sid had not recovered from the repercussions of his last trip to the States and Nancy was suffering from a kidney complaint.

Which didn't stop her from spending her last night on Earth trying to score.

Checking-out time

The various reports of what went on that evening mention different drug dealers coming to and from the couple's apartment in the

Chelsea until the early hours of the morning. Sid's account to the police was that he woke up to find a trail of blood leading from the bed to the bathroom, where Nancy was lying under the sink with a five-inch hunting knife in her side – a weapon she had bought him in Times Square as protection against the many New Yorkers eager to take a pop at him. She died at some point between 5 a.m. and 9 a.m., but the investigating police officers were never able to establish an exact time.

When he was arrested, Sid did claim responsibility. He was taken to the Third Homicide Division on 51st Street and charged with second-degree murder. Nancy's body was removed from the hotel at 5.30 p.m. on 12 October and the news of the crime soon spread far and wide.

Malcolm was made aware of what had happened by a *New York Post* reporter ringing him that afternoon. He flew out straight away and managed to get there in time for the bail hearing. Sid was remanded in Riker's Island prison, where he forcibly underwent cold turkey. While Malcolm started trying to raise his bail money from Virgin, Sid's mother, Ann Beverley, flew out on Sunday 16 October and was able to visit her son in the intimidating surroundings of his place of incarceration. On the same day, Nancy's physical remains were laid to rest in Philadelphia.

Sid was released into the custody of his mother on 17 October. He was in frail health from the detox regime and tried to kill himself five days later by taking all his supply of methadone and slashing his arm open with a knife from wrist to elbow. His mother, who found him but did nothing, later told Jon Savage that she had found a suicide-pact note in his handwriting in his pocket. It was Malcolm who got him taken into the psychiatric ward of Bellevue Hospital.

Being so far away and not knowing any of those details, my own response to hearing the news was awful, really, but it was a gut reaction. I burst out laughing when I was called from the shop with the news that Nancy had been found dead. It was Vivienne, I think, who phoned me, and if I remember rightly we both had a chuckle. Nancy had caused so much trouble and bad feeling, it felt like a relief that she had gone.

Vivienne designed a T-shirt saying, 'She's dead, I'm alive, I'm yours' that went on immediate sale at Seditionaries. She explained at the time: "You care about some people more than others, more about Sid than Nancy." She was also aware that the general public would probably find it distasteful: "and I did it for that reason too, because I like to upset people". As well as this, she made a Sid Action Man with a swastika vest, laid him in a little coffin and put him on display in the shop.

Whatever you think about this now, it fitted right in with the times. This was the season that would become known as the Winter of Discontent, when long spells of industrial action crippled the UK. Rubbish piled up in the streets of London and stacks of coffins lay unburied in cemeteries across the land. By the time the New Year came around, the docks were all closed too, but Prime Minister James Callaghan still managed to get right up the nose of the *Sun*, who reported him as coming back from holiday with the words "Crisis, what crisis?" on his lips.

Ants abroad

I had taken a break from the shop and the publicity for *Jubilee* that autumn when I joined the Ants on tour in Italy. They had already recorded their first single, 'Young Parisians'/'Lady', which Decca would release on 20 October with a single sleeve, designed by Adam and rendered by artists Wad and Clare, that he was very pleased with. The band began their first European tour in Germany at the end of September and found the place very much to their liking, especially Berlin, where Iggy Pop and David Bowie had recently been holed up, recording the classic albums *The Idiot*, *Low* and *Heroes* at Hansa Studios. Adam had devised a new look for himself, based on the Italian pre-war Futurist movement[2] and Japanese Kabuki theatre,

---

[2] The Italian Futurist movement, as opposed to the 1980s one led by Steve Strange, began life as a manifesto launched by Italian poet Filippo Tommaso Marinetti in 1909. He proposed an art movement that would forcefully shake off the past and declare "a new beauty, the beauty of speed". Futurist painting used elements of Neo-Impressionism and Cubism to create the impression of movement and energy. The Futurists often depicted conflict in their paintings and it was not long before they were drawn into the battlefields of the First World War.

Dance for your daddy

Lindsay Kemp (1938–2018), who sadly died during the writing of this book, came from a one-parent family in South Shields. His father Norman was killed onboard the *Patroclus* when it was sunk by a German U-boat in November 1940. This was the second tragedy to hit the family – Lindsay's older sister Norma had died at the age of 5 from meningitis. Norma had already been getting rave reviews for her dancing ability in the *Shields Gazette* for routines performed with kimonos and fans brought back from Japan by her father. Young Lindsay inherited these and wore the kimono to infants' school, until his headmaster wrote to his mother requesting he didn't. He was already dancing for his poor departed daddy long before his mother took him to the cinema to see Michael Powell and Emeric Pressburger's *The Red Shoes* (1948), which sealed his fate the way *Romeo and Juliet* did mine.

Linsday moved to Bradford as a teenager to study at the College of Art, where he met both fellow student David Hockney and dancer and life model Jack Birkett, with whom he would go on to form the first Lindsay Kemp Mime Company. It was Hockney who urged Lindsay to go to London, after they had seen their first ballet together, *A Rake's Progress*, at Sadler's Wells. Lindsay took lodgings in Bateman Street, Soho, and met the 19-year-old David Bowie in 1966. Bowie had seen Lindsay in a show, and two days later he started attending Lindsay's dance classes in Covent Garden. They embarked on an affair and wrote a show, *Pierrot in Turquoise*, which came to an abrupt end when Lindsay found his leading man in bed with their costume designer, Natasha Korniloff. He downed a bottle of whisky and slashed his wrists with a razor blade. Luckily he was found and taken to hospital. The pair would not collaborate together again until 1972, when they staged the two-hour live spectacular of Ziggy Stardust at the Rainbow, supported by Roxy Music – a gig I had the privilege of seeing with my own eyes.

After that, I followed Bowie's example and went to the Pineapple Studios in Covent Garden, where Lindsay was holding a course with Jack Birkett, and did a few sessions with them there. We would meet again on the set of *Sebastiane* and then, of course, *Jubilee*. Lindsay's accomplishments are too numerous to mention here; they include giving dance lessons to Kate Bush, Peter Gabriel and Mia Farrow and continuing to teach, perform and paint to his dying day. He had such an amazing vision of his own life, such a heart-warming perspective. He was a very dear man.

• Artist Garry Hunter interviews Lindsay about his life and times here: fitzrovianoir.com/home something that had probably first come from Lindsay Kemp and his early influence on Bowie. It certainly appealed to me; I was going to have a Kabuki wig made. I thought it would have looked really good. But, looking back on it now, maybe it would have made me look more like David Bowie in *Labyrinth*.

I can remember flying into Italy on 12 October, completely unaware of what had just gone on in New York, to join the Ants at the Modanosta Fashion Festival in Milan. When I got off the plane, my make-up fell straight off my face onto the tarmac, it was so bloody hot.

The band played two more nights at Cinema Nuevo in Milan, doing a set that ended with '(Send a Letter to) Jordan', before travelling on to play two nights at Rome's Titan Club on 20 and 21 October. There was a fantastic atmosphere in the audience, but the Ants' relationship with Megalovision was getting uncomfortable and it wouldn't be long before they parted ways. Dave Barbe ruefully recalls a source of friction – but also amusement – on the tour bus for those European dates.

DAVE BARBE: What happened was that Howard tried to get off with me and Adam loved it. Maybe I was just a phase for him, I don't know, but it amused Adam something rotten. He would engineer it so Howard always sat next to me on the bus. Because I was just with my first wife, Mandy, and on the night my first son was born, I remember Howard buying a bottle of champagne at the Roxy. So he knew Mandy, and he knew my situation. But I was so naive, I didn't know what a gay bloke was, seriously. So all the way through Europe, from southern Italy up to Rome, I was stuck next to this fucking bloke and Adam was just killing himself laughing.

Never trust a man with egg on his face

It was the end for Megalovision – and things weren't going as anticipated with Decca, either. 'Young Parisians', which Adam had chosen deliberately as the least representative single – "everybody was saying we were a hardcore punk band and this sounds like a 1920s Parisian jazz song" – had not sold well and he was certain that the company weren't pushing it properly, because the boss didn't get what they were trying to do.[3] They recorded 'Kick!' at Mickie Most's RAK Studios in St John's Wood and finished the year with some gigs at the Moonlight Club in West Hampstead under the name Adam y los Antos, with a feeling of uncertainty as to what the New Year would bring.

Which was an emotion shared by all of us who had been living at Buckingham Gate. After Nancy had brought Linda to the police's attention, the St James Hotel management tried to get her out by raising the service charge every five minutes. When that didn't work, they offered to buy out her lease. Linda was not in a position to refuse. By the beginning of 1979, the once happy band of punk campers had to go their separate ways.

Filthy lucre

On 10 November, John Lydon started High Court proceedings against Malcolm to wind up the Sex Pistols partnership and a date was then set for the second week of February. John had meanwhile signed an eight-album deal with Virgin for Public Image Ltd (PiL), so Richard Branson was hopeful this might be resolved out of court. The first incarnation of PiL, with Wobble on bass, Keith Levene on guitar and Jim Walker on drums, were all coexisting in John's house in Gunter Grove in not too perfect harmony. The first single, 'Public Image', was released in October, with the album of the same name following in December, by which time Jim Walker had left the band.

Paul and Steve came back to London from Rio in the winter of 1978 and worked on the recordings of the last Sex Pistols singles and the filming of *The Great Rock 'n' Roll Swindle,* to which they also contributed the songs 'Friggin in the Riggin' and 'Silly Thing', taking it in turns to do vocals on the latter. The messy end of the band affected Steve badly. Despite everything he had seen Sid do on that last tour, he too started to take heroin – which goes to show how insidious a drug it is. But within those final Pistols recordings lay what

---

[3] Despite turning down The Beatles with the famous line: "Guitar groups are on the way out, Mr Epstein", Decca was hugely successful in the 1960s, signing The Rolling Stones, The Zombies and The Moody Blues. But after the Stones left in 1970, a lot of other artists followed. The only other punk Decca signing was Slaughter and the Dogs, who enjoyed more in the way of success with their 'Where Have All the Boot Boys Gone' single in 1977 and *Do It Dog Style* album in May 1978.

would become Steve's lifeline – his production credit on 'My Way' led to an offer to go over to San Francisco and work with The Avengers and Joan Jett.

PAUL COOK: Steve had to go to America; otherwise he could have killed himself easily. My biggest regret is that we never did another album. When we were writing songs without Glen, it was more 'Bodies', 'EMI', 'Holidays in the Sun', so it could have been a great album. But we'd have had to do it without Malcolm. We could have done it without Sid, because Steve had done all the bass on the first album anyway; that wouldn't have been a problem. Just me, Steve and John could have done it. But we chose Malcolm over John. We didn't want to go down that avenue. I think John was ready to go off and do his own stuff, really. He was very driven and he had a good band around him.

Sid was arraigned at the Manhattan Supreme Court on 21 November 1978 – the $50,000 bail supplied by Virgin to Malcolm – and went straight into the arms of another disturbed girlfriend, Michelle Robinson. Michelle called herself an actress but she was performing in a different arena when I met her in New York, as we shall see in the next chapter. Ann Beverley, Sid's mother, remained in New York as Sid set about his next wave of chaos: getting into a fight with Patti Smith's brother Todd on 9 December at a disco and hitting him on the head with a broken bottle. The next day he was back in Riker's Island, where he remained while his next court hearing went ahead on 12 December. A new hearing was scheduled for 31 January, and until then Sid would stay inside and detox.

The final curtain

With Sid due in court on 1 February, Malcolm planned to meet him with the bail money and bring him to Miami. He aimed to make some more recordings with Steve and Paul to raise money for a defence fund. However, Malcolm was also due back in court in London the next week to begin the case John had brought against him. In the end, he was detained in England, powerless to stop what came next.

On 1 February, after an impassioned plea by his lawyer, James Merberg, Sid was let out on bail by lunchtime. Ann Beverley was there to greet him. They went back to Michelle Robinson's flat, where Ann cooked them a meal of spaghetti Bolognese and then Sid took his final overdose of heroin, purchased by his dear old mum. Many years later, she told Jon Savage: "I'm glad he died, in view of what happened. Nothing can hurt him any more."

I did meet Ann Beverley while Sid was alive, and I didn't like her very much. I thought she was kind of shallow and almost like a stage mum, in that she wanted him to be as famous as possible. But she didn't anticipate that this was how he would leave his indelible mark on the world.

Needless to say, the press had a field day. "SID VICIOUS DEAD" was the *Sun*'s headline, reflecting their palpable relief. 'DRUGS KILL PUNK STAR SID VICIOUS' pointed out the *Daily Mail* from their ever-vigilant position on the moral high ground. Five days later, while Sid's remains were being cremated in New York,[4] Malcolm and Lydon were back in the Chancery Court. Events were not going Malcolm's way and, on 13 February, after hearing about the tens of thousands of pounds it was alleged that he owed them, even the ever-loyal Paul and Steve changed sides.

Finally, the presiding Mr Justice Browne-Wilkinson ruled, on 16 February, that the only asset available to both parties (the Pistols and Glitterbest) was *The Great Rock 'n' Roll Swindle*.[5] He appointed a receiver. Malcolm flew to Paris the same day to stay with Jean-Charles de Castelbajac and lick his wounds at a safe distance. He would stay there for the best part of the next year, leaving Vivienne to steer 430 King's Road into its next direction alone.

Virgin rush-released *The Great Rock 'n' Roll Swindle* soundtrack only a week later, and the first single to be taken from it was Sid's

---

[4] Ann Beverley managed to drop Sid's ashes in Heathrow Airport when she came home. The story of his remains being sucked into the air conditioning and circulating for all eternity was the inspiration for a comic series called *Punk's Dead*, by David Barnett and Martin Simmonds, published by IDW Publishing in 2018.

[5] *The Great Rock 'n' Roll Swindle* was eventually given a theatrical release on 11 September 1980. Alan Jones remembers going to a preview of the film with Siouxsie: "We went together to that Rank screening cinema in Wardour Street and when we came out, someone tried to beat Sioux up. Even then! Four years after the event, we were still getting aggro."

version of 'Something Else', a song first performed by doomed rock'n'roller Eddie Cochran,[6] which managed to sell nearly twice as many copies as 'God Save the Queen' in the wake of the gory demise of punk's star-crossed lovers.

PAUL COOK: Malcolm was so obsessed about this film and he would fall out with Julien, he would fall out with the producer, and in the end he walked away from it and Julien had to finish it, or it never would have got made. Malcolm was destroying the whole thing he wanted to do. Looking at it now, you can see some of it's funny. Up to a point. The only good thing that come out of it was Julien never stopped working off the back of *The Rock 'n' Roll Swindle*, that made him. He's good at what he does. He done *The Filth and the Fury*, which I think is the best thing that's ever been done about us. But the less said about *The Rock 'n' Roll Swindle* the better, really. It was a really messy way to end the band, it was horrible. John hates it, despises it and despises us for being involved in it, which I can understand.

Blank generation

By the end of February it was all over for the Ants and Decca, too. Even though *Sounds* had given the band the front cover on their last issue in December and the band embarked on a tour of the UK at the beginning of January, Mike Smith, who had signed them, agreed with Adam to terminate their contract. By the time they had finished their gig commitments with a sell-out show at the Lyceum, they were the biggest unsigned band in the country.

They recorded another Peel session at the end of March: 'Ligotage', 'Tabletalk', 'Animals and Men' and 'Never Trust a Man with Egg on His Face'. Shortly afterwards, Adam was approached by Do It Records, the label founded by Robin Scott that was now being run by brothers Ian and Max Tregoning. They agreed to putting the band on a wage and giving them studio time at Olympus Studios

---

[6] Eddie Cochran was killed on Easter Sunday, 17 April 1960, from injuries sustained when the driver of the car he was travelling in lost control and hit a lamppost just outside Chippenham in Wiltshire. He was 22, just one year older than Sid was when he died.

314

in Primrose Hill to complete the recording of the first Ants LP, *Dirk Wears White Sox*.

The Winter of Discontent came to an end when, in February, the four largest public sector unions took 1.5 million employees out on strike. It became Springtime for Thatcher when a vote of no confidence in the government was announced for 30 March. Labour's resultant majority was so slim they were forced to call a general election for 3 May. Thatcher would be following my *Jubilee* fashion dictates of twinset and pearls when she came into office on 4 May.

Catching the red-eye

At this time, David Ireland arrived from New York and started working with Michael and me in Seditionaries. In contrast to the rest of the trauma recorded in this chapter, his recollections of the early months of 1979 are some rare moments of harmony at 430 King's Road.

DAVID IRELAND: I have one really lovely memory of the shop. It was winter, January or February, a very grey day, and just going into the shop and getting teas for everyone and you'd be sitting there brushing mohairs and Michael would be putting studs in Bondage trousers and it was just like being at home with your mum doing the ironing. It was a really lovely atmosphere. Seditionaries was like a magnet for me, but there were a lot of people who were just afraid of you, they found you intimidating... One of the things that stands out for me is that you were accepting of everybody. Because, when I came into the shop, there were people turning up asking for you. There was someone saying they wanted to be a prison warder when they grew up and so they wanted to come in and talk to Jordan.

We were a little hive of activity in there, doing hand sewing, putting in studs and using my little brush – how I loved making the mohair really fluffy. Those jumpers were a thing of beauty, and I actually hand-knitted several of them myself. They don't make mohair like they used to.

As David mentions, I had just decided on another radical change in style. I had my hair dyed a deep red at Robert Lobetta's salon.

315

It wasn't an easy look to achieve, because my hair was so highly bleached by then that it wouldn't hold the colour. But, always resourceful, Robert remembered somebody he knew who used to do hair for ballroom dancers and phoned him up at nine o'clock at night. Sure enough, this old hairdresser came round to Robert's salon on Berkeley Square and sorted things out.

This hairstyle was completely vertical and, to go with it, I ordered a pair of red contact lenses. With white theatrical PanStik covering my face, I think this was perhaps the most effective of all my looks in scaring the shit out of people, and it worked particularly well in cinemas. I was at a screening of *The Exorcist* in Los Angeles, with pale green make-up and those lenses, and when the interval came and I got up to look for my handbag the person sitting behind me nearly passed out.[7] It marked the start of another phase of rapid reinvention in my life.

---

[7] Judge for yourself if I look as terrifying to you as I did to the local mods in this 1979 television clip: www.youtube.com/watch?v=LcpT4Sz296Q

NEW YORK STORIES

From Needle Park to the Factory: my adventures in Gotham (1975 onwards)

Andy Warhol is a scream

I met Andy Warhol four times and I never spotted a chink in him. The person he appeared to be was his persona and he lived it. He was also very friendly and had a good memory for people. I think we had a great affinity for each other because we both invented ourselves from scratch into living works of art and never compromised what we first set out to do. What I think is so important and fundamental to that is that there were no perimeters on how you looked and how beautiful you were. Andy would not necessarily pick people who were really beautiful; a lot of them were misfits in some way or another. He was very derogatory about his own looks; probably as a child he thought he was the most awful gargoyle that you could ever meet. I mean, take someone like myself: I'm not tall, I've never been slim – you can make something else that catches people off guard. Make something better. I think the imperfections of people are just as important, and what you can make of them. Andy was great at that, at reinvention.

The first time I met him was in London in October 1975, when *The Philosophy of Andy Warhol (From A to B and Back Again)* had just been published and he was in town to promote it. On his last night in London, Lord Anthony and Lady Belinda 'Bindy' Lambton threw a party for him to which I was invited. This is not as bizarre a proposition as it sounds – their daughter, Lady Anne, had been working for Andy at the Factory in New York, and in the London of the mid-1970s many different worlds merged through the circles of fashion, art and music. Because I looked so completely different from everyone else in the room, I was on an A-list for events such as these. The Lambtons were no strangers to scandal, either. His Lordship, a Tory MP, had been forced to resign in 1973 over a sex scandal in which he was entrapped by a conman and photographed smoking a joint with two prostitutes. One of them was the smudger's wife, who worked in a stable of high-class call girls run by the aptly named Jean Horn, known to the tabloids as 'a society madam'.[8]

It was a wonderful party, not to be forgotten, and recorded in hilarious detail in Bob Colacello's *Holy Terror: Andy Warhol Close Up* (HarperCollins, 1990), where, with his fine eye for societal detail, Bob remembers me mingling with the Marquess and Marchioness of Dufferin and Ava, Lord and Lady Lichfield, Princess Elizabeth of Yugoslavia, Gunter Sachs, Lucien Freud, Lady Diana Cooper, Caroline Kennedy, Mark Shand, Keith Moon, Martin Amis and the ubiquitous John Paul Getty III.

I was wearing one of my favourite outfits, the Teddy Tinling tennis skirt, which was a little white mini-skirt with red tennis racquets all round the bottom – I'd added black fringing round the bottom of the hem and wore it with black tights. Andy was very taken with some earrings I had that were given to me by my Venezuelan friend Gustavo – they were real dried piranha fish. They were originally keyrings, and I adapted them; the ring goes right through their open mouths. I've still got them to this day and they're still in one piece, too.

I remember Andy took a shine to the teenage Charlie Tennant, who interviewed both of us that evening for the first and last issue of his underground magazine,

---

[8] Lord Lambton later left Bindy and their six children and went to live in Italy with his mistress, in a 400-year-old palace on the outskirts of Siena. When he died in 2006, he left this stately pile and his entire fortune to his son Edward Lambton, Seventh Earl of Durham, leading to a bitter court battle with his sisters, the Ladies Anne, Lucinda and Beatrix, about their share of the estate. Lady Anne became an actress – her first role was as precisely the kind of girl who got her father into trouble in *Sid and Nancy*, and her most recent was reporter Gloria in the Netflix series *The Crown*.

Chelsea Scoop. The eldest son of the Third Baron of Glenconner, Charlie's good looks caught the eye of many aesthetic types – he was photographed by both Robert Mapplethorpe and Patrick Lichfield – and many, like Andy, were to be disappointed that he wasn't gay. He fell from grace in 1978, when he stole photos of Princess Margaret to sell to the press for drug money and was subsequently disinherited.[9]

Lady Anne was described by Andy as his "best ever bodyguard" and he even once offered to marry her. She was an extremely nice person and put on loads of wonderful parties in her flat in Belgravia. She was a true socialite; a lot of people from all walks of life wouldn't have met up but for her.

At this first party at the Lambtons', I told Andy I was planning to come over to New York for the first time, to meet up with Frankie Savage, who I had been seeing all that summer. He invited me to come to the Factory to be photographed and profiled for his *Interview* magazine. Which was an exciting prospect all round. But nothing about that trip went exactly to plan…

Up in the old hotel

I went to the US Embassy to get my visa wearing one of the Snow White T-shirts we were selling in SEX – where only six of the seven dwarves attending to the princess are actually visible. The woman who saw me took one look and said: "Do you think we're going to let you in the country looking like that?" And I said: "Yeah. Stamp me up." It was perfect. These days you would be reported for saying that. I just laughed. "Stamp my visa, if you wouldn't mind."

Then, when I got to New York, they went through everything I had packed – what is it with planes, trains and rubberwear that just never works for me? When they finally let me through, Frankie had another surprise for me. I couldn't stay with him, as planned, because he had a rather overbearing girlfriend who objected to the idea. Instead, he had booked me into the Chelsea Hotel. I had never actually heard of the place before and, when I walked in, I was stunned by all the bizarre paintings. I learned later that people had given them in order to settle their bills. When I went to check in,

---

[9] After being disinherited by his father as a result of the Princess Margaret photographs, Charlie Tennant managed to turn his life around with the help of his wife, Shelagh Scott. But he had contracted hepatitis C from his wild years and this claimed his life in 2006. You can find his articles about both Andy and me archived at www.ideanow.online/chelseascoop.com

the bloke behind the bulletproof glass counter had his arm in a sling, so I asked him what happened. He said he'd been robbed while at work and run after the bloke who did it, who had kicked him down a whole flight of stairs in the subway. So that was my entrée to the place I had been dumped in.

Frankie did introduce me to some of his friends, who showed me around, but effectively I had been abandoned in Manhattan, leaving me to make up my own adventures as I went along. One of these was with a black woman I met in the Chelsea bar. It was a really nice bar and I remember thinking how sophisticated it was that they put coasters under your drink, because that never happened in London. This black woman was sitting next to me and we started talking; she was a resident in the hotel, but I don't know who she was. She asked me what my sexual orientation was and I said, "Well, I am attracted to men and women." And she said, "I've never been with a woman before; would you like to come up to my apartment?" So I did. It was a really nice apartment, a really beautifully decorated room. She could have been famous, for all I know. Afterwards she said I had made her life so much richer. I don't think that would have happened anywhere else.

All I knew about New York at that point was what other people had told me. Malcolm and Vivienne had spent most of their evenings there in Max's Kansas City with the Dolls. I decided to try my luck. I walked in and bumped straight into Sylvain Sylvain. At that moment, he had the sweetest, friendliest face on Earth, my saviour in New York, and he swept me straight on to the dancefloor, where we spent the rest of a fantastic evening.

The other person I spent a lot of time with on that trip was Michelle Robinson, who was one of the friends of Frankie's assigned to show me around. She didn't seem to be working as an actress then, but she sure did show me a whole other side of the city I hadn't quite expected to see.

A word to the wise guys

Michelle took me for a night out. She said, "We're just going to have dinner with these two guys", without explaining who our dinner dates would be. She took me to a very, very expensive hotel — I think it was the Waldorf Astoria — where our hosts turned out to be two gangsters, real New York Mafia boys. Over a lavish meal, liberally lubricated with fine wines, they explained what it was that they did. They called themselves "clearance", which meant that if a landlord or developer had problems evicting his tenants he would call on their services. They would start off with some major intimidation and, after that, if the people were still unwise enough to move on, they'd burn them out of their homes.

Why on earth they would want to be seen with me, I still don't know. Michelle looked like a hooker; I looked like something else. I'd got this great big beehive hairdo and black eyes, and obviously I was wearing rubber. You might think my appearance would draw so much attention to them that they really wouldn't like it. But no, they seemed oblivious. Perhaps that was because of the amount of whiskey they were putting away.

At the beginning of the evening Michelle said to me: "Don't drink too much, leave it to them, they'll drink everything. Act like you're drinking, but do it real slowly." She obviously knew what she was doing – they got absolutely plastered. Then she said: "Right, now we'll take them up to their rooms."

I was absolutely bricking it by now, thinking: I need to go. But Michelle kept reassuring me: "It'll be all right, it'll be all right", and because they were *so* drunk I went along with it. We went up to these unbelievably posh rooms, the like of which I'd never seen before. The guy I was with was just rolling around the place. He kept telling me how he wanted to take me in the bath to have sex with me, and I kept putting him off with another drink, thinking: If I bide my time, he's going to pass out. Thank God, finally he did. Then I heard a knock on the door and it was Michelle.

"You all right?" she asked, surveying the carnage.

"Yeah," I replied.

Then she said: "Have you got his money?"

And I said: "What?"

So I let her in and she systematically went though his wallet, took everything out and left the cleaned-out husk back inside his jacket. She'd already done her stuff with the bloke she was with. Took him to the cleaners.

So that's the sort of person that Sid ended up with after Nancy. More of an illusionist than an actress, I would say. Now you see it, now you don't.

The whole thing was like a Scorsese movie, it really was. The bath and the gangster. We were playing with people who kill for a living. Who have bags of lime and know how to mix it right. I was really naive. But it was so odd. All along, Michelle was edging me into doing what she thought was the best thing.

That wasn't the end of my surreal adventures with her, either. Michelle was staying at her mother's flat in Greenwich Village and she took me round there. It's one of those moments when you think you're walking into a dream. Everything was covered in plastic. The sofa, even the lampshades, had thick protective plastic coating all over them and I'm thinking: Are these new? They must have come straight from the warehouse or the furniture showroom. It was meant to stay like that for ever, I think.

Penguins and orange cake

But I did get to go to the Factory, which by then was in its third location, on 860 Broadway, a place that he had stuffed full of taxidermy animals – it looked a little bit like the Bates Motel when you went in there. He took pictures of me with a load of stuffed penguins – it made sense, as I was all in black and white, with white hair, white pixie boots,[10] black make-up, black leather cape and black leather gloves, the black leather pencil skirt with the D-rings at the back and black polo neck jumper.

I was wearing one of the Wigan coats we sold at SEX over the top of all that – it looked like a storm trooper's coat with the big belt and epaulettes. Andy must have thought the penguins would go well with that.

After he'd taken the pictures, he took me into his print room and showed me all his work. It was amazing; I couldn't believe it. They were in these big, wooden holders like architect's drawers and on trestle tables full of prints, as far as the eye could see. What crossed my mind was: I wish you'd just leave the room long enough for me to be able to take one of those prints. Oh, give us one, Andy. You know you want to. It would be very nice if he had – I'd be a millionaire by now.

But I did sit on his couch, the couch of couches, I'd say. And he shared a big orange cake with me. He was fond of his cakes, was Andy, and only bought the very best. It was worth crossing the Atlantic, and all the rest, for that perfect day with him.

Psycho parts I, II and III

That wasn't the end of my adventures in New York. You may imagine them if you have ever watched *Panic in Needle Park* (Jerry Schatzberg, 1971), *Mikey and Nicky* (John Cassavetes, 1976) or *Fingers* (James Toback, 1978). I credit the outfit I was wearing to the Factory with saving my life from the kind of lowlife evinced in those

---

[10] My white patent pixie boots had high stiletto heels, not those chunky ones everyone else had. To my shame, I sent them to be mended and never picked them up from a little shoe repair shop on King's Road. I came back after six months and they'd chucked them out. Although they're making them again now, it wouldn't be the same.

all-too-real early 1970s independent films, when, on my way back to the Chelsea, a bloke jumped out at me and tried to rob me – or worse.

Thinking back on it now, he was going to rob, rape or kill me. I turned and gave him the hardest look I could. It came totally out of fear. And it worked. I could see him change his mind. I suppose he just made a tiny calculation in his brain at that time: Was it worth it? Did I have a gun in my pocket? He didn't know I was English. Maybe he thought I was some tough New York broad. Which I could have been, seeing as I was walking around like that in the freezing cold. There was only me and him on the street. He must have thought it wasn't worth it, that I could do a death pinch on him or something.

But worse was to come. I went over to somewhere like Queens to try and get drugs and met this guy. We went back to the Chelsea, did the drugs… and then he wouldn't leave. He took my head and banged it against the wall. The only thing I could think of to get rid of him was to get his coat, which he'd taken off, open the door and throw it down the corridor as hard as I could. He went after it and I slammed the door, locked it and put my back against it. He didn't come back. Even Michelle thought I was insane going over to somewhere I knew nothing about and inviting back someone I'd never met before. I really could have paid for that one with my life, too.

While I was at the Chelsea, I had a phone call from London. I'd always really liked Anthony Perkins in *Psycho* and thought it would be great to meet him, as he seemed such an interesting guy. While I was out there in New York, recovering from my near misses with the local psychos and Andy's version of the Bates Motel, the actual Anthony Perkins had come into the shop. You just can't make this up, can you? Michael Collins phoned me and said: "You'll never guess what – Anthony Perkins is in the shop!" He was absolutely delighted.

I was about to blow my top. I said: "You lying toad!" But, sure enough, I got back and he'd taken a picture of him. What's worse, he never came back.

Mistaken identity

The next time I met Andy was in July 1978, when the ICA put on the *Athletes* exhibition, which included his iconic photograph of Muhammad Ali mid-punch that was used on all the publicity posters. I went to this event with Gustavo, too. This was the era of the tulip hairstyle and the Mondrian make-up I had devised for *Jubilee*, which I wore with a maroon suit and shirt from Harrods, and a little diamond necklace – again, I liked the juxtaposition between that and my hair and make-up. It was the same day I had encountered Michael Winner filming *The Big Sleep* in the Mall, on my way from Buckingham Gate to the ICA. There are some great photos of that private view of me, Andy and his dear friend, the *Vogue* Editor and socialite supreme Diana Vreeland, often credited with being the woman who took rubberwear to New York.

The last time I met him was when he spotted me in the middle of America on the Ants' 1985 *Vive Le Rock* tour at a party in Detroit and immediately came over. I looked totally different from the last time he'd seen me: I had a lemon-yellow beehive and was wearing a three-piece suit Adams Tailors had made for me. But Andy still remembered where we had been the last time we met. Only, this was the first time he realised that I wasn't Vivienne.

VIVIENNE WESTWOOD: I met Andy Warhol twice and each time I met him he was completely… well, he was always disinterested, he had the most bland, expressionless face, he kind of looks like that doesn't he, when you see a photo of him? Blank face, black glasses and blank. But the thing is that he was disappointed, because each time he expected Jordan, not me. 'Cos he had heard about the SEX shop and everything and met you, and so when I turned up he didn't like it, he wasn't interested. He'd got the wrong person.

Silver machine

Andy set up his first Factory on the fifth floor of 231 East 47th Street in Midtown in 1962. This is usually referred to as the Silver Factory: Andy got photographer Billy Name to redecorate the whole space, including the elevator, in silver, using foil and mirrors – the core materials of the early 1960s speed freak. Here Andy produced not just prints and paintings but films, sculptures, shoes and other commissioned work to be branded and sold in his name.

This was the location where the Superstars assembled: first Baby Jane Holzer, with whom he made his initial film experiments, then the tragic Edie Sedgwick, his Girl of the Year in 1965, who starred in a series of Warhol-directed shorts and movies, including *Poor Little Rich Girls*, *Kitchen* and *Chelsea Girls* (all 1965). She died from an overdose in 1971, aged 28.

It was at the Silver Factory that Andy began his collaboration with The Velvet Underground, going on to design the radical banana sleeve for *The Velvet Underground & Nico*, the band's debut, in 1967. He would later design another notoriously eye-catching record sleeve, for The Rolling Stones' *Sticky Fingers* in 1971, at the Silver Factory. The Silver Factory attracted the famous transvestite coterie that included Holly Woodlawn, Jackie Curtis, Robert Olivo (aka Ondine) and the transgender Candy Darling, who would make appearances in many of Andy's movies.

Andy's next location was at the sixth floor of the Decker Building on 33 Union Square West, round the corner from Max's Kansas City, which became the main hangout for all Factory denizens when they relocated in 1968. This was where his silk-screen and film production went into overdrive. Speaking to the *Guardian* in 2014, John Cale reflected: "It wasn't called the Factory for nothing… While one person was making a silkscreen, somebody else would be filming a screen test. Every day something new."

It was also here that Andy was shot by Valerie Solanas, founder of the Society for Cutting Up Men (SCUM) and author of *The SCUM Manifesto*. Solanas initially approached Andy in 1967 about producing her play *Up Your Ass*, which she later accused him of stealing and demanded financial recompense. Andy tried to humour her by casting her in his film *I, a Man* (1967) and paying her $25. Solanas's reply was to buy a gun, which she brought into the Factory on 3 June 1968 and shot Andy three times. In her rampage, she also hit art critic Mario Amaya in the hip and attempted to kill Andy's manager, Fred Hughes, but luckily the gun jammed as she took aim. Hughes ordered her out of the building, and she meekly complied. Andy was rushed into emergency surgery, and recovered – physically, at least. Solanas turned herself in to the police. She was diagnosed with paranoid schizophrenia and given a three-year sentence. Andy lived the rest of his life in discomfort from having to wear trusses and never recovered from the psychological effect of the shootings. Andy died on 22 February 1987, aged 58, from complications arising from an operation.

There are innumerable Warhol books, DVDs and artefacts out there – but perhaps the best way to experience the Factory at the height of its glory years is to watch John Schlesinger's *Midnight Cowboy* (1969), with hick from the sticks Joe Buck (Jon Voight) and smalltime Yonkers hustler Ratso (Dustin Hoffman) in party scenes based on Factory happenings and starring Viva, Ondine and Ultra Violet.

19

ON THE GOOD SHIP VENUS

Vivienne dreams of dandies and Malcolm returns (June 1979–June 1980)

London Year Zerox

With the backing of Do It Records, the Ants went into Roundhouse Studios to record 'Zerox/There's a Whip in My Valise', the first of a carefully planned set of moves by Adam, who had the cover artwork made up while the brothers Tregoning took out a series of ads in the music press, gradually revealing more details of the single each week in the countdown to its release on 6 July. Ron and Russell Mael of Sparks gave it a rave review on Radio 1's Roundtable and the band set off on a fifteen-date tour in July.

The challenges of the road did not improve relations between Adam and his charismatic new guitarist; neither did the love that the Ants fans were showing to this young rake. Adam brooded on removing Matthew and Andy even as they returned to the studio to record their debut album *Dirk Wears White Sox*.

DOROTHY MAX PRIOR: When they were recording *Dirk Wears White Sox*, that was quite difficult, I think. There wasn't much love between Adam and Matthew – it had never been that comfortable. I think Adam kept

327

re-doing Matthew's guitar and music stuff and Matthew and Andy were not happy with that. But I think the long and the short of it is, by the time *Dirk Wears White Sox* had been recorded, that version of the band just wasn't working.

Distant drums

Malcolm was recovering from the post-Pistols fall out in Paris. The city was full of his old friends at the time, including his art college comrade Robin Scott, now working with his brother Julian at Barclay Records. Robin had been producing some African musicians with a heavy drum sound called the Burundi beat, which immediately grabbed Malcolm's attention. Dividing his time between the Scott brothers, Jean-Charles de Castelbajac and his assistant Spider Fawkes, Malcolm moved between celebrity dinners with his fellow practitioner of musical outrage, Serge Gainsbourg, and hanging out with transvestites in Pigalle. Working with local musicians, he started trying to get together some music that reflected all these new sounds and stimuluses. He aimed to put together a movie called *The Adventures of Melody, Lyric and Tune* – not far off the title of Gainsbourg's 1971 concept album *L'Histoire de Melody Nelson*.

Meanwhile, Vivienne was dreaming of that same city's past from her bed in Nightingale Lane. She had found a book about an aristocratic movement of 1795–9 known as the *Incroyables* (Incredibles) and their female counterparts, the *Merveilleuses* (Marvelous Women), whose reaction to the Terror that had just ripped their country apart was to host hundreds of decadent balls and start the most outrageous fashion trends. Vivienne was inspired by the women's dresses and tunics, cut along Classical Greek and Roman lines, and the men's large earrings, green jackets, wide-legged trousers, thick neck ties and bicorn hats. These flamboyant, androgynous divas were worlds away from the post-war fashions she and Malcolm had mined for their previous collections, but completely in tune with the ideas that were now circulating in clubland, on the backs of such Seditionaries regulars as Boy George and Steve Strange. Enjoying the processes of researching and working out how to make such clothes, she immersed herself in the National Art Library of the Victoria and

Albert Museum, learning exactly how they were originally cut and constructed. The collection that would eventually appear as a result of all this research would mark her out as the first modern designer to put accurate reconstructions of historical clothing back on the rails and at the height of radical fashion.

MICHAEL COLLINS: What I liked about Vivienne was that she hadn't gone to university, she hadn't trained in that way. When she did the toga dresses, she had me lie on a piece of cloth, cut it around my body and then had me walk around to get the shape of how it would move.

I went to Liverpool with her so she could do a two-hour talk to the students at a fashion college there. They wanted to have some idea of how you design, and her approach was so different: "Let's look at the shape of this, what's so interesting about this is..."

She also took me to a factory in Manchester to get some corduroy for Bondage trousers and she kept going on to me about how wide the stripe of the corduroy had to be. She said it so many times that I couldn't remember. I ordered thousands of metres of corduroy with the wrong stripe! She sold them all, though.

Into the Grove

After I left Buckingham Gate, I moved into Michael's flat in Talbot Road, W11, where I stayed for about a year. We shared with Anna Melluso, a really lovely girl from Sicily, who was now working with us in the shop, and her little boy Luka. They had one room and Michael and I had another – like a marriage made in hell. It was right at the top of the house, so we always had to go past everyone else. The landlady was an old Polish Jewess who had a very strange daughter who was always stopping and looking up at the sky. We usually had a load of people coming up the stairs with us, like Adam and his girlfriend Mandy Donohoe, and the landlady would come out and just look at them, as if it was a zoo. It's hard to say who was the weirdest, really, them or us. Or our living arrangements, which now seem like a 1960s kitchen-sink drama.

Our bath was in the kitchen and we used to have a tabletop to put over it so we could sit round and eat off it. Sometimes people would have baths while others were in the kitchen, cooking. I did that many a time. When we'd finished work, we used to go out and do a big shop and come home and eat whatever we could lay our hands on. One night it was Mr Kipling's apple pies; we ate boxes of them. Then the next day, I woke up and found one staring at me from the pillow, where Michael had kindly left it. "Oh noooo…" I didn't know whether to eat it or be sick.

Another time I woke up so hungover it felt like I'd been in the desert for a thousand years. I put my hand out and there was this glass of water beside the bed. I just couldn't wait, really, I was too poorly to get up, and I thought: This is perfect, how kind of Michael. It was neat, warm gin – and I took a great big swig of it.

MICHAEL COLLINS: You had a wonderful knack of being able to throw up and then carry on like nothing had happened. I remember seeing you thousands of times when you'd be sick on the pot plant and then just carry on dancing.

Wherever I went, plants died in my wake. But somehow, we always got to work on time. God knows what we took to keep us going. A handful of coloured things, I think. Green Dospan (slimming pills) were terrible, they used to make you go up and down like a yo-yo. Black bombers (pharmaceutical amphetamine) were also terrible. Michael and I went to see Mum and Dad on black bombers and then went down to the Curtain Club in Brighton with Sally. We didn't sleep for two days after that: just stayed up in my old bedroom playing the same records over and over.

Taking care of business

Malcolm started coming backwards and forwards from Paris to London in July 1979. He was touting his film idea and had a meeting about it with Arista Records, who considered the premise – a soft-porn film for teenagers – too risqué and Malcolm's dreams for a Parisian location too expensive. But they told him to try again and he and Vivienne worked together on a rewrite, which they called *The Mile High Club*. It had characters with names that reflected both of their current obsessions, including Lieutenant Lush and Louis Quatorze, and a Homosexual Apache theme song. Arista read these endeavours and told them to sling their (Captain) hook.

Malcolm was ready to go back to France, but I had other ideas. By October, *Dirk Wears White Sox* had been recorded. As Dorothy Max earlier mentioned, Adam took the producer's role, so that he was able to take complete control of how the recording sounded. Since he wasn't happy with the way things were going, I had the bright idea of asking Malcolm to manage the Ants. In fact, I went on and on at him about it, thinking this would be the best thing for everyone. Malcolm used to do that Jewish thing of shrugging his shoulders and going: "Hmmm, Jordan, I don't know if it's right for me." But I kept saying: "Oh go on, you should have a go, even if it doesn't work." Eventually he buckled…

We were all at a wedding reception at the Portobello Hotel on 27 October when Adam and Malcolm had their first conversation on the subject. *Dirk Wears White Sox* came out on 30 November to a muted response from the press, if not the Ant fans, who had just enjoyed two sold-out shows at the Electric Ballroom in Camden. These would be Andy Warren's last before he left the band for his old friend Bid and The Monochrome Set. Matthew initially followed in his wake, leaving Adam and Dave to rehearse and audition new band members, but came back when Malcolm agreed to take over as the band's manager in the first week of December. According to Adam, Malcolm called it an Elvis/Colonel Tom Parker deal – meaning he would split everything 50–50. After a few weeks of auditions, Leigh Gorman joined the Ants on bass and Adam set off to make some personal appearances to promote *Dirk* during December, while the band rehearsed in Camden under Malcolm's watchful eye.

Malcolm had already given Adam his opinion on the first Ants album: he didn't think it was well enough produced or commercial enough to generate a hit single. He gave Adam a tape of songs to listen to and learn from.[1] These ran the gamut from surf to belly-dancing music, cool jazz to garage. But perhaps most telling of all was the inclusion of *Burundi Black* by Burundi Black.

When Adam returned, the band had been rehearsing with Simon Jeffes, the string arranger for Sid's version of 'My Way' and leader of the Penguin Café Orchestra, who was helping them with their beats and timing. It was clear the Burundi part of the equation on Malcolm's tape was the chief element in the sound he was driving at. He also urged Adam to read up about pirates, the idea being that the band would start their next phase wearing the clothes Vivienne had been working on. Another of Malcolm's favourite British Beat boom bands was Johnny Kidd and The Pirates, who used to go onstage wearing eyepatches and waving cutlasses.[2] I had taken to wearing a pair of doubloons that Adam had given me as earrings, and Michael Collins thinks this also helped to inspire the direction the pair would go in next.

---

[1] The full list, according to Adam, was: 'Wipe Out' by The Surfaris; *No Problem* by Chet Baker; 'He's the Fatman' by The Hawks; 'Mystery Train' by Elvis Presley; 'Blue Moon' by Elvis Presley; 'YMCA' by The Village People; 'Hot Dog' by Taps Miller; 'Cast Iron Arm' by Peanuts Wilson; 'Tear It Up' by Johnny Burnette; 'Hello! I'm Back Again' by Gary Glitter; 'Where Were You (On Our Wedding Day?)' by Lloyd Price; 'Broadway Jungle' by The Flames; 'Got to Pick a Pocket' by Ron Moody from the *Oliver!* Original Soundtrack Recording; 'I'm Not Tired' by Cliff Bennett and The Rebel Rousers; 'Rave On' by Buddy Holly; belly dancing music by Farid El Atrache; *Burundi Black* by Burundi Black.

[2] Adam remembers Malcolm telling him: "Forget about David Bowie, you want to listen to Johnny Kidd and the Pirates." Johnny's crew included drummer Clem Cattini, who would later join The Tornados, and Joe Moretti, who played guitar on the original 'Brand New Cadillac'. Like many of Malcolm's favourites, Johnny Kidd was destined to die worryingly young, in a car crash in 1966 at the age of 30.

Feed me to the lions

As the New Year dawned, the only trouble Malcolm had with his new protégés was Adam himself. While the younger Ants were knuckling down and learning to do things his way, Adam already had a lot of set ideas of his own that he didn't need advice on. Behind his back, Malcolm got in a friend, Dave Fisher, who specialised in manufactured pop bands; Dave watched a rehearsal and agreed with the management analysis that Adam was surplus to Malcolm's requirements.[3]

On 26 January 1980, as Adam arrived in the pub basement in Camden that the Ants had been using to rehearse in, Dave Barbe, his faithful lieutenant for all those years, stood up and told him that he was leaving the band. Matthew and Lee followed suit. Saying nothing, Malcolm watched from a chair in the far corner of the room.

DAVE BARBE: I had no good role models in my life. I had an abusive father who tried to destroy me. Adam and Malcolm were like my two dads. Adam taught me discipline, self-respect. To have this amazing man who could rule a crowd, turn round and say, "You're my right-hand man", was fucking unbelievable; it made me the man I am.

I had been with Adam about four years up to that point. Life's like that. Three or four years is how long a band normally lasts. Adam was a genius, a unique artist and I was teacher's bird, he gave me carte blanche to do whatever I wanted. He did give everyone else a hard time, but I never had a cross word from Adam.

Then Malcolm turned around and said: "You can be your own right-hand man, you can have a band based around your drums and go around the world." They had two diametrically opposite attitudes…

Both Malcolm and Adam gave me a direction when I had nothing; when I was just a kid on the dole. Adam was incredible; he really was a man's man, which was what my dad tried to be and failed. But Malcolm was a liberator; he opened my horizons. They were the two most important men in my life, really.

---

[3] Details about Dave Fisher from *The Wicked Ways of Malcolm McLaren* by Craig Bromberg (Omnibus Press, 1991), p. 215.

That night Adam called me and told me what had happened with Malcolm and the Ants. He was absolutely distraught. I went straight over to his flat, this tiny little bedsit room in Earl's Court, and we went right into a brainstorming session. I said: "You've got to get all this stuff out that Malcolm's given you, get it all in your head. You've got to get a record out really quickly and really well, you can't drag your heels on it. And it's got to be better than anything Malcolm could do."

We sealed our plan by having sex for the first time. It had taken him years to woo me, because I had seen for my own eyes what a womaniser he is. Though Mandy Donohoe was ostensibly his girlfriend, he'd had hundreds of women and I knew he would never be able to commit. Adam punched a hole in the headboard in triumph.

The final frontier

Adam had a different take on the tape Malcolm had given him, his own tastes leading him in a different direction, one that Malcolm probably would have objected to anyway. The material that would become *Kings of the Wild Frontier* was born out of opposition and adversity, and, in the end, was all the stronger for it.

While Adam had been doing those personal appearances the previous December, he had already started writing the song 'Kings of the Wild Frontier', first calling it 'Shade Too White'. Malcolm had been telling him to read up on pirates; he had instead been immersing himself in books about Native American culture and the passage of rites of a warrior – the same impulse that led to me carving his back for him just prior to *Jubilee*. What he needed now was somebody to collaborate with, the way he had always done with Dave Barbe, but this time someone more experienced musically, who could take his vision to the next level. I was sure I knew who that person was: Marco Pirroni.

Marco had been in two bands since his appearance at the 100 Club with the first line-up of The Banshees and then Rema-Rema,[4]

---

[4] Rema-Rema spawned a number of other notable outfits: when Marco left, Asquith, Allen and Cox went on to form Mass, which then divided into Renegade Soundwave and The Wolfgang Press. Dorothy Max subsequently joined Psychic TV, the band founded by Genesis P-Orridge after the demise of Throbbing Gristle. More at http://4ad.com/artists/remarema

Wedding of the year, *Honey* magazine.

Rest in peace, Darby Crash – a sweet but troubled man.

Before blackjack was finally banned in our house.

Oh, those lovely Madras Pirate trousers. [Derek Ridgers]

RCA

15th February, 1984

Ms J Mooney
5 Bonchurch Road
LONDON
W10

Dear Jordan

I am getting increasingly concerned about some of the supposedly "small"
items I am being asked to pay for on behalf of Wide Boy Awake. Whilst I
appreciate that some of these are indirectly connected with the forthcoming video and/or press photo session, there are a number of items that
I do not feel are necessarily RCA's responsibility and I would like to
discuss these with you at your earliest convenience. In the meantime,
I do not feel I can give you the "go-ahead" on a couple of items of
expenditure, these being haircuts for yourself and Kevin and the £200 cash
requested for the purchase of accessories to go with the "tiger stripe"
outfits.

Incidentally, I do feel that the hire charge of £300 for the "tiger stripe"
outfits should have been cleared with me before any arrangements were made
to fly them from the United States. In the event, I have been left with
the choice of picking up the bill or having no costumes for this Friday's
press session and I have, therefore, agreed to pay it but I am not happy
about the way the whole situation was handled.

The other thing that I need to make quite clear to you is the matter of
the armorlite rifles for the photo session. I fully understand why you
want the guns used but after consultation with the Press Office and other
interested parties, I am convinced that no weapons should appear on anything
connected with Wide Boy Awake. I am sure you will appreciate that their
presence on advertising and posters could cause us unnecessary problems
at radio and TV levels.

Yours sincerely
RCA RECORDS LIMITED

P PRESKY
Product Manager

cc P Robinson, I Groves, G Harris, R Semon
A Company Registered in London, Number 242246
Registered Office :- Lincoln Way, Windmill Road, Sunbury-on-Thames, Middlesex TW16 7HW

I am a very naughty girl... NOT.

My orphan lamb, Penelope.

In the cockpit of a B-1 bomber, Edwards Air Force Base, 1985.

Supreme UK and Gold Olympian Imperial Grand Champion and Supreme UK and Silver Olympian Imperial Grand Premier Mainman Kisschase, aka Berry.

Lucky shot.

Looking to the future. [Etienne Gilfillan]

The hand of Marco Pirroni on my shoulder. At Vivienne's V&A exhibition, 2004.
[Richard Young/REX/Shutterstock]

Outside Posh Teckel, Berlin, 2018. [Martyn Goodacre]

The beginning of this adventure with a wonderful woman. Cathi Unsworth and me.
[Etienne Gilfillan]

with singer-guitarist Gary Asquith, Mick Allen on bass, Mark Cox on keyboards and his then-girlfriend, Dorothy Max Prior, on drums. They had recorded one four-track EP, *Wheel in the Roses*, for the new 4AD label. Adam had seen Marco play in The Models and considered him the best guitarist he had ever seen. All I had to do was put them in touch with each other. It was an idea that didn't go down too well with one member of Rema-Rema.

DOROTHY MAX PRIOR: I went straight from Exhibition Road with Andy to living at Marco's in Harrow. Andy and I had a slightly odd relationship at the best of times; he always described me as his husband! So I did start going out with Marco when I was still going out with Andy, but by then we were more like siblings. Marco and I were a very sweet, old-fashioned kind of couple, almost like my first normal relationship. I got on really well with his family: I went to Sicily with them every year and we've kept in touch; his parents are now my elder son's godparents. Rema-Rema had played at the Rainbow with The Banshees and Human League; there was some more cross-pollination going on there[5]... Then Adam turns up in Harrow and wants to speak to Marco.

Marco was not that happy with how Rema-Rema was going. He wanted to be in Roxy Music, basically. He saw it as too experimental, too far left for his pop sensibilities. So, fair enough, I think it was inevitable that he was going to leave; it was just how it happened. For me it was an action replay of when Adam persuaded me and Andy to leave the Band With No Name. This was an odd thing. I was a bit: "Adam, can you leave my boyfriends alone?"

Get it on

But when Marco and Adam got together, magic happened. They were both massive fans of Roxy Music, as well as the Glitter Band's use of two drummers, a notion Malcolm had also been getting at in

---

[5] John McKay and Kenny Morris walked out on The Banshees mid-tour on 7 September 1979 in Aberdeen, the same day that the second Banshees' LP, *Join Hands*, was released. Robert Smith from The Cure, who were supporting them, stepped up to play guitar for the rest of the tour and Budgie was recruited from The Slits to play drums.

his list of records for Adam to ingest, and one which they would work on to fashion the next incarnation of Ant Sound. For Marco, there was one other important double act to follow.

> **MARCO PIRRONI:** It worked with me and Adam in the way I always dreamed it would be with David Bowie and Mick Ronson. He didn't particularly want to play guitar and I didn't want to be the singer, so we were just two blokes who did our stuff and we complemented each other. As much as I love Ronson, he was never gonna eclipse Bowie, not in a million years. He was just going to make Bowie look better. And I was happy to do that. Very happy, because that worked with Ziggy Stardust…

Falcon Stuart, who had been the second person to want to audition the original Ants, came back on the scene when he heard what had happened with Malcolm. He agreed to work with Adam and Marco without a contract. The first thing the pair did together was rewrite 'Car Trouble' to fulfil their contract with Do It,[6] which they recorded to go with the B-side 'Kick!' at Rockfield Studios. At Marco's suggestion, Chris Hughes produced the record – he was also a drummer and he agreed to join the new band, under the name of Merrick. Terry Lee Miall, who had been in The Models with Marco, soon became drummer number two. The single was released on 7 March.

What's inside a girl?

Because I was still working at the shop and listening to Malcolm's schemes, I knew exactly what he had planned with the remainder of the original Ants. He was meeting them daily in his favourite Soho locale, an Italian café called Centrale, where he'd reprised his *Expresso Bongo* routine. Unable to let go of the Homosexual Apaches idea he'd had for *The Mile High Club*, he at first tried to get them to pretend to be gay, despite the fact that none of them were and that Dave was married with a young child. When that didn't

---

[6] Do It Records folded after the departure of the Ants and sadly it left a permanent rift in the Tregoning brothers' relationship. Dave Barbe: "I still see Ian all the time. He ended up being an engineer and then part of the management company for Yello. He fell out massively with his brother, because Ian wanted to put everything into Adam Ant and Max said no. So they fell out and they've never talked to each other since."

work, he turned back to his helpful friend Dave Fisher, who found just what Malcolm needed, singing along to Stevie Wonder on the radio at his local dry cleaner's on West End Lane, West Hampstead. Her name was Myant Myant Aye Dunn-Lwin, she was half Burmese and had only just turned 14.[7]

Malcolm would always claim to have found Annabella Lwin (as she would be restyled for the press) himself, singing in his local launderette. But Annabella's mother, Amy Dunn-Lwin, who was very much the social climber, was always miffed at this misrepresentation of her much more classy dry-cleaning business. The band were going to be decked out in Vivienne's forthcoming new Pirates collection – Dave would henceforth assume the mantle 'Dave Barbarossa' after the famous Red Beard – and the name, after a line from Malcolm's treasured Homosexual Apaches song, was Bow Wow Wow.

DAVE BARBE: Are you talking about the years I strode across the world looking like a bowl of fruit?

By April, Malcolm had a demo tape, including the songs 'Homo Sex Al Apache', 'C30' and 'Sun, Sea and Piracy', that he touted around the record companies to little avail. After what had happened with the Pistols, door after door slammed in his face. But one of his few friends at EMI, Terry Slater, who had been in charge of publishing when Malcolm made his original deal with them, did listen and did agree to a £50,000 advance.[8]

I reported everything I heard back to Adam and Marco.

MARCO PIRRONI: In hindsight, you can look back and go: Adam's gonna piss all over Annabella any day of the week. But we weren't sure at the time.

Hoist the Jolly Roger!

Perhaps it is a coincidence, but as soon as Malcolm had that deal signed, Vivienne and Malcolm set about changing the identity of the

---

[7] *The Wicked Ways of Malcolm McLaren* by Craig Bromberg (Omnibus Press, 1991), p. 225.
[8] *Ibid.*, p. 230.

shop in readiness for the Pirates collection. Vivienne already had someone in mind to refit the premises.

Roger K. Burton's second hand clothes business had run into trouble by 1977. When people stopped buying vintage, he had begun buying military clothing from army surplus stores in Holland, Germany and France – a risky business that at one point led to him being held by the police on suspicion of being part of the Baader-Meinhof gang. Then he opened a shop called PX in an old fruit-and-veg warehouse in Covent Garden, found for him by Andy Czezowksi, with his business partner Rick Carter and Leicester friends Steph Raynor and Helen Robinson, to sell all this gear. Going with the military theme, Roger fitted out the space with metal ducting and cages salvaged from the former MI5 building in Mayfair for the princely sum of £20. It quickly attracted the attention of the *Sunday Times*'s Michael Roberts, who penned an article called 'Strange New Shops, Stranger Faces' in January 1978.

ROGER K. BURTON: I got a phone call one night from Jack English, an old friend from Leicester who was also great friends with Vivienne. They'd been having a drink in the Chelsea Potter and she was discussing with him that they were just about to close down Seditionaries. She really liked what I'd done with PX, so she asked if she could meet to discuss doing the new shop. I actually was living very close to Vivienne at the time, in Clapham, so I just cycled round the corner to Nightingale Lane and spent the day brainstorming. She was constantly pulling out reference books with Native American Indians wearing bowler hats and Western gear, just trying to give me a feeling for the shop. Malcolm was on the phone the whole time to record companies. It was a pretty crazy day, but by the end of it I had come away with a clear picture of what she wanted this thing to be.

Roger took further inspiration from William Hogarth's 1764 engraving *The Bathos*, which featured the figure of Old Father Time breathing his last beside a pub sign for the World's End.[9] From this he got

---

[9] This was Hogarth's last engraving, published eight months before his death and intended by him to "…serve as a Tail-Piece to all the Author's Engraved Works, when bound up together". It is currently owned by the Royal Collection Trust and you can find out more at www.royalcollection.org.uk/collection/913466/the-bathos

the idea of the backwards-running clock with thirteen hours on it. He knew a man from the BBC's special effects department who could put the timepiece together. The idea for the interior came from a pub he used to drink in, the Crooked House in Himley, in the Black Country.

ROGER K. BURTON: It was built in Victorian times and there had been so much mining underneath it that the whole thing had subsided. It looks ridiculous – the floors are going one way, the doors are going another and it's such an optical illusion that you can put a bottle on a table and roll it and it will look like it's going up instead of down. I've still got the original set of postcards from the 1970s that I very excitedly showed to Vivienne and Malcolm, and they were very pleased with it. So that just left the problem – how am I going to do it?

Never mind the pallets

Roger had to work out the cheapest possible way of transforming the shop. He had a warehouse in Borough Market, which was at that time an old fruit-and-veg market, active from midnight until six in the morning, when piles of wooden pallets would be left lying about in the streets. He loaded his van up with them over a series of days, dropped them all off at World's End, and staggered them, so they were going down in tiers. Then, he and his accomplice, Big Tony, screwed them all together, utilising the gym bars from the old Seditionaries to somehow make everything fit. Being experienced in the antiques game, Roger went to an architectural salvage place and found a load of oak flooring that was very beautifully gnarled and weathered. He bought a stack of this very cheaply, along with all the slates for the roof and a little iron staircase. He started to bolt it all together and screw it all down, looking over his shoulder for a visit from building inspectors.

ROGER K. BURTON: But in fact they didn't come along until we started to take out the front of the shop, and we'd got all the floors sorted by then, so they couldn't see how it had been built. They were quite happy with it.

339

They just took a few photographs, took some notes and things, and I was told to get them back in again when it was finished. But I don't think they ever did come back.

Vivienne kept a check on his progress, but it wasn't until they got round to painting the shop that she made any objections.

ROGER K. BURTON: She gave me the colour – that turquoise paint, almost the Fortnum & Mason's colour – and we painted it. The first time we did it, she said: "No, it's too dark. Can we just make it one shade lighter?" So we made it a shade lighter. Then it was too light. We repainted that shop probably about six times before we ended up back where we started, with the original colour. That was the only time she really took issue, and she was really adamant about it.

Over at Nightingale Lane, Vivienne had me and Michael painting light-bulbs to go with this decor. We had a turquoise one, then a brown one, then a terracotta one, Indian Earth, then we came back to turquoise. And we had to sit and paint them all by hand because you couldn't buy those shades in the shops. Vivienne also had me making clothes again, while Michael had to keep the place clean. Which wasn't easy. I went to boil up some milk on the hob and it all went turquoise. Vivienne had been using the pan to dye clothes. In the same way, she used to produce plates full of black potatoes. It was hit-and-miss what type of poisoning you could have died from in there.

A bright spark

Roger's idea for the pièce de résistance of the shop was to be the lighting. He wanted copper pipes, all different lengths, covered in verdigris, with elongated bulbs like strip lights stuck on the end of them, so that it looked like something from the future. And he knew the very man who could pull off this most unusual job. He had employed him before, to sort the wiring out in his warehouse.

340

The revolution's here

Andy Newman (1942–2016) got the nickname 'Thunderclap' while still at school for his distinctive manner with a keyboard. The band that became Thunderclap Newman was put together by Pete Townshend, who wanted to create a vehicle for his friend, drummer and singer-songwriter John 'Speedy' Keen; he recruited Mr Newman, who was working as a telephone engineer for the GPO at the time, alongside guitarist Jimmy McCulloch, who would later join Wings. The single that made their name, 'Something in the Air', was released in May 1969 and has never really gone away. Central to its appeal is Mr Newman's honky-tonk piano – New Orleans jazz was his first love.

Roger K. Burton: "The road where he lived was always getting filmed because it was so run-down it really did look like Dickens's time. It was run by a housing co-op and he was in charge of the community, looking after everything there. He had a heart of gold, this man, as well as being a genius. The reason he was so reluctant to admit his real identity was that he'd had such a bad deal with the record company, they'd ripped him off completely and, apart from his jazz gig in Hampstead, he swore he would never get involved in music again. But he eventually did; he even reformed the band in later years."

The song he will always be known for has featured in *The Magic Christian* (1969), *The Strawberry Statement* (1970), *Kingpin* (1996), *Almost Famous* (2000) and *The Girl Next Door* (2004), as well as ads for TalkTalk, Coca-Cola and British Airways.

ROGER K. BURTON: I used the small ads in the back of *Time Out* for electricians, and I saw one for a Mr Newman in Clapham, which I rang because he was local. Went to meet him at Borough Market and found this giant of a man. With very little hair but long, lank and receding, National Health glasses all Elastoplasted together and a big belly, all wrapped up in a lovely old army coat. Massive army boots and a ladies' shopping trolley with the tiniest little dog on it: a Yorkshire terrier called Miss Thing with a bow in her hair.

341

I was showing him the job, thinking: Who the fuck is this guy? And my mate who was there, Jack's brother Will, said: "I think he's someone famous." I said: "Get away, he's a tramp." Anyway, we're chatting away and I can hear this retching going on – the dog is throwing up all over the floor. I said: "Mr Newman, your dog's just been sick." And he said: "That'll be the duck à l'orange I gave her last night." Later on, Will said: "I know who this guy is: he's Thunderclap Newman."

At first he denied it. But later, as our relationship developed, he did admit that he was Thunderclap Newman and he used to play piano in a bar in Hampstead on a Friday night, where they paid him in food. Which was how he got the duck à l'orange for Miss Thing!

The ring cycle

Roger asked Mr Newman – as he always liked to be called – to design the lighting for World's End. He made it all in his Dickensian house in Clapham, just down the road from Nightingale Lane, and got it into the shop in time for the grand opening. Which was when our unconventional electrician really lived up to his former stage name.

ROGER K. BURTON: We worked through the night to get the shop ready for its ten o'clock opening. People were arriving in their droves, Vivienne was shouting at us: "Come on! We've got to let them in!" and there was someone in a wheelchair trying to manoeuvre up the slope to get through the front door, when suddenly there was this God-almighty explosion and all the lights went out. People ran out shouting and screaming like it *was* the end of the world! What had happened was that, with the backwards clock and all the fancy lighting, we had overloaded the ring circuit. I could hear Mr Newman coughing and spluttering, there were sparks flying, but he managed to plug it all back together and get it working again. It was quite a moment. I remember this person in the wheelchair trying to get out and Little Helen trying to assist...

It was better than *The Great Rock 'n' Roll Swindle* by miles. And the shop that Roger, Big Tony and Mr Newman built still exists in this incarnation to this day. It's the only original shop left on the King's Road from everyone who was there in punk's heyday. It's an icon, there's absolutely no way anything could happen to it now – so, next time you go in inside, look up and wonder how Thunderclap Newman made that lighting with his own hands.

20

JOIN OUR INSECT NATION

**A new royal family with its very own usurper prince
(April 1980–February 1981)**

A war dance

Having played the bass himself for the re-recording of 'Car Trouble', Adam now needed to recruit a permanent bassist to complete the new line-up. Kevin Mooney was living with Adam's former wife Eve, in a squatted former bus depot in North Street, Islington, that was also shared by Toyah. The first time they met each other, Kevin told Richard Cabut,[1] he was working out the bassline Glen Matlock had used on 'Don't Gimme No Lip Child', which, if true, should maybe have sounded a warning note to Adam. At the time, though, he was impressed enough with Kevin to offer him the final vacant slot in the new version of the Ants, and Kevin was more than happy to go along for the ride.

Adam lined up a new tour to begin in May, with a modest advance of £500 from Falcon Stuart, who told him EMI were ready to make an offer for their publishing. Perhaps they were hedging their bets on

---

[1] Richard Cabut, 'The World's Forgotten Boy', *3:AM* magazine, September 2004. 3ammagazine.com/musicarchives/2004/sep/interview_kevin_mooney.html

which part of the original Ants would turn out to win the battle between the two new factions of Pirates and Braves. Adam's new band was now assembled, and they got straight on with recording the single 'Kings of the Wild Frontier' on 19 April at Matrix Studios. The effect of Merrick and Terry Lee's drumming was instant: "It sounded like ten thousand Zulus banging their shields," Adam thought.[2] Terry Lee had improvised with the same sort of genius that had created the Glitter Band's literally foot-stomping trademark sound, by banging on drum cases and lumps of wood to create a phenomenal wall of primal sound. Hearing that back through the monitors for the first time was nothing short of revelatory. The air was alive with sound.

After a showcase gig for potential new record company suitors, Adam got a new look ready for the Ants Invasion Tour. He hired a jacket from Dave Whiteing at the theatrical costumiers Berman's and Nathan's which had originally been made for David Hemmings in Tony Richardson's 1968 film *The Charge of the Light Brigade.* He wore it with his black leather trousers and his warpaint, a thick white stripe painted straight across the bridge of his nose, with braids and feathers in his hair, Geronimo-style. Although Adam was worried at the lack of mainstream press attention going his way, the first night at the Electric Ballroom on 22 May was a sell out and 'Car Trouble' went into the top 10 of the Independent charts.

The new Ants mixed material new and old at their debut gig – the set started with 'Physical (You're So)' and 'Kings of the Wild Frontier' and ended with 'Plastic Surgery'. There were trials along the way – Adam dedicated their Manchester Poly gig to Joy Division's Ian Curtis, who had committed suicide the week before, and then two days later, in Bournemouth, a girl named Janet Hayworth died during their gig at the Stateside from an asthma attack. There was trouble in Edinburgh from a bunch of Glaswegian punks and a surprise appearance in his native Sheffield from Dave Berry, of the original 'Don't Gimme No Lip Child' fame.[3] Adam was so delighted, he

[2] *Stand & Deliver*, Adam Ant, p. 151.
[3] Sheffield-born Dave Berry recorded 'Don't Gimme No Lip Child' as the B-side to 'The Crying Game' in 1964, which provided him with his biggest UK hit, getting to number five in the charts – it's used as the theme song for Neil Jordan's 1992 film *The Crying Game.*

asked Berry and his band The Cruisers to support them on their final date, at the Empire Ballroom, Leicester Square, on 8 June – by which time half the audience had white stripes across their noses, too.

The next day, as Falcon Stuart had promised, Adam and Marco were offered a publishing contract from EMI for £22,000. Armed with some cash at last, they started demoing songs for the album.

Burned by The Germs

That same month, we had a visit from one of Adam's biggest fans, Darby Crash, singer of the cult LA band The Germs. He and I had a mutual friend called Amber in Los Angeles, a fashion buyer who had bought a lot of clothes from Seditionaries. Amber was an unusually proportioned woman: very, very short and almost as wide as she was tall. When I took her measurements for a pair of Bondage trousers, Mr Mintos phoned me up. "You must have made a mistake with the measurements for these trousers," he said, "because they are as wide as they are long – the inside leg is as long as the waist and the rise is ridiculously huge." And I said: "No, I haven't made a mistake, those are her measurements. I took them myself, I know this lady."

While World's End was being refitted, Amber had taken me to LA for the first time – I was a bit of a catch for her to have at all the parties she threw there. Among her guests had been the extremely handsome singer and dancer Spazz Attack, who appeared in Devo's 'Satisfaction' and 'Peek-A-Boo!' videos and went on to work with David Bowie on the Glass Spider Tour. But there wasn't so much of a punk scene in LA at that time as just a smattering of individuals trying to stand out from the crowd, and Darby – with his audacious five-year plan to become a superstar and then kill himself – was at the forefront of that.

Darby came to see Adam play at the Empire Ballroom. There's a great photo of Mandy Donohoe and me with him on a staircase behind us, when he'd just gone and got himself a Mohican, or a Mohawk as he called it. It has been claimed elsewhere that I did that haircut for him, but I can't take the credit for that. Although I did pass the one test of endurance he put me through.

347

The natural messiah type

The Germs were formed in 1975 in the mind of the then 17-year-old LA native Paul Beahm, in an idea based on Bowie's apocalyptic 'Five Years'. That was the time Paul, who renamed himself Darby Crash, gave himself to form a band, become outrageously successful and then kill himself. He got the first part of the act together in 1977, teaming up with bassist Lorna Doom, guitarist Pat Smear (later of Nirvana and Foo Fighters) and drummer Dan Bolles, who considered Darby "...the new Jesus/Bowie/Manson/Hitler/L. Ron Hubbard... he was a natural messiah type". They played their first gig at the Los Angeles Orpheum in April 1977 and soon became notorious. The riot police were regularly sent to try and break up the mayhem. The Germs recorded their debut single, 'Forming', considered the first punk record to come out of LA, five months later, with the album *(GI) (Germs Incognito)* following in December. It was produced by fan Joan Jett, who apparently passed out during the recording of 'Shut Down'. "An aural holocaust" was the *LA Times'* opinion of it.

In January 1980, producer Jack Nitzsche recorded six Germs songs for William Friedkin's controversial *Cruising*, about a serial killer at large in the New York gay community. He also widened Darby's appetite for potential destruction, according to Jonh Ingham: "Nitzsche was very much a connoisseur of the chemicals. Darby was telling me about this conversation they had in the studio and he said Nitzsche was basically a pharmacological index." Appropriately enough, The Germs' track 'Lion's Share' was featured during a murder scene in the movie.

By May of that year, the band had been banned from every venue in their home city. Fortunately, their live act had been recorded for posterity as the centrepiece for Penelope Spheeris's seminal 1981 documentary *The Decline of Western Civilization*, and an image of Darby passed out onstage was used in promotional flyers for the film.

The Germs split up in July 1980, but Darby got his former band back together a few months later so that, as he told Smear, he could get the money to buy his fatal heroin dose. On 7 December, he took an OD with his girlfriend Casey Cola, who survived their suicide pact. A day later, John Lennon's murder outside the Dakota building ensured Darby's death would be eclipsed in the annals of rock legend. However, in 2007, the film *What We Do Is Secret*, directed by Rodger Grossman, revived interest in Darby and The Germs for a new generation. It was co-written and produced by Darby's close friend Michelle Baer Ghaffari, and Shane West did such a spookily convincing job of bringing the singer back from the dead that he was asked by Pat Smear and Lorna Doom to front a reformed Germs, as Shane Wreck.

Anna Melluso and I had by now moved on from the rather intimate confines of Talbot Road and Michael's unusual neighbours to a bigger flat in Hyde Park Square, not far from Buckingham Gate, and this is where Darby came round to meet me for the first time. He insisted that I had a Germs burn: he put a cigarette out on my wrist. Another of Darby's many obsessions was with circles – he wore an armband with a circle on it on-stage – which he derived from reading the works of dodgy German social theorist Oswald Spengler. He believed that if he branded you with a circular scar from a cigarette, it would encourage loyalty. Only the initiated would have them, the people he wanted. There was no getting out of this unless I was to tell him to leave the flat – and he just went on, and on, and on at me. He held the cigarette on my wrist for as long as I could take it. He was so pleased that I'd done it, but it hurt like hell. I've still got a small scar there.

Only six months after I met him, Darby went ahead with his plan and committed suicide on 7 December. He had made a pact with his girlfriend Casey Cola, who, in a weird reversal of Nancy's fortunes, survived being shot up with a supposedly lethal dose of heroin but had to be institutionalised after she came round to find Darby dead in her arms. Jonh Ingham, who had by this point left London for LA and was managing bands The Weirdos and The Go-Go's, also knew Darby well and remains mystified by his final act.

> **JONH INGHAM:** He was very self-destructive and yet he was so smart. You think: Why did he elect to do that? You couldn't see any reasons that he would be so self-destructive – except that he really liked doing it.

My secret life

After *Jubilee*, Malcolm always encouraged me to work on my acting, and for a while that's what I did. In July 1980, I was in a radical play staged one lunchtime at the ICA by the playwright Jonathan Gems, called *The Secret of the Universe*. Jonathan, son of the famous playwright Pam Gems, was someone I met through Derek Jarman, who designed the set with Steve Meaha and Christopher Hobbs. I performed an improvised ballet in this, with actor Keith Hodiak, and I also had some dialogue which caused a bit of consternation when Mum, Dad, Sally, Roger and Linda came to see it. One of my lines was: "She died of cancer of the cunt." I remember the hush in the auditorium when I said it.

> **ROGER ROOKE:** I don't particularly remember that, but I do remember you getting lifted by a dancer... I don't remember the swearing stuff. Maybe I fell asleep!

Jonathan Gems went on to co-write *White Mischief* (Michael Radford, 1987) and *Mars Attacks!* (Tim Burton, 1996). It was a great play and I really enjoyed doing it. Derek shot some footage of Keith and me dancing that appeared in his *B2 Movie*, a collage of home movie clips.

Not quite so successful was the offer I had from an American casting agent, who had seen a tiny article about me in *Time* magazine and somehow got my number at Hyde Park Corner. He said he was a casting agent and wanted me to be in this film with Charles Bronson – but would I send him some photos of me in tennis wear.

Now, these days, we'd think: Oh yeah. But at the time, I told my friend, the film costume designer Norma Moriceau,[4] about it, and she offered to do a session. So we found a tennis court, did the shots and sent them off to him. Then, a few weeks later, he asked me to do something in ballet wear. And of course, in those days, we believed it. Then I got a phone call from the CIA at Hyde Park Square asking me if I knew this man, and what connection did I have with him? He might have been one of those big serial killers, Henry Lee Lucas or something. So much for Hollywood.

Walking the dog

On 25 July 1980, Adam's hard work appeared to have paid off: the Ants signed to major label CBS, the 'Kings…' single was cut and manufactured, and the band went into Rockfield Studios in Monmouthshire, Wales to record the album. But, as good as it was, on its first release, the single only got up to number forty-eight in the charts. Meanwhile, Malcolm was baiting Adam from the pages of the music press, calling him an old man (he was all of 27). Bow Wow Wow had just released their first single, 'C30, C60, C90, Go!' – a paean to home taping with which he intended to infuriate the industry that was feeding him. Despite the urging of the lyrics, people bought the single in enough quantities to get it to number thirty-four in the singles chart – a lot of original Ants fans, including Matthew's army of admirers, took sides with Bow Wow Wow. However, despite all his influence over the band, Malcolm had a problem with his singer that would only get worse as Adam continued to get better.

---

[4] Norma Moriceau (1944–2016) was a friend of Malcolm and Vivienne's, who lived around the corner from 430 King's Road. At the time of SEX/Seditionaries she was working in fashion and shooting a lot of advertising campaigns and she contributed some of her Super-8 films to the footage that went into *The Great Rock 'n' Roll Swindle*. She returned to her native Australia to style *Mad Max* (George Miller, 1979) and its sequels, *Mad Max 2* (1981) and *Beyond Thunderdome* (1985), drawing on the imagery of the shop and the punk milieu and reflecting her own nomadic lifestyle.

For a start, Amy Dunn-Lwin didn't trust Malcolm as far as she could throw him, and insisted on her under-age daughter being chaperoned everywhere. I got a taste of her overbearing maternal nature when she accompanied Annabella into World's End to select her outfits for their forthcoming tour. She said to me: "You will look after her, won't you?" And I said: "Of course I will – she's only young." I picked out some gold brocade Pirate trousers for her and her mother went: "No, we ought to have the red ones, in case she starts her you-know-what…" And I was thinking: What? You're worried about her having a period when she was wearing a pair of Pirate trousers? The other problem was that Annabella couldn't really sing.

> **SIMON BARKER:** Annabella's mother was too much – she was brilliant. She kept telling us: "I could have been a star! Otto Preminger wanted to turn me into a star!" All those tiger-head diamanté tops, that was her. But Annabella herself was really untalented. Malcolm used to have to make her sing the songs over and over again. She was picked because of how she looked. Malcolm wanted that exotic look. But she couldn't hold the stage, either, so Malcolm had to get dancers to go on stage with her.

As he so clearly demonstrated with the stream of ideas that eventually led to the formation of Bow Wow Wow, I think Malcolm thought the key to success was all to do with young girls. He was obsessed with youth and he wanted to be around young people at all times. Unlike Annabella, Adam wasn't a blank page, he wasn't malleable. He knew exactly where he wanted to be.

Adam was inspired to write 'Dog Eat Dog' by a line used by Margaret Thatcher that he felt could equally apply to his situation with Malcolm. The record company liked the song and released it as the next single on 3 October. This time, it got as far as number thirty-seven, breaching the top 40, and the band were asked to go on *Top of the Pops*.

Many years later Adam saw me in the audience at a gig just as he was about to start doing 'Dog Eat Dog' and he said: "Jordan's here. She'll know exactly what this means. Our world changed when we went on *Top of the Pops*. Everything changed."

That one show was so important in those days that it could literally steer your destiny overnight, turn a bedsit room in Earl's Court into a rock star's mansion. Though, like everything else for Adam, even appearing on that show was a triumph over adversity.

Before we had even set foot inside the studios at Wood Green, the band, Mandy and myself were met by the skinhead band 4" Be 2", who started taunting and jeering at us as we walked down the corridors, finally kicking Adam in the back, causing him to topple down some stairs. Mandy, Kevin and I managed to smack their arses back before security guards intervened to escort them off the premises.

Adam was to meet his next manager, Don Murfet, as a result of this altercation. Don was the head of the security firm the BBC were using, Artists Services, and at first Adam hired him to be his own head of security on the autumn/winter Frontier tour. Don, who was a friend of the legendary Led Zeppelin manager Peter Grant, made Adam feel safer as his celebrity suddenly skyrocketed. Feeling that Falcon Stuart hadn't come up to scratch,[5] Adam replaced him as his manager with Don in December 1980, a position he would keep for the next three years.

'PUNK STARS IN TOP OF THE POPS RIOT' was the front cover of the next day's *Daily Mirror*. The single shot up the charts to number four.

Unplug the jukebox

A couple of weeks later, in November, *Kings of the Wild Frontier* was released and went into the album charts at number four. Adam and Marco had set out to make an album that was the equal of those records that had inspired them as teenagers. Looking back now, Marco feels that they did achieve all they had intended with the album.

MARCO PIRRONI: I think albums that don't date are *For Your Pleasure*, *Ziggy Stardust*, *Never Mind the Bollocks* and *Transformer*. But that's just our generation. I don't know if other bands try to make albums like *Kings*

---

[5] Adam distrusted Falcon Stuart so much in the end that he had all of the 'Kings...' demo tapes secretly copied.

of the Wild Frontier, but we tried to make an album – well, I did that was like *Ziggy Stardust* and *Transformer*, that would stand the test of time.

It certainly did a whole lot better than Bow Wow Wow's mini-album *Your Cassette Pet*, which, released in cassette-tape format only, didn't qualify to be included in the albums chart and peaked at number fifty-eight in the singles chart instead. Malcolm had managed to infuriate EMI a second time, when they realised the lyrics of the first Bow Wow Wow single had been advocating piracy of the audio kind, and the British Phonographic Industry (BPI) launched an official complaint against the record company in retaliation. Malcolm had made hay in the press with this, but actual sales figures meant the battle between the two bands was clearly now over in Adam's mind, as Marco remembers it:

MARCO PIRRONI: I remember him coming round my house with *Cassette Pet* saying: "You've gotta listen to this, it's great!" 'Louis Quartorze' was the song. The rest of it I didn't think was that good, but that track was brilliant. I said: "Yeah, it's really good. But I thought you hated them." He said, "Oh yeah, but I don't hate them now." What, because we've sold 1.6 million records more than they have? Because you're no longer in competition? When we'd surpassed them to the point of 500 times, Adam was like, "OK, that doesn't matter now." He'd even gone past the "I've beaten you" stage, he just became magnanimous and thought: Yeah, they're all right.

'Antmusic' was chosen to be the next single and, for the first time, CBS gave the band the money to make a video to go with the song, which was filmed in our old haunt Sombrero's, scene of my almost run-in with Freddie. You can see the flashing, star-shaped dancefloor in the video, and maybe some shreds of Lycra floating around on the breeze that were all that was left of the long-departed winged messenger. The single got all the way to number two that December, only being held off the number one position by the same event that robbed Darby Crash of any notoriety for his suicide – the assassination of John Lennon outside the Dakota Building in New York on the evening of 8 December.

354

Antmania had begun. And so, on the Ants autumn tour of the UK, had something else.

We need to talk about Kevin

When I first met Kevin Mooney, we really, really seriously clicked. The trouble was the clandestine relationship I'd been having with Adam, which had been carrying on since that night in Earl's Court. Then, on the night of 15 November, after the Ants had just played West Runton Pavilion in Norfolk, that all changed.

I had actually had sex with Adam that night, before the gig. He had been given what was probably the best room in the bed and breakfast we were staying in – Antmania may have been in its first flush, but we were still being put up in the pokiest dives on the UK gig circuit, one of the reasons that Falcon Stuart got the push. This room had a mirror, in front of which we'd had sex. And after the gig Adam went back there to sleep. He didn't drink and he was never one for hanging out afterwards. But the rest of the band were in the mood for a bit of an aftershow and there came that moment when Kevin and I were the last people left in the bar. We just looked at each other and knew we were going to go upstairs.

The only trouble was, the B&B was so awful that to get to Kevin's room you had to go through the one occupied by Marco – we had to go and tiptoe round his bed. Once we had successfully navigated that obstacle and got safely into Kevin's room, he said the immortal words: "What shall I call you?" I replied, "Just call me Venus," as I devoured him.

I always wondered if Marco ever knew what we'd done that night. So, when I set about writing this part of the story, I asked him.

MARCO PIRRONI: Not really, being asleep at the time. But once Adam found out about it, it upset the dynamic of the band pretty quickly. Because bands have a hierarchy, and that doesn't often change. I don't think I understood that then. The dynamic was different and it was weird, but for me it wasn't the end of the world. But, for Adam, he couldn't control it.

Marco is putting it mildly. Adam went completely bonkers when he heard. It was at the next day's soundcheck – somebody had told him that Kevin and I had been together the night before. He screamed at the top of his voice: "FUCKING HELLLL!"

Even though he could never commit to me, Adam didn't want anyone else to have me. Also, he really didn't like being upstaged in any way and that's how he must have felt about Kevin. He was really, really riled, to the point that he even told Mandy Donohoe and really upset her, too. So there was all this interplay going on…

MARCO PIRRONI: He said the usual, "What the fuck does she want to be with him for?" sort of thing. Then there was: "They're doing this to undermine me." But, to be fair, that was only for about five minutes. My point was, either we chuck him out or we don't. We can't come to you and say you mustn't see him. But Adam had this thing that I had to have a talk with Kevin about how he mustn't see you any more. And I said: "Adam, look. That's not going to work with grown-ups." I wasn't going to say it and, even if I had, Kevin wasn't going to take any notice. Can you imagine: "You're absolutely right, I'm so sorry. I'll get rid of her." He might have said that, but I didn't think that was really going to happen. I thought he would probably tell me to fuck off, which is what I would have done. Either you put up with that, or you don't.

Adam wasn't the only one who was angry. Eve called me over at the Ants gig at the Hammersmith Palais on Christmas Eve and said: "I want to talk to you upstairs." We went up to the toilets on the first floor. "Explain yourself", I offered, "before I hit you."

She blamed me for first taking Adam away from her and then for Kevin, said I was breaking her life to pieces. But Adam had split up with her before I even knew him. I let her finish, not saying anything, just looking at her. During that time, she must have decided against having a fight.

She had already tried to do a lot of things to get Adam back, but when I came along she saw me as the end of all that. It was the same with Kevin. She thought that the two loves of her life had ended up with me.

DOROTHY MAX PRIOR: She knew that the marriage was not what it was, which was a normal, straight marriage and that they had moved into this open relationship, but she wanted to keep him as her husband. That's why she changed her name to Eve. If Stuart was going to be Adam, then Carol was going to be Eve. All of her forays into bands and things were to prove she could do it, too. But I don't think that was really what was driving her. I think it was jealousy. I got that sense from her that she was hanging on.

A right royal carve-up

By the New Year of 1981, *Kings of the Wild Frontier* was number one in the album chart. Following hot on its heels, CBS re-released the single of the title track, which climbed to number two in February. The Ants would get their first number one in April, with 'Stand and Deliver', for which I made some emergency ringlets for the Dandy Highwayman when he was asked to go on *Top of the Pop*s at the last moment and couldn't grow his own in twenty-four hours. I got some bits of real hair from a salon on the King's Road, but they only had a brown wig that I could use, so I dyed them black with a Sharpie felt-tip pen, put little bows in them and tacked them to my door at Hyde Park Corner to dry. I clipped them onto his head for the performance and, all the way through, I was praying he wouldn't sweat all that marker-pen dye off on his face.

But by then, Kevin was not part of the band any more. Not after the Ants were invited to play *The Royal Variety Show* at the Palladium, in front of Princess Margaret on 5 February, a night that turned into a disaster all round.

Adam had by now already appeared on Noel Edmonds' *Multi-Coloured Swap Shop*, while no less an authority than the *Sun* had decided he was going to be the biggest pop star of 1981. So, already, he was going in a direction that was far, far away from my original vision of the Ants when he first asked me to manage him. Many stories and much speculation surround the performance the band did on *The Royal Variety Show* and what followed as a result of it. This is how I saw it.

I styled Kevin for his performance that night; he was wearing a pair of culottes from Vivienne's Pirates collection at World's End. When we arrived at the Palladium, there was a moment when I saw

357

in Adam's face that he knew Kevin's look was my influence and that was it, the last straw. Kevin was young, handsome and dressed in a skirt. What Adam couldn't ever stand was someone who upstaged him.

But Kevin did even worse than that. During their performance – which was only miming, anyway – Kevin dared to walk in front of him on stage. He was doing the whole bass-slinger thing and Adam was furious. Then the strap broke on his guitar. Adam was convinced that Kevin did it deliberately, but it was an accident. He started to play it like a double bass for a little while. He didn't know what else to do, you can't hold the bass up for long without a strap; it's a heavy thing.

The writing was on the wall anyway, I think. There is a line that you draw and that line has to begin with Adam being at the front of the stage and everyone else behind him. Kevin had irked Adam a few times on tour with his onstage flamboyance and now they'd reached breaking point. How can you ask somebody not to be good at what they're doing?

When the Ants came off stage, Kevin was fired.

DOROTHY MAX PRIOR: Afterwards, Adam was really, really cross about Kevin. He thought he was completely drunk and drugged up, behaving like a complete fool. I said: "Oh, I thought it was quite funny." And Adam just went absolutely spare.

MARCO PIRRONI: I knew it was bollocks, that Kevin hadn't done it on purpose, but Adam thinks everything is about him. It's all about control. I did have a very long conversation about it once in America when he said something like: "Do you know that bloke called Dave that's on the crew? The one with the glasses who works in the lighting crew? I think he's smoking dope!" I said: "What the fuck are you talking about? They're all smoking dope. The only two people who aren't smoking dope are you and me. And it's not just on this tour – it's in the world!"

That's why Kevin wanted out. Kevin wasn't in the least bit bothered about being sacked, because he knew that was the last thing he was going to do with the Ants, who had gone too far in a direction that neither of us agreed with. Adam had won the war with Bow Wow

Wow, but my ideal for Adam and the Ants when we put that game plan in place in his Earl's Court bedsit had been for them to become a really hard-hitting, groundbreaking band. There were two choices for Adam to make, and the one he picked was to go for the teeny market that would give him lots of money. I can't argue with that: if you want money, then you want money. But other things he could have done might have given him even more. When you've got power, you've got a chance to make something, you've already done that hard work in the right way. That's how I looked at it.

RICHARD CABUT: Also, Adam had been through a very similar thing as he did with Kevin before with Matthew Ashman, exactly the same thing and exactly the same animosity. Adam must have had a big flashback and thought: Shit!

Adam and I also disagreed about 'Prince Charming'. It was very, very hard, that. I didn't like that formulaic, let's-look-at-people-through-history, the highwaymen, Prince Charming, aiming it at children, when they had so much more to give. They'd turned into a pantomime act. It took Adam a long time to forgive me for that.

But Kevin and I were in love and had other ideas about the future of music. We were going to take things somewhere else entirely – and we were going to do it together.

21

OVER THE MOONEY

Love, marriage and leaving King's Road
(February 1981–September 1982)

Ducking and diving

Kevin and I had big plans for putting a new band together, around a nucleus of Kevin's West London mates that included John Keogh, Lenny Brazier and Horace Carter-Allen. Things moved quickly – Kevin and John had been close since they were kids; they were at school together and played in The European Cowards before Kevin joined the Ants. John was a brilliant guitarist, even though he had been in a terrible accident in his youth. He was getting some washing for his Mum from the launderette, when a spin-dryer that he'd just reached into malfunctioned and started up again, taking his arm with it. He broke his elbow and hand, and all the ligaments and muscles were twisted; he could never straighten his arm out properly again. But he became a guitarist, and a good one, too.

Kevin was always a cunning wordsmith, interested in all forms of argot, and he and John invented their own secret language along the way that Kevin used for his lyrics. The name of this new collaboration was the nickname he had for John – Wide Boy Awake.

Lenny, who was enigmatically described to the press as 'the Spinning-all-over Man' in WBA slang, had already made a name for himself at my place of work:

DAVID IRELAND: He came into the shop and almost instantly I could see that something had disappeared. You could tell by the way he was standing that he had a pair of trousers up his coat. I said: "Lenny, the trousers you've got there, put them back." He said: "What?" He used to be a model, didn't he? There was that agency that did star lookalikes, and he was David Essex. He did look the spitting image of David Essex.

Lenny once presented me with a lovely dark blue and gold Cartier lighter, which got nicked from the dressing room at the London Palladium, of all places. You'd believe that people were good there. But no, off it vanished again, for at least the third time in its existence.

Spinning and weaving

With the World's End shop now launched, Malcolm and Vivienne decided to try something they had never done before – show the Pirates collection formally on a catwalk. Having made such a powerful statement with the transformed shop and its revolutionary new line, Vivienne wanted to prove herself in fashion's 'Premier League', so Malcolm decided they should stage the collection at the Pillar Hall in Olympia in March 1981. As they had no idea what putting a runway show together entailed, they took on two people who had that experience: Michael's pattern-cutter friend Mark Tarbard, who had worked on shows with Jeff Banks, and Marysia Woroniecki as public relations officer and the show's producer. Marysia had previously been employed by Lynne Franks, the PR who would help to establish London Fashion Week and head one of the most prestigious fashion PR agencies of the 1980s.

MICHAEL COLLINS: I had some knowledge of catwalk shows. Not much. But the first big show at Olympia, the Pirate show, it went down so well because it was the only show that had colours. It was wonderful – great models and great music.

Michael was put in charge of the running order, and both of us got in models' portfolios. One of the new faces we chose was Nick Kamen, future star of the 1985 Levi's shrink-to-fit ad that would propel a short-lived pop career. Wide Boy Awake's Horace Carter-Allen was also picked, a Rastafarian pirate among the Mohicans, plaits and multi-hued plumage of the crew.

MICHAEL COLLINS: One of the models had quite a big forehead that you covered up quite successfully with a hat, and Malcolm said: "This is great. We'll put a World's End logo on her forehead." This is years before tattoos on the face became big.

The night before the show, Malcolm and I were up all night at Nightingale Lane, pressing an endless pile of cotton Pirate shirts with an ironing board each and equipment so ancient, it brought back that old childhood favourite of mine, 'Dashing Away with the Smoothing Iron'. Even Bernie Rhodes had been roped back in to help with the music, which, naturally enough, was entirely comprised of Bow Wow Wow.

The day itself was madness. On his way up the steps to Olympia, Simon Barker was accosted by one of Vivienne's knitting ladies, Maureen from Mitcham, who had been delayed because her dog escaped and she'd had to spend the morning trying to find him. She presented Simon with a bag of clothes Vivienne had been expecting. Vivienne emptied this out onto the floor and asked the models to choose which ones they wanted to wear. She hadn't thought of doing a running order.

If anybody's been backstage at a fashion show, they wouldn't have seen anything like this day. To do a running order, you really need two people to keep an eye on who's coming off and who's going on, plus the order of the clothes. What people don't realise is that, quite often, we had to sew people into their clothes. Not everybody could fit into Vivienne's shoes, either, which is why a lot of the models went barefoot.

MICHAEL COLLINS: There was fighting backstage, as well. And Mr Mintos turned up to sew all those beads on the jackets at the last minute.

363

The catwalk itself was a long white oblong, but all around it Malcolm covered the auditorium, including all its massive pillars, with World's End wrapping paper, printed with the logo of an arm brandishing a cutlass above the words 'BORN IN ENGLAND'. He had got Walkmans out of Sony for the models to wear as they snaked down the catwalk through dry ice and the sound of cannon fire, while an audience that included Mick Jagger, Adam, Boy George and Michael Costiff looked on, delighted.

> **MICHAEL COSTIFF:** It was so exciting. After the punk period, when the colour palette was strictly black and white with maybe a bit of red, to go from that to a sort of pirate/Caribbean fantasy was something amazing. In a way, punk had also been very white working class, whereas this was a multicultural extravaganza. We knew most of the models in the show and the amazing make-up by Yvonne Gold with gold and orange, the models leaping around and swirling through the dry ice – it was really high-energy and we didn't know where to look next.
>
> Vivienne and Malcolm looked so happy at the end – and they'd never really appeared together in public like that before. We wanted absolutely everything – and we got most of it. 'Swashbuckling' was the word!

The show succeeded in grabbing all the attention Vivienne needed. The hugely influential trade magazine *Women's Wear Daily* called her "the hottest designer of the new look", prompting American buyers to follow that lead up the King's Road. British *Vogue*'s Liz Tilberis dared to come in and was astonished by Vivienne's clothes. Her tip-off to senior fashion editor Grace Coddington led to a four-page feature in the fashion bible that August. Anna Piaggi, as editor of *Vanity*, based in Milan, commissioned an entire feature on pirates. *Italian Vogue* quickly followed suit, printing extensive photos of me in the bicorne hat – the only piece of headwear that has ever actually suited me.

By May, even the *Sunday Times* was revealing how the look was catching on with the Sloane Ranger set, including the soon-to-be Princess Diana, who had all taken to wearing ruffled pirate shirts. But you can spot the difference quite easily if you look at the cover of *Style Wars*, the book of Peter York's collected style journalism, which was published at the height of all this. There's me, with red eyes and hair, sharing the split-screen front cover with headscarved Sloane Arabella Scott.

Before long, that style would be labelled in the pages of the emergent style press[1] as New Romantic, along with the movement that Boy George, Steve Strange and Leigh Bowery, among many others, were involved with. I must admit that I didn't have much time for Steve, because I considered him and Pete Burns as groupies, for want of a better word. I didn't go along to any of his nights at Browns or the Mud Club, either, but I did really like the Camden Palace. He had a good do going there. On the whole, though, I thought the whole New Romantic thing was over-thought and over-cooked. Everyone was trying to outdo each other without there actually being any meaning behind it.

George, I do have a lot of time for. He wasn't a singer then, but he used to come into SEX all the time – and he would freely admit how all that early stuff resonated with him.

You can see me in my full Anne Bonny get-up, with red ringlets, being photographed by Ted Polhemus and Lynne Proctor in the film *Posers: New Romantics in the Kings Road* (Carlos Pasini-Hansen, 1981), standing outside World's End and explaining the ethics behind Vivienne and Malcolm's Pirates collection, as a reaction against Margaret Thatcher's government, a revolt into a new style inspired by pirates, Native Americans and Louis Quatorze.[2]

That was the last snapshot of my life on King's Road before Vivienne and I finally parted ways.

Wedding of the year

This is an example of how my friends found out that I was no longer working at no. 430. Bertie Marshall phoned up the shop one day

---

[1] *The Face* magazine launched in 1980, the brainchild of former *NME* editor Nick Logan, who created the blueprint of a "well-produced, well-designed and well-written monthly with music at its core". The New Romantic era was heralded by Robert Elms with a piece called 'The Cult with No Name' in November 1980 and the title became synonymous with the rapidly mutating, intertwined music and fashion worlds of the early to mid-1980s. Hot on its heels in 1980 was *i-D*, founded by former *Vogue* art director Terry Jones, and launched first as a fanzine, then rapidly morphing into a glossy monthly.

[2] You can watch *Posers* at www.youtube.com/watch?v=w8eklDJKDRE&t=28s

and Vivienne asked him: "Did you know, Jordan's getting married?" Bertie said, "No," and she said: "Yes, well she is. And I've got a wedding present for her – the sack!"

She was furious. She could never get over the fact that I was the kind of person who could get married. But on 23 June 1981, my 26th birthday, Kevin and I tied the knot at Marylebone Registry Office and had a wedding party to remember at Andrew Logan's warehouse. The whole event was filmed by Derek Jarman, and exists today as the short film *Jordan's Wedding*.

Vivienne wasn't the only one put out by my relatively sudden nuptials – my family didn't like the situation very much either. They thought it was too quick and Kevin was too young – he was 18 at the time – but while we didn't need to get married, we were genuinely in love. It was my idea to tie the knot and Kevin said yes without any hesitation – he had probably been worried about asking me himself. We saw it as a great big party to invite all our family and friends to, there was no religious reason behind it, although Kevin did come from a big Irish family, where all the women ran around the blokes – or should I say the *bloke*, his father. But the event was covered as Wedding of the Year in *Honey* magazine by the

---

Snap happy

Robyn Beeche (1945–2015) came to London from her native Australia in 1974 and, after working as an assistant to the fashion photographer Harri Peccinotti, set up her own studio in Thurloe Square in 1977. She documented the work of other highly creative women, including Vivienne and Zandra Rhodes, as well as the emerging New Romantic scene at The Blitz in Covent Garden. She travelled with Rhodes and Andrew Logan to India, a country she fell in love with and where she settled in 1992, with her partner, independent filmmaker Michael Duffy. Beeche was involved in many charities and was working on a commission for Mumbai airport at the time of her death. See *Robyn Beeche: Visage to Vraj* by Stephen Crafti (Images, 2009) and Lesley Branagan's 2013 documentary *A Life Exposed.*

photographer Robyn Beeche, a friend of both Andrew Logan and Boy George, who took some of the most memorable images of the era.

The day before the wedding, Dad had an accident with the hedge clippers and nearly took his finger off. On the day, our dear friend from the shop, Ozzie, who was one of our witnesses, was almost not allowed into the wedding venue when she pulled up on her chopper, dressed in her road rat colours. And my best man, Michael Collins, turned up sporting a fetching black eye that had been given to him by his boyfriend, Ted, the night before.

MICHAEL COLLINS: I looked like Kevin Keegan with my permed hair and my black eye. Fucking Ted had punched me in the eye the night before and I was so out of it, I didn't even notice. But I'm from Peckham, so what do I care? Everyone in Peckham turns up with a black eye. Especially the women.

When I looked back over my wedding photographs with my family, there were surprises in there for all of us. David McDonald, my old clubbing partner from Brighton, was one of the guests. Lenny and John from Wide Boy Awake were there, with sometime band member Harley Price, who was wearing a German army helmet. Malcolm and Vivienne didn't attend, and nor did Adam – I thought it was inappropriate to ask him, something that I regret now. I was shocked to see that, somehow, Eve had managed to be there on the day!

ROGER ROOKE: A lot of people thought it was a film set, and people were taking photos. The guests at the other weddings were all taking photos of your wedding, on the steps of Marylebone Registry Office. It was a wonderful fashion show, the whole thing.

Afterwards, Andrew Logan greeted us at his warehouse with a lit-up model Pegasus. Michael set about making another of his trademark punches for the occasion, an entire dustbin full of the stuff. Dad drank so much of it, he pulled one of the pillars over. He went to lean on one, thinking it was made of stone, and they were made of polystyrene – they came from a film set. Somebody caught it in time, though.

MICHAEL COLLINS: There were tears at bedtime that night. It's funny. That punch seemed to be my pièce de résistance. I used to leave the fruit soaking in brandy for a few days, then add lots of white wine and sugar so it turned into some sort of psilocin that sent people over the edge. I called it Fruit Cup. It was the worst place to have it, at Andrew Logan's, you could just drop over the side and kill yourself. He had a balcony and I was running along it. Lenny was there and he pulled me off. I was so out of it, I don't even remember.

Jeannie remembers that, at one stage, Michael put his shoe in the dustbin full of punch and drank from it. But she still doesn't remember how she managed to drive home after sharing a spliff with Ted.

LINDA ROOKE: I took your mum and dad and Sally to the station in the car while Roger stayed at the party with Jeannie. I got back from Liverpool Street and, because I knew the way, I was going to guide them back to where we lived in Ilford at that time. But when I got back to the party, Roger and Jeannie had already left with Jeannie driving, and they had left some time ago. I drove all the way back to Ilford and they still hadn't appeared. When eventually they did, Roger said: "Don't ask me how we did that."

By her own admittance, Jeannie didn't know what she was doing. She nearly hit three roundabouts, she could have gone into anything. Things weren't much better at the other end of the tracks back in Seaford, either.

SALLY REID: I nearly abandoned your dad on the train after the wedding. He'd had so much to drink, he couldn't move. Mum and I had to drag him off and into a taxi.

After the ball

After the party, Kevin and I went off to Venice on our honeymoon. It wasn't until we got back that I learned that Ozzie had been killed on her motorbike. She came through Kensington and went into a traffic island, being chased by police because one of her lights was out. She was decapitated.

MICHAEL COLLINS: I went to work one day and they took me to one side and said: "We've got to tell you, Ozzie's dead." It was Bella Freud, I think. I was devastated. I think that was when I began to resent Vivienne, because she didn't understand and just expected me to carry on. I was really close to Ozzie and I went to her funeral and Vivienne only gave me a couple of hours off to go to the crematorium. I had to sort that out. None of her family could do it; all her brothers were in prison.

I've still got the twisted silver bangle that she was wearing when she was killed. Ironically, I found out many years later that Anna Melluso was also killed in a bike accident and it was her friend Maurizio, who we had stayed with on our honeymoon, who told me. He had known about Ozzie's death at the time and hadn't been able to tell us. Anna was an absolutely lovely person and I was devastated when I found out. I knew she had gone back to Italy and I had been trying to get back in touch with her for years. Like I say, looking back at my wedding photographs was a humbling experience. There were a lot of faces smiling back at me from the scenes of my big day who are now no longer with us.

At the safer distance of over three decades, I asked Vivienne why she had given me such a special going-away present by sacking me. To give this more perspective, I should also point out that at the time Kevin and I got married, Malcolm had finally left Nightingale Lane for good, moving in with a young German designer called Andrea Linz. Though he had often strayed before, this time he would not be coming back to Vivienne.

VIVIENNE WESTWOOD: I had a horrible relationship with Malcolm, just leave it at that. I was extremely loyal to him, you see, but he just had to hurt you every day – he was an awful, awful person to live with. I'd definitely fallen in love with him to start with, I just thought he was an amazing person. But the more you invest in the hardship and everything, the more terrible you feel when it all comes down. Betrayed, if you like, to feel that it didn't work. When it broke down, I was in a terrible way, but that was because I'd suffered so much, that's what I'm saying. And the reason I suffered is because I was so loyal to him because I thought I was a stupid person who didn't know anything and didn't understand the world, didn't know enough, I'd better learn about it, I'd better listen to Malcolm when he told me this, that and the other. Mothers shouldn't be anywhere near their own children, send Ben off to live with his dad. I listened to everything. So that's one reason why I became so loyal to him. Therefore I suffered terribly with Malcolm and I wasn't nice when you were getting married. I really thought: I've got to give her the sack, this is terrible. She's betrayed us by getting married, we belong to these people who suffer and don't get married. We don't want to contribute to the system by having these approved-of relationships. I was really angry with you about it.

When I was young, you couldn't experiment and see if it worked, you had to get married. I'd been married once before and I kind of associated my suffering with Malcolm as being the price I was paying not to be working for the Establishment. All his rebellion and what he was against, I believed in that. It was all tied in. If someone else was getting married, it was like you were doing something bad against me. I'm just working it out now, because you don't want to put up with suffering like I've had to.[3]

MICHAEL COLLINS: I remember when she and Malcolm split up. Malcolm was going with that girl Andie from Germany. Me and Vivienne went to the cinema in the West End and she had a bottle of whisky in her bag and we got really quite drunk. She was just swigging it – it was all or nothing with her. Then we walked down to Craven Terrace, which is where Malcolm was living, and she picked up the biggest brick and her aim was immaculate – it went straight through the window and landed on Malcolm! He was in there with Andie, as well.

---

[3] Vivienne is, of course, now married herself, to her former student Andreas Kronthaler. They were married in 1993 and now design collections together.

Unaware of any of this, when we got back after our honeymoon, Kevin and I moved out of Hyde Park Gate and in with John Keogh, to his big housing co-op flat off Portobello Road. I was wearing one of Vivienne's wonderful Matisse toga dresses, which had a long train on it, and we were really happy, Kevin and I, as he lifted me up over the threshold and kicked the door shut behind us. He kept on walking with me in his arms, not realising that he had caught the end of the train in the front door... And the whole back of the dress ripped off. A moment that should have been absolutely wonderful turned to: "Shiiiiiiit! That's my favourite dress!"

From dusk till dawn

On Christmas Eve 1980, I went back to the Portobello Hotel, which always shut over the festive season, to make a film with the Ladbroke Grove/Berlin-based director Robina Rose called *Night Shift*. It was shot over five nights in the hotel and featured Heathcote Williams, Jon Jost – who was also the cameraman – and Jacob Rees-Mogg's Aunt Anne, who taught at Chelsea School of Art. I played the receptionist, watching the activities of the others in a dreamlike, slow-motion state.

ROBINA ROSE: While I was at the Royal College of Art Film School, I worked at the Portobello doing night shifts, and I was able to shoot the film there because they lent it to me over Christmas. I got the keys from the girl who was doing the last shift, which I handed over to the next girl on shift five days later, and my mum came over and did the cooking, so it was like spending one long night there! It was a different universe then.

I was quite influenced by Japanese Noh theatre and a face that is a catalyst, and you had the perfect one – without your make-up and without the hair standing up, wearing one of my beige dresses. It was a double mask and you were mesmeric. You only had one line: "Reception." You couldn't have someone do something without speaking unless they were a very powerful person, and you had total command of your own image.

We shot it in real time, at night, all night – Jon does very long, slow takes – and it never occurred to me to black out the windows. But there is a shot at the end, with you walking out of the door into the dawn, which wouldn't have been half so good if we hadn't done it that way. So it was a very extreme shoot, and it added to it, doing it in real time. The whole film cost five grand and everyone worked for nothing but a bottle of wine a night. You are the star of the film, the silent star.

Night Shift was bought by the Museum of Modern Art New York archive and, at time of writing, was being digitised by the BFI. So hopefully you will be able to find a copy of it by the time you are reading this.

Cajun chicken outlaws

Kevin got a big pay off when he left the Ants. He got £50,000, in a settlement I negotiated myself with Don Murfet, who was about as heavy a presence as you could have to deal with. I honestly thought Wide Boy Awake were the future – an unconventional dance band that incorporated a mash-up of tribal beats, hip-hop and Cajun music, which we were both heavily into and which had never really been used in that way before. My position with them was a more intensified version of the role I had with the Ants – I managed them and got them a deal at RCA Records. I had initially gone to talk to a subsidiary label of RCA who wanted to sign Wide Boy Awake, but, as soon as RCA heard of this, they gazumped them. They wanted to get the band before anyone else did, even though that label was part of their own organisation.

Wide Boy Awake started working on songs for what would become their first EPs right away – 'Slang Teacher', 'Bona Venture', 'Whooping on the Roof', 'Chicken Outlaw' and 'Raver's Red Light'.[4] They worked very hard on those songs: Kevin wrote them all in my presence and he had the same 100 per cent sense of commitment that I had seen before in the Pistols and Adam, the same excitement of conjuring up a new sound and spirit. Part of that was the slang as Kevin was really into the idea of spontaneous prose and he was really talented as a lyricist; and part of it was the mixing up of different

---

[4] All these tracks were collected on US-only mini-album *Wide Boy Awake* in 1982.

forms of music, all those rhythms that we both really liked – getting out on the dancefloor was and will always be such a special thing for me. We wanted to generate a feeling around them that would make people get up, go out and be part of it.

RCA released two singles off the album in 1982, 'Chicken Outlaw' and 'Slang Teacher'. We had a great MD at RCA, David Betteridge (who co-founded Island with Chris Blackwell), and a brilliant publisher at Warner Bros., Rob Dickens, who was a real inspiration to me. Derek Jarman was involved from the off, directing the video for their first single, which both Sally and I helped to style, a day both of us look back on with really fond memories. Things were looking so good…

RICHARD CABUT: I thought you were a really great couple, really suited each other, coming from the same place and bouncing stuff off each other. You had the connections and the clothes and he had a whole bunch of energy to move it forward. I loved Wide Boy Awake.

But, if you look carefully at the cover of that twelve-inch of 'Chicken Outlaw', you will find a clue as to where all that money was actually going, laid out on the mirror.

Beyond the fringe

Malcolm was always encouraging me to be an actress, telling me that was my way of staying the public image of punk. He was so business-minded he always had to see the money-making angle, but in truth, I've never been anyone but me. Obviously people have misconstrued me as being an exhibitionist, an accusation that has been aimed at me many times. But no: I always just wanted to be comfortable, be happy and be myself. Make a difference. I didn't want to become the type of person who would do anything to have money and to get attention.

I enjoyed all my dalliances with film and theatre because they were so unconventional and required me to think on my feet, something I've always been good at. Which was why I took another challenge when it came my way, to perform a two-hander comedy play, *Farque*, in Edinburgh during September 1982. Before you rush to look that one up in the *Urban Dictionary*, the meaning it gives doesn't have anything to do with what the playwright, James Maw,[5] meant by it – it was supposed to be a posh person saying "Fuck".

James was a friend Kevin and I had made from living around Ladbroke Grove – we had got our own flat in Bonchurch Road by then, and he lived nearby in Holland Park. The play was a satire about the Falklands War that had revived the fortunes of Margaret Thatcher that summer, turning her from the most unpopular prime minister in our history in April 1982 to the vanquishing Britannia who won the 1983 general election with the most votes since Clement Attlee in 1945. All it had taken was 74 days, 252 British, 3 Islanders and 649 Argentinian dead – sometimes satire is the only answer you can give to that. I played the daughter of an artificial-limb-maker whose business has undergone a similar reversal of fortune in the conflict, while James played my dad and several other roles. A lot of it was akin to mime, but there were still a lot of lines to learn, which I am really bad at – I've always been much better at improvisation. Still, after a preview at Battersea Town Hall, we took it to the Edinburgh Fringe, where it seemed to go down well at the time. I performed my role in a stunning £10,000 Zandra Rhodes gold dress.

It was while I was in Edinburgh with *Farque* that I realised I was pregnant with Kevin's baby. We did talk about it and consider what to do, but I just could not see either of us, with our lives and careers at the time, being able to bring up a child properly. So I had an abortion. It was my second in two years and weighs heavily on me to this day; I can still remember how much my body wanted to go against my decision. The first one was the result of a relationship I'd been having

---

[5] James Maw (b. 1957) wrote his first play at the age of 8, imagining the last moments of King Charles I and what happened on the block. He called it *Why Am I Not the King, Wentworth?* He continued to grapple with his metier at junior school, composing *Have Them All Out*, in contemplation of his teeth, and *Bedlam*, which was performed by his classmates in 1975. Following *Farque*'s run at Edinburgh, he wrote the comic novel *Hard Luck* (1986), which has since been followed by *Jack and Sarah* (1995), *Year of the Jaguar* (1996) and *Nothing But Trouble* (1998), the latter two inspired by travels in Mexico and further afield in South America.

with another musician at the same time as Adam. Adam thought that one was his and was desperate to pay for anything I needed; I knew it wasn't, and thought I was doing the right thing for similar reasons. But it's not easy, because something does kick in inside you; your body's meant to have babies. I just never wanted to have a child that I couldn't have looked after properly. In retrospect, I did make the right decision.

Night must fall

Christmas that year was a portent of things to come. I went back to Seaford with Kevin and Lenny on Christmas Eve for the traditional knees-up. My family can remember what happened over the Brussels sprouts that year a bit better than I can.

SALLY REID: You were awful. You gave us hell about the tree – it was either too slender or bushy in the wrong place, not enough things on it, somebody hadn't dressed it properly... We all sat and watched a Christmas film, but Kevin had earphones on and he listened to music all the way through the film, so we didn't hear what was going on in the film, all we heard was 'Sssstttttthhhhhhh-Ssttttthhhhh'. Mum, Dad and me all wanted to kill him.

ROGER ROOKE: I think the worst time was Christmas dinner, with the drummer, Lenny. We were all sitting around and he went out, got a taxi to London, I presume to buy something to get high on. Then he came back as high as a kite, and we were sitting around the dinner table with all these expletives coming out in front of Mum. He completely lost all inhibitions. I didn't know where to put myself or how to deal with it. It was so unexpected.

The worst thing was, Alex and his wife, who were still our next-door neighbours, had offered to let people sleep at their house, as they were going to be away that year. So we let Lenny stay in their house, reading the riot act to him first about what he couldn't do in there. Unbeknown to any of us, he plugged his hairdryer in, taking out the plug from the freezer, which he forgot to replace afterwards. All of Alex's frozen food was ruined. I was absolutely mortified. He had been my Maths teacher! But maybe I've got a fault in me, being so attracted to people who are only obsessed with themselves. The sort of lifestyle I lived with Kevin was not one that could ever have lasted for long.

22

IT'S COMING DOWN FAST

Bad drugs juju and the dirty rotten music business (1982–84)

The thin red line

The last really great hair challenge I ever laid down was for the look I had put together to go with Wide Boy Awake's 'Billy Hyena' single release in May 1984. I went to a guy called Lester who worked at Joshua and Daniel Galvin and said I wanted concrete-coloured hair. He looked at me and said: "I don't think this can be done. I don't think the dye exists to do it. But leave it with me; I'm not going to get beaten." I went back a couple of weeks later and he'd worked out how to do it. He got it that concrete colour and he was very proud of it. He mixed about five or six different hair dyes together to achieve it. The hair – which I had close-cropped – was to go with this fantastic camouflage outfit I had found in Kensington Market.

It was very small, as I was then, about a size eight or ten – which was unusual because it was the original tiger-stripe American Vietnam combat gear. Apparently, what that means is that it had been appropriated either from an American soldier who had died, or had been stolen by the Viet Cong, who had altered it to wear themselves as a disguise. You could see where it had been altered, taken in – no way would it have ever fitted anyone who was in the American army.

To complete the look, I drew a thin red line around my neck – it was a symbol from the French Revolution, when aristocrats cropped their hair and added a line as a sick joke. It was when I kitted the band out in similar camouflage gear that I got a real insight into the workings of the music industry. I found a letter recently, from one of the A&R guys, absolutely furious about the money we'd spent on things and having to foot the bill for these camouflage outfits. I had really bad experiences with the record company. Very sexist, awful things were said to me. And it was always one-to-one, so no one was ever around to witness it.

We wanted to hire real helicopters to get the noise for the single, rather than use the *Apocalypse Now* soundtrack noise, and they wouldn't do it. So I argued the point privately with someone at RCA and he said: "Why don't you just fuck off out of here, go home and open your legs like all women do and you probably do best." That's what he actually said. "That's all women are good for."

I saw the industry change from being run by people who really knew a good band when they saw one to people who only counted the money they'd be getting. If you looked carefully, you could find lists of people they were promoting each week, it was that cut-throat. There was a list of priorities, and if you found out you weren't on top of it, you knew immediately something was wrong. I remember when it was us on top and JoBoxers second or third, and thinking: I hope they don't find that list.

The worst thing was that you'd come in and find people you liked had just been sacked, people you'd had a rapport with for months who were right behind the band – you'd walk in and their desk would be empty. They have to get rid of them really quickly because of all the data they might take with them. So they'd get them out of the door and then deal with their desk for them.

Those were the days when the recording industry was awash with coke, which didn't help with this kind of attitude. I've walked into

380

RCA in the past and whoever it was has just taken my hand and given me a wrap. You only knew what it was by looking at the colour. If it was all white, it was coke. It was really, really prevalent in the 1980s. They all had so much money, those people.

But it wasn't the coke that did it for Wide Boy Awake, or myself and Kevin. It was the heroin.

Something for the weekend

What I had begun dabbling with in the shop with Michael went totally full-blown when Kevin and I got together with all that filthy lucre. I did

381

love Kevin – I never would have married him otherwise. But then you start to think. You love somebody when they're normal and when you're in a normal state of mind. Then you suddenly realise you've spent two years in a drug-induced stupor and you don't know who they are. Honestly, you don't know what happened, if any of that was real or if all of it was just a dream.

To give you an example, there was this late-night chemist in Willesden Lane where you could go when everywhere else was closed – it was a real faff to get to but they were lax enough. I once went up there on a Friday night and asked for thirty syringes, thinking: I'm never going to get this. But the chemist handed them over with the words: "Looks like it's going to be a good weekend."

It was the same for Michael. Like siblings who had always dared each other on to greater feats of outrage, we had engineered our own crash landings from a great height. Everything coalesced around the fate of 430 King's Road and Malcolm and Vivienne's relationship. When that went pear-shaped, so did everything else.

The thick of it

But, like the beginning of Wide Boy Awake, things seemed to be getting much better for my erstwhile employers. Vivienne had followed Pirates with the Savage autumn-winter collection of 1981–2 and Buffalo in 1982–3, which echoed Malcolm's next direction – after Bow Wow Wow also failed to make him a millionaire,[1] he had gone back to clubland, this time in New York, to investigate B-boy culture and scratching techniques. Despite their personal split, he and Vivienne expanded their business into another shop, Nostalgia

---

[1] Bow Wow Wow released the album *See Jungle! See Jungle! Go Join Your Gang Yeah! City All Over, Go Ape Crazy* on RCA in November 1982, with its controversial cover that recreated Manet's *Le déjeuner sur l'Herbe*, with Annabella as the nude. By then, Malcolm had lost interest in the project, having failed to oust Annabella in favour of Boy George, or outwit her tenacious mother. The album spawned two hits, 'Go Wild in the Country' and their cover of The Strangeloves' 'I Want Candy', neither of which was sanctioned by their increasingly distant manager. By August 1982, Malcolm had got himself a recording contract. Bow Wow Wow made one more album without him – *When the Going Gets Tough, the Tough Get Going* in 1983 – before going their separate ways.

of Mud, which opened in the heart of the lucrative West End couture district, in St Christopher's Place, in the summer of 1982.

Once again, the crack team of Roger K. Burton and Mr Newman was hired to design the new shop.

ROGER K. BURTON: Nostalgia of Mud was an even greater challenge for Mr Newman, but he did it. I enjoyed doing that shop more than World's End, because they left me alone completely and I came up with loads of ideas, around an architectural dig and this thing that had burst out of the floor from a bubbling pit of pus...

Again, we didn't get planning permission to do anything – not that we needed anything for the inside, but we did need building regulations and the Westminster planning architect came down and said: "You can't do this on that floor, it will never stand the weight." We were going to put a ton of earth on the floor of the shop that people had to walk through – the mud. So I found out about this material that they used in the Underground, an epoxy cement that they line the inside of the underground tunnels with, which was 100 times stronger than normal cement but very lightweight. So I sculpted this floor in there using that substance – there was no problem with the floor being able to bear the weight – but they'll never be able to get it off again, because it's stronger than concrete. I'm sure it is still there now.

I built this scaffolding walkway, so you went in on this and you could look down into this precipice of mud. We had hidden treasure under the floorboards – broken floorboards sticking out of the wall. I was trying to give the impression that there's this beautiful Regency building above us, and this thing had come out the ground that Mr Newman had created and broken all the floorboards, an alien that was chucking out bubbling oil. Then, under the floorboards was all this treasure in chests. Vivienne wanted them full of gold and jewels. That wasn't going to happen, but we did manage to get some old tat from somewhere and chuck it in there to look like treasure.

John Tiberi had these lovely paintings from the inter-war periods of kids on bombsites – we had those in there, as well. And the other thing was, the horrible tiled ceiling with spotlights coming through it. Malcolm said: "I can't have that, get rid of it – call Mr Newman!" I found these old tank tarpaulins and draped a load of them from the ceiling. Then we got these iron railings from a salvage yard and made them into flagpoles and drove them into the building, and hung these tarpaulins off them with the name of the shop stamped on them.

Nostalgia of Mud was an impressive-looking building, hailed by Peter York as the most innovative design of the decade. The St Christopher's Place Preservation Society did not agree, and came round with a petition trying to get everything removed. They thought it was going to be temporary and, four months down the line, they were very unhappy about it. Then the council got involved and wanted to close it down. But that wasn't Malcolm and Vivienne's only problem. They had staffing issues, to boot…

Hubble, bubble, toil and trouble

Nostalgia of Mud was where it got serious. The famous quote was that you'd go in there and someone would tell you that you could have anything for a hundred quid. You know, 'cos that hundred quid would be going in their pocket… People just wandered in there and you could just barter or bargain, and whatever wasn't stolen was paid for and pocketed. Malcolm and Vivienne must have lost a fortune.

David Ireland, who was working at World's End and living with Michael in the flat he had then in Church Street, off Edgware Road, paints a vivid picture of what life was like in the duration of the second shop's existence.

DAVID IRELAND: God. It was spring, it was March or April, and Michael would be stoned out of his gourd, zipping about on that Vespa he had. In hot pants! He would go to World's End and Nostalgia of Mud and say: "Vivienne wants you to send money up to the office." Then he would go through this whole thing of cleaning the counter and the cubby holes and everything underneath, looking for the hiding place. Which was horrible, actually.

This was about the time, that transition from when I left World's End and Nostalgia of Mud opened, when Vivienne phoned me up and asked me to please come back and work with her because she couldn't trust anybody on the staff.

384

I would say of both Malcolm and Vivienne that if either of them did find someone of good character, it was by luck instead of judgement. They had no idea, really, of the good people who have worked for them, who they might not have appreciated enough, and the bad people, who were just out to get something off them. Neither of them had any empathy. They never paid good wages and no one who worked there got given any clothes; by the same token, they never did a stock take, either, so how were they to know if people were stealing from them? The main people Vivienne had working in the shops for her, Gene Krell at World's End and Michael at Nostalgia of Mud, all had the same problem. By 1983, most of the assistants working in St Christopher's Place, including Anna Melluso, were addicts, too. David Ireland saw the whole thing with clear eyes.

DAVID IRELAND: Gene Krell used to use it to deal with the stress of what he was going through with Vivienne, when she had real money problems through leaving Malcolm; that's when I was there. She had won her first award, stopped paying anybody. "I'm so good, you should be paying to work with me!" Gene was getting pushed every which way from the Nostalgia of Mud shop.

The other thing was that Michael got annoyed with me about something, went out and got some [psychiatric drug] Largactil and went: "Hey, take some of this!" And I, being stupid, did. And then was falling down, nodding out and all sorts of things. You were there and you were concerned: "Is he OK? Should he be rolling round the floor in front of the TV drooling?"

MICHAEL COLLINS: That was a very difficult situation, because Malcolm and Vivienne were still business partners but really not getting on. Vivienne had World's End and Malcolm had Nostalgia, although she was still involved with that because the clothes were coming from her. She assumed that if you decided you wanted to work there, you were siding with Malcolm. I was in a real state then. I was heavily into drugs and so many people died in the club scene around that time.

Michael lost his job and a lot else besides. I think that Michael got cast in the same place as Malcolm – the two men Vivienne really loved; two pivotal relationships that came crashing down at the same time. The last collection Malcolm and Vivienne ever did together was Witches, inspired by a book she had found about voodoo – draw your own conclusions. At the end of the catwalk show for autumn/winter 1983–4, they appeared together in public for the last time as partners in a business. Vivienne had made almost all of this collection herself; Malcolm's major contribution was the soundtrack of his latest album, *Duck Rock*.[2] Nostalgia of Mud closed soon after, and Vivienne retreated to Italy with her new lover, Carlo D'Amario, much to Malcolm's chagrin.

Besides everything else, that sort of shop suddenly going up in St Christopher's Place was a big jump at the time. You've got to attract people who pass by. Although 430 King's Road was difficult to get to, it never had that problem. Vivienne now has three shops in that area – but, at the time, the world was just not ready for that kind of vision.[3]

On Vivienne's abrupt departure, World's End was closed and stood empty for a year. Holly Johnson, who was by then living nearby, can remember walking up the King's Road in July 1986 and finding the shop lit by candlelight, with Vivienne's mother Dora sitting in a corner stitching buttons on, just like I had once done. Michael Costiff helped Vivienne pick up the threads of her existence and get back on her feet.

MICHAEL COSTIFF: Vivienne had no money; she asked us for a loan. Gerlinde's theory was, only lend people half of what they ask for and never lend money if you expect to get it back. But Gerlinde said she'd have the money back in clothes and she did get it back that way.

---

[2] Malcolm had first been exposed to hip-hop culture in New York in August 1981, on a visit to the New Music Seminar, when he was taken to see Afrikaa Bambaataa and was amazed by what he saw. He began styling himself as an expert, finding out all he could about B-boy culture and spinning a line about it to RCA that would eventually bear fruit in *Duck Rock*, the album he fashioned with producer Trevor Horn that would finally come out in January 1983, spawning the hits 'Buffalo Girls' and 'Double Dutch'. The front cover was by Keith Haring, another New York find who at the time was being represented by Malcolm's chum Robert Fraser.

[3] Vivienne has her flagship shop at 44 Conduit Street, plus Vivienne Westwood Couture on 6 Davies Street and Vivienne Westwood Man on 18 Conduit Street, as well as World's End.

Dream a little dream

What was I doing while all of this was going on? David Ireland can remember large chunks of things I had long forgotten. After Vivienne sacked Michael, she put David up in the Columbia Hotel in Paddington, a notorious rock'n'roll hangout popular with visiting musicians from the States, which was how David had heard about it. Apparently, Kevin and I spent a lot of time with him there and even had our own suite – but I can recall nothing of the following:

DAVID IRELAND: The Columbia was like the Chelsea Hotel in Paddington. It was a huge hotel, but it had this run-down ambience. The lift would stop between floors and you'd have to kick it to get it to open. You came with Kevin and stayed for a bit. In fact, you were in there for longer than I was. I remember Kevin buying this all-in-one entertainment unit, which was a TV on one side, a stereo system on the other, a radio on this side and a tape player on the other side. One of those gadgets that was big at that time, when they were trying to get things to be a smaller size, as people's living space got smaller and more compact. You had a huge room in the hotel. You used to ask me to come down to the room with you and then you'd both slump on the sofa. I'd sneak down to my room on my own so I could do something, and you'd come running down the hall going: "David! Come back!"

I asked David how he had managed to ward off the narcotic spell that we had all fallen under.

DAVID IRELAND: It was just something Gene Krell said to me once. I asked him what it was like being on smack. He said, having given up, you just go through life comparing everything else to it. Because it is so good. And I thought: Well, I just don't want that.

It is such a dangerous thing. More so than anything else. While taking it and after; psychologically and physically. You dice with death each time you take it, because you don't know what's in it. It's potentially lethal. It's a very strange thing with heroin, that it's never a solitary drug. There's always someone who wants to get you into it and keep supplying you, they want to be in your company when they take it, and it becomes an insidious group of people, who die when they're on their own. It's this thing of: I'm in hell – so I want you, you and you to join me. But what sort of life is it, when you look back on it? What I see about that junkie time is just people dreading the mornings, dreading something ruling their lives.

Wide boys never work

Kevin and I managed to spend our way through all that £50,000 from the record company in about a year. Bought lots of drugs, lots of clothes, lots of things. And then, when there was no money left, he sold all of my clothes – except the ones that I had left at home, which fortunately for me were the prime ones from SEX and Seditionaries. We had to move everything out of the flat in Bonchurch Street. We then moved back to Kevin's mum and dad's house in Kidbrooke and we had so many bags full of clothes that he said he would get them put in storage. A person came round and picked them up in this truck, along with all my press cuttings, a big artist's portfolio stuffed with cuttings, and a lot of my jewellery – including that pendant of Antonio's that Gustavo had given me and a beautiful little gold heart Sally gave me for our wedding day. Not long after, people started telling me they had seen other people wearing my clothes out at clubs. When I realised what he'd done and confronted him, Kevin just said: "Well, what's yours is mine, so I can do what I like with all your stuff." When he said that, I knew I had to save my own life and get away from him.

A lot of this was to do with what happened when we were still at Bonchurch Street. I had two kittens then: Al, who was a Burmese, and Bat, who was a little moggy Anna Melluso had bred. We named him after Homunculus in *Clash of the Titans*, who was a little bat-like thing. One night, when I was asleep, Kevin smacked Bat so hard that he gave him brain damage. That's the thing that I can't ever take back, I can't ever forget. He didn't hit him; he threw him against the wall. It didn't kill him, but I woke up in the morning and the cat was in a terrible state. Kevin told Richard Cabut in that *3:AM* interview that we split up because he'd killed my cat. But he didn't kill him outright. This is what drugs do to you.

I know that it was in a fit of anger, because he wouldn't play with him or something petty like that. But you just don't get over those things. Kevin was never, ever nasty to me. Not once in our relationship had he ever shown any aggression towards me. But what he did to my cat, he could have done to a baby, and I had been pregnant by Kevin twice by then. Once, I had the abortion; the second time, I lost the baby because I was doing drugs. This was my final wake-up call.

I wanted to take the cat to the vet, but he kept saying: "Oh, don't take him; they'll know I've done something to him." So I had this massive dilemma about whether I should take him, and I let Kevin talk me out of it. They wouldn't have been able to do anything – I know that now I'm a veterinary nurse myself, so at least I've got that to hold on to. But, even then, I couldn't leave Kevin straight away; things were just too difficult. I could have just walked out with the two cats but I'd have been leaving everything I'd ever worked for my whole life. Instead, I waited until we got to Kidbrooke before I rang my mum and dad up and asked if I could come home. From there, I got on a train back to Seaford and never came back.

I walked out on Kevin to save myself. But I did it without any rehab. My parents didn't know anything about it; it was all a secret and they never found out. Sally did know, but that was it, and even she couldn't fully understand, because unless you've been in that situation, you don't know how painful it is, or how dangerous. I had no idea how perilous it was to go cold turkey without any medical help. There was no methadone or anything.

I went through massive pains for about two weeks – those are the times when you can't sleep, you ache all over and the vomiting lasts for quite a while. Then it's the psychological thing that hits you hard. I just told my parents I had flu. But it's one of the proudest things I've ever done in my life. I walked away from Kevin and heroin at the same time. They were the same thing, really.

When I look back, so many of the people I have been close to who died – Dee Dee Ramone, Johnny Thunders, Jerry Nolan and, of course, Sid – all died because they could never get away from it. They were stuck. Even if they'd wanted to get away, they were entrenched. Like George Best and everyone wanting to buy him a drink. They're all drinking one drink and he's drinking thirty. It's a life of total shit.

But, of course, Kevin didn't want to let it go at that. He came back down to see me, and he tried to get back with me. He walked into my house and my little cat just fled. No word of a lie, Bat took one look at Kevin and ran. If anyone ever tells you animals don't have memories... And you could see in Kevin's eyes that he knew what he had done to him. That injury did kill my cat in the end: he got run over because he couldn't react fast enough to get out of the way. He was always slipping, and if he jumped up he'd always miss where he thought he was going to land. I begged my dad not to let him out, but he came from that generation where they wouldn't keep cats in. So Kevin didn't kill him that day, but...

When he realised that he couldn't get me back, he tried to get my wedding ring and engagement ring, that famous David Morris yellow and white diamond, back instead. He almost tried to ransack the house to find them. I had to be really steadfast: I knew where they were, but I'd hidden them. He was desperate to get them off me, but I've still got all of them. That's what happens when people are that strung out. It's a form of torture, really.

After all that, I walked back to Seaford station with him. While he was buying his ticket – this is very *Brief Encounter*, but in the opposite way – he had his back to me and I slowly backed away so he couldn't hear me, and ran as fast as I could. I ran right down to the sea, to a pub called Beachcombers on the seafront that he didn't know and I knew he wouldn't be able to find me. So I didn't even watch him get on the train.

The party's over

People often ask me why I haven't changed my surname – because people get to know you. Kevin and I did get divorced. For about two years after we split up, he sent me letters begging me to come back. A lot of them were lyrics, some of them were poems, and I'd get them very often. They were very sad, actually. But I made my mind up that I couldn't go back. I would have died, I think, if I'd stayed in that life. I would be no more.

Like John Keogh – that was tragic. He was one of the nicest people you could possibly meet. He'd do absolutely anything for you. He continued to work with Kevin, in the band Max, which Matthew Ashman joined after he left Bow Wow Wow. The last time I saw him was when they played together at Brighton Zap Club, in the early 1990s. I was very reluctant to go, but in the end I was glad I did, because Leee Black Childers and Leigh Bowery were both there; they had got a coachload of people down from London. I left early because the whole show ended in chaos, all the equipment broke down, but I went backstage and said hello to everyone first. That was the last time I ever saw John. From what I gather, he died not that long afterwards, nodding off in the bathtub from taking drugs, and drowning.

The first I heard about Lesley Winer was that she was a top model for Yves Saint Laurent and a friend of William S. Burroughs – you can see the attraction for Kevin. She was absolutely beautiful. There were mutterings that her and Kevin were going out, but I didn't want anything to do with him. A couple of years later, after all these love letters and pleas to come back, I suddenly got a letter from a lawyer asking for a divorce. The reason – and it's funny this; I couldn't believe what I was reading – was because his new fiancée needed milk coupons for the baby that she'd had. That's when I realised he was intending to marry her and needed me to divorce him, which I did straight away. There was no problem at all about that, because there was no feeling left. Because of the time that had elapsed, it all went through really quickly. But I thought it was very funny. Milk coupons!

The next time I heard from him was about fifteen years ago. Normally, I wait for the answerphone to kick in, but for some reason I picked up the phone and it was Kevin. I hadn't heard a single word from him since those divorce papers. He and Lesley had had five children since then, but he'd left her and he was back in Kidbrooke because he had nowhere else to go. The main reason for him phoning me after all those years was to say: "Please forgive me."

After all that time, what can you say? You can't block it out from your mind. He said there was no excuse for what he did, but he was just so out of it he didn't know what he was doing. And when he said he would love to come and see me, I was so caught on the hop I didn't know what to do. So I said, "Yeah, come and visit."

I thought: I'll just get this out of the way. Again. I cleaned the house from top to bottom – and he never came. Which was such a relief. I spoke to Marco about it and he said Kevin had probably just drunk half a bottle of brandy and that's what prompted him to ring me. Looking back at it now, it would have been just after Richard Cabut's article was published.

In those types of situations, relationship-wise, I am very unforgiving. We did have some great times. It's just very hard, in these distant years, to remember those great times again. It always seems to be that I end up with people who have to be entertained the whole time. Those hyperactive types – John Rotten was like that, Sid was like that, like ADHD children, the whole bored generation. You should never be bored if you've got something in your head. If somebody harms me, hurts me, is cruel or nasty, anything like that, I will walk away, I will not stay in that situation. I'm too proud. If anybody tries to disrespect or demean me, I couldn't stay with them. I never look back, you see.

But, there is a question Ted Polhemus asked me that still needs answering. What happens to the people who perform on *Top of the Pops* and then have to go back to working at a petrol station or something? How do you deal with that?

MICHAEL COSTIFF: You inspired so many people with your utter fearlessness. I can still remember seeing you for the first time, putting my book down to stare at you through the window of the bus – it was just like seeing a unicorn on the King's Road. You were so absolutely striking – and then, just like Greta Garbo, at the height of your powers, you just disappeared.

The way you deal with it is by reinventing yourself all over again.

23

MY FAMILY AND OTHER ANIMALS

New vocations (1984 onwards)

Turning Burmese

Buckingham Gate gave one lasting gift to me. It was because of the Burmese kitten called Lana, which Simon Barker and Derek Dunbar bought when we were all living together there that I first got interested in this type of cat. My love of them has since led to a thirty-year ongoing adventure for Sally and me, breeding and showing Burmese.

I had to go in disguise to get my first one, because no one would have sold me a kitten looking the way I did in 1977, with my spikes and Mondrian make-up. It was winter, so I borrowed a sheepskin jacket from Linda – she didn't always wear fetishwear – and I wore a bobble hat, with all my hair flat and tied back underneath it, and no make-up on.

Simon, Derek and I went to a village called Good Easter in Essex, where we were picked up from the station in a Mini Traveller by this really gung-ho country lady. She took us to her house to see a litter of kittens and I picked one. But I hadn't got enough money to pay for him. He was £35 and I only had £20 on me. Derek paid the extra £15 and he's never let me pay him back to this day.

His stud name was Easter Ways Superstar – I got to choose that, because at the time I picked him he hadn't been registered. But around the house, I called him after Jerry Nolan. Because he had really sharp nails, he was Needles Nolan – a double entendre on the needles side – but he was always Nollie. So my first Burmese was named after a Heartbreaker, and he's the one you see in Simon's lovely pictures in the flat from *Punk's Dead*, with a big Sex Pistols poster and me kissing him on the nose.

Al was my second Burmese, the one I bought in 1984 when I lived in London with Kevin. He was named after Alex in *A Clockwork Orange*, and over the time I had him he taught all of our other kittens how to be a Burmese, the way Lana had taught Nollie. It was because of Al that Sally and I started showing cats in the first place – when I went to pick him, he'd already been entered into a show by the breeders and they wanted us to take him to the event in Maidstone. We were so inexperienced, we didn't think to even buy a basket to take him home in.

The breeder, Sheila Harris, who is the sweetest, kindest person, took him from her house in Walthamstow and bought us a basket because we didn't have one. They were so generous. I don't know if we would ever have got involved if it hadn't been for that, and it was purely an intuitive thing, too – I liked Sheila more on the phone than another person I'd spoken to, who was offering a kitten for less money. If I had chosen that other person, it would have been a completely different story. A first introduction to something is so important and that's what Sheila gave us. After that first show we were hooked; we met such a lovely lot of people there.

Mainman is the name of my cat-breeding activities. All the cats Sally and I have bred since then have got Mainman in front of their names, every single one. Nobody knew what it meant in the cat world and they all went wild when I told them it was the name of David Bowie's old management company. It's another link to the past and another juxtaposition between two worlds that I am passionate about.

We have had many adventures doing the shows over these years, but this incident remains Sally's favourite:

SALLY REID: Do you remember when you got such bad sunburn that time when your hair was yellow? You went to a big cat show looking like eggs and bacon.

The worst of it was that I was booked to do *Women in Punk* for the BBC that week and I couldn't do it because my face blew up like a balloon, my eyes looked like slits. I had to cancel because I didn't know how long it would take me to get better. As it was, at the cat show there were hundreds of people at all looking at me going: Whaaaat?

But my love of breeding and showing Burmese comes back to the old adage – if you're going to do something, do it really well. That's what my motto has always been. You want to excel at something. And you've got to be your own biggest critic in order to make it as good as it can possibly be.

Sister act

Both my sisters played a big part in how I reshaped my life after I came back to Seaford. It was through Jeannie, and the unlikely direction that her life also turned in, that I discovered a vocation I never knew I had in me, and that I have since turned into a career.

Jeannie has not had the easiest of lives. She lost her first husband, James – the maths genius who used to help me with my homework – while they were still living in Scotland. He died very suddenly and very young. A few years later, she met Michael, a great, strong Lincolnshire man, who had become a sheep farmer in Huby, just north of York. He could hold two really big buckets in one hand and jump over a fence with ease – so nothing was woman-friendly on the farm. Jeannie, who is both a lady and a carpenter, had to adapt everything, make sure that gates actually opened, because there was no way she could climb over them. She conceived Alwyn, my only and much-beloved nephew, on her honeymoon, I believe. Mum said: "People will talk!"

So Jeannie got thrown from being a teacher to being a farmer's wife, and she literally had to take the sheep by the horns when Michael had a heart attack at the time of her first lambing season. I came up to help her, though neither of us really had a clue what we were doing. Michael was there, but wasn't fit enough to help us.

It was a three-month stint and we knew absolutely nothing about keeping the lambs alive. That you have to keep a record of their weights and times they are born, and try not to drop the book you're noting that down in in the water trough while you're doing it. That the lambs can get infections really quickly and their mother's milk is absolutely vital for antibodies – at one point, we were trying to feed formula to them. We had to learn all of these things very fast. Truthfully, I thought we were amazing.

JEANNIE CRAVEN: You were, you took to it straight away and delivered the lambs, which I didn't do. I only did the other end. You've never not taken on a challenge, have you? That's your weakness and your strength. You never hesitate, do you?

398

It was certainly true of lambing. You just have to use your imagination to visualise what's happening inside the mother sheep. You have to be really patient and feel for the head and the shoulders, get used to doing this. Because, when you're getting lambs out, normally you've got two or even three, all backed up against each other. If you pull the wrong leg, it's all going to go a bit David Lynch. So you have to work out who's first. You have to see it in your mind's eye, feel around for the head, the shoulders, know for sure it's the first one. Find the shoulder, find both legs and the head and pull it out that way, slowly, with the mother's contractions, or you can do a lot of damage.

It's normally either a really large lamb or it's triplets. I have very small hands, so that helps. But you have to take your time. A lot of people would start to panic in that situation and just start pulling. And this goes on around the clock. You do get sleep deprivation and everything starts blowing out of proportion. Jeannie and I didn't know what day it was, whether it was a Monday or a Tuesday; we lost all reference points. You start arguing for no reason not big arguments, just squabbling. Both of us realised fairly early on that we were suffering from exhaustion.

Something else happened while we were lambing: a feral cat had kittens. I didn't even know the cat was pregnant, except that she was fat. Then we came out one morning and found her with these tiny kittens – two gingers, two tortoiseshells – and they were all covered in a load of afterbirth and one of them had it all twisted around his back leg and his leg had turned purple. I unwound it, got it off, along with a load of straw it was twisted up in. I thought his leg might drop off; I knew absolutely nothing – but he got better. That was when I thought: I could do this. After that, I trained to become a veterinary nurse, my career for the past thirty years.

Lambing was something really great to learn – and it brought out the masochist in me. Because you really look forward to it every year, and then dread it carrying on, because it's so much hard work. Then, by the time the next year comes round, you're looking forward to it again. All the memories are good ones. It's what people say about childbirth, isn't it? You forget the pain. Which is just as well, because by the time the next year came round, Michael had to have a major operation on his aorta and Jeannie and I had to go through the whole routine by ourselves again.

Prince Charming

As for my Ant family, well, after Kevin, it took Adam a long, long time to forgive me. But when he did, he treated me so beautifully. When he knew Kevin and I had split up, he phoned me up and said: "Can we meet in London and I'll take you to a really nice restaurant and we can just talk? I'm sure you're hurting, but we'll talk and have a really nice time." You've got to take your hat off to him. Adam does know how to forgive. He even forgave Malcolm in the end.

> **DAVE BARBE:** And me. I was playing in Italy for Beats International. I was their drummer for four or five years. And Norman Cook said: "Dave, Dave! Come to the dressing room!" giggling conspiratorially. I come in and he pushed me and there I was, face-to-face with Adam for the first time in all those years, and we fell into each other's arms. It brings a lump to my throat to think of it. He was a big enough man. It really was emotional. That was a big history for our tribe – we fell out, it was all in the papers – but he was a bigger man than many men ever are. Then he took me on the road with him and Marco, big shows. Then we did *Dirk Wears White Sox* when it was the anniversary, as we never did it live at the time. We did a big show at the Hammersmith Apollo and then toured it around the country.

Adam and I resumed our friendship and it became stronger than ever. He loves animals as much as I do, and they feel the same way about him. One time when he was coming round to stay, I had been waiting for months for one of my cats to come into call and, the moment he arrived, she took one look at him and started calling. He gave the cat the horn. So I had to get her to stud and he offered to drive. I rang the stud owner to let her know that it wasn't just me turning up, but Adam Ant was coming as well. Which put her into a bit of a panic. But by the time we got there, she'd laid on a full dainty tea and he got a whole tour of her stud cats and kittens.

400

Unfortunately, it was a different story when, after he had started seeing the American actress Heather Graham, he brought her over to Seaford. Poor Heather had a massive asthma attack because she's allergic to cats. I had to put all these infusions into a bowl to help her breathe – it was good old Friar's Balsam that did the trick in the end. I've still got the bowl. I use it for porridge now, but every time I use it, I think of her!

Adam even ended up coming to the farm with me to help with the lambing that second year when Michael had to have his operation. He bought my nephew Alwyn a stuffed toy dog that he still has to this day – Doggard, because Stuart Goddard gave it to him. Adam didn't do any lambing, but he had to do a lot of mucking out and proved to be a dab hand with the wheelbarrow. There was a little orphan lamb that we used to feed and he christened her Doris. He got really upset when she died. It was heartbreaking to start with, learning how to deal with things like that. There was another orphaned lamb, Penelope, who I used to play games with, running up and down, and she'd chase me.

ALWYN CRAVEN: She still played that game until she was old. She was one of the last ones to go. She would have been 15, I think.

Struwweljordan

As soon as Alwyn could talk, it would be his task to wake me in the middle of the night in the lambing season, because Jeannie and Michael knew I couldn't ever be cross with him. I used to put my head on the pillow, have twenty minutes, then get an: "Auntie Pamela!" That was my alarm. So I'd fall out of bed – almost like *The Wrong Trousers* – and jump into my clothes, which were so stiff with all sorts of fluid that had got onto them, and run back outside.

I did start off with my big, spiky hair, but when you're working on a farm there's no way you can maintain that, so within a few days I looked like Andy Warhol on a bad day, with a gale blowing. We were on our way to buy some feed when Alwyn, sitting next to me in the back of the Land Rover, looked up at me and said the immortal line: "Auntie Pamela, your hair really looks very much like straw!"

This was another time I was asked to do a big TV programme and couldn't make it. It was the Jonathan Ross show this time and I was right slap bang in the middle of lambing. They asked me what I looked like at the moment. I said: "Do you really want to know?" I could have told them: "Lumps of straw and shit hanging out of my head. Trousers that would stand up on their own if you took them off." You have to wear dirty things, because the sheep feel comfortable with you, you've got to smell nice to them, and the farmhouse was basically just a trail of straw and hay. Instead, I merely made the understatement: "It's probably not a good moment. I'm not looking my best."

I had a bad rash on the inside of my thighs from lambing, from the amniotic sac that breaks when you're delivering lambs and feeding them. If you hold them between your legs to bottle-feed, you often get this. It was only the castor oil for my inner thighs and QC sherry – "Quality Counts", as Jeannie and I always say – that kept us all going throughout the lambing seasons.

A roll in the hay barn

One of the most frightening things that ever happened to me was on the farm. Jeannie had gone out for a while and tasked me with looking after Alwyn, who was 4 by then, and cleaning all the sheep out. She left me with the words: "Whatever you do, don't let him get on those straw bales. 'Cos, at the drop of a hat, he'll do it – just keep an eye on him."

Alwyn came to help me muck out, which was something he was really good at by then. Like Adam, he was handy with a wheelbarrow, had very good balance, and he was willing. I remember telling him what a good boy he was and then, in the blink of an eye, I turned my back on him and he disappeared. When I called for him, there was no answer. I went all over the farm, calling everywhere – and got not even a peep in reply. Only when I went over to the big building where all the bales were stacked up did I hear a tiny little muffled sound.

I was standing in front of a wall of bales about 30 feet high, which looked like an immense wall of bricks that hadn't been finished off properly. And I had no idea whereabouts in this whole, huge construction I could find Alwyn. I could just hear a sound. All these panicked thoughts rushed through my head: The bales are very heavy, so where do I start to move them? And, if I do, will I be treading on him?

Eventually I located the source of the sound. Alwyn had fallen all the way down from a tiny gap in the side of the big building and was a long way down behind the bales. I had to move them to get him out, because I thought he was going to suffocate. All the time, I was thinking of Jeannie saying: "If you turn your back, he'll be on there…" Eventually, I pulled out a bale and found him, but I couldn't manage to dislodge the final bale between us, so I had to drag him out of there. I was really worried I was going to pull his arms out of their sockets. He was absolutely covered in straw. I hugged him and burst out crying. I have never felt relief like that in my life. If that had been my mum, she would have whacked me down the farmyard. He obviously could not help himself going up there; it was too tempting. He was prowling around, pretending to be a cat. Then he started crying, too.

Poor Jeannie got the hang of being a farmer's wife only to become a widow for the second time. After the groundbreaking operation Michael had to create a new aorta, which they put through his arm, Michael developed non-Hodgkin's lymphoma. Jeannie nursed him at home and the doctors were amazed he survived so long – he probably wouldn't have done, if he had been in hospital. Gradually, everything packed in, his kidneys, his bowel. So in the end he had no bodily functions: he was fed by a tube to the stomach and everything else came out in bags. Jeannie made a whole downstairs annexe for him, so that he could look outside and see the birds, and she could wheel him into the shower more easily. She's not one to give up. I guess that's part of our family strength. She wasn't going to let him go into hospital and die, because he would have succumbed to some infection or other. He survived for quite a few years like this. He would occasionally have a crisis and have to go back in. But he always had his marbles and he always enjoyed looking at the birds and the fields outside. He had the best wake you can ever imagine, a real Yorkshire do with lovely great big pork pies – but how sad to think how much he would have enjoyed that.

Alwyn, who studied Biological Science at Oxford and Horticulture at Kew Gardens, runs the farm now, and has transformed it into a wildlife woodland.[1] He's planted 42,000 trees so far, helped by the group Muslims for Humanity, who all came and volunteered and planted trees, as well as the Forestry Commission, the Woodland Trust, Thorpe Trees and Landlife Wildflowers.

About ten years ago, I saw the most remarkable thing at the farm. I was on holiday with Sally and her partner Evan, but I'd gone out on my own one morning. I was walking around the fields when I heard this chuckling sound coming from the hedgerow. I stopped and turned my head really, really slowly. There was a mother stoat and three little babies making the nearest thing I've ever heard to an animal laughing. They were climbing up on the branches of the hedgerow, falling off, rolling over and doing it all over again, giggling away. I stood stock-still, hardly breathing – I knew if the mum realised I was there, they'd be gone in an instant. It was a really precious moment. When they ran off, I was just dumbstruck.

As I set off back for the farm, I saw another stoat – whether it was Dad, I don't know – but he crossed the path right in front of me, in that looping way they run. By the time I'd got back down to the farm to tell Sally and Evan, there was no chance of them seeing anything. It was a once-in-a-lifetime chance. Jeannie said she's never seen anything like it and she's been there thirty years.

Venus rides again

Being friends again with Adam soon led to him asking me for help with the band, which, just like the early days, turned out to be a joy and an adventure. One of the most exciting days was styling him and the band – Marco on guitar, Chris De Niro on bass and Count Bogdan Wiczling on drums – before they played Live Aid on 13 July 1985. What a day that was. You had a choice of how you got there: you could either be limousined up to the entrance of Wembley Stadium, where there was a special green room for all the bands, or

---

[1] For more details about what Alwyn has achieved on the farm, see Ben Westwood's blog about him, Punk Farming, at: worldsendshop.co.uk/punk-farming/

you could fly in by helicopter. I hate flying and I don't like helicopters either, so I went by limo.

This was the last time I ever wore my famous Venus shirt. I brought it out as a treat for the shirt: you're coming out today, out of the cupboard. Its reward was my second meeting with David Bowie, as he was coming out of the tunnel at Wembley and I was coming in with Adam. I said "Hi" to David and he immediately knew we'd met before. He came over, but before he gave me a kiss he took a good look at the shirt.

Adam had got me back in to style the cover of his *Vive Le Rock* album, released in September 1985, which we did with photographer Nick Knight and was based on our fixation with NASA and the space race, which goes all the way back to my childhood and staying up all night to try and see the men land on the Moon. Adam was so pleased to have me back, because he trusted my judgement on matters of taste more than anyone else. He had re-recorded the whole of the preceding 'Apollo 9' single that came out in September 1984, because I didn't like it. With *Vive Le Rock* he had Tony Visconti as producer, who gave the record that whole David Bowie/Spiders from Mars 1973 feel – exactly what he had always wanted.

Adam was going through some troubles of his own by then. He had taken on the role of the title character in a revival of Joe Orton's 1964 play *Entertaining Mr Sloane*[2] for director Greg Hersov at the Manchester Royal Exchange, for which the press was giving him a bit of a panning. While he was in the middle of this, his stepfather Les was arrested on child abuse allegations.[3] At times like that, he needed his friends around him and he took me on tour with them to America, which was a real eye-opener for me. As well plenty of highs along the way – including meeting Andy Warhol again – I got to see for myself what the Pistols had been up against when Malcolm sent them into the Deep South.

---

[2] One of my favourite plays, Joe Orton's *Entertaining Mr Sloane* first premiered at the New Arts Theatre in 1964, starring future SEX customer Dudley Sutton as Sloane; he remained in the cast when it transferred to Broadway the year after.

[3] Les was eventually charged with conspiracy to commit gross indecency against a minor, to which he pleaded guilty at the Old Bailey on 4 June 1987 and was sentenced to two years.

Dining with Jordan

Here are my most memorable meals remembered, in order of greatness:

1 Quality time with Quentin Crisp: I met Quentin twice in 1977. I went to his flat and we had a dainty tea – I think the cups and saucers were fairly clean – but there was an enormous amount of dust everywhere. He made a lovely cup of tea. Then we went to a lovely little Italian and sat outside for dinner. He had extremely interesting ideas; after all, he was kind of a punk himself.

2 Buffet with Bette Midler: It was the premiere party for *The Rose* in February 1980. They had one of those cascades of champagne and a buffet to die for. Jack Nicholson was there and we were standing on this big, sweeping staircase, both knowing what the other one was thinking – What would happen if we pulled the bottom glasses out? I was tempted, but it would have ruined the whole party. Bette was very, very funny, and we got some good profile photos taken together.

3 Breakfast with Burroughs: This was around the time that *Jubilee* came out in 1978 and we met at the Chelsea Arts Club. He had scrambled egg, bacon and toast. He liked the way I looked and he spoke a bit about the film – didn't say one way or the other if he liked it; he isn't that kind of guy. He mainly spoke of London.

4 Pancakes with Divine: Divine was also in London at the time of *Jubilee*, and it may have been Derek who introduced me to him, or Jayne Rogers. But I was asked if I would like to go for breakfast with him at the Portobello and you have never seen anything like it. When English people think of a stack of pancakes, they maybe think of two or three. His was a teetering tower of pancakes and he ate the lot. Drowned in maple syrup. I think there was bacon to go with it – and I'm not sure if there wasn't egg, too.

5 Texas rib-tickler with Adam in Houston: On the *Vive Le Rock* tour of 1985, we were at a rib bar when I made the mistake of saying: "I'm more hungry than you." So I had a dozen snails to start with. Then we both had so many ribs we were nearly sick.

6 High tea with Adam on his daughter Lily's christening: Beautiful high tea, with champagne, in 1998.

7 Lady Anne Lambton's parties: Fabulous parties at her Belgravia flat circa 1976–7, around a long table, like a medieval banquet with about seventy guests, all of them from very different spheres of life.

8 French Valerie's gourmet grub: Valerie O'Ferrell used to come in the shop when Sid worked there and she really wanted to impress us, so she cooked us a gastro-French assault course for the senses. She started off with calves' brains. Then it was smoked eel. Then it was andouillettes, those sausages made with pig's intestines, followed by ortolans, those little birds that are eaten whole. The pièce de résistance was stuffed pheasant – a friend of hers owned a truffle farm in France and she had stuffed the bird with about ten truffles. Jamie Oliver would be content with a tiny sliver. Sid and I were just looking at this meal, but we had to eat it, it was a pact. We burped quite a lot after that lot.

9 Pilchards at primary school: I was the only kid at school who liked pilchards, so I ate everyone's else's on the whole table. And, at about half past three, I started to feel really sick. I kept asking the teacher if I could be excused and she kept replying, in a Joyce Grenfell voice: "We're nearly going home now." I was sick at every gate on the way home, left a little pile of pilchards at each one.

10 No more Monkee business: The Monkees' manager – whose name escapes me – invited me out for dinner in 1977. He took me to a really expensive restaurant for a wonderful fish meal and about three-quarters of the way through it became obvious what he was after. I wanted to go to the Embassy Club but I didn't want him to come with me, so I said I needed to get some cat food from the late-night store and go home to Buckingham Gate to feed the cats. He said, "Oh, don't worry about that", and went back into the kitchen and asked for a large piece of turbot to take away, uncooked. It was about thirty quid's worth, even in those days. So then I had to go to the Embassy Club with him, I had no more excuses. I had my black Wigan mac on and I put the fish in my coat pocket, left it in the cloakroom and danced the night away. I was keeping an eye on this bloke, hoping to make a getaway at some stage – I could have danced out of the door if it hadn't been for the turbot in my mac. God knows what the cloakroom must have smelled like! I managed to lose him in the melee and he didn't follow me. I went home and cooked the fish, and I've never seen cats eat like it! It was the caviar of the cat world.

I see a lot of America's problems as based around religion, and I got my strongest taste of that in the heart of Texas's Bible Belt. We went from New Orleans, which is really liberal and free – well, so long as you are in the centre – across the desert, through swathes of Texas, like those endless cabbage fields at the start of *Midnight Cowboy*. I walked into truck-stop places on that tour and I think if I hadn't been with the band, their manager Barry Mead and, perhaps more importantly, the driver, who had a Stetson with a dead snake hanging off it, God knows what might have happened to me. When you walk in somewhere wearing a sunshine blonde beehive and a handmade Savile Row three-piece suit out there, everything just goes silent. They look at you with real menace.

A completely different scene greeted us at the Rainbow Rooms in Los Angeles. It was the height of the Mötley Crüe hair metal years and everyone inside the venue looked like Spinal Tap. They were all staring at me and, as I walked through them, they parted like waves. "What's the matter with you?" I asked. "You're all Gonks." They thought it was a compliment. We had a better time at Edwards Airforce base in California, which I really enjoyed despite my fear of flying. I had my photo taken in the cockpit of a DC-10.[4]

In remembrance of Sid, I took to the saddle for the second time in Arizona. We were trekking up a mountain, so when they asked me if I was experienced, I knew I wouldn't get a ride if I wasn't, so I said: "Oh yeah, I've ridden before." Which wasn't a lie. It was just across Hyde Park with Sid.

I thought I was going to die that day. Adam didn't do it because of insurance purposes: if he had gone and hurt himself, that would have been the end of the tour. When I got off the horse after two hours' ride, I hobbled into the bar in our hotel hardly able to walk, my legs all shaking – and he laughed his head off.

"Told you not to do it!" he said.

And I said: "Shut up! Just buy me a drink."

---

[4] A pilot once let me take the controls of a DC-10 on a flight to America, to try and help me conquer my flying fear. It was in the middle of the night and I had already downed six whiskies by then to try and keep myself calm. He told me never to tell anyone…

We all had a brilliant time on that tour, except for Marco. He was starting to get fed up with life on the road.

MARCO PIRRONI: It is actually an ego thing, but someone who was in a band with me once said: "You don't want to play live because for you it's too easy." And yeah, it is a bit boring, really. You always need the challenge of doing something new. I mean, how many more times can I play 'Dog Eat Dog'? After you've played it ten times, your mind starts to wander. You start to think: What should I do about them spotlights in the kitchen? That is literally what I would think of: Should we do the kitchen all 1950s? That is what I'm thinking when you see pictures of Adam and the Ants on tour. I would go back to the hotel, phone my girlfriend and say: "I've got it! If we just paint the ceiling red…"

Still falls the rain

Another card that fate dealt me was that if I hadn't moved back to Seaford when I did, I might have missed out on my parents' last years – and my mother's end, in 1987, came all too shockingly quickly. Because of what happened to my poor brother Michael, my mother had a great lack of faith in doctors, and, despite some fairly persistent health problems that she was suffering by then, it was virtually impossible to get her to seek help. When she did eventually go, it was a really rainy day and I had to ring her a taxi and put her in it – I think the only reason she did was because I had paid for her fare. You wouldn't think twice about it now, but a taxi was a really big issue in those days, like going out for a steak dinner, a treat we just couldn't afford.

So she got in the taxi to the doctor, but, when she arrived, the doctor she wanted to see wasn't in. If I had only gone with her, I would have insisted she saw any doctor, but the next thing I knew, she had come back home without seeing anyone. She still tried to carry on as normal. She gave me a list of things to buy for dinner that night, but she did a very strange thing: she emptied all the change out of her handbag to give me, as well as the notes.

That was on the Thursday. Two nights after that, Sally was with us and we were in the living room when she came downstairs to get a cup of tea in the kitchen and went back up to bed. Then she called for me, really loudly. I ran upstairs and she was unable to breathe. It was really very shocking. So I yelled for Sally to come and take over, and I remember running downstairs three steps at a time, just flying down the stairs. Got to the phone and rang the ambulance and described the symptoms.

While I was waiting for them to arrive, I got totally and utterly disorientated. I didn't know the front of the house from the back. I went into the back garden and looked up to where I thought her bedroom was, which was at the front. Then I went in the greenhouse. I just couldn't cope. When the ambulance came, they didn't have the right equipment and had to then phone a specialist paramedic ambulance – that was how things were in 1987. When they arrived, they tried loads of resuscitation techniques. Then they stretchered her into the ambulance and asked us not to follow too soon, to give it some time.

Dad was so stressed, he started scrubbing the kitchen, scrubbing down the walls and everything, so it would be all clean for her to come home. When we finally got to the hospital, she had already gone. She was 71.

They told us she had died from a pulmonary embolism, a blood clot that had gone from her leg to her lungs, which was why she couldn't breathe any more. It was devastating for me, but my dad went completely to pieces. Mum had been the driving force in the family – everything Dad had ever done was for her, and without her he was lost. They had both liked a good drink and they did have heart problems and several other issues to do with drinking. But he started drinking really heavily then and things got very difficult for both Sally and me.

I have had, over the years, a few bouts of unexplainable tachycardia, which is now called panic attacks. There was no seeming trigger for it and I can't say it was drug-induced. Once it happened when I was walking through Fortnum & Mason, once was when I was just in the street, and I had a few others where I thought I was dying, that my heart was going to burst out of my chest.

What happened after my mother's death brought another bout on. It was a kind of post-traumatic stress, and I had to get the doctor out because I couldn't control it. He recorded my heart rate as 150 beats per minute. I was on beta blockers for a long time, which work on your brain to slow your heart down. They were tested on concert pianists and people like that who get stage fright but can't take anything that dulls their senses. That was the beauty of them: they wouldn't change your mood or your capabilities.

In the aftermath of Mum's death, I tried to find out how much she had suffered at the end of her life. I was furious about what happened to her and wrote a massive long letter of complaint about the service we had received in the lead-up to her passing. We could never get through to the surgery on the phone and there wasn't even any answerphones, just this constant, unanswered ringing, when it was hard enough to get her to call in the first place. For someone like my mum, who hated doctors anyway, that was not good enough.

I have learned to master this tachycardia now, although there is still no way of controlling when it happens.

Ridicule is nothing to be scared of

If my problems had physical manifestations, Adam's stress took a different form. As he has recorded in his own memoirs, he had a bad problem with a stalker called Ruth Marie Torries, who had been terrorising him at his Los Angeles home from October 1992 to January 1993. At the same time, he and Marco had been toying with the idea of making an album of covers called *Persuasion* – at one point, he had considered recording a duet with Morrissey of Johnny Thunders' 'You Can't Put Your Arms Around a Memory' – then ditched that idea and started recording new material instead. But when he returned to London between August and December to record what would become the *Wonderful* album, he was beset with depression and fear.

He'd been holed up in his flat in Primrose Hill, behind the fridge, in the cupboard underneath the sink. Marco suggested he came to Seaford to recover. He thought I would be a calming influence and my dad helped me look after him, cooking him food and letting him sit in the garden. It seemed like a good idea at the time.

But I just didn't know how to get away for work. My dad was there and made him tea, didn't ask him to do anything, gave him his own space, and that did help a bit. I had such a fear of leaving him when he was clinging onto my hand every morning, literally like his life depended on it. Like I was the last life raft on the *Titanic*. How could you take your hand away and go to work?

He was so ill, he had all his drugs laid out in my spare room and it was all mixed up, Prozac, Xanax, and in between it all these homeopathic cures. We look at his condition now and think, of course, he's always been like that. If I went to his place in London, he wouldn't know where to go to eat, he'd stay up all night writing unbelievable lists, trying to plan out everything in advance. But at the time, it was so hard – no one knew what to do for the best. Marco went through a hell of a lot with him.

MARCO PIRRONI: But there was nothing we could have done. When Adam first got ill, my friend Hugh said: "Would you like to speak to my father?" He was Sir Ismond Rosen, then the head of the Royal College of Psychiatry. I went to his house in Hampstead and he took two hours to talk to me about Adam. He said: "Your friend is lost to madness. There is nothing you can do and you have to disengage now. Otherwise, he will take you down with him." He told me everything he was going to say and everything he was going to do and everything he'd just done. He told me everything, and I didn't say a single word. Because, of course, I knew better than Sir Ismond Rosen.

When the *Wonderful* album was being prepared for release, Adam couldn't even decide what shots to use for the cover. Marco and I had to take over. We picked the picture of him with the roses that was eventually used. But, at the time, whatever we chose was the wrong one. He kept going round in circles.

By the time Adam was arrested by armed police outside the Princess of Wales pub in Camden Town on 12 January 2002, waving his father's 1940s starting pistol around, his public breakdown had been a long time in the making. Adam is a lot better now, and that has a lot to do with being on the road with a really good band, working all the time. Sadly, his relationship with Marco, both professionally and as friends, did not survive the traumas they both went through in those years.

MARCO PIRRONI: I try and get it across to people that I'm not just being difficult. But they [all think they] know him better than me. If I went on tour with him again, the past would all come out. Because he remembers every single thing… That's what Sir Ismond said: "Your friend is lost to madness." He isn't just being stupid in a Kenny Everett way. He's mentally ill, he doesn't see things the way they really are.

Soldiering on

My dad's drink problems never got any better after Mum died, no matter how hard Sally and I tried to hide his poison from him. Once, Sally found him lying on the floor and thought he had died. But he was just drunk. Another time, Sally and I came home from a cat show and found him with a great big gash on his head and so much blood on the carpet it had gone through the underlay. I bet if a forensic pathologist went through there now, they'd still find blood. And a trail of boiled egg, all the way through from the kitchen to the dining-room table. So he'd obviously tried to cook himself something, but he was too out of it. He needed an awful lot of care. I had a job at the vet by then and was terribly worried about him, because his legs wouldn't work properly, and he couldn't walk any more. Even commando legs let him down in the end.

Jeannie would have him up to stay with her while he was still mobile. Sally and I sent him off on the train once – he looked like a little schoolboy who'd been sent back to boarding school and didn't want to go. We waved goodbye to him and his head was bowed. He had his small bag, which just had the crib board, a pack of cards, a toothbrush and his cherry blossom shoe polish. That was all that was in there. I still pack very light now; maybe that's to do with him. Though I don't bring the crib board or the cherry blossom. And in his pocket he'd have his nail file. Had to have that.

JEANNIE CRAVEN: As he walked towards me, I thought: Goodness, here comes a little old tramp. And then he said to me: "You look like a tramp." It was so funny, me thinking it and him saying it. That was lambing time, as well. He would drop out, wouldn't he? Whether it was what happened

413

to him in the war, I don't know, but without Mum, he would have dropped out completely.

When he eventually went into a nursing home it was a massive relief, because someone was there for him all the time. I mean, I'd come home from work and find him watching children's programmes on the telly because he'd dropped the handset and he couldn't stand up to reach it back. He was a very gregarious person, so it was better for him to be around people all day. He passed away on 22 April 2003, in his 91st year (he was born on 3 February 1913), and to my immense relief, unlike Mum, he died very peacefully.

Beat the clock

When Julien Temple's *The Filth and the Fury* came out in 2000, there was a gathering of the tribes at the premiere that put me back in touch with some faces I hadn't seen for a very long time. As I've said previously, this was the last time I ever saw Little Helen, and I had such a good time talking to her, Steve Jones and Simon Barker in the pub over the road before the screening that we were late to our seats and the cinema was full. Boy George saw me coming down the side aisle, waved me over and walked me through to his seat, then went and stood at the back himself. He was always a real gentleman. To me, anyway. Sally has her doubts.

> **SALLY REID:** At the party after *The Filth and the Fury*, I was abandoned into the care of Boy George. "You stay with George," you said, "He'll look after you." It was like asking a fox to look after the chickens, wasn't it?

The last time I saw George was only in the distance. He came to Simon Barker's *Punk's Dead* London book launch in 2016 and somebody said to me: "George is over there." But when I went over, he ran off. I think it was because of what he looked like at the time: he was overweight and didn't want me to see him not looking his best. Looking back at it now, *The Filth and The Fury*'s moving re-evaluation of the madness of those heady years between 1975 and 1977, and the honesty with which the surviving Pistols spoke about the

414

torments and tragedies that had torn them apart, was the beginning of a massive renaissance of interest in punk from all quarters.

> **PAUL COOK:** People only started to understand how significant the whole period was twenty years later. At the time, they got rid of all us lot and then they had the lovely New Romantics and, oh great, everything's back to normal – almost. They were glad to see the back of us.

The Pistols' original line-up had reformed as a direct result of making the documentary, going through the archive material that had been used to make *The Great Rock 'n' Roll Swindle* and seeing each other on friendly terms again. The *Filthy Lucre* tour of 1996, aimed at recouping some of the money that had been lost to them, lasted six months and put them back in front of a much more appreciative American audience. They rode out again for the Queen's Golden Jubilee in 2002, celebrating their own Silver Jubilee at the Crystal Palace National Sports Centre, and a dance remix of 'God Save the Queen' by Leftfield's Neil Barnes was released on the twenty-fifth anniversary of its original release. More gigs and official record releases followed, and the band last played together in 2008.[5] By then, some of the old war wounds had started to flare up again.

> **PAUL COOK:** We thought about making another album when we did our reunion, but it didn't take long for all the old resentments to resurface. No one could sit round with each other long enough to write a song, you know.

The next time there was a reunion on such an epic scale would be for Malcolm's funeral.

---

[5] For everything you need to know about the Pistols, see sexpistolsofficial.com

24

THE HISTORY OF THE VOID

Funeral games for Malcolm and rising from the ashes of Chaos

Too fast to live too young to die

Malcolm would never have wanted to be old, that's the only consolation I can take from his death, on 8 April 2010, from cancer, at the age of only 64. He was obsessed with young people being around him, as if being surrounded by youth would keep him younger. His funeral was on 22 April, at the deconsecrated St Mary Magdalene church that stands opposite Great Portland Street tube station. I was invited by Joe Corré and I went with Marco. As Malcolm would have wanted, it was a very interesting and unusual day. There were a lot of people there who shouldn't have been there; and another lot should have been there, but weren't.

Vivienne – wearing a headband emblazoned with the word 'CHAOS' – called me over to the front row, where she was sitting with Andreas. We were chatting like it was just a normal party or something, which was rather lovely. And she was busily scribbling some words down because she was going to speak about Malcolm, do the eulogy. She asked me if I was going to be saying anything – I hadn't even thought that you could.

She was just trying to work out what she was going to say herself. Then, when she started talking, Bernie Rhodes went: "Oh shut up, Vivienne. It's always about you." I felt so sorry for her. She went: "Bernie, Bernie, I was just trying to get my thoughts in order and it's really difficult." And he said: "It's Bernard, actually." At that point, I stood up and said: "Bernard? You've never been Bernard!"

JON SAVAGE: When I went to Malcolm's funeral, you, Boogie, Paul [Cook] and Sophie [Richmond] were the nicest people there, because you were natural and human. There were so many people posing. I remember Vivienne trying to be human and almost succeeding. She was trying to be nice. But I was furious with Bernard, because he was so disrespectful. Have some fucking humanity.

Adam was there, and at that point I hadn't seen him for a long time, a lot of water had passed under the bridge. He was dressed very strangely, looking a bit like the Mad Hatter with a big hat that had ripped pictures, including one of himself, sticking out of it and a great big bunch of flowers, as if he was presenting an award. It was a difficult moment, because I was with Marco, and Adam was three or four rows in front of us. I think Adam was on a lot of medication that day.

There was some comedy relief when Joe Corré read out a message from Steve Jones that went: "Dear Malcolm, did you take the money with you? Is it in the coffin? Do you mind if I come back tomorrow and dig you up?"

DAVE BARBE: What was interesting to me, all the people that stood up, all the [Alan] Yentobs, all those kind of nobs, everybody was so passionate who got up and spoke. And I realised, I knew Malcolm for three years, that's all I had him in my life for, I never saw Malcolm again after Bow Wow Wow. And I missed him, because he was such a brilliant geezer to me. But at the funeral, I realised he did that to everyone.

After Malcolm's death came an exhumation of the remains of punk, with anniversaries noted and what began as a bunch of misfits meeting on the King's Road to dream and scheme of something better becoming the subject of university courses, symposiums and huge retrospective exhibitions around the world. Vivienne got her tribute at the V&A in 2004, at the same time as John Rotten appeared on *I'm a Celebrity, Get Me Out of Here* with another woman called Jordan – "A woman who's written more books than she's read", according to the *Times Literary Supplement* – prompting Vivienne to tell a *Guardian* reporter to call up the original and find out what I had been up to lately. But it wasn't until two pivotal events in 2015 that I started to think it was time to say something for myself.

Vive Le Punk: Vivienne and Malcolm's last stand

When Roger K. Burton moved his clothes archive, the Contemporary Wardrobe Collection, to the Horse Hospital in Bloomsbury, in 1993, he had an idea that turned into one of the most important documents of punk: the last ever interview of Malcolm and Vivienne, discussing the biggest collection of their work to have been assembled by any museum or archive since their parting of the ways.

ROGER K. BURTON: I wanted to stage an exhibition of punk clothing, which I've got quite a large collection of. I contacted Marco, who's got tons of stuff, and various other collectors that I knew, and they all agreed it was a good idea – not for any money, just to put the place on the map and celebrate that whole era. As it was coming in, I was in quite regular contact with both Malcolm and Vivienne and I'd tell them: this is going to be quite a big show and I'd like you to be involved in it. Vivienne would say: "No, no, I'm not interested, I endorse what you're doing, but that was then and I don't want to be involved." Malcolm was pretty much saying the same thing.

But, as it was coming in, it was becoming more and more apparent that we had pretty much an example of everything they'd ever designed between 1971 and 1979. I found this collector who used to visit the shop every weekend and had a photographic memory of what went that day or that month. He'd go: "Yeah, that was the second week of June 1976." So he helped write the catalogue.

So I got hold of Vivienne and said: "You've got to come and see this; you'll probably never ever see it all together like this again." It was twenty-five years ago, before she was really famous. And she was: "No, no, no, I'm really busy working on my collection. I'm too busy."

So I got onto Malcolm again and he was in France recording with Françoise Hardy and he was: "Oh well, I think I'm actually going to be in London just the day before, so I'll drop in and have a look." It turned out he was coming the night before we opened, and we were still putting the thing up – Mr Newman was doing the lighting with his dog running about, Miss Thing. And I thought: If I've got him, I've *got* to get her. So I rang her again. I said: "Vivienne, you've got to come, it's really important." And she said: "Oh, is Malcolm coming?" And I said: "No, absolutely not." I had to lie. And she said: "OK, well I'm going to be late, because I'm not going to be finished until late." I said: "It doesn't matter – just come."

So, as it happened, Malcolm turned up about seven o'clock and immediately went over to the Cambridge Rapist T-shirt and started talking about how Bernie Rhodes had done a really cheap job on it with the printing ink, it was so thin and really crap, and so on. And I said: "Hang on a minute, Malcolm. Do you mind if we film you just talking about this?" Anyway, about ten minutes goes by and the buzzer rings – and it's Vivienne. She's stood in the doorway and we both turned round. I was going, "Oh, hi, Vivienne," and Malcolm's going: "Oh, hi, Vivienne." And she didn't say a word – she just stood there chain-smoking.

So I said: "Can I get you a cup of tea, Vivvie?" And she said: "No, but I'll have a double brandy." So we sent across to the pub for a double brandy for her and she stood there for another ten minutes while Malcolm went on and on and on about: "I designed this and I designed that." All very interesting stuff, until he got to one of the very early T-shirts, which had the pin-up girl in a pocket, and he was talking about them being his works of art, and then his son Joe having a John Bull printing set and having run a little tractor over it... And then suddenly Vivienne started to speak.

> She said: "Yes, that's right, it was Joe." And then they sort of – it
> was a bit like a Pinter stand-off – but they kept coming together
> and agreeing about stuff and disagreeing about stuff, and she'd go:
> "No, Malcolm, that isn't right!" And they ended up talking about
> the entire thing. Then, in the end, she went into her manifesto. She
> said: "You can't do anything unless you've read a book." And she
> went into that, and it's ten minutes of pure gold – very coherent,
> very focused.

Selling SEX

On 23 June 2015, my entire collection of Westwood-McLaren
originals from SEX, Seditionaries, World's End and Nostalgia of
Mud went under the hammer at an auction arranged by Kerry Taylor
called Passion for Fashion.[1] The lot included such iconic pieces as
my Anarchy shirt, the horsehair earring Frankie Savage gave me, my
turquoise mohair 'Chesty Morgan' sweater that Michael loved so
much, my Bondage jacket and Destroy T-shirt and my Pirates shirt
and trousers.

Despite the enormous number of memories attached to all those
items, seeing them gone actually felt like a weight lifting off me. The
fact was, I had realised if I didn't do something about it, it was all
going to go to nothing. It would fall to pieces, like Alan Jones and his
chicken bones; the whole lot would go to dust.

All of my clothes were bought by either museums, fashion archives
or collectors who will always keep them properly preserved. You don't
have to keep the garment to keep the memories; I can remember
every time I wore any of those things. Now I don't have the worry of
not knowing how best to preserve them.

Before the auction, I spent about £3.75 renovating my clothes. It
was spent on a J cloth, water – which I won't count – and two pots
of very cheap leather restorer. I didn't dare wash anything, because I

---

[1] You can see the full catalogue of the Passion for Fashion auction here:
https://issuu.com/jammdesign/docs/kerry_taylor_-_23_june_2015

didn't know what was going to happen if I did. When I took the Venus shirt, which was the major piece, out of the cupboard, it was looking very poorly. I had to brush it down with a damp J cloth because it was covered in cobwebs and dry mould. I had kept it very dry, which was lucky, because if it had been wet... On the day – which, as you may have noted, was my birthday – there was a bidding war for Venus, and a private collector outbid a museum for her.

Suffice to say, I had a bottle of champagne on ice for the occasion.

Summoning Ariel

I did my first ever public talk about my past that same summer, at the Crypt in Seaford, with Kate Parkinson, committee member of the gallery, who worked really hard on her research. The event was sold out, they couldn't fit any more people in, and the historic venue lent itself beautifully to the talk. We ended with a big Q&A session where a lot of local people asked some really good, insightful questions. What was most touching of all was to see Mrs Scott, my Art teacher from Seaford Head, sitting there in the front row. It made me realise that this was something I could do, and do well – and really enjoy myself at the same time.

After that, I set up my Facebook page, through which I have found so many photographs and other treasures that I had once thought were lost for ever in the bags of my belongings that Kevin sold. These really were the foundations that led to writing this book. And, from the Crypt Gallery talk onwards, events started to spiral.

At the British Library's *Punk 1976–78* retrospective in May 2016, I was asked to give a talk about The Ramones with their hilarious and wonderful manager, Danny Fields. I also got to put Bernie Rhodes straight when he claimed to have "stormed the stage" when Vivienne was speaking at Malcolm's funeral in the long, rambling talk he gave about his memories. I didn't envy John Robb the job of trying to chair that one.

Then in November of that year I took part in the Museum of London's 'Punk.London' debate with Richard Boon and Joe Corré, who was about to stage his *Burn Punk London* event, where he claimed he was going to set fire to his archive of Malcolm and Vivienne's clothes on a barge in the Thames. There had been a lot of talk on Facebook about the SEX door handle, the blown handkerchief, which he really should have given to me, seeing as I was the one who touched it more than anyone else. There had been a picture of him with it in the press, and it opened the floodgates.

In the end, it was a fairly chaotic evening. Chair Vivien Goldman did not manage to control Joe, who has learned that he'll get listened to if he does this big oration thing, and who wasn't interested in anything anyone else had to say. It was a shame – a lot of people were disappointed, because they wanted to have a discussion. Vivien Goldman should have just shouted at him; she was too polite – I had to tell him instead. Then again, maybe it's a family trait. He always looks at me at those moments as if to say: We know what the game is, don't we?

At the end of the event, I found myself face-to-face with my own past – a girl had turned up dressed as Amyl Nitrate, complete with Britannia helmet and trident, and promptly burst into tears when she met me. A few days later, I attended Joe's ceremonial bonfire on the banks of the Thames at Chelsea. It was a strange echo of my scene in *Jubilee*, dancing around the flames as the old world burned.

Afterwards, we all got taken off in this old van, which was belching out all sorts of fumes, very 'Save the Planet'. To this day I have no idea where we went; we just got taken to this pub. Then, when we arrived, they couldn't get the door open to the party area upstairs. Nobody had a key. Joe had booked it, apparently, but they had forgotten the booking. Does this remind you of anything?

So then they had to find a key and set it all up. There was no food, but at least they had a bar ready there, small, basic: the tables were old barrels. We had some drinks and they found some tacos to eat and it was all very good fun. Vivienne sat down next to me and wouldn't talk to anyone else all evening – she was shooing people off if they tried to come up and talk to her. "Get away! I'm talking to Jordan!"

We had a huge catch-up as we shared a plate of tacos between us. I dropped something on my top, which I often do, and she leaned over and went, "Oh, Jordan, d'you not want this?" and ate a bit of cheese off my top. She's so funny. She had a bag full of books with her, and at the end of the evening I had to remind her to take it with her. "Oooh, yes, me bag!"

Then she just cycled off into the sunset.

Defying gravity

Punk was born of a lot of things. It was born out of the total misery and poverty of the time. Everything was really, really dark, politically oppressive, and a small group of people led the way. My argument against Joe burning all his stuff – although that was a stunt and I know why he did it – was that it wasn't what it was meant to be. You only ever learn from the art, literature and science that has gone before. All of these things move on, become different versions. Ours was a pretty good one, though.

SIMON BARKER: The real creative force behind punk was women. All the blokes would have been in rock'n'roll bands anyway, I think. It was you, Vivienne, Sioux, Poly Styrene, The Slits who were the real originals. They're the ones you think: Where did that come from? You couldn't identify what the points of reference were. You couldn't explain where the look came from. You've seen it since, but you'd never seen it before. The only bloke there wasn't any reference points for was John Rotten; no one had ever spat at the audience like he did. But all the others would have just been in bands anyway. After I did my book, *Punk's Dead*, I realised all the true originals of that time, apart from Malcolm and John Rotten, were all the women of the time.

DAVE BARBE: I basically say that punk rock was an art movement. It wasn't about the Socialist Workers' Party, it was about people looking beautiful and unique and outdoing each other in outrageous styles and attitudes. I don't think it was the music, either. I think it was the attitude and the spirit. It's not like Tamla Motown or dub reggae. There were some great albums made, but you can't look back on double, treble albums of great punk rock, because there weren't that many. There were some brilliant songs and about three brilliant albums, but it wasn't even about that – it completely changed society. They didn't like us, the industry. We threatened it, we overthrew it.

BERTIE MARSHALL: I thought it would have influence, but how could we have known that it would have such an impact? In hindsight, forty years later, it's not just been about music and clothes, really. The whole ideology or aesthetic has really swamped the world. It has been a total cultural change. I can't think of another. The hippies didn't really do it in those terms.

ROGER K. BURTON: It's a funny old period, because it was so enlightening, so exciting. I can't even summon up enough expletives to do it justice. But it affected people in so many different ways. I screen my film of Malcolm and Vivienne quite regularly to students, which of course goes down very well, because they get a bottled history in an hour. The senior tutor at London College of Fashion who asked me to do it, he's written various historical books, and his take on it is this. Punk is the only fashion phenomenon that so many people have claimed ownership over. He'd written about couture, about high street fashion, and, even with the bitchiness of couture, everybody's in their own camp. But punk seems to belong to everybody, and everyone who talks about it, or writes about it, claims ownership over it in some way. Probably because they all see it from different angles...

Because it changed their lives and they think they lived it, so they own it. I can't imagine any other phenomenon which gives people that feeling. Maybe because it was encapsulated within a very short time and it burned very brightly. It was fleeting. People who weren't there just wish they were in that capsule, hurtling towards the edge of the known universe, not knowing where or if they were going to land, or whether they were going to just crash and burn.

I was always determined that I was going to excel: at sport, at ballet and as the living work of art I fashioned myself into on my journey to, and my time at, the epicentre of punk. As Jeannie said, I never turned down a challenge, never compromised my belief in always doing something to the best of my ability.

I wanted to dance and I did defy gravity.

SELECTED BIBLIOGRAPHY

Adam Ant, *Stand & Deliver* (Sidgwick & Jackson, 2006)

Michael Armstrong, *A Star Is Dead: The Screenplays* (Paper Dragon, 2017)

Simon Barker, *Punk's Dead* (Divus, 2016)

Craig Bromberg, *The Wicked Ways of Malcolm McLaren* (Omnibus Press, 1991)

Roger K. Burton, *Rebel Threads* (The Horse Hospital in association with Laurence King Publishing Ltd, 2017)

Richard Cabut and Andrew Gallix, *Punk Is Dead: Modernity Killed Every Night* (Zero Books, 2017)

Bob Colacello, *Holy Terror: Andy Warhol Close Up* (HarperCollins, 1990)

Michael Costiff, *Michael & Gerlinde's World* (Slow Loris Publishing, 2012)

Jayne County, *Man Enough to Be a Woman* (Serpent's Tail, 1995)

Max Décharné, *King's Road* (Weidenfeld & Nicolson, 2005)

Tony Drayton, *Ripped & Torn* (Ecstatic Peace Library, 2018)

Steve Jones with Ben Thompson, *Lonely Boy* (William Heinemann, 2016)

John Lydon with Andrew Perry, *Anger Is an Energy* (Simon & Schuster, 2014)

Legs McNeil and Gillian McCain, *Please Kill Me* (Little, Brown, 1996)

Bertie Marshall, *Berlin Bromley* (SAF Publishing, 2006)

Barry Miles, *London Calling* (Atlantic Books, 2010)

Jane Mulvagh, *Vivienne Westwood: An Unfashionable Life* (HarperCollins, 1998)

Tony Peake, *Derek Jarman* (Little, Brown, 1999)

Keiron Pim, *Jumpin' Jack Flash* (Jonathan Cape, 2016)

Ted Polhemus, *Street Style* (Thames & Hudson, 1994)

Ted Polhemus, *Boom! A Baby Boomer Memoir* (Lulu, 2012)

Daniel Rachel, *Walls Come Tumbling Down* (Picador, 2016)

Jon Savage, *England's Dreaming* (Faber and Faber, 1991)

Jon Savage, *The England's Dreaming Tapes* (Faber and Faber, 2009)

Deborah Spungen, *And I Don't Want to Live This Life* (Penguin, 1983)

Sylvain Sylvain and Dave Thompson, *There's No Bones in Ice Cream: Sylvain Sylvain's Story of the New York Dolls* (Omnibus Press, 2018)

Fred and Judy Velmorel, *Sex Pistols: The Inside Story* (Omnibus Press, 1987)

Harriet Vyner, *Groovy Bob* (Heni, 2016)

Curt Weiss, *Stranded in the Jungle* (Backbeat Books, 2017)

Jah Wobble, *Memories of a Geezer* (Serpent's Tail, 2009)

Matthew Worley, *No Future: Punk, Politics and British Youth Culture 1976–84* (Cambridge University Press, 2017)

Peter York, *Style Wars* (Sidgwick & Jackson, 1980)

ACKNOWLEDGEMENTS

Jordan Mooney and Cathi Unsworth would like to thank Roger K. Burton, for his genius idea of putting us together in the first place; Caroline Montgomery, the late Doreen Montgomery and Fenris Oswin at Rupert Crew Ltd, and David Barraclough, Imogen Gordon Clark and Matthew O'Donoghue at Omnibus Press, for believing in this book and giving us so much support and encouragement along the way. Special thanks to Jon Savage for letting us use interviews from his *England's Dreaming* sessions with Derek Jarman and Debbi Wilson, as well as his incisive interview and follow-up help and encouragement; and to Dave Barbe for writing so thoughtfully about his departed friends Matthew Ashman and Mark Ryan after our initial interview. The following people were generous enough to give us lengthy interview time and, in lots of cases, also share archive material and assist on other important matters to the text and photos: Simon Barker and Derek Dunbar, Anton Binder, Richard Cabut, Michael Collins, Paul and Jeni Cook, Michael Costiff, Alwyn and Jeannie Craven, Duggie Fields, Simon Fisher Turner, Lesley Foster, David Ireland, Jonh Ingham, Holly Johnson, Alan Jones, Bertie Marshall, James Merifield, Jane Palm-Gold, Marco Pirroni, Ted Polhemus, Dorothy Max Prior, Sally Reid, Roger Rooke, Robina Rose, Sylvain Sylvain, John Tiberi, Dame Vivienne Westwood and Peter York – muchas gracias to you all. Graham Humphreys made our cover dreams come true. Billy Chainsaw kindly gave us his thoughts on Nils Stevenson; Ossian Brown helped us track down his late friend Peter Christopherson's Pistols photographs to Xavier at Timeless Press; Damon Wise let us use his Roger Ebert quote and was helpful with film assistance; Geoff Cox helped us track down Robina Rose; and Marc Albert, Keith Cameron, Nicky Charlish, Max Décharné, Pat Gilbert, Etienne Gilfillan, Barney Hoskyns, Julian Stanislaw Kalinowski, Richard Newson, Tony Stewart, Tom Vague, Mark Wardel, Matt Worley and Ray Yates provided essential archive assistance, enthusiasm, support and good advice.

Jordan Mooney would also like to thank all of those who have enriched my life and shown me kindness, support, friendship and inspiration along the way: Cathi Unsworth, Adam Ant, Jon Savage, Vivienne Westwood, The Sex Pistols, Simon Barker, Derek Dunbar, Sally Reid, Evan Cardy, Michael Collins, Jayne Rogers, Buzzcocks, Julian Stanislaw Kalinowski, Roger and Linda Rooke, Rosalind and Alwyn Craven, Sue Tovey, all of my many friends in the world of cat showing and my colleagues at my wonderful veterinary surgery.

And those no longer with us: Derek Jarman, Malcolm McLaren, David Bowie, Sid Vicious, Johnny Thunders, Jerry Nolan and all of The Heartbreakers, Dee Dee Ramone, Lou Reed and the Velvet Underground, Nils Stevenson, Andy Warhol, Poly Styrene, Divine, Lindsay Kemp, Angela Bolsch, Margot Fonteyn and dear Mum and Dad.

Cathi Unsworth would also like to thank Jordan Mooney for trusting me to do this. My solid gold friends: Ann Scanlon, Benedict Newbery, Pete Woodhead, Joe McNally, Emma Murphy, David Knight and Ruth Bayer, Kriss and Lynn Knights, Paul Willetts, Marc Glendening and Chris Simmons. My dear family: Mum, Dad, Matt, Yvette, William, Tom and Sophie. My biggest thanks, as ever, go to Michael Meekin, for everything.

INDEX

432

A SONG BY JOR—D—

LOU. (A TRIBU[T...]

① You lost your U-N-P-R-E[...]
they said you were an "a[g...]
~~[crossed out]~~
You "stockPILED all your [...]
But now / ~~my friend~~ / you [...]

② I know you used to sh[...]
you ~~felt~~ but never hur[...]
FELL

You never stagger in [...]
The baliff put you on the [...]

/chorus/
Andy warhol   V — I-D—[...]
Four QUID for a T—[...]
Wrap up your arse an[...]

— / Lick — it! (oh[...]

NO
~~A~~ tribute to you — Kevi[...]